Research Methods for Social Justice and Equity in Education

Kamden K. Strunk • Leslie Ann Locke

Editors

Research Methods for Social Justice and Equity in Education

Editors
Kamden K. Strunk
Educational Psychology and
Research Methodologies
Auburn University
Auburn, AL, USA

Leslie Ann Locke
Educational Policy and
Leadership Studies
University of Iowa
Iowa City, IA, USA

ISBN 978-3-030-05899-9   ISBN 978-3-030-05900-2   (eBook)
https://doi.org/10.1007/978-3-030-05900-2

Library of Congress Control Number: 2019930472

This Palgrave Macmillan imprint is published by the registered company Springer Nature Switzerland AG
The registered company address is: Gewerbestrasse 11, 6330 Cham, Switzerland

Contents

Part I Theoretical and Philosophical Issues

1   Re-positioning Power and Re-imagining Reflexivity: Examining
    Positionality and Building Validity Through Reconstructive
    Horizon Analysis   3
    Meagan Call-Cummings and Karen Ross

2   Considering Positionality: The Ethics of Conducting Research
    with Marginalized Groups   15
    Laura Parson

3   Flipping the Paradigm: Studying Up and Research
    for Social Justice   33
    Elena Aydarova

4   Framing Critical Race Theory and Methodologies   45
    Kenzo K. Sung and Natoya Coleman

5   Disentangling the Complexities of Queer Theory and
    Intersectionality Theory: Research Paradigms and Insights for
    Social Justice   59
    Christian D. Chan, Sam Steen, Lionel C. Howard, and Arshad I. Ali

6   Using Critical Theory in Educational Research   71
    Kamden K. Strunk and Jasmine S. Betties

7   Viewing Research for Social Justice and Equity Through the Lens
    of Zygmunt Bauman's Theory of Liquid Modernity   81
    Danielle T. Ligocki

8   Thinking Critically About "Social Justice Methods": Methods as
    "Contingent Foundations"   91
    Lucy E. Bailey

9   Institutional Review Boards: Purposes and Applications
    for Students 109
    Leslie Ann Locke

Part II   Approaches to Data Collection and Analysis

10 Typical Areas of Confusion for Students New to Qualitative
    Research... 117
    Leslie Ann Locke

11 Youth Participatory Action Research: The Nuts and Bolts as well as
    the Roses and Thorns 125
    Shiv R. Desai

12 Advancing Social Justice with Policy Discourse Analysis 137
    Elizabeth J. Allan and Aaron R. Tolbert

13 Through Their Eyes, in Their Words: Using Photo-Elicitation to
    Amplify Student Voice in Policy and School Improvement Research   151
    Jeff Walls and Samantha E. Holquist

14 Using Photovoice to Resist Colonial Research Paradigms 163
    Susan Cridland-Hughes, McKenzie Brittain, and S. Megan Che

15 Re-introducing Life History Methodology: An Equitable Social
    Justice Approach to Research in Education 177
    James S. Wright

16 Quantitative Methods for Social Justice and Equity: Theoretical
    and Practical Considerations................................. 191
    Kamden K. Strunk and Payton D. Hoover

17 Large-Scale Datasets and Social Justice: Measuring Inequality in
    Opportunities to Learn...................................... 203
    Heather E. Price

18 X Marks the Spot: Engaging Campus Maps to Explore Sense of
    Belonging Experiences of Student Activists 217
    Carli Rosati, David J. Nguyen, and Rose M. Troyer

19 Propensity Score Methodology in the Study of Student
    Classification: The Case of Racial/Ethnic Disproportionality
    in Mild Disability Identification and Labeling.................. 227
    Argun Saatcioglu and Thomas M. Skrtic

20 Transformative Mixed Methods: A Missed Opportunity 241
    Carey E. Andrzejewski, Benjamin Arnberg, and
    Hannah Carson Baggett

Part III   Developing a Research Agenda

21   Writing, Race, and Creative Democracy 255
Timothy J. Lensmire

**22   Beyond White: The Emotional Complexion of Critical
Research on Race** 263
Cheryl E. Matias

**23   I Pulled Up a Seat at the Table: My Journey Engaging in Critical
Quantitative Inquiry** 275
Lolita A. Tabron

**24   Working with Intention and in Tension: Evolving
as a Scholar-Activist** 283
Kristen A. Renn

**25   Collaboration, Community, and Collectives: Research
for and by the People** 289
Erica R. Dávila

Terminology 295

Index 305

Notes on Contributors

Arshad I. Ali, PhD, is Assistant Professor of Educational Research at The George Washington University. Ali is an interdisciplinary scholar who studies youth culture, identity, and political engagement. His research engages questions of decoloniality, race, religion, and political liberalism. He is co-editor of *Education at War: The Fight for Students of Color in America's Public Schools* as well as numerous research articles on Muslim youth identities and politics.

Elizabeth J. Allan, PhD, is Professor of Higher Education at the University of Maine. Her scholarship on campus cultures and climates includes qualitative and mixed methods studies about teaching, equity, student engagement, and student hazing and its prevention. Drawing on critical theories and feminist poststructuralism, she developed policy discourse analysis as a hybrid methodology for both unthinking policy and advancing social justice.

Carey E. Andrzejewski, PhD, is a former mathematics teacher with a research and outreach agenda focused on equity and reform in schools. She is an associate professor in the College of Education at Auburn University. She joined the faculty there after completing her PhD in Teacher Education from Ohio State University.

Benjamin Arnberg is a PhD candidate in Higher Education Administration at Auburn University. His research uses queer and feminist theories to address campus climate, inclusion policy and practice, and research methodology in higher education research.

Elena Aydarova is Assistant Professor of Social Foundations at Auburn University in Auburn, Alabama. Her interdisciplinary research examines the interactions between global social change and the work of teachers, teaching, and teacher education through the lens of equity and social justice. Her projects have explored teacher education reforms in Russia and the US, education privatization and commodification, as well as internationalization of education. She has written about conducting ethnographic research in elite settings and in postsocialist contexts.

Hannah Carson Baggett, PhD, is a former high school teacher and current assistant professor in the College of Education at Auburn University. Her research interests include critical theories, race and education, and educator beliefs. She holds a PhD in Curriculum and Instruction from North Carolina State University.

Lucy E. Bailey, PhD, is Associate Professor of Social Foundations and Qualitative Inquiry and the Director of Gender and Women's Studies at Oklahoma State University. She teaches a variety of qualitative methodology and diversity courses. Recent research has focused on family methodology and body politics in education.

Jasmine S. Betties is a doctoral student in Educational Psychology at Auburn University. Her research interests include social justice, democratic and alternative approaches to schooling, and education policy.

McKenzie Brittain is a doctoral student in Curriculum and Instruction at Clemson University where she focuses on Secondary Mathematics Education. Her research interests include single-sex education, photovoice methodology, and teacher support of argumentation in the mathematics classroom.

Meagan Call-Cummings is Assistant Professor of Qualitative Methods at George Mason University's Graduate School of Education. She writes on critical, participatory, and feminist qualitative methodology, with a specific focus on how validity and ethics are conceptualized. Her most recent work has taken youth participatory action research forms.

Christian D. Chan, PhD, NCC, is Assistant Professor of Counseling at Idaho State University. His interests revolve around intersectionality; multiculturalism in counseling, supervision, and counselor education; social justice; career development; critical research methods; acculturative stress; intergenerational conflict; and cultural factors in identity development and socialization.

S. Megan Che is Associate Professor of Mathematics Education at Clemson University. Her research foci include humanizing pedagogies in mathematics teaching and learning, and the roles of social context in student mathematical thinking.

Natoya Coleman is a PhD student in Urban Education at Rowan University where she focuses on decolonizing curriculum and instruction in urban and diverse learning environments. Her research interests include mentorship among black women in higher education, feminist pedagogy, critical literacy, and equity-based pedagogical practices in secondary English classrooms.

Susan Cridland-Hughes is Assistant Professor of Secondary English Education at Clemson University. Her research centers on the intersection of critical literacy and pedagogy, specifically exploring how critical literacy is taught and enacted both in schools and outside of schools.

Erica R. Dávila, PhD, is Associate Professor in Educational Leadership in the College of Education at Lewis University outside of Chicago. Her research interests are educational policy, critical race theory, sustainability, and Puerto Rican studies. Dávila holds her doctorate in Educational Policy from the University of Illinois Champaign Urbana.

Shiv R. Desai is an assistant professor in the Department of Teacher Education, Education Leadership, and Policy in the College of Education at the University of New Mexico. Desai is currently working with system-involved youth where he is helping them conduct a youth participatory action research (YPAR) project that examines the school-to-prison pipeline as well as how YPAR can be utilized to inform new policies to shape a more socially just juvenile justice system.

Samantha E. Holquist is a doctoral candidate in Organizational Leadership, Policy, and Development at the University of Minnesota. She also advises Oregon Student Voice, a student-led organization that empowers students to be authentic partners with education decision-makers. Her research interests include the incorporation of student voice into education policymaking.

Payton D. Hoover is a PhD student in the Educational Psychology program at Auburn University. She earned a BA in Psychology from Hanover College. Her research interests include community-based participatory research, specifically with schools and after-school programs.

Lionel C. Howard, EdD, is Associate Professor of Educational Research at The George Washington University, in Washington DC. Howard's research interests include, broadly, racial and gender development and socialization, motivation and academic achievement, and qualitative research methodology.

Timothy J. Lensmire is Professor of Curriculum and Instruction at the University of Minnesota, where he teaches courses in race, literacy, and critical pedagogy. His current work examines how white people learn to be white, as part of a larger effort to develop more effective antiracist pedagogies.

Danielle T. Ligocki is Assistant Professor of Education in the Department of Teacher Development and Educational Studies at Oakland University in Rochester, Michigan. She spent 11 years teaching junior high school in a high-needs area before making the move to higher education.

Leslie Ann Locke is Assistant Professor of Educational Policy and Leadership Studies at the University of Iowa. She received her PhD from Texas A&M University in 2011. Her research interests include leadership for social justice, schooling for students from marginalized groups, equity-oriented education policy, and qualitative methodologies.

Cheryl E. Matias is an associate professor in the School of Education and Human Development (SEHD) at the University of Colorado Denver. She is the faculty founder of Research Advocacy in Critical Education (R.A.C.E.). Her research focuses on race and ethnic studies in education, critical race theory, critical whiteness studies, critical pedagogy, and feminism of color.

David J. Nguyen is Assistant Professor of Higher Education and Student Affairs at Ohio University. He holds his PhD in Higher, Adult, and Lifelong Education from Michigan State University. He incorporates visual research tools when studying his research interests, which focus on access and equity issues facing underserved and underrepresented college students.

Laura Parson is an assistant professor in the Higher Education Administration Program at Auburn University. Her research interests focus on identifying the institutional practices, processes, and discourses that coordinate the experiences of women and underrepresented groups in higher education, explored through a critical lens.

Heather E. Price, PhD, is an assistant professor in the Leadership Studies doctoral program at Marian University. Her research focuses on sociology and educational policy. Price previously worked as a senior analyst at the University of Notre Dame and the private educational policy sector, and taught for years in the Milwaukee District.

Kristen A. Renn, PhD, is Professor of Higher, Adult, and Lifelong Education at Michigan State University, where she also serves as Associate Dean of Undergraduate Studies for Student Success Research. She studies student identities, learning, and success with particular focus on students who are minoritized in higher education by their race, ethnicity, sexual orientation, gender, gender identity, socioeconomic class, or first-generation college student status.

Carli Rosati is Assistant Director for Student Success Initiatives at Rice University. She holds a BA in Political Science and Women's, Gender, and Sexuality Studies and an MEd in College Student Personnel, both from Ohio University. Her research interests center on student activism and feminist theory.

Karen Ross is Assistant Professor of Conflict Resolution at the University of Massachusetts-Boston, where her work focuses on conceptual and methodological issues at the nexus of peace-building, education, and sociopolitical activism. She is also a dialogue practitioner and trainer.

Argun Saatcioglu, PhD, is Associate Professor of Educational Leadership and Policy Studies and (by courtesy) Sociology at the University of Kansas. He studies educational inequality and school organization. His recent work has appeared in *Teachers College Record*, *Du Bois Review: Social Science Research on Race*, and *Sociological Inquiry*.

Thomas M. Skrtic, PhD, is Williamson Family Distinguished Professor of Special Education at the University of Kansas. His interests include disability policy and politics and critical policy inquiry. He has published his work in several books and in journals such as *Harvard Educational Review* and *Disability Studies Quarterly*.

Sam Steen, PhD, is Director of the Counseling Program at the University of Arizona, Associate Professor, and a practitioner-researcher. He served as a school counselor for ten years before entering academia and has spent approximately eight years consulting, collaborating, and conducting school-based research within public schools in Washington, DC.

Kamden K. Strunk, PhD, is Assistant Professor of Educational Research at Auburn University, where he teaches quantitative methods coursework. He holds his PhD in Educational Psychology from Oklahoma State University. His research focuses on intersections of sexual, gender, and racial identities in higher education, and broadly on social justice and equity in education.

Kenzo K. Sung, PhD, is Assistant Professor of Urban Education and Education Foundations, and affiliated faculty with Africana Studies and American Studies, at Rowan University. His research areas include urban education and policy, ethnic studies, critical race theory, history of education, political economy, and social movements and reforms.

Lolita A. Tabron, PhD, is Assistant Professor of Educational Leadership and Policy Studies in the Morgridge College of Education at the University of Denver. Through critical policy analyses and critical quantitative inquiries, she studies how systemic racism and other forms of oppression are perpetuated and sustained through policies, politics, and statistical data.

Aaron R. Tolbert, PhD, currently serves as the Dean of Liberal Arts at SUNY Schenectady County Community College. He also serves as the college co-chair for the Achieving the Dream Core Team. He holds a PhD in Higher Education from the University of Maine, and an MA in English from the University of Vermont. Tolbert's research interests are highly varied, including discourse, policy analysis, agency, access to higher education, and equity in higher education.

Rose M. Troyer is a Community Coordinator at Denison University. She holds a BS in Journalism and an MEd in College Student Personnel, both from Ohio University. Her research interests focus on student activism and civil discourse within the academy.

Jeff Walls is Assistant Professor of Educational Foundations and Leadership at the University of Louisiana at Lafayette. His research interests include caring school environments, school-level policy implementation, and how school leaders and teachers collaborate in their efforts to produce more equitable schools.

James S. Wright, PhD, is Assistant Professor of Educational Leadership at San Diego State University. His research agenda is highlighted by the ways in which educational administration and leadership are positioned to rewrite historical inequities across the educational landscape. He holds a master's degree in Business Administration (MBA), which he leverages to broaden understandings of organization and economic currents that impact schooling and educational reform.

List of Figures

Fig. 14.1 "Discipline from the teachers can be difficult because sometimes the guys (or girls) in the class don't want to listen" 170

Fig. 14.2 "Students seem more focused and on-task" 172

Fig. 14.3 "In a unisex class, we always thought that we were bigger than each other. Our egos were high" 172

Fig. 17.1 Within-group student shutoff along the Advanced Placement curriculum pipeline. Source: Civil Rights Data Collection, pooled school years of 2011–12 and 2013–14 210

List of Tables

Table 1.1   Validity horizon for Example 1 7
Table 1.2   Validity horizon for Example 2 8
Table 1.3   Validity horizon for Example 3 10
Table 1.4   Validity horizon for Example 4 11
Table 17.1 HHI scores along the Advanced Placement curriculum
            pipeline 211
Table 19.1 PSR-adjusted multinomial estimates for odds of mild disability
            labels 234

Introduction

Typical instruction in research methods in education can be detached from real issues and real problems in education; it often focuses on the nuts and bolts of research processes, and sometimes with examples that are less than substantive. Similarly, students often progress through their research methods coursework with no real sense of how those methods can contribute to moves toward (or away from) equity. Our goal with this book is to provide theoretical, methodological, and practical information on how to mobilize educational research and research methods for social justice and equity in education.

Our experiences teaching similar content have guided our decisions about the structure of the text. We have observed that students often come to these classes with very static and uncritical ideas about research methodologies. They often think of those methodologies as set, natural, and unquestionable. So, we open the text with chapters that challenge those assumptions, and push students to think critically about the nature of the methodologies they are already familiar with and how those could be adapted for the purposes of social justice and equity. Further, we firmly believe that research must always be theoretical, and that without theory, research becomes reductive and meaningless. Because of that, the text next highlights several central and commonly used theoretical frameworks in research for social justice an equity. In introductory methods courses, students usually next arrive at questions around the practicalities of getting approval for this kind of research, collecting data for social justice and equity ends, and how they can analyze those data. So, the second section of the textbook includes chapters addressing these very practical, procedural questions about the conduct of social-justice-oriented and equity-oriented research. Finally, as students usually then want to understand how to apply those theoretical perspectives and research procedures to various areas of content, the culminating section of the book includes narratives from scholars articulating their research agenda and how they have worked with various methodologies in service of that research agenda. They also describe how they found a place and made careers as scholar-activists. The three sections of the textbook are titled, Philosophical and Theoretical Issues: Liberating Frameworks and Methodologies; Collecting and Analyzing Data for Social Justice and Equity; and Approaches to Social Justice and Equity in Educational Research.

We hope this textbook helps to guide students and researchers through the most typical sequence of questions they generate while exploring research for social justice and equity. In addition, the rationale for and structure of this book is guided in part by focus group interviews with current and former students. We have both taught these courses and debriefed with students the kinds of materials they would have found most helpful in the course. Thus, our goal was to create a textbook structure that meets most of those needs.

There are also a number of instructional supplements included in the text. One such supplement is that most authors have suggested further readings related to their chapters. A book like this is, necessarily, more of a survey text, and will not fully explore the depths of any theory or methodology. But we suggest that students who find they resonate with a particular approach that is introduced in this text take the next step of exploring the suggestions for further reading. These authors have thoughtfully selected readings that would help someone learn more and go deeper with their content. In addition to those suggestions for further reading, we have also collaborated with the chapter authors to produce a terminology section, found at the end of this text. That terminology section defines many terms and we hope provides some clarity on commonly misunderstood terms. Finally, we provide an index at the end of the text. We hope that is helpful in cross-referencing the ways that different approaches take up the same kinds of issues and problems. We appreciate the time and thought that the authors included in this textbook have taken to explain their approaches to research for social justice and equity in education. Below we provide a brief synopsis of each chapter.

Meagan Call-Cummings and Karen Ross explore how researchers might engage in reflexivity. The authors engage in reconstructive horizon analysis (RHA), which is an approach for examining taken-for-granted claims made by ourselves and our research participants. They find that by engaging in RHA, we build moments for dialogue and communication into the research process that allow assumptions, structures, and roles to be made explicit.

Laura Parson outlines the ethical concerns and potential methodological obstacles that can occur when conducting research with underrepresented, marginalized, or minoritized groups. Prioritizing the implications of conducting this research as a member of a dominant group and/or with privileged outsider status, she describes key methodological strategies to use when conducting social-justice-oriented research to address or mitigate ethical concerns and methodological obstacles.

Elena Aydarova notes that social justice research most often focuses on the voices, experiences, and practices of underserved and marginalized groups. While this focus produces important insights, it disregards the actions of those in power who create and maintain systems of inequality and injustice in the first place. To address this gap, she examines methodological approaches for studying up or researching the powerful. It describes the challenges faced by researchers who study those in power, such as problems of access, interview pitfalls, dangers in data analysis and interpretation, ethical concerns, and dissemination of findings. She also provides suggestions for how researchers can address those challenges.

Kenzo K. Sung and Natoya Coleman note that critical race theory (CRT) is now a prominent framework for critical scholarship on race and racism in the field of education. They trace CRT's trajectory in educational research and analyzing the significance of its legacy, and provide an alternative framework to analyze how racism is institutionalized through research-based or legalized "truths" that too often continue to perpetuate the oppression of minoritized communities. Further, they illuminate the significance of critical race analysis in educational research and the implications to reframe current discussions regarding the relation of research and the struggle for social justice.

Christian D. Chan, Sam Steen, Lionel C. Howard, and Arshad I. Ali explore the complexities of queer theory and how it might integrate with and diverge from intersectionality. They suggest ways in which to use both theoretical approaches in educational research, as well as implications for studying genders and sexualities in education.

Kamden K. Strunk and Jasmine S. Betties provide an introductory overview of critical theory. They particularly work to differentiate this theoretical approach from other similarly named approaches such as critical race theory. They explain some of the basic concepts of critical theory and how those might be applied in educational research.

Danielle T. Ligocki notes that understanding the power that research holds to advance the need for social justice and equity is a crucial step in making real societal, institutional, and educational change. In her chapter, she sought to explain Zygmunt Bauman's theory of liquid modernity and provide a new understanding regarding how this theory works to frame and explain this current historical moment and how all areas of society have been impacted, but specifically the work of the researcher.

Lucy E. Bailey offers reflections on emancipatory research methods and examples of maneuvers in feminist qualitative methodology that are oriented toward social justice, crystallizing in the specific space, time, and moment of inquiry. She casts a critical eye on "social justice methods," and argues that all researchers are subject to shifting forms of normalization and that we should work toward keeping methods as contingent and dynamic, to serve educational projects with varied allegiances and aims.

Leslie Ann Locke has two chapters in this volume. In the first chapter, based on her experiences teaching introductory qualitative methods courses, she highlights some of the questions students who are new to qualitative methods struggle with in her courses. Specifically, she identifies ideas around objectivity and multiple truths, generalizability, positionality, and ambiguity as particular areas where students are challenged. In the second chapter, she details human subjects review and its purpose, some of the processes associated with applying for institutional review board (IRB) approval for research studies involving human subjects, and the main elements required of an IRB application.

Shiv R. Desai discusses youth participatory action research (YPAR) to challenge traditional social science research as it teaches young people how to inquire about complex power relations, histories of struggle, and the consequences of oppression directly related to their lives. Additionally, Desai explains the central critiques of YPAR and provides insights and challenges from a YPAR study with system-involved youth.

Elizabeth J. Allan and Aaron R. Tolbert discuss policy discourse analysis (PDA) which draws from critical and poststructural theories to provide researchers with an approach to identifying dominant discourses shaping policy problems and solutions. They define PDA, describe the conceptual principles of the approach, and detail the research methods for implementation of a PDA study. Examples of studies employing PDA are used to illustrate the utility of the approach.

Jeff Walls and Samantha E. Holquist highlight the promise of photo elicitation-based data collection to authentically leverage student voice in research on policy and school improvement in ways that promote equity and critical social justice. These authors highlight methodological choices researchers must make in utilizing photo elicitation, and how these choices bear on the equity implications of this method.

Susan Cridland-Hughes, McKenzie Brittain, and S. Megan Che explore a critical version of photovoice to describe a study of single-sex middle school classrooms in a small school in the Southeast (a term used by the school district). They share a critical analysis of the implementation of photovoice and their imperfect research process. Their analysis is guided by recommendations by members of historically marginalized communities for reframing research to be collaborative and responsive to community needs.

James S. Wright argues that life history methodology can be used as a counter to traditional research methodologies and provides space to collect and analyze data in a way that counters past traditions. He notes that life history provides real opportunities for educational researchers to develop new knowledge by listening to and validating the experiences of the most vulnerable populations. Life history challenges the idea of a universal truth—stemming from Eurocentric positionalities.

Kamden K. Strunk and Payton D. Hoover note that quantitative methods, both in their historical and contemporary use, have been mobilized from hegemonic, positivist perspectives with implicit assumptions of whiteness and cisheteropatriarchy. In their chapter, they highlight some of the historical, theoretical, and practical challenges in using quantitative methods in equity-oriented scholarship and suggest practical ways to humanize those methods.

Heather E. Price argues that large-scale datasets allow for the tracking of persistent patterns of inequality and inequity in education. In her chapter, she demonstrates how inequality in students' learning opportunities compound in high schools through the use of the Civil Rights Data Collection (CRDC) of Advanced Placement (AP) and International Baccalaureate (IB) curricula to demonstrate how a four-part chain of events in curriculum opportunities exacerbate inequality of education in the US. She works to move forward the educational opportunity and tracking discussions in the twenty-first century to understand the nested spaces of opportunity along curricular pipelines.

Carli Rosati, David J. Nguyen, and Rose M. Troyer demonstrate how campus maps tend to illustrate places and spaces, and also hold stories and experiences that may alienate students. They share how pairing campus maps with a semi-structured interview protocol can yield new insights into campus life.

Argun Saatcioglu and Thomas M. Skrtic illustrate a "propensity score" procedure as a research alternative. Their chapter focuses on disproportionate racial/ethnic representation in mild disability labeling, using a large federal dataset. They discuss testing labeling differences and find evidence of strong racial/ethnic disproportionality, which varies by grade and disability type. Other potential applications of this approach are highlighted.

Carey E. Andrzejewski, Benjamin Arnberg, and Hannah Carson Baggett explore the applications of mixed methods approaches to social justice and equity-oriented research. They describe some of the common ways of thinking about mixed methods, as well as ways to integrate this work with social justice paradigms. They also offer illustrative cases of "missed opportunities" in educational research and mixed methods.

Timothy J. Lensmire traces how his critical teaching and scholarship has sought to contribute to what John Dewey called creative democracy. He explores how the teaching of writing might serve radical democratic ends, and discusses his examination of the complexities and conflicts of Whiteness and White racial identities. He also notes his connection to the works of Mikhail Bakhtin and W.E.B. Du Bois (among many others) as well as how his hatred of school and love of basketball are significant influences on his living and learning.

Cheryl E. Matias discusses an exploration of life in the academy while doing racially just work, and the associated difficulties. She explains that those who relay their experiences in the academy as a way to improve the professoriate are incorrectly labeled whistleblowers and are often met with resistance, passive aggressive bullying tactics, or find themselves and their scholarship constantly under scrutiny. She notes that instead of listening and learning from the stories shared about academy life, administrators who do have the power to make changes belittle and minimize the stories as if they are just mere whines of a baby. To combat this, she shares three essays that paint a picture of academy life while doing racially just work. She also shares the trials, tribulations, and simple successes of this path so that professors and administrators can create more racially just educational systems that is inclusive to faculty of color and scholars of race.

Lolita A. Tabron notes that historically, statistical research has been used as a tool of oppression attempting to "prove" the intellectual and cultural inferiority of communities of color (i.e. bell curve, Tuskegee Syphilis Study, eugenics, IQ testing) and obscure the reality of racism. Such scientific racism is the foundation of the US education system and contextualizes many of the contemporary issues of racial and social stratification today. She discusses the need for critical quantitative inquiry, where researchers disrupt and push for the re-imagining of ways to engage in more culturally inclusive and sustaining approaches to quantitative inquiry and argues that statistics is a powerful tool that can be used to resist oppression through community-driven, justice-oriented work.

Kristen A. Renn recounts the pathways she followed in developing a line of LGBTQ research and her identity as a queer researcher. Specifically, she traces the parallel pathways of becoming an LGBTQ activist and focusing her research on LGBTQ topics, in the process coming to terms with the ways that she was socialized to follow rules, not to draw attention to herself, and not cause trouble. She further describes how she came to understand herself as a scholar who works intentionally to create a more socially just version of higher education while also being in tension with the idea that higher education is itself inherently unjust.

Erica R. Dávila reflects on her research trajectory, which is rooted in collaboration, community, and collectives. She includes a discussion of her development as a scholar-activist and her work with justice-centered research projects. Overall, she highlights her work with and for our people, lived experiences grounded in struggle and hope, and the power that schools and universities have to liberate as well as oppress.

While there are scholars from a broad mix of educational fields, and who apply a variety of methodological approaches in their work, included in this textbook, we do not intend this to be a comprehensive treatment. Rather, we hope it is the beginning of a conversation, and that students and faculty are able to go deeper with methods and theories that resonate with them through the suggestions for further reading. Further, we hope *Research Methods for Social Justice and Equity in Education* is useful for faculty and graduate students alike, as they conduct their work, and that it provides a meaningful exploration of social justice and equity-related research across educational contexts.

University of Iowa   Leslie Ann Locke
Iowa City, IA, USA
Auburn University   Kamden K. Strunk
Auburn, AL, USA

Part I
Theoretical and Philosophical Issues

Chapter 1
Re-positioning Power and Re-imagining Reflexivity: Examining Positionality and Building Validity Through Reconstructive Horizon Analysis

Meagan Call-Cummings and Karen Ross

Abstract In this chapter, we explore how researchers might engage in reflexivity. Reflexivity is closely related to the concept of positionality, which refers to the way we as researchers view our *position* in the world in relation to others, especially those who are involved in or may read our research. Often reflexivity is issued as a call—an important step to take to establish the validity, rigor, or ethical nature of the research being done. Here we engage in reconstructive horizon analysis (RHA), which is an approach for examining taken-for-granted claims made by ourselves and our research participants. We find that by engaging in RHA, we build moments for dialogue and communication into the research process that allow assumptions, structures, and roles to be made explicit.

Over the past 20 years, much discussion and debate in methodological literature has revolved around reflexivity: what it means, what it looks and feels like, and how it is best "done." Linda Finlay and Gough, in her (2008) edited volume, *Reflexivity: A Practical Guide for Researchers in Health and Social Sciences*, defines reflexivity as "thoughtful, self-aware analysis of the intersubjective dynamics between researcher and the researched" (p. ix), acknowledging that "reflexivity both challenges treasured research traditions and is challenging to apply in practice" (p. ix).

Both authors contributed equally to this manuscript.

M. Call-Cummings (✉)
George Mason University, Fairfax, VA, USA
e-mail: mcallcum@gmu.edu

K. Ross
University of Massachusetts Boston, Boston, MA, USA
e-mail: karen.ross@umb.edu

K. K. Strunk, L. A. Locke (eds.), *Research Methods for Social Justice and Equity in Education*, https://doi.org/10.1007/978-3-030-05900-2_1

In this chapter, we explore these issues by focusing on *how* we as researchers can engage in reflexivity, a concept we define as purposeful, often challenging reflection about ourselves, how we identify, and what we take for granted as true or right. Reflexivity is closely related to the concept of positionality, which refers to the way we as researchers view our *position* in the world in relation to others, especially those who are involved in or may read our research. In particular, positionality requires us to think about how our background and experiences play a role in our relationships with participants and in how we carry out research: for instance, how might one's gender/race/class/religion or other aspect of one's identity affect the choices one makes about what questions to ask an interview participant or how one interacts with participants of similar or different backgrounds during the interview? Being explicit about our positionality is important as a way of helping readers understand how the lens through which we see the world is reflected in our research.

As our opening paragraph suggests, there is agreement among many (though not all) methodologists about the importance of exploring positionality and reflexivity, especially in order to be transparent about how our backgrounds shape both the process and results of our research. However, there is much less agreement about how to engage in reflexivity in productive ways. Scholars have illuminated challenges to doing so through discussions of reflexive practice as well as through what scholars have learned from engaging reflexively. Most often, reflexivity is issued as a call—an important step to take to establish the validity, rigor, or ethical nature of the research being done, especially for scholars who are determined to engage in knowledge production that is critical, participatory, emancipatory, and democratized. Often these calls relate to concerns about the representation of participants. For example, Milner (2007) charges researchers to engage in the process of cultural and racial introspection in their research in order to avoid some of the potential dangers of (mis)representation that can occur in varying research contexts. He argues that researchers in the process of conducting research "pose racially and culturally grounded questions about themselves," and that attention to these questions can "bring the researcher awareness and consciousness of known (seen), unknown (unseen), and unanticipated (unforeseen) issues, perspective, epistemologies, and positions" (p. 395). By researching the self in relation to others, Milner (2007) maintains, researchers can better understand issues of power and self-interest, which can overshadow the interests of participants. This kind of "engaged reflection and representation" (p. 396) can allow researchers and participants to explore together what is happening in that particular research community, allowing the research findings to become products of shared interpretation and perspective.

Pillow (2003) calls for researchers to work toward an uncomfortable reflexivity—a reflexive practice that seeks to "know while at the same time situate this knowing as tenuous" (p. 188). Her work highlights the often vulnerable and personally challenging aspect of reflexivity, and she urges researchers to understand reflexivity as a "methodological tool interruptive of practices of gathering data" to produce what she acknowledges are likely uncomfortable "tellings" (p. 192). She suggests that reflexivity is about more than just an accounting of researchers' struggles with representation but should also attend to accountability to that representation.

Guillemin and Gillam (2004) advocate for a kind of reflexivity that they connect to the concept of "ethics in practice" (p. 262). They suggest that ethical engagement in the research process requires a constant monitoring of the ethical implications of one's choices as a researcher. This practice of continuous scrutiny—of relationships between researcher and participant, research context, and the purposes of research, in addition to methods—is, in Guillemin and Gillam's view, a form of reflexivity.

This idea expands the role of reflexivity beyond the examination of epistemological aspects of research, to its use as a conceptual tool for understanding how researchers might exercise ethical practice in research. Guillemin and Gillam (2004) say that researchers should develop ways to address and respond to ethical issues that arise in the research process. By so doing, researchers can prepare for potential problems and even prevent them. Framing reflexivity as a skill in this way—the ability to recognize and effectively navigate ethically important moments—is exciting, but still begs the question: how? How can researchers examine and account for their positionalities in research that works toward equity and social justice? And when? Is reflexivity only called for upon completion of a study? Or, like Milner (2007) and Pillow (2003) seem to suggest, is there something about the role of reflexivity that demands its use throughout the process of knowledge production? Lastly, we ask, with whom? Finlay and Gough (2008) is explicit that reflexivity allows intersubjective understandings and dynamics between and among the researcher and the researched to emerge. Yet the literature on reflexivity as a whole emphasizes internal introspection focused on *oneself*, thus leaving it unclear how self-reflection might occur in a way that opens up possibilities for position-taking and deeper intersubjective understanding of meaning.

Reconstructive Horizon Analysis: An Introduction

Carspecken's (1996) reconstructive horizon analysis (RHA) is a methodological tool that can help researchers in this quest to "do" reflexivity in a way that is meaningful. In particular, RHA is a tool that requires individuals to position-take, that is, to explicitly take the position or perspective of other actors (such as research participants) in a way that is conscious and explicit rather than in the tacit, implicit manner that is characteristic of most interactions (Carspecken, 1996). Moreover, as Dennis (2017) states, "when we listen to the claims of others, our interpretations involve position-taking, which intrinsically require our self-commitments and positionings within the interpretations" (p. 112). As a tool used to deepen understanding of a participant's speech acts, RHA can be understood as a form of "listening" to the claims of others, wherein the attempt is made to hear those claims more clearly. As such, it requires position-taking from the perspective of the participant as well as from one's position—this inherently creates a *dialogic* approach to reflexivity, wherein a researcher is moving through multiple positions in attempting to bring tacit claims into explicit discourse.

According to Carspecken (1996), who bases his work in Habermas' (1984, 1985) Theory of Communicative Action, the implicit reasons behind an action or communicative claim fall into one of four categories of validity claims: objective (based on the principle of multiple access), subjective (based on the principle of unique access by the communicator), normative-evaluative (relating to norms by which we operate in a given society or culture), or identity claims (references by the communicator to who that person is in the world); these reasons also differ based on "how immediately they are referenced in the original act (foregrounded) or how remotely they are referenced (backgrounded)" (p. 111). RHA is an approach for examining taken-for-granted claims made by ourselves and our research participants that allows us to locate the source of discomfort that is central to reflexivity.

We offer four examples from our fieldwork to highlight how this can be done. Our use of RHA entails the creation of what Carspecken (1996) refers to as a *validity horizon*, which puts into explicit discourse the tacit validity and identity claims articulated in a specific communicative act.

Example 1

In the midst of an interview with Bayan,[1] a Palestinian woman, I (Karen) found myself discussing enlistment in the Israel Defense Forces (IDF). Our conversation had focused on Bayan's experiences, several years prior, in a program designed to bring Jewish and Palestinian youth together for joint learning and education toward activism. As we spoke, Bayan discussed the issue of enlistment among her Jewish friends from the program, how some had enlisted and some had not, and how this had helped her understand that there is more complexity among the Jewish population in Israel than she had previously thought. In the midst of discussing this, Bayan suddenly asked me, "Did you enlist?" I found myself extremely uncomfortable in that moment and unsure how to respond. Ultimately, the conversation went like this:

> *Karen*: Yes, I enlisted. I enlisted out of a belief that I could try to change things from… inside the military.
> *Bayan*: Yes, one of my friends, I heard the same thing from her, about trying to change things from the inside.
> *Karen*: Yes. I'm not totally sure it's possible, to be honest.
> *Bayan*: That's exactly what I told her.
> *Karen*: But, anyway, for me, it was a long time ago, and the way I see things now is not the same way that I saw things then. Today if I were in the same position I am sure that I would not enlist. But it's something that…it's a process that takes time, for everyone.

By reconstructing the validity claims and identity claims in this example, we can better understand the discomfort I experienced in this conversation and its source (Table 1.1). In particular, the source of this discomfort can be addressed through a validity horizon focusing in the statement,

> But, anyway, for me, it was a long time ago, and the way I see things now is not the same way that I saw things then. Today if I were in the same position I am sure that I would not enlist. But it's something that…it's a process that takes time, for everyone.

Table 1.1 Validity horizon for Example 1

	Objective claim	Subjective claim	Normative-evaluative claim	Identity claim
Foreground	The IDF requires Jewish citizens of Israel to enlist.	I am uncomfortable telling Bayan that I enlisted.	Researchers should be honest with their research participants.	*I am an honest person.*
Mid-ground	There are ways for Jewish citizens to avoid enlisting.	I am concerned about how Bayan will react to my response. *I want Bayan to feel comfortable narrating her authentic self.*	Researchers should value relationships with their participants. Jewish citizens should not enlist without understanding why they do so.	I am a person who is willing to challenge the status quo.
Background	Enlistment in the IDF is not something that all Israeli citizens agree with.	I do not want Bayan to think I blindly submit to societal pressure.	*It is appropriate for research participants to ask researchers questions that make them uncomfortable.*	I am a person who is willing to acknowledge poor decisions in my past.

Using RHA to create a validity horizon allows for a much better understanding of where my discomfort, as a researcher, came from, *as well as* my own normative beliefs and the role they played in creating discomfort. Although this validity horizon focused on a comment *I* had made, the tacit claims it put into explicit discourse highlight how in the process of speaking these words, I was engaged in a process of trying to reconcile my perspective with Bayan's, based on my presumed understanding of her position. Specifically, the italicized subjective, normative-evaluative, and identity claims illustrate a situation where my desire for authentic interaction with Bayan stood in tension with my sense of self as an honest individual. Ultimately, it is difficult to know whether my response facilitated or mitigated a sense of comfort on Bayan's part to express herself honestly; however, the validity horizon makes clear the different pulls on my sense of accountability to her as a research participant and to myself in the process of data collection.

Example 2

After the conclusion of a semester-long participatory research project with English Language Learners at a local middle school, my (Meagan's) graduate research assistant interviewed me about my experience as one of the faculty leaders of the group. We were conducting these interviews with all those who were involved in the project because some of the graduate students who acted as "mentors" to the research participants had expressed frustration about their roles and the roles faculty members played during the project. They felt like there were power dynamics that

Table 1.2 Validity horizon for Example 2

	Objective claim	Subjective claim	Normative-evaluative claim	Identity claim
Foreground	I am a new faculty member here.	I am aware that I put my professional needs first.	People should be honest. People should not be selfish.	I am an honest person.
Mid-ground	My main focus at the beginning of this project was my career, not you or the participants.	Sometimes I feel torn between my needs and attending to my students' needs.	Sometimes it's okay to be selfish if it's for a good reason.	I need others to think I am honest. I am not really selfish, I am just trying to move my career forward.
Background	New faculty members need to begin to conduct research quickly in order to be competitive for tenure.	*I didn't think this through fully before I signed on for this project. I was not being transparent about whose needs I was attending to and the role I was taking in this project.*	*Researchers should clarify their expectations before engaging in research. Researchers should be transparent and intentional about their goals and their roles as they engage in research.*	I am an ambitious person. *Sometimes I am not as thoughtful or intentional or transparent as I should be.*

were not explicitly attended to. Overall, they felt like the project did not live up to its full potential. Conducting these interviews became an opportunity to reflect on what happened, understand each other's perspectives on what maybe went wrong, and plan for more ethical work in the future. During my interview, Marie, my research assistant, asked me about the expectations I had coming into the project (Table 1.2).

> *Marie*: So you said your expectations were kind of undefined, when you went in. But what did you hope to gain from it, or what was your objective in joining?
>
> *Meagan*: This is probably really selfish, but as a new faculty member, honestly I was just trying to get into a school or into a space. I was trying to start research and hit the ground running. Coming here as a new assistant professor. Trying to get contacts in schools, start working with you, you guys as students, doctoral students. Get some research under my belt. That type of thing. I mean, of course I love photovoice, and of course I wanted to work with students, but I think that was kind of secondary or different than really just wanting to get into schools and start—start doing good research.

Focusing in on my first sentence here helps to illuminate more backgrounded truth claims:

> *This is probably really selfish, but as a new faculty member, honestly I was just trying to get into a school or into a space.*

The act of constructing this RHA table allowed me to see the validity claims that I had taken for granted when I was speaking. When I spoke these words, I was aware that I was speaking about professional priorities. After examining the horizon of these claims, however, I realized that I was also indicating my lack of intentionality, thoughtfulness, and transparency as I took the project on. This realization makes me extraordinarily uncomfortable, even now as I write. I see an implied act of power in my original dismissal of my lack of thoughtfulness and intentionality as I put my own needs ahead of the needs of my students. Engaging in RHA allowed me to see my actions and understand the justification of those actions from others' positions. Through this exercise, I clarified my need to be accountable not only to my own professional needs but also to those of my students.

Redistributing Power Through Reflexive Reconstructions

The preceding examples are meant to illustrate that researcher engagement with RHA can allow for a better understanding of one's own positionality (through the process of making backgrounded validity claims explicit), as well as for articulating points of tension in the data collection (and larger research) process that can shape the validity of findings. RHA is useful not only for making explicit issues of power and other taken-for-granted claims that arise in research contexts but also for position-taking and thus making the reflexive process more dialogically oriented.

Yet, we wonder about the challenge of using RHA in a fully democratized and dialogic way that moves the researcher and the researched toward greater intersubjective understanding. In our experience, the use of RHA almost always happens as a retrospective or reflective/reflexive analytical exercise (i.e., after "being in the moment" of discomfort in a fieldwork situation). Engaging in this analysis allows us to learn from what has happened in the past, and even potentially think about how we can "do better" the next time around as a result of what has been learned. But, if we think back to Guillemin and Gillam's (2004) idea that, by building the skill of reflexivity, researchers can prepare for and even prevent moments that are ethically troubling, we wonder how RHA might offer a clear path for examining and accounting for our own positionalities "in the moment"? Is that even possible? And how can engaging in RHA "in the moment" and *with* our participants build a stronger intersubjective understanding of each other's positions and positionalities?

One possibility we suggest is to use RHA not only as a tool for better understanding one's positionality in an intersubjective way but also as a tool that can help us be more accountable to our participants. Specifically, we suggest that RHA might become a part of a multilayered member checking process, and thus a basis for dialogue and a more explicit position-taking process with our participants. In the following examples, we illustrate situations where we believe dialogic engagement *with* RHA could potentially have been used as the basis for developing a deeper understanding of our own and our research participants' perspectives.

Example 3

In 2012, I (Meagan) conducted several interviews with people in Jamaica who were involved in peace education, either as teachers, principals, school counselors, non-profit staff members, or other members of civil society. Principal Nathan, the principal of a high school renowned for students that "behaved badly," agreed to be interviewed but did not want to have her interview audio recorded. Therefore, I wrote notes during the interview and then wrote up everything I remembered immediately following the interview. Any verbatim speech I had captured in my notes were set off in italics:

> She is talking about talking to teachers, giving them advice on how to treat difficult students. *Treat the issue like a Doberman or* (other dog, comments missed) *comes to attack you. Don't show your fear. Treat it with authority. Spare the rod, spoil the child.*
>
> *I beat. You can write that.* (A few seconds pass as she talks more.) *My warning: I'm not going to back off from any student.* (She puts more force into the word "any" with more volume, and more depth, as if she's punching someone with her voice.)
>
> *Pickney fi' afraid of adult.*

I emailed the notes to Principal Nathan for her comments. She responded to the section above:

> Thank you for sending this to me. It seems like you are doing good work; however, your notes indicate that you possibly do not understand Jamaica or the children I am charged with educating and controlling as well as you might think. The only words you wrote down or remembered paint a picture of me as a person who only wants control or vengeance.

Although I knew she might have been upset seeing the transcription and notes, I was still taken aback by her comments. I did not know what to do. Now, I envision working through an RHA on her comments emailed back to me to try and take Principal Nathan's perspective (position-take) to understand better points where there has been a breakdown in meaning and thus in validity (Table 1.3).

Table 1.3 Validity horizon for Example 3

	Objective claim	Subjective claim	Normative-evaluative claim	Identity claim
Foreground	You do not understand me.	It is important to me that you understand me.	You should try to understand me.	I am an educator who works hard to serve students.
Mid-ground	You do not understand my job or this context.	My job is really hard and it is frustrating that you do not seem to understand that.	Researchers who do not fully understand a context should not conduct research on that context.	I am misunderstood.
Background	You did not fairly represent me or what I said.	I do not feel understood and that is hurtful.	*Researchers should be understanding. Good and valid research reflects understanding.*	*I am someone who is often misunderstood.*

After working through the process of parsing out the various validity claims implicit in her statements, I attempted to try to take Principal Nathan's position so as to understand better her perspective instead of jumping to my conclusions and feeling defensive. Doing so, and narrowing in on the backgrounded normative and identity claims Principal Nathan may have implied through her email, I clarified for myself the possible justifications she may have made for her words. Looking back, I could have delved deeper into my assumptions through RHA and then met with Principal Nathan to discuss the backgrounded claims and taken-for-granted assumptions I had uncovered. In this way I could have engaged more dialogically, reaching toward intersubjective understanding. Discussing these assumptions *with* Principal Nathan would have also enabled her to comment on my interpretation of her words and mitigate the power imbalance that exists when researchers make monological decisions about the meaning of their participants' statements.

Example 4

At the end of one of my (Karen's) interviews when living in Tel Aviv conducting my dissertation research, Neta, the woman I had spent the evening conversing with, offered me a ride part-way back to my apartment. As we sat in the car, we spoke about my research, and I mentioned that some participants had told me they enjoyed the opportunity to reflect on some aspects of their lives. Neta nodded her head and then said to me, "The reason I agreed to do this interview was because I knew it would help you out, and I'm the type of person who helps people out, always."

Neta's statement gave me pause. I found myself wondering, what did her statement suggest about the authenticity of her words? About the power dynamic between us? What should I take away from what she said? A validity horizon helped clarify my understanding of Neta's comment (Table 1.4).

Table 1.4 Validity horizon for Example 4

	Objective claim	Subjective claim	Normative-evaluative claim	Identity claim
Foreground	I helped you tonight with your research.	I feel good about helping you.	It is important to help other people.	I am a helpful person.
Mid-ground	Researchers need help in order to do their work.	It is important to me that you understand I did this for you.	*Researchers should appreciate the help they get from their participants.*	I am a person who is willing to do things for others even if they don't benefit me.
Background	Participants' choice of whether to help or not affects the end result of the research process.	*I am confident that I helped you tonight more than you helped me.*	*Research participants should be explicit about their reasons for participating in research projects.*	I am a person who is not afraid to share my thoughts.

It was only through going through the process of creating this validity horizon and attempting to understand Neta's position better that I had a sense of why her statement gave me pause: the highlighted mid-grounded and backgrounded normative-evaluative claims, and the backgrounded subjective claim, clarified for me what I understood to be Neta's perspective, and helped me realize that I had not spent sufficient time considering my own perspective on what the benefits of research participation should be and for whom. Engaging in the process of RHA, therefore, helped me clarify my perspectives on this issue. However, had I shared this validity horizon with Neta, I believe it would have been the basis for a rich dialogue about shared assumptions and misunderstandings that would have both allowed for a more accurate interpretation of her words *and* provided Neta with an opportunity to participate in the process of meaning-making and interpretation. In other words, using this validity horizon as the basis for a joint conversation could have served as a powerful tool for democratizing the meaning-making process that is an inherent part of interpretive research.

Conclusion

The examples above point to the utility of RHA as a tool for carrying out the "engaged reflection and representation" that Milner (2007) suggests is necessary for better understanding issues of power and self-interest. In particular, we believe RHA is an important tool because it requires researchers to position-take with respect to their research participants. This makes RHA unique as a tool for reflexivity, which generally occurs only as an introspective, self-focused exercise where researchers better aim to understand *their* perspectives. Because RHA requires making explicit the backgrounded claims that are central to one's understanding of both self *and* others, it moves us closer toward a communicatively based, intersubjectively structured understanding of meaning and process of sensemaking. Thus, RHA not only deepens the process of reflection but it also enables a potentially more accurate understanding of meaning and thus a more precise interpretation in the (intersubjective) analytical process.

We suggest that beyond its utility for researchers, moreover, RHA can be used to democratize the analytical process itself if used as part of member checking with participants. While it is not necessarily possible for us to engage in RHA during specific moments of fieldwork, it is possible for us to share and engage in dialogue about validity horizons with our research participants. Doing so provides an opportunity for participants thus to be part of the conversation about the assumptions that are made, and therefore to address the power imbalance that generally exists within the interpretive process. By engaging in RHA, we build moments for dialogue and communication into the research process that allow taken-for-granted assumptions, structures, and roles to be made explicit (Call-Cummings, 2017). Thus, this process carries with it the potential to enhance the validity of our interpretations as well as of the larger meaning-making projects in which we are engaged.

Suggestions for Further Reading

Berger, R. (2015). Now I see it, now I don't: Researcher's position and reflexivity in qualitative research. *Qualitative Research, 15*(2), 219–234. https://doi.org/10.1177/1468794112468475

This article is useful because it explicitly addresses how a researcher's social position, lived experiences, and beliefs interact with the process of reflexivity.

Chan, A. (2017). Reflection, reflexivity, reconceptualisation: Life story inquiry and the complex positionings of a researcher. *Reconceptualizing Educational Research Methodology, 8*(1), 27–39. https://doi.org/10.7577/rerm.2544

This is an example of reflection and reflexivity that can be useful, especially for those just starting to engage in qualitative inquiry, as well as for those interested in learning new approaches to become more reflexive.

Note

1. We use pseudonyms for all individuals referenced in this chapter, in order to protect confidentiality.

References

Call-Cummings, M. (2017). Establishing communicative validity: Discovering theory through practice. *Qualitative Inquiry, 23*(3), 192–200. https://doi.org/10.1177/1077800416657101

Carspecken, P. F. (1996). *Critical ethnography in educational research: A theoretical and practical guide*. New York, NY: Psychology Press.

Dennis, B. (2017). Validity as research praxis: A study of self-reflection and engagement in qualitative inquiry. *Qualitative Inquiry, 24*(2), 109–118. https://doi.org/10.1177/1077800416686371

Finlay, L., & Gough, B. (Eds.). (2008). *Reflexivity: A practical guide for researchers in health and social sciences*. New York, NY: John Wiley & Sons.

Guillemin, M., & Gillam, L. (2004). Ethics, reflexivity, and "ethically important moments" in research. *Qualitative Inquiry, 10*(2), 261–280. https://doi.org/10.1177/1077800403262360

Habermas, J. (1984). *The theory of communicative action* (Vol. 1). Boston, MA: Beacon Press.

Habermas, J. (1985). *The theory of communicative action* (Vol. 2). Boston, MA: Beacon Press.

Milner IV, H. R. (2007). Race, culture, and researcher positionality: Working through dangers seen, unseen, and unforeseen. *Educational Researcher, 36*(7), 388–400. https://doi.org/10.3102/0013189X07309471

Pillow, W. (2003). Confession, catharsis, or cure? Rethinking the uses of reflexivity as methodological power in qualitative research. *International Journal of Qualitative Studies in Education, 16*(2), 175–196. https://doi.org/10.1080/0951839032000060635

Chapter 2
Considering Positionality: The Ethics of Conducting Research with Marginalized Groups

Laura Parson

Abstract In this chapter, I outline the ethical concerns and potential methodological obstacles that can occur when conducting research with underrepresented, marginalized, or minoritized groups. Prioritizing the implications of conducting this research as a member of a dominant group and/or with privileged outsider status, I describe key methodological strategies to use when conducting social justice-oriented research to address or mitigate ethical concerns and methodological obstacles. Finally, I describe strategies for the ethical use and reporting of research findings by providing examples of existing and proposed social justice research projects.

Conducting research through a social justice lens is key to identify and explore the factors that marginalize and minoritize underrepresented groups and individuals. Historically, however, research procedures and reporting have often served to reinforce and exacerbate the marginalization of research participants and members of marginalized groups even when research was conducted with the intent of "helping" them (Goodkind & Deacon, 2004). Considering positionality allows one to identify how the research process has the potential to marginalize research participants and perpetuate structural and systemic discrimination of the researched population. By interrogating one's role, placement, and motivation, identifying one's positionality prompts researchers to explore the power and privilege inherent in one's identity. This consideration allows researchers to make decisions to mitigate the pitfalls of conducting research with marginalized groups, which includes an evaluation of if one is positioned such that they should not be conducting that research.

L. Parson (✉)
Auburn University, Auburn, AL, USA
e-mail: ljp@auburn.edu

© The Author(s) 2019

15

K. K. Strunk, L. A. Locke (eds.), *Research Methods for Social Justice and Equity in Education*, https://doi.org/10.1007/978-3-030-05900-2_2

Researchers hold a privileged status within the research process, regardless of their other salient identities. One's status as a researcher influences the research process from the selection of research questions, who is invited to participate, the selection of research methods, and decisions about how to report and share findings: "Strategies, tactics, and procedures that characterize power dynamics in research include participant selection, privacy, disclosure, interviews, observations, analysis, and the (re)presentation of research participants and their communities" (Vanner, 2015, p. 2). The ability to make these decisions in the research process represents the significant power of the researcher. Further, this decision-making power means that researchers have a significant role in creating and reifying knowledge: "Academic researchers represent centers of power, privilege, and status within their formal institutions, as well as within the production of scientific knowledge itself" (Muhammad et al., 2015, p. 1046). Reporting research results, such as through the publication process, defines what is considered knowledge, which is why decisions about what to study, how to conduct research, and what is reported convey significant power to researchers. Through a system of rewards and recognition, the research reporting and publication process confers power both to the reported "knowledge" and to the researcher/author.

The power of researchers in the power/knowledge process is significant. As a result, it is especially important to be mindful of one's place in the research process in order to identify how research might be reproducing existing power/knowledge frameworks that marginalize underrepresented groups (Muhammad et al., 2015). First, beyond selecting research parameters, researchers rebuild participant stories in ways that conform to the dominant ideology because they are recontextualizing the stories of research participants through their own lens as a member of the oppressor class. Without considering the bias inherent in one's worldview, "participants in the study are silenced, and that the last word remains with the uncontested and privileged interpretations of the author" (Arber, 2000, p. 45). Second, researchers often exploit participants in very colonizing ways. For example, if I publish a participant's words (accurate or misrepresented), then I profit via job security, accolades, or merit raises. Meanwhile, participants gain very little, if anything. I have, in essence, turned participants' "struggles in society" to my own personal gain. Considering positionality means identifying one's motivation for doing research and identifying how that research could be implicitly reinstantiating the very dynamics one hoped to document and interrupt.

Positionality prompts researchers to ask if this research should be done and if one is the researcher to be conducting this research. If one cannot really represent stories of people of color without them being implicitly and intrinsically reframed through a whiteness-infused worldview, then this is perhaps not the research that this researcher should be conducting. Further, even if researchers believe that their research is emancipatory, simply by speaking for participants in one's reports and writing, a researcher is still objectifying participants (Gordon, 2005, p. 280). Considering one's positionality is the first step toward conducting research that contributes to more equity in society, instead of reproducing inequity or diminishing it.

In this chapter, I begin by discussing the implications of conducting research from a position of privilege and critiques around privileged group members doing research with or "on" marginalized populations. Next, I define and discuss positionality, insider/outsider status, reflexivity, and the relationship between power and knowledge. Second, I discuss key strategies in the research process, beginning with research questions, the nature of participation, and reporting results. Finally, I suggest several research methodologies that incorporate ethical and participatory research methods, research methods designed with the goal of empowering participants that result in meaningful change.

Positionality

To understand the potential harms that come from doing research on marginalized populations without considering power/privilege, it is important to understand positionality and how to identify one's positionality in the research process. Suffla, Seedat, and Bawa (2015) define positionality as "the researcher's social location, personal experience, and theoretical viewpoint, the relational and institutional contexts of the research, and the bearing of these elements on the research process itself" (p. 16). Thinking about and identifying one's position in the research process is the first step toward understanding the impact of personal bias, because one's position limits them from seeing things from the perspective of someone in a different position: "One's position in the field is situated within a social hierarchy vis-à-vis other groups and individuals with regard to class, gender, ethnicity, and race, each of which potentially limits or broadens one's understanding of others" (Milgram, 2012, pp. 178–179). One's position impacts how a researcher anticipates participant needs in the research process, crafts research questions that truly seek to understand the participant's lived experiences and interprets participant's words.

To begin the process of considering positionality, one starts by identifying the salient and non-salient aspects of personal identity and the power and privilege embedded in the intersection of one's salient identities. The process of identifying one's position rejects the idea of a post-racial, post-feminist society. While one's identity, and therefore their positionality, is not limited to race, it is important that one first acknowledges that race, ethnicity, gender, sexuality, and other identities do exist:

> Colorblindness is a complex ideology in which White people are taught to ignore race, a stance that ends by reinscribing existing power relations that privilege White people. Colorblindness maintains that race does not exist as a meaningful category and posits that the benefits accrued to White people are earned by (gifted) individuals rather than systematically conferred. (Gordon, 2005, p. 281)

Ignoring the power and privilege that come along with racial identity and perceived racial identity virtually ensures that the research one conducts will, at the very least, perpetuate the marginalization of minoritized groups: "By pretending these implications are not real, we become complicit in reproducing them" (Gordon, 2005, p. 299). Similarly, one must also identify how their identity relates to class, ethnicity, gender, sexuality, and age, and the power/privilege inherent in those intersecting identities.

Indeed, in social-justice-oriented research, research should seek to improve the lives of the marginalized groups of individuals whose experiences the researcher is exploring. Yet, one cannot hope to make recommendations to improve their position if the researcher does not truly understand what marginalized persons are challenged by. Defining one's identity is the first step of that process. As an example, consider *The Immortal Life of Henrietta Lacks*, the movie based on Rebecca Skloot's book of the same name. In *The Immortal Life of Henrietta Lacks*, Skloot's (played by Rose Byrne) exploration of the life of Henrietta Lacks and the Lacks family provides an example, both positive and negative, of the difficult and often problematic ethical issues associated with conducting research as a White, privileged outsider with a disadvantaged group. The Lacks family, whose experiences Skloot is exploring, are Black, poor, and lack formal education as evidenced by degrees. While Skloot is disadvantaged by her gender because of systemic sexism in academia and journalism, she is simultaneously privileged by her race, education level, and socioeconomic status. In contrast, the Lacks family is disadvantaged by their race, socioeconomic status, and formal education level; the men in the Lacks family may be privileged because of gender, but the stereotype of Black men as criminals that is perpetuated throughout the movie serves to disadvantage the Lacks men. Skloot's power and privilege are witnessed when she can gain access to medical records that the family has not been able to access, despite repeated attempts. As one considers Skloot's positionality, this should raise questions about whether Skloot can truly understand the experiences of the Lacks family, how she can ethnically gain access to speak to them, and if she can speak for them. If Skloot cannot gain access or she cannot understand the experiences of the Lacks family, when she speaks for them, is she really speaking for them or continuing to marginalize them?

Considering Skloot's identity in the research process is just the first step. After defining one's identity, the next step in considering positionality as it impacts the research process is to identify how one's identity is related to the identities of those whose experiences one's research seeks to explore. This is not an exercise in describing how a group of individuals are different from the researcher and therefore deficient, which is the traditional way of viewing members of marginalized groups. Instead, exploring one's identity as it relates to the identities of the group whose experiences one hopes to improve is an exploration that acknowledges differences in order to consider how the intersection of power and privilege impacts a researcher's ability to conduct research ethically. Considering positionality in order to conduct research ethically is more than identifying how one might be less able to anticipate the methodological challenges of conducting research with marginalized groups. Considering positionality also includes identifying how the privileged aspects of one's identity have structured their life such that they view others through the lens of being in power. The privileged aspects of one's identity structure their relationship with power, and the ways in which one has been a beneficiary of asymmetric power relations may have conditioned them to see the world in ways that reproduce the goodness of their values, characteristics, and culture. That understanding of the world will impact the research process and knowingly or unknowingly impose that worldview on the data and those from whom the data originate.

To understand the identities of marginalized groups, it is important to understand the history of how they have been exploited and marginalized. Returning to *The Immortal Life of Henrietta* Lacks, the Lacks family has been exploited multiple times by researchers or people claiming to want to help the family or tell their story. Understanding how the Lacks family had been victimized in the past could have helped Skloot to approach the family differently or, perhaps, led her to reconsider the research project completely so that she did not contribute to their exploitation. In addition to considering immediate factors, it would also have been important for Skloot to consider the larger history of research and exploitation. Black Americans have been made unwilling participants in medical research since before slavery, such as the Tuskegee Syphilis study. Like many underrepresented groups, Henrietta Lacks was exploited as a patient when her cells were taken and used in research without her consent and acknowledgment. This medical invasion and ethical violation of her body is a history that was important to consider as Skloot decided how to approach the family to ask them to participate in her research.

Positionality does not just include identity differences that are apparent in how one presents themselves to the world but also research context and the researcher's role in the research process. Researchers, as a part of their identity, have power in the research process in the decisions they make about the research project. In traditional research methods, researchers decide whom to talk to, the questions participants are asked, where the research occurs, how participants' voices are used, and where to publish research results. In each step of the research process, researcher decisions take agency, and therefore power, away from participants. Researchers control the process, and therefore, the ways participants are involved, represented, and presented. This power is especially dangerous if one has not considered positionality and has not considered how one might not understand the experiences and perspectives of participants. If researchers are not asking the right questions, researcher recommendations and implications may not address the problematic, or, worse, address problems that do not exist. Further, a lack of awareness of researcher bias may lead one to frame participants, findings, and recommendations through a lens of privilege that views participants as deficient because they are unlike the researcher.

Making decisions in the research process, especially as it is designed within the modern, western university, researchers may still make decisions that marginalize participants, even if they share other characteristics with participants. Traditionally, research has been a colonizing practice even when occurring in decolonizing spaces:

> These spaces are officially decolonized but are usually characterized by a new imperialism shaped by the economic, political, military, and cultural hegemony of the West within the context of globalization. Therefore, the Western researcher represents not only a colonial past but also a neocolonial present. (Vanner, 2015, p. 1)

In addition to the researcher role, one's positionality also includes nationality. National privilege, as a western researcher, is an additional layer of identity that may impose western knowledge, culture, and values on non-western participants (Falcon, 2016, p. 176). Considering nationality is important, especially in cases where one shares certain aspects of their identity with research participants, such as race.

The intersection of one's identity interacts to privilege them in multiple ways (Crenshaw, 1991). For example, as a researcher, I am a White, middle-class, woman professor. My privilege from my race and social class interacts with my role as a professor. The power I derive by determining the research process privileges me in multiple ways and gives me even more power in the research process than I might have as a woman professor within the higher education institution. Similarly, research participants might be marginalized by their race, gender, or sexuality and then they may be further marginalized in the research process when they are identified, sometimes reductionalistically, as "subjects" and stripped of agency in the research process and control over how their voice is used. Intersectionality provides additional perspective on how a researcher's identity will influence the research process, even for researchers who identify as a member of a marginalized group. A researcher still holds power and privilege in the research process because of other aspects of their identity, like nationality or the power inherent in their roles as research decision-maker. This leads me to the concept of insider/outsider status.

Insider/Outsider Status

Researchers are often insiders as members of groups whose experiences they are exploring and outsiders by their status as academics or researchers simultaneously (Wiederhold, 2015). Suffla et al. (2015) describes the complicated navigation of considering positionality as insiders and outsiders: "In the space between, we were insiders as Blacks, as Africans, and as community-based researchers whose work centers on underrepresented and oppressed groups, and insiders through our established and recognized partnerships with the local research teams" (p. 17). Similarly, in the case of my work with women in Science, Technology, Engineering, and Math (STEM) education in the United States, I am an insider inasmuch as I am a woman, but I am an outsider as a researcher, a professor, and because of my education level. This made me simultaneously an insider and an outsider. However, without reflecting on positionality, it was hard to identify when my status as an insider shifted to outsider and how that impacted data collection and analysis: "At times as researchers we are so embedded within our work, it is difficult to determine how our insider/outsider status changes and how this impacts our research" (Kohl & McCutcheon, 2015, p. 753). Further, there were conflicts that came into play because of my role as a researcher, and I was only able to identify those conflicts because I considered the bias of my position as a researcher and the power and privilege that resulted from my position (Hoskins, 2015). If I had assumed that because I was a young(er) White woman I understood the experiences of participants, I would have neglected to explore how my experience changing majors from STEM to political science as an undergraduate student may have been dramatically different from the experiences of participants who were majoring in math, computer science, or physics. That could have meant that I took for granted certain characteristics of my participants or did not probe for deeper meaning because I assumed I understood what participants were experiencing, leading to flawed conclusions and results. Additionally, I also ran the risk of assuming insider status and equal footing with participants and the relationship norms that went along with that, when in reality my relative power and privilege would have made that both an impossible and unethical assumption.

Racism, sexism, ableism, cisgenderism, and ethnocentrism interlock to complicate systems of oppression and exacerbate the marginalization of those who are disadvantaged because of the different groups without whom they identify. Again, intersectionality provides insight to understand how "various layers of inequality that are present in the field" (Caretta & Jokinen, 2017, p. 277). Systems of oppression influence researcher and participant power and privilege, so understanding how identity impacts the research process is complicated by one's identification as an insider and an outsider, "multiple identities can be simultaneous, inter-related and sometimes contradictory" (Muhammad et al., 2015, p. 1047).

Limitations of Positionality

Positionality is, like one's identity, a construct: "Positioning is often discussed as if it is something natural, authentic, timeless, essential, primordial; something which can fully explain and categorize them and us. Yet we find ourselves saying there is something more; that we are not just that" (Arber, 2000, p. 45). However, while identity itself is a construct, it is still important to consider; without identification, however tenuous, one might fall back into the more problematic "colorblind" view that neglects to admit or acknowledge that meaningful differences exist between members of privileged and marginalized groups, which we know they do. The goal, in the positionality process, is to understand the multiple ways that privileged aspects of a researcher's identity act as "power over" research participants. Although identity is constructed, considering positionality prompts researchers to understand where they are positioned in relationship to participants. The key is not to define participants, especially not within a deficiency framework, but to analyze the "influence of social position and the politics of identity on the interactions between researcher and research participants and the role of power and identity in everyday lives and research" (Kohl & McCutcheon, 2015, p. 752).

Similarly, defining oneself as an "insider" is problematic because it neglects to acknowledge how individual characteristics differentiate members of the same social group:

> Asserting that a meaningful difference exists between those researchers who connect with the participants due to general commonalities and those researchers experiencing the specific mutual familiarity of sharing a personal history, a social network, and an assumed

place-based investment in the future with their participants—as experiences by those scholars who conduct their research in the places they call home. (Wiederhold, 2015, p. 602)

Negotiating identity is an imperfect and tenuous process. Instead one considers
identity in order to create a space between insider and outsider while acknowledging that this process is imperfect and imprecise but better than refusing to accept
that a power differential exists (Muhammad et al., 2015; Suffla et al., 2015).
Identifying positionality is not about a blind relativity of choice about the place
where one wants to be positioned, but "it is about finding the place where one has
been put. It is about defining the practices which have defined this 'putting.' It is
about stating the place from where one can speak" (Arber, 2000, p. 58).

Considering positionality is simply an expectation of doing research with marginalized groups, and it does not need to be shared or "confessed" with to peers or
participants, especially those who have been traditionally underrepresented or marginalized (Falcon, 2016, p. 177). Researchers must accept their position and our
privilege without expecting an award or recognition for doing so. There is not an
award given to the most aware White person doing research with non-White individuals. Similarly, confessing alone does not lead to the undoing of privilege nor
does it allow one to think their way into a new position. Instead, research should
create structures that dismantle systems of oppression. Indeed, this is the obligation
of researchers: "Thus although responsibility is possessed by all toward all, those
who have benefitted from structures of power bear a greater responsibility for those
who lack privilege" (Goering, Holland, & Fryer-Edwards, 2008, p. 50). Whether or
not it is identified, the identity of the researcher and the researched is part of every
study, and examining it makes the work richer and more comprehensible for readers
(Gordon, 2005, p. 280).

Strategies for Conducting Research as a Privileged Outsider

Identifying one's positionality influences the research process by guiding research
questions, research methods, participants, data analysis, and reporting.

Research Questions

Every project begins as an inquiry, and researchers cannot hope to conduct research
that promotes social justice if they start from a place that has not identified social
justice as a key goal of that work. While this is discussed in detail throughout this
text, an inquiry should "*start* by considering whether such research is likely to meet
the needs of the underserved" (Goering et al., 2008, p. 46). Researchers will not
know if the research will meet the needs of the underserved as an outsider if they
have not first asked what the challenges and problems are from members of the
group whose experiences they hope to explore. A researcher is an outsider even if

they are a member in some way of the group they are exploring, because of the power associated with leading a research project. Further, it is more likely that an insider will be blind to some challenges experienced by participants because they have neglected to consider experiences outside of their own context.

If seeking to identify how an individual or group of individuals is challenged, research questions should guide the exploration of the experiences and challenges of the groups whose experiences we would like to improve. Secondarily, or in subsequent projects, findings from that research can help the researcher to craft questions that seek to flush out understanding of the experience or challenges identified in response to the initial research question. One example is from an institutional ethnography of STEM in higher education I conducted from the standpoint of undergraduate women majoring in math and physics (Parson & Ozaki, 2017). The theoretical underpinning of an institutional ethnography is feminist standpoint theory. Standpoint theory views members of underrepresented or marginalized groups as epistemically privileged because they are able to see more clearly the institutional structures and systems that marginalize them (Smith, 2005). An institutional ethnographic exploration begins by asking participants to describe their daily activities, where they go, what they do, why they do it, and how they know where, why, how, and when to do those things in order to identify the institutional processes, practices, procedures, and discourses that coordinate their descriptions of their daily lives; a second research question then asks participants to describe the challenges they face accomplishing their daily work. By building on participant description of their daily work, the researcher seeks to identify exactly when, during the day, those challenges arise as a junction, or problematic that guides subsequent data collection to identify the institutional process or discourse that is coordinating their work. By identifying where the institution coordinates the work of participants, the goal of an institutional ethnography is to understand how the institution is creating challenges for participants. Once participant challenges are identified, subsequent research questions or projects can explore the nature of the institutional processes and procedures to identify if and how they unfairly marginalize individuals and groups (the third set of research questions). Only after identifying the institutional structures that marginalize participants can a researcher make recommendations to remedy those practices or identify structural areas that require changes (potentially, a fourth research question).

However, had I begun with the third research question, to identify if a certain institutional practice was gendered, sexist, or racist, I would have run the risk of creating a research question that was not exploring the practice or area of participant's lives that was marginalizing. Worse, if I had started with the fourth research question and developed a program or made recommendations without gathering the answers to questions one through three, I might have made an irrelevant or harmful recommendation. While a researcher does not have to ask all four questions in one research project, as I did in this institutional ethnography, a researcher does need to know the answers to the prior questions from insider sources. Insider sources could include the researcher, but the researcher should not be the sole source of information guiding a research inquiry and developing research questions.

Consider Whom We Invite to Be Participants and Researchers

When one chooses who to invite to participate in a research project, they need to consider both representation and misrepresentation: "representation involves the exercise of researcher power in making decisions about which of the participants' experiences and stories to include and on what basis these choices are made" (Hoskins, 2015, p. 398). This does not require that one include individuals from the group they are exploring as participants in their research. For example, a study on bias in STEM might ask White, men scientists to describe what a scientist looks like in order to explain how they view the ideal scientist. However, much of the research that is socially oriented will seek to include, at the very least, members from the group whose experiences the research is exploring.

Similarly, if one is exploring the experiences of multiple groups, it is especially important that the research includes the voices of those who have not frequently been included in the literature or have traditionally been misrepresented: "If claims about misrecognition can be met without introducing serious new harms or compromising the participation of other groups, meeting them is a requirement of justice" (Goering et al., 2008, p. 47). If a group is underrepresented or misrepresented in the literature, researchers have an obligation to invite participants from that group of people. However, even if a researcher has identified an individual or group that they believe will help them to respond to their research question(s), researchers need to remember that participants are not obligated to participate despite the researcher's obligation to invite them to participate in the research. Participants need to be able to decline participation (Goering et al., 2008, p. 45).

There is an important opportunity here, and some might say an integral one, to include participants in the research process. Indeed, just like insiders can confirm the validity of one's research questions, they are also able to be participant-researchers. Participatory research (McGarry, 2016; Salmon, Browne, & Pederson, 2010; Vanner, 2015) provides space for participants to influence the research process (design, data collection, analysis, and writing stages). Participatory research requires a flexible design and a fluent definition of what is means to be a researcher and a participant, "within the context of ensuring a diverse academic research group, allow teams to form organically," and "establish a system for continual self-reflexivity" (Muhammad et al., 2015, p. 1058). It also requires that researchers empower participants by engaging them in research design, data analysis, and discussion of findings (Vanner, 2015) in order to co-produce and collaborate in the research process (Oldfield & Patel, 2016). Participatory research, while non-traditional, is a powerful opportunity to influence the research process positively. Including participants in the research process also has a powerful opportunity to improve reflexivity and validity of results. Further, insiders, if they are willing, can help the research to identify who might be appropriate participants.

Finally, considering and engaging participants in the research process requires a redefinition of what it means to be a researcher. The idea of a researcher is typically designed with a gendered, classed, and raced ideal in mind, but the reality is that "researcher" looks different for everyone. Similarly, one also needs to re-evaluate how participation is defined (Salmon et al., 2010). Participation might not look the same way, and participant dedication to the project should not be assumed. This might mean a researcher needs to understand what outside obligations might prohibit a participant from arriving on time, being at every meeting, or might lead to frequent absences: "A woman's capacity to participate consistently should not be assumed, not should any single incident be taken as an indicator of her ability or willingness to participate" (Salmon et al., 2010, p. 340).

Ethics

While ethics is discussed in more detail throughout this text, there are certain considerations when seeking to mitigate positionality. First, the minimum requirement for every study with human subjects requires approval from the ethical board that governs the researcher's institution, typically an Institutional Review Board (IRB). However, context matters, so a simple review from a western institution's IRB board might not suffice as ethical approval for the research because one must also consider cultural and linguistic sensitivity. Always, but especially in cases of linguistic differences, researchers need to use multiple formats to receive consent, referred to as interactive consent. Interactive consent should be sought from each participant in every setting, "I typically adopt a multi-level form of consent, which includes written and oral consent, with an understanding that it can be withdrawn at any time" (Falcon, 2016, p. 183). Further, receiving informed consent means that a researcher also helps participants to understand not just what they are consenting to by participating in the research project but also discusses the ramifications of participating in the research study.

Finally, researchers also need to consider cultural and national norms when seeking permission for access to research sites and when requesting permission to contact participants. Some countries have national procedures and laws governing research. Additionally, different institutions may require additional permissions and forms of consent to conduct research than those required by a researcher's home institution. For example, one's IRB may just require a letter from an institutional representative giving permission to conduct research at another institution, but the institution itself may require additional permissions before a researcher can access and conduct research at that site. IRB approval is the minimum ethical requirement for a study with human subjects. The researcher must "consider the repercussions of her decisions, particularly for the most vulnerable participants or affected parties, ask whose voice is being privileged and why, and always prioritize the safety and requests of community members over the depth of data collection" (Vanner, 2015, p. 6). Researchers also need to consider cultural and national norms and ensure that permission is obtained from all involved people, sites, and institutions.

Reflexivity

Considering positionality and navigating insider and outsider status continues throughout the research process through reflexivity. The process of reflexivity facilitates continual exploration of one's power and privilege as it impacts research. Reflexivity is a process where one examines their place in the research process through reflection. Ongoing reflection helps to mitigate identity constructed as static and unchanging. "Ongoing negotiations indicate that the relationship between researcher and research participants cannot be reduced to somewhat fixed or frozen positionalities based on social categories such as gender or class; rather they unfold over the course of the encounter" (Kaspar & Landolt, 2014, p. 109). Reflexivity often includes feedback from critical peers that can identify where and how one might not be aware of differences and conflicts between their assumptions and the lived experiences of participants. Reflexivity should ensure that one is constantly evaluating their position within the research.

The three principles of reflexive research as defined by Bourdieu (as cited in Hoskins, 2015):

> First, to avoid projecting my 'values, dispositions, attitudes and perceptions' onto the participants' social realities; second, to reflect on and acknowledge the impact of the bias of my field location; and third, to examine the epistemological and social conditions that make possible social-scientific claims of objectivity. (p. 397)

Reflexivity goes beyond identifying social place and requires that one critically identifies and explores their "assumptions, values, discourses, and practices that we deploy to portray reality and create knowledge" (Suffla et al., 2015, p. 10). Through reflexivity, researchers identify their biases and seek to understand how other contextual and power relations are influencing research. This is critical to create new knowledge and situate it in the literature (Suffla et al., 2015).

Researchers need to continue to be reflexive throughout the research process to ensure that they are mindful of their position (and ethics) and to continue to engage with research participants and fellow researchers. One such reflective strategy is kitchen table reflexivity where researchers explore and navigate their positionality with co-researchers and participants (Kohl & McCutcheon, 2015). In kitchen table reflexibility, researchers ensure that continual reflection on positionality occurs throughout the research process through informal conversations that occur naturally and fluidly (Kohl & McCutcheon, 2015). This ill-defined process is messy and may not have a satisfactory resolution. Researchers have to accept the idea of a "good enough" reflexive relationship and "accept rather than defend against healthy tensions in fieldwork" and be attuned to these questions and how they inform and may even possibly be data (Muhammad et al., 2015, p. 1050).

Data Collection Methods

Selecting methods that consider the implications of ethics, positionality, and place requires reflection, perhaps through memoing, in order to identify which research methods are the best and most ethical way to explore your research question. To guide method selection, a researcher should reflect on their reasons for conducting the study, who should participate, and the knowledge the researcher has about their own identity development. Specific methods for data collection are discussed at length at other locations through the text, so my discussion of specific methods in this chapter is framed through positionality, approach, and ethics. Some questions to ask as one chooses their research methods might include the following questions adapted from Pennington and Prater (2016).

What Role Is Privilege Playing in the Research Design?

Exploring the role of privilege in one's research design requires that they ask who has access to the site/who does not, what theory is informing the research questions, and who will benefit from the study. Whether conducting interviews, observations, or focus groups, it is important that researchers make the process safe and comfortable for participants. First, it is important that researchers conduct our research in "safe spaces." A safe space does not look the same for everyone, and it might not look the same for one's participants as it does for the researcher—in this case, I refer to safety as comfortability and freedom from potential harms such as a loss of confidentiality or physical harm (Salmon et al., 2010). Again, it behooves researchers to ask participants or other insiders where it would be safe to conduct the research and if there is a place where it is safe. While it may be most convenient to conduct the research in one's offices or even a coffee shop, that might not be where the participant is the most comfortable. Returning to *The Immortal Life of Henrietta Lacks*, the first meeting between Lacks and Skloot takes place in a fancy restaurant. It was clear that Lacks was unfamiliar with the setting and not comfortable, and her discomfort set the tone for the meeting and, possibly, the entire future of their relationship by reinforcing the class difference between Lacks and Skloot. When choosing research settings, choose spaces that are safe and comfortable for participants, but do not neglect one's own safety in that process, such as by entering a site where the researchers feel emotionally or physically unsafe.

Second, when possible, match researcher identity with that of the interviewee (Muhammad et al., 2015, p. 1057). A researcher should seek to include academic team members whose identities intersect with those of the community partners as members of the research team. Awareness requires that researchers pay attention to ethical and cultural sensitivity. Finally, researchers should not prioritize the needs of the research field or the individual researcher (e.g., getting an interview) over the needs of the community or the participant (Falcon, 2016).

What Role Is Silence Playing in Research Implementation and Data Analysis?

Researchers need to "identify a methodological design that will minimize the negative effects of power on the research participants and maximize their empowerment" (Vanner, 2015, p. 2). This can be done by integrating participatory and collaborative data collection and analysis which can be sustainable and cultivate co-learning and alignment with community partners (Muhammad et al., 2015). By involving participants in the research design, analysis, and reporting, researchers can ask who is promoting dialogue about privilege and what are the opportunities for honest privilege/power discussion.

Involving participants in the research design and analysis process can help researchers to ensure that participants' needs are being met in the research process, help researchers to continually interrogate whether the research project is continuing to consider positionality, power, and privilege, and help researchers to examine analysis and conclusions critically. One methodological example is feminist participatory action research (FPAR) (Salmon et al., 2010). FPAR blends participatory action research and critical feminist theory. In FPAR women are involved in all stages of the research process. Salmon et al. (2010) conducted an FPAR project exploring effectiveness of nursing practices in marginalized communities and involved affected women as researcher-participants. Through the involvement of researcher-participants, Salmon et al. (2010) found that researcher-participants allowed them to connect research to the community in order to address lived inequities: "congruence between the concerns of nursing with people who are marginalized and the commitments of FPAR to continually redress power inequities, hierarchies, and health and social inequities" (p. 336).

Even if the decision is made not to involve participants directly as researchers in the research process, allowing participants to shape the direction of data collection allows them continued access to the research process. For example, McGarry's (2016) exploration of the experiences of Muslim teens involved teen participants in decisions about how they represented their knowledge. Multiple forms of situated knowledge led to an understanding of the fluid and flexible power dynamics that characterize youth experience, "allowing participants to shape power dynamics and positionalities throughout the research process led to the generation of unexpected forms of situated knowledge" (McGarry, 2016, p. 352).

Finally, one's data collection methods can give control to participants to direct the nature of data collected. One example is photovoice, a method that asks participants to take pictures of the things that are most salient in their lives: "[Photovoice] espouses the idea that individuals' realities, and therefore their narratives, are situated in social configurations of class, gender, race, geography, sexuality, kind, and the like, and that their portrayal is negotiated through culturally available forms of representation" (Suffla et al., 2015, p. 12). Participants choose to take pictures of what is important to them and their lives, which directs the research process, context, and data collected.

Similar to photovoice is mobile interviewing (Wiederhold, 2015). In mobile interviewing participants talk to a researcher while physically guiding them to places that demonstrate or indicate an example of what they are talking about, similar to a community tour. Mobile interviewing can also help a researcher to build familiarity with local places and interpretations, and capitalize on participants' local knowledge. Through the processes of mobile interviewing and photovoice, researchers and participants mutually construct an understanding of the research setting through and direct the type of data collected.

What Type of Academic White Talk Is Performed by and Between the Researchers?

Finally, researchers must continually ask how participants are positioned/discussed in the analysis and reporting process by critically examining the analytical tools used to interpret the data. After a researcher has collected data, analyses and reporting begin, and it is critical that the reflexivity process continues as one checks the validity of results. One way to check validity is through member checking or asking participants to read analyses and discuss if they feel the analyses are accurate representations (Falcon, 2016; Vanner, 2015). Member checking is a requisite part of research conducted with marginalized groups by privileged outsiders to ensure that researcher representation of the participant's words reflects the participant's lived experiences from their standpoint.

When considering positionality, the practical considerations of where to publish, what conferences to present at, and status differences in different academic areas are important to consider as well (Hoskins, 2015). In reporting research findings, researchers must "incorporate the voices of others without colonizing them in a manner that reinforces patterns of domination" (Suffla et al., 2015, p. 15). As researchers report their findings, they need to ensure that they "embrace personal narratives as 'counter-storytelling' to assure minority voices are heard" (Muhammad et al., 2015, p. 1049). Similarly, researchers must explore catalytic validity, or "the extent to which research 'moves those it studies to understand the world and the way it is shaped in order for them to transform it" (Vanner, 2015, p. 8). One's reporting on research conducted to achieve social justice must report on the research with the intention to recreate a more equitable society (Falcon, 2016).

Conclusion

It is not the responsibility of one's research participants or those traditionally marginalized to assuage a researcher's guilt or congratulate them for acknowledging their privilege. If the process seems difficult, that is because it is. However, choosing not to do research or ignoring concerns of positionality and insider/outsider status are not acceptable alternatives. Instead, researchers have to reflexively and continually interrogate their positionality and resultant power and privilege in the research process in order to ensure their research does not replicate participant marginalization.

There is a complicated balance to draw between considering positionality and using it as a rationale not to conduct research with marginalized or underrepresented groups. One's positionality should not be an excuse not to conduct research; research centered around the experiences of underrepresented and marginalized groups is critical and necessary; indeed, I argue that all research should be conducted while considering positionality and this is the future of all research with "human subjects." Dismantling the White, patriarchal, cisgender, straight structures of society cannot be done by applying the same research methods that one has always used. When researchers do that, they continue to replicate the same systems that marginalize. If researchers continue to conduct research according to existing academic and social structures, they will continue to find participants lacking. This deficiency-based view of marginalized groups has resulted in the continued labeling of those different from the White, privileged norm as deficient because they do not fit into the current structure.

Considering positionality is just one step in the process of rebuilding the research process in order not only to explore and understand the experiences of traditionally marginalized groups truly but also to make recommendations to improve their experiences. Doing that requires a new approach to research, research participants, what it means to participate in research, and how researchers discuss their results. Just like "we are never done with justice, and we are always working toward it" (Goering et al., 2008, p. 49), researchers should always be working toward greater social justice in their research processes.

Suggestions for Further Reading

Pennington, J. L., & Prater, K. (2016). The veil of professionalism: An autoethnographic critique of White positional identities in the figured worlds of White research performance. *Race, Ethnicity & Education, 19*(5), 901–926.

Pennington and Prater critically examine their shifting positionality and unacknowledged White privilege as it influenced their research 12 years after the study concluded.

Sawyer, R. D., & Liggett, T. (2012). Shifting positionalities: A critical discussion of a duoethnographic inquiry of a personal curriculum of post/colonialism. *International Journal of Qualitative Methods, 11*(5), 628–651.

Sawyer and Liggett reflect on the colonizing practices of ethnographic research and discuss strategies to decolonize ethnographic research.

Laker, J. A. (2016). What's a nice, straight, White guy doing in an essay like this?!!! Privilege, oppression and the binary politics of positionality. *Social Alternatives, 35*(3), 57–60.

Laker calls for a critical examination of the identity, power, and privilege that comes from the positionality of being a White, cisgendered, man or woman in higher education. In his essay, he reminds White men and women in higher education that this critical examination is an obligation.

References

Arber, R. (2000). Defining positioning within politics of difference: Negotiating spaces 'in between'. *Race, Ethnicity & Education, 3*(1), 45–63. https://doi.org/10.1080/13613320050000583

Caretta, M. A., & Jokinen, J. C. (2017). Conflating privilege and vulnerability: A reflexive analysis of emotions and positionality in postgraduate fieldwork. *The Professional Geographer, 69*(2), 275–283. https://doi.org/10.1080/00330124.2016.1252268

Crenshaw, K. (1991). Mapping the margins: Intersectionality, identity politics, and violence against women of color. *Stanford Law Review, 43*(6), 1241–1299.

Falcon, S. M. (2016). Transnational feminism as a paradigm for decolonizing the practice of research. *Frontiers, 37*(1), 174–194.

Goering, S., Holland, S., & Fryer-Edwards, K. (2008). Transforming genetic research practices with marginalized communities: A case for responsive justice. *Hastings Center Report, 38*(2), 43–53.

Goodkind, J. R., & Deacon, Z. (2004). Methodological issues in conducting research with refugee women: Principles for recognizing and re-centering the multiply marginalized. *Journal of Community Psychology, 32*(6), 721–739. https://doi.org/10.1002/jcop.20029

Gordon, J. (2005). White on White: Researcher reflexivity and the logics of privilege in White schools undertaking reform. *Urban Review, 37*(4), 279–302. https://doi.org/10.1007/s11256-005-0015-1

Hoskins, K. (2015). Researching female professors: The difficulties of representation, positionality, and power in feminist research. *Gender and Education, 27*(4), 393–411. https://doi.org/10.1080/09540253.2015.1021301

Kaspar, H., & Landolt, S. (2014). Flirting in the field: Shifting positionalities and power relations in innocuous sexualisations of research encounters. *Gender, Place & Culture, 23*(1), 107–119. https://doi.org/10.1080/0966369X.2014.991704

Kohl, E., & McCutcheon, P. (2015). Kitchen table reflexivity: Negotiating positionality through everyday talk. *Gender, Place & Culture, 22*(6), 747–763. https://doi.org/10.1080/0966369X.2014.958063

Laker, J. A. (2016). What's a nice, straight, White guy doing in an essay like this?!!! Privilege, oppression and the binary politics of positionality. *Social Alternatives, 35*(3), 57–60.

McGarry, O. (2016). Repositioning the research encounter: Exploring power dynamics and positionality in youth research. *International Journal of Social Research Methodology, 19*(3), 339–354. https://doi.org/10.1080/13645579.2015.1011821

Milgram, B. L. (2012). Tangled fields: Rethinking positionality and ethics in research on women's work in a Hong Kong-Philippine trade. *Critical Arts, 26*(2), 175–191. https://doi.org/10.1080/02560046.2012.684438

Muhammad, M., Wallerstien, N., Sussman, A. L., Avila, M., Belone, L., & Duran, B. (2015). Reflections on researcher identity and power: The impact of positionality on community based participatory research (CBPR) processes and outcomes. *Critical Sociology, 41*(7–8), 1045–1063. https://doi.org/10.1177/0896920513516025

Oldfield, S., & Patel, Z. (2016). Engaging geographies: Negotiating positionality and building relevance. *South African Geographical Journal, 98*(3), 505–514. https://doi.org/10.1080/037 36245.2016.1217255

Parson, L., & Ozaki, C. C. (2017). Gendered student ideals in STEM in higher education. *NASPA Journal about Women in Higher Education*. https://doi.org/10.1080/19407882.2017.1392323

Pennington, J. L., & Prater, K. (2016). The veil of professionalism: An autoethnographic critique of White positional identities in the figured worlds of White research performance. *Race, Ethnicity & Education, 19*(5), 901–926. https://doi.org/10.1080/13613324.2014.885431

Salmon, A., Browne, A. J., & Pederson, A. (2010). 'Now we call it research': Participatory health research involving marginalized women who use drugs. *Nursing Inquiry, 17*(4), 336–345. https://doi.org/10.1111/j.1440-1800.2010.00507.x

Sawyer, R. D., & Liggett, T. (2012). Shifting positionalities: A critical discussion of a duoethnographic inquiry of a personal curriculum of post/colonialism. *International Journal of Qualitative Methods, 11*(5), 628–651.

Smith, D. E. (2005). *Institutional ethnography: A sociology for people*. Lanham, MD: Altamira Press.

Suffla, S., Seedat, M., & Bawa, U. (2015). Reflexivity as enactment of critical community psychologies: Dilemmas of voice and positionality in a multi-country photovoice study. *Journal of Community Psychology, 43*(1), 9–12. https://doi.org/10.1002/jcop.21691

Vanner, C. (2015). Positionality at the center: Constructing an epistemological and methodological approach for a western feminist doctoral candidate conducting research in the postcolonial. *International Journal of Qualitative Methods, 14*(4), 1–12. https://doi.org/10.1177/1609406915618094

Wiederhold, A. (2015). Conducting fieldwork at and away from home: Shifting researcher positionality with mobile interviewing methods. *Qualitative Research, 15*(5), 600–615. https://doi.org/10.1177/1468794114550440

Chapter 3
Flipping the Paradigm: Studying Up and Research for Social Justice

Elena Aydarova

Abstract Social justice research most often focuses on the voices, experiences, and practices of underserved and marginalized groups. While this focus produces important insights, it disregards the actions of those in power who create and maintain systems of inequality and injustice in the first place. To address this gap, this chapter examines methodological approaches for studying up or researching the powerful. It describes the challenges faced by researchers who study those in power, such as problems of access, interview pitfalls, dangers in data analysis and interpretation, ethical concerns, and dissemination of findings. The chapter also provides suggestions for how researchers can address those challenges. The significance of this chapter lies in a systematic presentation of methodological tools necessary for studying the powerful in research for social justice.

Equity and social justice research often focuses on oppressed or underserved groups (Griffiths, 1998). Many of the classical and contemporary ethnographies in the field of education attend to marginalized populations (see Ferguson, 2010; MacLeod, 2008; Valenzuela, 1999; Willis, 1977). Other works compare the experiences of the privileged and underprivileged groups, juxtaposing how they engage with schooling in ways that lead to different educational outcomes (see Anyon, 1981; Heath, 1983; Lareau, 2000). The overall focus on marginalized groups leaves out of consideration the actions of those in power who create and maintain systems of inequality and injustice in the first place. This omission is unfortunate because dominant groups that hold power in the society—be they White middle-class parents, policymakers, or conservative think tanks—create, advocate, and promote practices and policies that protect their privilege, reproduce inequality, and retrench social hierarchies. In other words, by limiting research to the oppressed, we leave the oppressors unaccountable

E. Aydarova (✉)
Auburn University, Auburn, AL, USA
e-mail: eza0029@auburn.edu

© The Author(s) 2019
K. K. Strunk, L. A. Locke (eds.), *Research Methods for Social Justice and Equity in Education*, https://doi.org/10.1007/978-3-030-05900-2_3

for their actions. Exceptions exist, but they are rare (see Demerath, 2009; Tompkins-Stange, 2016). Overall, if scholarly investigations do not examine the oppressors' voices, experiences, and practices more consistently, the pursuit of liberation and alternative futures that could be more just for all will be greatly undermined.

This chapter explores possibilities for addressing this gap through researching the powerful, also known as studying up or researching elites. While there is a sizable body of scholarship on studying up, little of it focuses on equity and social justice. Thus, this chapter considers methodological tools helpful for social justice research.

Defining Power, Conceptualizing Elite Status

In researching the powerful, an important question to consider is what assumptions of power guide the research project. Historically, researchers equated power status with participants' structural positions in the society: those who occupied higher positions in the social hierarchies were believed to have more power. Recently, this approach has been problematized. Smith (2006), for example, argued that post-structural conceptions of power that recognize its fluid, dynamic, and context-dependent nature are necessary to disrupt the assumptions about fixed and static positions of power. Yet while this observation is helpful for attending to power in particular social settings, it does not address the dynamics of how dominant groups use their power to create injustice and inequality through their daily actions (Ayers, Quinn, & Stovall, 2009).

Smith's (2006) argument stems from the observation that there is a significant variation in how different scholars identify their participants as elites. Some of them rely on the status differentials between the researcher and the participants (Hunter, 1995; Mikecz, 2012; Stephens, 2007), while others take into account participants' position of power, professional status, and sphere of influence (Fitz, Halpin, & Power, 1994; Harvey, 2011). For example, in educational research, some scholars identified policymakers (Phillips, 1998; Gewirtz & Ozga, 1994), philanthropic organizations' employees (Ostrander, 1995), or NGO heads (Straubhaar, 2015) as elites. In many cases, the upper-class background of the participants or settings where research is conducted is enough to designate participants as elites (Priyadharshini, 2003). Such conceptual profusion is misleading as research approaches differ if participants are politicians or students in elite high schools. For this reason, this chapter uses examples from research in policy circles as actors in this area have a significant influence not just on maintaining their privilege (as elite participants in other settings do) but also on recreating oppressive and unequal social structures more broadly through their policy initiatives. Despite this focus, the challenges in conducting research with the powerful and ways to address them described in this chapter are useful for researching other social groups that hold power in the society, such as parents from elite backgrounds, lobbyists that promote neoliberal approaches to education, or conservative groups that promote dominant ideologies.

The variation in definitions and conceptualizations is a useful reminder that social positions are relative, relational, and are in the process of constant negotiation. In that regard, it is helpful for researchers to be reflexive about their positions throughout the research project and to recognize the fluid subject positions available to both the researchers and the study participants (Priyadharshini, 2003).

Challenges in Researching the Powerful

Research with the powerful is wrought with numerous methodological challenges. In researching the powerful, problems of access leave much uncertainty in the process of conceptualizing the study. When scholars collect and analyze the data, the veracity of verbal data becomes suspect, and intentionality of participants' actions emerges as a puzzling riddle. Considering a study's ethics, scholars juggle the responsibility to treat their participants with respect and care at the same time as they contemplate how such treatment makes them complicit in maintaining systems of injustice and oppression. In what follows, I will address each of the challenges in more detail.

Access and Flexible Designs

One of the first challenges that a researcher has to consider is the problem of access, as those who occupy positions of power and privilege may be hard to access. Busy schedules, the sensitivity of the topic, or sheer unwillingness to meet with a researcher can undermine one's attempts to collect data (Welch, Marschan-Piekkari, Penttinen, & Tahvanainen, 2002). To mitigate some of those challenges, researchers can delay the study until the most severe struggles are over or focus on those who held power in the past, such as retirees or those who moved on to other projects (Lancaster, 2017; Phillips, 1998; Selwyn, 2013). Some scholars, however, argue that challenges of access may be exaggerated and that many respondents are willing to find time in their busy schedules for interviews with researchers (Walford, 2012).

In tackling the challenge of access, one has to consider whether the inquiry can proceed if access is denied. In that regard, developing a study with maximum flexibility and multiple data sources is highly advisable. Another point to consider is whether interviews alone are sufficient for the study. In ethnographic studies often judged by one's prolonged immersion in participants' cultures, interviews alone may not be enough. To have access to observations, one has to consider what roles one can play in the organizations with which most participants are associated. In elite studies of international corporations or law firms, anthropologists took up positions of apprentices or full-time employees. Where possible, this could be a worthwhile option to consider for educational researchers.

Most studies with the powerful do rely on interviews as the primary source of data. First, one has to consider how to identify and access key participants. Farquharson (2005) proposed the method of reputational snowball, whereby researchers ask powerful participants to identify and, if possible, introduce the researcher to other actors in their networks. In elite studies, the recommendation is to "start at the top" (Ostrander, 1995, p. 136), contacting the most powerful individuals or groups first. To gain access to those who hold power, some researchers draw on their established networks and relationships. For example, previous work for a government agency (Gewirtz & Ozga, 1994) or friendships with those who know someone in elite circles (Ostrander, 1995) can provide a useful entrée for the study. Other possibilities include requesting interviews by email, phone, or letter (Duke, 2002; Ostrander, 1995), using networking opportunities during conferences, summits, or research seminars (Stephens, 2007), or even establishing contact through LinkedIn, Facebook, or Twitter (Straubhaar, 2015).

As one embarks on scheduling interviews, one needs to consider the logistics of the process. First, there is the question of navigating busy schedules and research project timing. Most interviews have to be scheduled weeks and months in advance. It is also common for participants to cancel interviews or delay them for hours, days, or even weeks. In the situations when the researcher has to travel domestically or internationally for data collection, such delays can be detrimental for the study's timeline. To mitigate these challenges, some scholars suggest using phone or Skype interviews as an alternative to face-to-face interviews (Stephens, 2007).

Another logistical consideration is interview locations. Many participants prefer to meet in their offices but spaces where interviews are conducted shape the information shared. More formal settings create conditions where answers to interview questions are stilted and lifeless (Duke, 2002; Fitz et al., 1994). Public spaces with onlookers around can heighten participants' concerns about being watched or overheard. Acknowledging the context of the interview and the role of others in it enhances the quality of research and allows the reader to critically assess researchers' claims.

Collecting Data, Conducting Interviews

An important matter to consider before scheduling interviews is how much a researcher can learn about the topic and study participants from other sources. Many scholars note the importance of doing one's homework before the interviews (Berry, 2002; Harvey, 2011; Thuesen, 2011). Various sources of data could be used for this purpose: policy documents, reports, participants' interviews or opinion pieces in popular media, archival materials, national or local newspapers, participants' articles in mainstream or academic outlets, organizational newsletters, financial reports, participants' (auto)biographies or publicly available CVs, and even Twitter or Facebook conversations. All of those resources could help researchers strengthen their study, deepen their understanding of the issue, and tailor interview questions for the participants' specific areas of expertise.

For interview design, it is often recommended to use semi-structured interviews (Leech, 2002) with open-ended questions that invite participants to share their personal perspectives (Duke, 2002; Harvey, 2011). Close-ended questions can significantly stifle the conversation as elites are used to sharing their opinions at length (Aberbach & Rockman, 2002). Many scholars suggest adopting maximum flexibility in the interview process, arguing that interviews are more productive and data are richer when interviewers adopt a more conversational style and allow the interview to flow between topics, instead of strictly following a list of questions in an interview schedule (Aberbach & Rockman, 2002; Stephens, 2007).

One of the most important challenges of interviewing the powerful is that many of them are familiar with the interview process (Duke, 2002). Unlike participants from underprivileged groups for whom the experience of being asked questions about personal views or being listened to can be relatively new, the powerful may have gone through this process multiple times. This means that when a researcher arrives at the interview, the interviewee can have a polished performance that represents "the official line" and does not offer any new insights beyond the publicly available information (Duke, 2002). Learning how to probe and how to ask difficult, shocking (Ostrander, 1995), or "presuming" questions (Leech, 2002) is important to move the interview beyond the official storyline.

During the actual interviews, the researcher's ability to navigate power differentials plays an important role in determining the study's success. Those who occupy positions of power in the society may attempt to exert greater control over the interview process than researchers anticipate (Duke, 2002). This can take the form of controlling the conversation, providing extended utterances with no questions asked, refusing to answer questions, criticizing interview questions, evading questions to redirect the conversation, or using the interview to pose questions to the researcher. Many of these moves are a part of a "performance" (Aydarova, forthcoming; Lancaster, 2017) meant to reassert power hierarchies. Observing the variation of these behaviors in his interviews with powerful policymakers, calls for the researchers to "recognize and explore more fully the interview as an extension of the 'play of power' rather than separate from it" (p. 113). To address these differentials, the researcher can assume a more assertive role or play along to learn more about participants' perceptions of the topic of inquiry.

In research for social justice, the researcher also has to consider how to address sensitive issues and political topics. Thuesen (2011), for example, invites qualitative researchers to move between dialogue and confrontation when interviewing elites about topics related to discrimination. Kezar (2003) argues that researchers should engage the powerful in transformational interviews that will help the elites see the issue from different perspectives and recognize their position as the oppressor. In choosing a confrontational approach or engaging powerful participants in the exploration of their involvement in maintaining the system of injustice, researchers have to consider how the study will proceed, especially if the study design requires a large number of interviews with elites in the same network. Those in power share information about the researchers who approach them for interviews. A negative experience that one person in the network has with a researcher can foreclose opportunities for future interviews and terminate the study prematurely.

Overall, it is recommended to deploy maximum flexibility during the data collection stage. One can pretend to know less about the topic of research or one can use one's lower social status to present oneself as less of a threat (Duke, 2002). The main point here is to be responsive to the situation and adjust one's presentation accordingly. In situations where participants are likely to disclose more to a graduate student, and the researcher is one, that identity can be emphasized over others (Stephens, 2007). In the community where one's professional status and prestige matters more, it would be beneficial for the researchers to highlight their credential, academic position, or university affiliation (Hunter, 1995). If the researcher adopts more fluid and flexible positions (Priyadharshini, 2003), the study is more likely to move forward, potentially advancing the well-being of those who are marginalized and underserved when it is complete.

Analysis and Interpretation

The area that has received less attention in the literature on researching the powerful is analysis and interpretation. This omission is unfortunate, however, because, as Briggs (2003) cautions, studies that do not attend to the contextualization and substantive interpretation of interviews run the risk of reproducing social inequalities and power hierarchies. To avoid this risk, the researcher first has to consider carefully the truthfulness of the accounts collected. One step undertaken by scholars working with elites is to share interview transcripts or summaries with the study participants for a check. Some participants will appreciate the opportunity to check the interview text while others might request to delete parts or the entirety of the interview they gave (Lancaster, 2017). In considering whether transcripts will be shared with participants, the researcher needs to be mindful of the fact that interaction with the transcript, as Briggs (2003) notes, is useful as a new set of data but unlikely to shed more light on the original exchange. Other scholars recommend cross-checking stories that emerge from interviews and observations with other data sources (Berry, 2002; Mikecz, 2012; Phillips, 1998). Particularly helpful in this case can be meeting minutes, detailed records of decision-making, or internal reports if those are available to the researcher.

As was mentioned earlier, many powerful participants share "official responses" during interviews (Fitz et al., 1994; Walford, 2012). It is important for the researcher to recognize that polished stories of benevolent intentions, exaggerated roles, and altruistic motives can be used to justify actions leading to pernicious outcomes for vulnerable populations. Powerful participants often co-opt the language of social justice to justify policies that entrench inequities and further marginalize underserved groups. The burden on the researcher then, as notes, is to engage in the inquiry reflexively in order not to reproduce dominant narratives. Ball argues that researchers working with the powerful should be mindful of the agendas that the powerful bring to the interview and be attuned to what is being said and how it is being said—not just the content of the interview, but also its form.

In this regard, Briggs (1986) provides two stages for interview data analysis that can be useful in research with the powerful. The first stage attends to the interview as a whole and considers the overall context of where the interview was conducted, who was present, how the conversation was flowing, and whether there were any break-ups in that flow. It also includes the process of chunking interview transcripts into major components to create an overall outline of the conversation. This stage contextualizes the content of the exchange within broader sociopolitical trends. During the second stage of analysis, the researcher attends to the details of how the message was conveyed, focusing on the mechanics of how individual utterances were produced (intonation, prosody, syntax, and semantics, etc.). If a record of body language or eye contact during the interview exists, it is useful to analyze those elements as well. In conducting this level of analysis, the researcher seeks to identify how the interviewees intended the message to be read and responded to.

Qualitative inquiry guides often suggest that a researcher identify recurrent themes and consider data collection completed when themes become saturated because "any additional data collection will result only in more of the same findings" (Marshall & Rossman, 2016, p. 229). This approach may be treacherous when researching the powerful because elite participants can repeat the same official story that is shared in their networks. The researcher's task is not to take interview narratives at face value but to look for cracks in the facades even if those cracks do not appear with any regularity in the data. Critical discourse analysis (Fairclough, 2003, 2013) can be particularly useful for identifying those cracks as it helps the researcher locate discrepancies in the elites' narratives, ruptures in their timelines, or distortions in their presentations. Additionally, Boucher (2017) provides tools from sociolinguistics to analyze how power is constructed, negotiated, and perpetuated through language in interview settings. In sum, whatever tools of analysis the researcher deploys, in conducting research with the powerful, one has to be mindful of the agendas elites pursue and use the analysis stage to preclude the possibility of becoming complicit in recreating unequal structures or unjust causes (Baez, 2002; Berry, 2002; Briggs, 2003; Hunter, 1995; Lancaster, 2017).

Ethical Considerations

Even though there are some disagreements on the matter, research with the powerful differs from researching marginalized groups. Because elite participants are often well-known to the public, ensuring anonymity or confidentiality can be difficult to accomplish (Lancaster, 2017; Walford, 2012). Some elite participants, in fact, prefer to have their interviews fully attributed to them and scoff at researchers' offer to use pseudonyms. At the same time, some participants feel that positions of power they occupy place heightened responsibilities on them and discuss the pain involved in engaging in high-profile activities (Lancaster, 2017).

The vulnerability of participants from elite circles suggests that they are not impervious to the attacks from the media, the public, or peers in their networks (Lancaster, 2017). Research findings can damage people's careers and undo the projects into which they invested much time and energy. It is important for the researcher to take precautions not to cause unnecessary harm.

At the same time, one has to consider what the study reveals about elites' involvement in creating and maintaining systems of oppression. One of the common themes in reports on the powerful is comments "off the record," "for background knowledge," and other information shared in confidence that represent insights into the inner workings of power. While ethics recommendations require that scholars do not divulge this information, there is danger in helping the powerful keep their secrets. As Baez (2002) observes, "hidden power arrangements are maintained by secrets—the secrets of those who might benefit from those arrangements… Qualitative research contributes to this disenfranchisement if it prevents the exposure of hidden power arrangements" (p. 52). In that regard, researchers have to consider carefully to whom they are accountable for their research (Aydarova, in press). If the study seeks to shed light on the processes in which the powerful perpetuate injustice, inequality, and marginalization of subordinate groups, it is important to reconsider obligations to the participants.

Sharing the Findings

The final point to consider is how research findings will be disseminated. Observing how neoliberal transformations increase the suffering of marginalized groups worldwide, Bourdieu (2000) called for social scientists to use their scholarship to join social movements and activist groups in their struggle for social justice. In that regard, research findings should be shared with the groups that can put them to use in their work. Additionally, the field of qualitative inquiry is seeking to bring research findings to the public sphere through blog posts for national newspapers, articles in popular magazines, submissions to open source journals, podcasts for series with wide reach, or community performances of (auto)ethnographic studies (Denzin & Giardina, 2018). These are potential outlets to consider so that research findings can reveal many of elites' activities hidden from the public view. The path to liberation in this regard is not through giving voice to those who lack power (if the subaltern speaks, who is there to listen? (Spivak, 1988)), but through equipping those who struggle for justice with the resources needed to take down systems of oppression and injustice. A word of caution, however, is that researchers have to be aware of the dangers that ensue from their work. As Lee-Treweek and Linkogle (2000) show, powerful participants can use lawsuits, public shaming, and other intimidation strategies to silence the researcher. The possibility of retribution calls for a more thorough process of inquiry, careful collation and storage of data, peer debriefing, and audit trails to ensure high quality of research (for more information on these techniques, see Marshall & Rossman, 2016).

Conclusion

This chapter described methodological approaches for addressing the challenges in social justice research that focuses on the powerful. The chapter provided strategies for gaining access to elite participants, preparing and conducting interviews, analyzing data, and sharing research findings with broader communities. The key point for researchers to consider is how flexible designs, expansive understandings of what constitutes evidence, as well as multi-stage approaches to data analysis can shed light on the activities of the powerful that may otherwise remain invisible. The importance of this research cannot be underestimated because, as Nader (1972) argued, those in power make decisions that affect all of our lives, but bear most pernicious outcomes for the most vulnerable groups in our society. In striving toward equity and justice, it is important to engage in the type of inquiry that will reveal the inner workings of power and to turn the tides of justice to serve those who need it most.

Recommended Readings

Briggs, C. L. (2003). Interviewing, power/knowledge, and social inequality. In J. F. Gubrium & J. A. Holstein (Eds.), *Postmodern interviewing* (pp. 242–255). Thousand Oaks, CA: SAGE Publications.

This reading provides a useful critique of "research-as-usual" by showing how interviews can reproduce dominant paradigms and retrench social inequalities unless researchers attend to power in study design and data analysis.

References

Aberbach, J. D., & Rockman, B. A. (2002). Conducting and coding elite interviews. *PS: Political Science & Politics, 35*(4), 673–676. https://doi.org/10.1017/S1049096502001142

Anyon, J. (1981). Social class and school knowledge. *Curriculum Inquiry, 11*(1), 3–42. https://doi.org/10.1080/03626784.1981.11075236

Aydarova, E. (in press). Jokers and fools in the public square: Ethnography in the age of spectacle.

Aydarova, E. (forthcoming). *Teacher education reform as political theater: Russian policy dramas.* Albany, NY: SUNY Press.

Ayers, W., Quinn, T. M., & Stovall, D. (2009). *Handbook of social justice in education.* New York, NY: Routledge.

Baez, B. (2002). Confidentiality in qualitative research: Reflections on secrets, power and agency. *Qualitative Research, 2*(1), 35–58. https://doi.org/10.1177/1468794102002001638

Berry, J. M. (2002). Validity and reliability issues in elite interviewing. *PS: Political Science & Politics, 35*(4), 679–682. https://doi.org/10.1017/S1049096502001166

Boucher, A. (2017). Power in elite interviewing: Lessons from feminist studies for political science. *Women's Studies International Forum, 62*, 99–106. https://doi.org/10.1016/j.wsif.2017.05.003

Bourdieu, P. (2000). For a scholarship with commitment. In *Profession* (pp. 40–45). New York, NY: Modern Language Association.

Briggs, C. L. (1986). *Learning how to ask: A sociolinguistic appraisal of the role of the interview in social science research.* Cambridge, UK: Cambridge University Press.

Briggs, C. L. (2003). Interviewing, power/knowledge, and social inequality. In J. F. Gubrium & J. A. Holstein (Eds.), *Postmodern interviewing* (pp. 242–255). Thousand Oaks, CA: SAGE Publications.

Demerath, P. (2009). *Producing success: The culture of personal advancement in an American high school.* Chicago, IL: University of Chicago Press.

Denzin, N. K., & Giardina, M. D. (Eds.). (2018). *Qualitative inquiry in the public sphere.* New York, NY: Routledge.

Duke, K. (2002). Getting beyond the "official line:" Reflections on dilemmas of access, knowledge and power in researching policy networks. *Journal of Social Policy, 31*(1), 39–59. https://doi.org/10.1017/S0047279402006505

Fairclough, N. (2003). *Analysing discourse: Textual analysis for social research.* London, UK: Routledge.

Fairclough, N. (2013). Critical discourse analysis and critical policy studies. *Critical Policy Studies, 7*(2), 177–197. https://doi.org/10.1080/19460171.2013.798239

Farquharson, K. (2005). A different kind of snowball: Identifying key policymakers. *International Journal of Social Research Methodology, 8*(4), 345–353. https://doi.org/10.1080/1364557042000203116

Ferguson, A. A. (2010). *Bad boys: Public schools in the making of black masculinity.* Ann Arbor, MI: University of Michigan Press.

Fitz, J., Halpin, D., & Power, S. (1994, April). *Brief encounters: Researching education policy making in elite settings.* Paper presented at the American Education Research Association Annual Meeting.

Gewirtz, S., & Ozga, J. (1994). Interviewing the education policy elite. In G. Walford (Ed.), *Researching the powerful in education* (pp. 186–203). London, UK: University College London Press.

Griffiths, M. (1998). *Educational research for social justice: Getting off the fence.* Buckingham: Open University Press.

Harvey, W. S. (2011). Strategies for conducting elite interviews. *Qualitative Research, 11*(4), 431–441. https://doi.org/10.1177/1468794111404329

Heath, S. B. (1983). *Ways with words: Language, life and work in communities and classrooms.* Cambridge, UK: Cambridge University Press.

Hunter, A. (1995). Local knowledge and local power: Notes on the ethnography of local community elites. In R. Hertz & J. B. Imber (Eds.), *Studying elites using qualitative methods* (pp. 151–170). Thousand Oaks, CA: SAGE Publications.

Kezar, A. (2003). Transformational elite interviews: Principles and problems. *Qualitative Inquiry, 9*(3), 395–415. https://doi.org/10.1177/1077800403009003005

Lancaster, K. (2017). Confidentiality, anonymity and power relations in elite interviewing: Conducting qualitative policy research in a politicised domain. *International Journal of Social Research Methodology, 20*(1), 93–103. https://doi.org/10.1080/13645579.2015.1123555

Lareau, A. (2000). *Home advantage: Social class and parental intervention in elementary education* (2nd ed.). Lanham, MD: Rowman & Littlefield Publishers.

Leech, B. L. (2002). Asking questions: Techniques for semistructured interviews. *PS: Political Science & Politics, 35*(4), 665–668. https://doi.org/10.1017/S1049096502001129

Lee-Treweek, G., & Linkogle, S. (2000). Putting danger in the frame. In G. Lee-Treweek & S. Linkogle (Eds.), *Danger in the field: Ethics and risk in social research* (pp. 8–25). London, UK: Routledge.

MacLeod, J. (2008). *Ain't no makin' it: Aspirations and attainment in a low-income neighborhood.* New York, NY: Routledge.

Marshall, C., & Rossman, G. B. (2016). *Designing qualitative research* (6th ed.). Thousand Oaks, CA: SAGE Publications.

Mikecz, R. (2012). Interviewing elites: Addressing methodological issues. *Qualitative Inquiry, 18*(6), 482–493. https://doi.org/10.1177/1077800412442818

Nader, L. (1972). Up the anthropologist: Perspectives gained from studying up. In D. Hymes (Ed.), *Reinventing anthropology* (pp. 284–311). New York, NY: Pantheon Books.

Ostrander, S. (1995). "Surely you're not in this just to be helpful." Access, rapport, and interviews in three studies of elites. In R. Hertz & J. B. Imber (Eds.), *Studying elites using qualitative methods* (pp. 133–150). Thousand Oaks, CA: SAGE Publications.

Phillips, R. (1998). The politics of history: Some methodological and ethical dilemmas in élite-based research. *British Educational Research Journal, 24*(1), 5–19. https://doi.org/10.1080/0141192980240102

Priyadharshini, E. (2003). Coming unstuck: Thinking otherwise about "studying up". *Anthropology & Education Quarterly, 34*(4), 420–437. https://doi.org/10.1525/aeq.2003.34.4.420

Selwyn, N. (2013). Researching the once-powerful in education: The value of retrospective elite interviewing in education policy research. *Journal of Education Policy, 28*(3), 339–352. https://doi.org/10.1080/02680939.2012.728630

Smith, K. E. (2006). Problematising power relations in 'elite' interviews. *Geoforum, 37*(4), 643–653. https://doi.org/10.1016/j.geoforum.2005.11.002

Spivak, G. C. (1988). Can the subaltern speak? In C. Nelson & L. Grossberg (Eds.), *Marxism and the Interpretation of Culture* (pp. 271–316). Urbana, IL: University of Illinois Press.

Stephens, N. (2007). Collecting data from elites and ultra-elites: Telephone and face-to-face interviews with macroeconomists. *Qualitative Research, 7*(2), 203–216. https://doi.org/10.1177/1468794107076020

Straubhaar, R. (2015). The methodological benefits of social media: "Studying up" in Brazil in the Facebook age. *International Journal of Qualitative Studies in Education, 28*(9), 1081–1096. https://doi.org/10.1080/09518398.2015.1074750

Thuesen, F. (2011). Navigating between dialogue and confrontation: Phronesis and emotions in interviewing elites on ethnic discrimination. *Qualitative Inquiry, 17*(7), 613–622. https://doi.org/10.1177/1077800411413998

Tompkins-Stange, M. E. (2016). *Policy patrons: Philanthropy, education reform, and the politics of influence*. Cambridge, MA: Harvard Education Press.

Valenzuela, A. (1999). *Subtractive schooling: US-Mexican youth and the politics of caring*. Albany, NY: SUNY Press.

Walford, G. (2012). Researching the powerful in education: A re-assessment of the problems. *International Journal of Research & Method in Education, 35*(2), 111–118. https://doi.org/10.1080/1743727X.2012.669523

Welch, C., Marschan-Piekkari, R., Penttinen, H., & Tahvanainen, M. (2002). Corporate elites as informants in qualitative international business research. *International Business Review, 11*(5), 611–628. https://doi.org/10.1016/S0969-5931(02)00039-2

Willis, P. (1977). *Learning to labor: How working class kids get working class jobs*. New York, NY: Columbia University Press.

Chapter 4
Framing Critical Race Theory and Methodologies

Kenzo K. Sung and Natoya Coleman

Abstract Critical Race Theory (CRT) is now a prominent framework for critical scholarship on race and racism in the field of education. Our goal is to introduce CRT as a formative theoretical and methodological framework for social justice and equity-minded educational researchers. The chapter is divided into three sections: (1) key terms and concepts, (2) broader history of CRT, and (3) critical race methodologies in education. By tracing CRT's trajectory in educational research and analyzing the significance of its legacy, we provide an alternative framework to analyze how racism is institutionalized through research-based or legalized "truths" that too often continue to perpetuate the oppression of minoritized communities. In doing so, we illuminate the significance of critical race analysis in educational research and the implications to reframe current discussions regarding the relation of research and the struggle for social justice.

In today's "education can fix all" political climate, it is important for social justice and equity-minded researchers to critically reflect on how society functions and the role of schools within it. One theoretical framework that education scholars have substantively drawn from to both analyze and challenge existing social conditions regarding race and its intersections is critical race theory (CRT). Growing in influence over the past two decades, CRT is now a prominent framework for critical scholarship in the field of education among those studying the role of race and racism in educational policy, practice, and the relation between schooling and society.

Our goal is to introduce CRT as a formative theoretical and methodological framework for social justice and equity-minded educational researchers. This chapter is divided into three sections: (1) key terms and concepts, (2) broader history of CRT, and (3) critical race methodologies in education. By tracing CRT's trajectory

K. K. Sung (✉) · N. Coleman
Rowan University, Glassboro, NJ, USA
e-mail: sungk@rowan.edu; colemann1@rowan.edu

© The Author(s) 2019
K. K. Strunk, L. A. Locke (eds.), *Research Methods for Social Justice and Equity in Education*, https://doi.org/10.1007/978-3-030-05900-2_4

in educational research and analyzing the significance of its legacy, we provide an alternative framework to analyze how racism is institutionalized through research-based or legalized "truths" that too often continue to perpetuate the oppression of minoritized communities. In doing so, we illuminate the significance of critical race analysis in educational research and the implications to reframe current discussions regarding the relation of research and the struggle for social justice.

What is Critical Race Theory?

As a theoretical and methodological framework, CRT has no canonical doctrines or methods. Rather, as Ladson-Billings (1998) explains, CRT research is unified by "two common interests: (1) understand white supremacy and subordination of people of Color; (2) change the bond that exists between law and racial power" (p. 14). Yet the range of critical and activist scholarship within the umbrella of critical race studies is anchored by what are commonly understood to be central tenets regarding the study of race and racism. Before outlining these central tenets of CRT scholarship, it is important to note some key definitions as connected to the overarching goal of CRT.

As critical race studies views knowledge as power, CRT is both an intellectual and political project that aims to illuminate and challenge racism simultaneously. Within this framework, the overarching purpose of CRT that is most often referenced is the eradication of racism as part of a larger goal of eliminating oppression in all its axes and forms (Matsuda, Lawrence, Delgado, & Crenshaw, 1993). Though there are multiple definitions for race among CRT researchers, all focus on the fact that race itself is socially constructed, rather than stemming from natural differences, in ways that are both historically specific and contested manners. As Omi and Winant (2015) state, "race is a concept that signifies and symbolizes social conflicts and interests by referring to different types of human bodies" that are characterized as distinct through various contested racial projects they describe as the process of racialization (p. 111).

The fact that race is socially constructed does not mean that it does not have real effects in society. Rather, as Banks (1995) explains, race is "a human invention constructed by groups to differentiate themselves from other groups, to create ideas about the 'Other,' to formulate their identities and to defend the disproportionate distribution of rewards and opportunities within society" (p. 22). The real material and ideological effects of race's social construction is key for critical race scholars. Likewise, racism can be characterized as a racial project that "creates or reproduces structures of domination based on racial significations and identities" (Omi & Winant, 2015, p. 128). In modern US society, White supremacy is the dominant racializing ideology that produced and legitimated various racial projects including Black slavery, Native American genocide, and segregation and anti-miscegenation laws separating and privileging those deemed "White" from "non-White." Thus, CRT scholars like Solórzano, Allen, and Carroll (2002) often posit that in US society today racism is largely synonymous with the support and maintenance of White supremacy.

Drawing from these concepts of race and racism, there are a few central tenets that have broadly shaped CRT research from its nascent first years in the field of education. In what is understood to be the foundational CRT article in education, Ladson-Billings and Tate (1995) argue for a CRT perspective in education based on three propositions: (1) race continues to be significant in the US; (2) US society is based on property rights rather than human rights; and (3) the intersection of race and property creates an analytical tool for understanding inequity. Ladson-Billings (1998) expands on this initial thesis by positing that there are four central tenets for CRT-based research: (1) race as normalized; (2) critique of liberalism; (3) interest convergence; and (4) use of storytelling and experiential knowledge. While it is beyond the scope of this chapter to fully develop each of these tenets, we offer a brief explanation for each below:

Race as Normalized

CRT centers on the seeming permanence of race as a significant, institutionally embedded part of US society and institutions in such a way that people take the idea of race and racial difference to be normal or natural rather than socially constructed and contested. For example, when studying the school-to-prison pipeline, a CRT scholar would likely focus on why US schools normalize the racialized disparities in disciplinary rates rather than take as normalized fact that Black and Brown students are "naturally" predisposed to behavioral issues (Fasching-Varner, Mitchell, Martin, & Bennett-Haron, 2014).

Critique of Liberalism

CRT centers on critiquing the limits of liberalism privileging of value of liberal ideas of individual freedoms and rights as the primary tool to combat racism, and instead emphasizes the material relations embedded in racism, or what is referred to as "race realism" (Bell, 1992), including the relation of property and human rights in US law such as the valorization of whiteness as property (Harris, 1993). For example, when studying the Civil Rights Movement, a CRT scholar would likely focus on its contradictory history by addressing the material legacies of racism, rather than accepting the liberal narrative celebrating the triumph of enlightenment over the supposed irrational racism of Jim Crow (Crenshaw, 1988).

Interest Convergence

CRT centers on race and racism as materially determined such that people of Color historically have made significant gains only to the extent that their interests aligned with White interests. For example, when studying the origins of the 1968 Bilingual Education Act, a CRT scholar would likely focus on how 1960s federal policymakers' interests aligned with Latinx activists such that policymakers gained more from redi-recting activists more radical demands into educational reforms, rather than view the bill as a singular victory for Latinx activists or ability of liberal policymakers to sim-ply recognize and do right (Sung, 2017).

Storytelling and Experiential Knowledge

CRT centers on the importance of legitimating the voices and experiential knowl-edge of people of Color that are too often minimized in traditional research through methods such as counter-storytelling. For example, when studying the history of Latinx student protest movements in Los Angeles, a CRT scholar would likely focus on developing analyses that center on how Latinx youth explain their own school experiences rather than statistical demographic data that too often lead to patholo-gizing Latinx students by defining them through a deficit discourse (Solórzano & Delgado Bernal, 2001).

As an example of how CRT can be understood as an umbrella movement, another of the earliest major CRT scholars Solórzano (1997) offered what has now been regularly referenced as five key tenets of CRT as a theory and methodology: (1) the centrality and intersectionality of race and racism, (2) the challenge to dominant ideology, (3) the commitment to social justice, (4) the centrality of experiential knowledge, and (5) the utilization of interdisciplinary approaches. Clearly some of these tenets overlap with the four previously offered, including the centrality of race in modern society, the challenge to dominant ideology (which typically is under-stood to be the ideology of liberalism in the academy, though this could obviously apply other mainstream ideologies such as conservatism, nativism, neoliberalism, etc.), and centrality of experiential knowledge. However, Solórzano also explicates three additional points in his list that CRT scholarship in education consistently references:

Intersectionality

CRT centers on illuminating how marginalization and oppression often occur at the intersections among the social systems that fundamentally structure modern society such as racism, capitalism, heteropatriarchy, as well as expanded to nationalism, ethnocentrism, and ableism. For example, when studying disproportional inclusion practices for African American students, a CRT scholar would likely focus on the intersection of race, class, culture, and language with the assumptions made regard-ing ability/disability, rather than assuming a student's placement in special educa-tion as the single unitary marker of importance separate from these other intersecting axes within which schools are structured and students are categorized (Zion & Blanchett, 2011).

Commitment to Social Justice

CRT centers on race research based on a social justice-based praxis that simultaneously aims to illuminate and actively challenge racism and intersecting axes of domination. For example, when studying the educational protests of Black and Brown communities in Chicago against choice of school openings that benefit urban gentrification, a CRT scholar would likely highlight their dual role as both a researcher and participant who actively stands in resistance to oppression as part of their scholarship, rather than seeing research as necessarily "objective" and deciding to take a "neutral" position when studying manifestations of racism (Stovall, 2016).

Interdisciplinary Approaches

CRT centers on moving beyond artificial disciplinary boundaries or canon, and toward researching race by engaging in a multitude of schools of thought and traditions including those often marginalized from traditional academic spaces in the US. For example, when studying the community cultural wealth that minoritized youth of Color often draw from, a CRT scholar would likely examine culture through a range of disciplinary perspectives and schools of thought including Ethnic Studies, Women and Gender Studies, Marxism, Sociology, and Critical Legal Studies, rather than taking a single disciplinary lens in isolation as the best strategy to do the research (Yosso, 2005).

While the above list obviously does not cover the full range of key ideas and influences, it does offer the central tenets that are most commonly referenced across critical race research in the field of education along with one characteristic example of CRT-based scholarship that adhered to each tenet. Like any theoretical framework, understanding the significance of CRT for social justice and equity-minded scholars studying race today requires taking stock in the origins of CRT and its expanding trajectory in the education field over the past two decades.

Critical Race Theory's History and Trajectory

Derrick Bell is widely recognized as a founding figure in CRT. Prior to his tenure at Harvard Law School, Bell was a civil rights lawyer with the National Association for the Advancement of Colored People (NAACP) where he worked under Thurgood Marshall at the height of the Civil Rights Movement. Pivotal to Bell's early academic work during the 1970s was understanding why the early civil rights efforts like the *Brown v. Board of Education* (1954) US Supreme Court case succeeded during a conservative period best known for anti-communist McCarthyism, while civil rights gains stalled in the 1970s after an unprecedented decade of legal successes and broader social change. Among his seminal studies, Bell's (1980) analysis of the decision via the thesis of interest convergence has become one of the leading frameworks within *Brown* historiography and, in doing so, helped create the new interdisciplinary subfield of CRT.

According to Bell, *Brown* occurred due to an interest convergence between Black communities struggling for racial justice and White elites concerned about Soviet propaganda regarding Jim Crow that dissipated by the 1970s with declining Cold War anxieties. By focusing on race as the central analytic, CRT grew as a response during the 1980s to Critical Legal Studies that Bell and others critiqued as being too centered on class-based analyses (Delgado & Stefancic, 2012). However, the origin of CRT in legal studies belies the important social and scholarly movements that heavily influenced CRT's analyses. As Crenshaw (1988) notes, she and other early critical race scholars borrowed from several traditions including cultural nationalism, postmodernism, and Black feminist thought. These schools of thought also drew from various 1960s–1970s social movements for inspiration including the Civil Rights Movement, Black and allied (Brown, Yellow, Red) Power Movements, Second and Third Wave Feminist Movements, and the Third World Liberation Front's movement for Ethnic Studies.

CRT has since grown into other social science and allied areas starting in the 1990s including ethnic studies, women's studies, education, sociology, art history, public health, and social work (Delgado & Stefancic, 2012). However, the primary residence of critical race scholarship beyond legal studies is currently the field of education, which seems to be a natural fit as education continues to be the principle CRT topic in legal studies including racial desegregation (Bell, 1980; Singleton, 2007), school finance reform (Adamson, 2006), educating undocumented youth (Lopez, 2005), affirmative action (Bell, 2003), or school choice (Dickerson, 2005).

The rise of CRT in the field of education in the 1990s can be traced to a similar critique of Critical Pedagogy that was leveled in the 1970s toward Critical Legal Studies, arguing that both marginalized the fundamental significance of race in their analyses (Leonardo, 2013). As outlined in Ladson-Billings and Tate's (1995) foundational article, CRT provides an analytic tool to better focus critical scholarship on racial justice and equity in education. Critical race studies is now the dominant framework for scholarship among critical education scholars studying race and racism including research on teacher education and preparation (Juarez & Hayes, 2014; Leonardo & Boas, 2013; Milner, 2008), college athletes (Donnor, 2005), desegregation (Leigh, 2003), inclusion (Zion & Blanchett, 2011), intercultural education (Caraballo, 2009), affirmative action (Park & Liu, 2014), undocumented students (Allen, 2015; Buenavista, 2018), educators of Color (Blaisdell, 2016; Davila & Aviles, 2018), and media on education (Gillborn, 2010).

Over the past two decades, CRT in education studies has also developed into an umbrella for a range of analytic branches that both draw from critical race scholarship and highlight the often intersecting and contradictory racial geographies present in schooling (Dixson & Rousseau, 2005; Ledesma & Calderón, 2015; Lynn & Parker, 2006). These "sister crit" frameworks include LatCrit (Davila & Aviles de

Bradley, 2010; Solórzano & Delgado Bernal, 2001; Yosso, 2006), AsianCrit (Buenavista, Jayakumar, & Misa-Escalante, 2009; Curammeng, Buenavista, & Cariaga, 2017; Iftikar & Museus, in press; Museus & Iftikar, 2014), BlackCrit (Dumas & Ross, 2016), TribalCrit (Brayboy, 2005; Haynes Writer, 2008), and critical whiteness studies (Leonardo, 2009; Hayes & Hartlep, 2013; Matias, 2016). In addition, critical race scholarship has intersected with other scholarly traditions including feminism and particularly critical race feminism (Childers-McKee & Hytten, 2015; Evans-Winters & Esposito, 2010; Sampson, 2016), critical social theory (Melamed, 2011; Leonardo, 2013), antiblackness (Dumas, 2016; Parker, 2017; Sung, 2018), settler colonialism (Snelgrove, Dhamoon, & Corntassel, 2014; Tuck & Yang, 2012), and coloniality (de los Ríos & Seltzer, 2017; Hsu, 2015; Patel, 2014) and dis/ability (Annamma, Connor, & Ferri, 2013).

Critical Race Methodologies in Education

Methodologically, CRT has also grown from its legal roots as it develops in the field of education. While CRT was originally used in legal studies as a framework to analyze patterns in court cases and legal precedent, in the field of education focus on methodology that highlights experiential knowledge and voice has been key. As such, the primary narrative of critical race scholars in education has traditionally focused on counter-storytelling or *testimonios* of students and communities racialized as non-White (Bernal, 2002; Pérez Huber, 2008; Solórzano & Yosso, 2002; Yosso, 2006). Solórzano and Yosso (2002) employ counter-stories to reframe the study of race and racism by starting with the experiences of those who have been minoritized through daily racial microaggressions (Alvarez, 2017; Pérez Huber & Solórzano, 2015). Originating from LatCrit, *testimonios* is another method that draws on experiential knowledge as a means to both critique traditional research that privilege the scholar's perspective and validate the personal and collective knowledge among minoritized communities (Pérez Huber, 2008), as well as those racialized as non-White who are in institutional positions of power (Alemán, 2009; Sampson, 2018).

Critical race scholarship in education also employs the study of history and historical cases as a critical method, similar to the revisionist historical study of the *Brown* decision and other legal cases that Bell (1980) and others researched in the field of law. As Ladson-Billings and Tate (1995) note, the power of historical storytelling and historiographical revision is important to properly understanding and challenging injustices past, present, and future. One example of this critical race history method is the study of the historical context surrounding racially segregated schools in Oxnard, California, and the stories of the lived experiences of Mexican American youth during the early twentieth century (Garcia, Yosso, & Barajas, 2012). A second example is the study of the 1968 Bilingual Education Act and its origin as a hegemonic interest convergence between the 1960s federal policymakers and Latinx activists, formatively shaping the contradictions that bilingual education still struggles with today (Sung, 2017).

Another methodological tool employed by critical race educational scholars is the interrogation and reframing of curriculum and pedagogies across different subject areas in teacher education. For example, Critical Race English Education (CREE) focuses on challenging antiblackness and White supremacy in English and Language Arts (ELA) classrooms through studying the value of Black literacies as part of reimagining classrooms as sites for healing and racial justice (Baker-Bell, Butler, & Johnson, 2017; Johnson, Jackson, Stovall, & Baszile, 2017). Other examples of CRT methods being employed in the study of subject matter areas include everything from bilingual education (Flores & Rosa, 2015; Rosa & Flores, 2017) and Teachers of English to Speakers of Other Languages (TESOL) education (Crump, 2014; Liggett, 2014) to math education (Larnell, Bullock, & Jett, 2016; Terry, 2011).

In addition, critical race scholarship has recently expanded from more qualitative, interpretive methods as central to critical race praxis (Stovall, 2016) toward reimagining how to include quantitative methodology, which was typically critiqued as privileging a seemingly objective, essentialistic analysis. The recent evolution of QuantCrit challenges the notion that the "numbers can speak for themselves" and encourages researchers to question the assumptions that result from the analysis of big data (Garcia, Lopez, & Velez, 2018; Gillborn, Warmington, & Demack, 2018). QuantCrit builds on the work of other critical race scholarship including TribalCrit's work in Indigenous Statistics that challenges the absence of indigenous populations in aggregate data (Brayboy, Fann, Castagno, & Solyom, 2012; Walter & Andersen, 2013) as well as Critical Race Spatial Analysis that uses geographic information system (GIS) mapping tools to represent race and how racialized oppression is manifested geographically (Solórzano & Velez, 2016; Morrison, Annamma, & Jackson, 2017).

Conclusion

While not nearly long enough to comprehensively cover the explosive growth of critical race scholarship in the field of education, this chapter provides an introductory survey of CRT's central terms and tenets, history of CRT prior to and within education studies, and the range of critical race methods currently employed in educational research. The goal of this chapter is for social justice and equity-minded educational researchers to find inspiration in critical race scholarship as a theoretically and methodologically valuable way of doing research. If so, we hope you will explore CRT further through the selected referenced readings that follow, and contribute to CRT's continued development in the field of education as a means of both illuminating and challenging dominant race narratives and racist structures.

Suggested Readings

Richard Delgado, R., & Stefancic, J. (2012). *Critical race theory: An introduction.* New York, NY: New York University Press.

Popular Critical Race Theory primer is concisely written with lots of clear examples. Book is intended to be a first introduction in legal studies, but easily readable and adaptable for the field of education.

Lynn, M., & Dixson, A. (2013). *Handbook of critical race theory in education.* New York, NY: Routledge.

Edited collection of essays from foundational Critical Race Theory scholars in the field of education. Book will provide reader a strong understanding of CRT's influence in educational research on race and racism.

Crenshaw, K., Gotanda, N., Peller, G., & Thomas, K. (1996). *Critical race theory: The key writings that formed the movement.* New York, NY: The New Press.

Edited collection of early Critical Race Theory foundational articles and essays from the field of legal studies. Book will provide reader a strong understanding of CRT's historical trajectory.

References

Adamson, B. L. (2006). The H'aint in the (school) house: The interest convergence paradigm in state legislatures and school finance reform. *California Western Law Review, 43*(1), 173–202.

Alemán Jr., E. (2009). LatCrit educational leadership and advocacy: Struggling over whiteness as property in Texas school finance. *Equity & Excellence in Education, 42*(2), 183–201. https://doi.org/10.1080/10665680902744246

Allen, A. (2015). Leveraging the cultural wealth in family and friend networks: An examination of undocumented Latino college students' support systems and academic achievement. In D. Mitchell, E. Daniele, K. Soria, & J. Gipson (Eds.), *Student involvement and academic outcomes: Implications for diverse college student populations* (pp. 219–236). New York, NY: Peter Lang.

Alvarez, A. (2017). "Seeing their eyes in the rearview mirror": Identifying and responding to students' challenging experiences. *Equity & Excellence in Education, 50*(1), 53–67. https://doi.org/10.1080/10665684.2016.1250686

Annamma, S. A., Connor, D., & Ferri, B. (2013). Dis/ability critical race studies (DisCrit): Theorizing at the intersections of race and dis/ability. *Race Ethnicity and Education, 16*(1), 1–31. https://doi.org/10.1080/13613324.2012.730511

Baker-Bell, A., Butler, T., & Johnson, L. (2017). The pain and the wounds: A call for critical race English education in the wake of racial violence. *English Education, 49*(2), 116–129.

Banks, J. A. (1995). The historical reconstruction of knowledge about race: Implications for transformative teaching. *Educational Researcher, 24*(2), 15–25. https://doi.org/10.2307/1176421

Bell, D. A. (1980). Brown v. Board of Education and the interest-convergence dilemma. *Harvard Law Review, 93*, 518–533. https://doi.org/10.2307/1340546

Bell, D. (1992). Race realism. *Connecticut Law Review, 24*(2), 363–379.

Bell, D. A. (2003). Diversity's distractions. *Columbia Law Review, 103*, 1622–1633. https://doi.org/10.2307/3593396

Bernal, D. D. (2002). Critical race theory, Latino critical theory, and critical raced-gendered epistemologies: Recognizing students of color as holders and creators of knowledge. *Qualitative Inquiry, 8*(1), 105–126. https://doi.org/10.1177/107780040200800107

Blaisdell, B. (2016). Exorcising the racism phantasm: Racial realism in educational research. *The Urban Review, 48*(2), 285–310. https://doi.org/10.1007/s11256-016-0354-0

Brayboy, B. (2005). Toward a tribal critical race theory in education. *The Urban Review, 37*(5), 425–446. https://doi.org/10.1007/s11256-005-0018-y

Brayboy, B., Fann, A. J., Castagno, A. E., & Solyom, J. A. (2012). *Postsecondary education for American Indian and Alaska natives: Higher education for nation building and self-determination: ASHE higher education report 37:5*. San Francisco, CA: Jossey-Bass.

Buenavista, T. L. (2018). Model (undocumented) minorities and "illegal" immigrants: Centering Asian Americans and U.S. carcerality in undocumented student discourse. *Race Ethnicity and Education, 21*(1), 78–91. https://doi.org/10.1080/13613324.2016.1248823

Buenavista, T. L., Jayakumar, U. M., & Misa-Escalante, K. (2009). Contextualizing Asian American education through Critical Race Theory: An example of U.S. Pilipino college student experiences. In S. D. Museus (Ed.), *Conducting research on Asian Americans in higher education. New Directions for Institutional Research* (Vol. 142, pp. 69–81). San Francisco, CA: Jossey-Bass. https://doi.org/10.1002/ir.297

Caraballo, L. (2009). Interest convergence in intergroup education and beyond: Rethinking agendas in multicultural education. *International Journal of Multicultural Education, 11*(1), 1–15.

Childers-McKee, C. D., & Hytten, K. (2015). Critical race feminism and the complex challenges of educational reform. *Urban Review, 47*(3), 393–412. https://doi.org/10.1007/s11256-015-0323-z

Crenshaw, K. W. (1988). Race, reform, and retrenchment: Transformation and legitimation in anti-discrimination law. *Harvard Law Review, 101*(7), 1331–1387. https://doi.org/10.2307/1341398

Crump, A. (2014). Langcrit: Critical language and race theory. *Critical Inquiry in Language Studies, 11*(3), 207–224. https://doi.org/10.1080/15427587.2014.936243

Curammeng, E. R., Buenavista, T. L., & Cariaga, S. (2017). *Asian American critical race theory: Origins, directions, and praxis*. Center for Critical Race Studies at UCLA Research Briefs. Retrieved from http://issuu.com/almaiflores/docs/ec_tlb_sc_asianam_crt?e=25160478/49582421.

Davila, E., & Aviles, A. (2018). Afro-Puerto Rican primas: Identity, pedagogy, and solidarity. In S. A. Shelton, J. E. Flynn, & T. J. Grosland (Eds.), *Feminism and intersectionality in academia: Women's narratives and experiences in higher education* (pp. 117–130). New York, NY: Springer International Publishing.

Davila, E., & Aviles de Bradley, A. (2010). Examining education for Latinas/os in Chicago: A CRT/LatCrit approach. *Educational Foundations, 24*(1–2), 39–58.

de los Ríos, C. V., & Seltzer, K. (2017). Translanguaging, coloniality, and English classrooms: An exploration of two bicoastal urban classrooms. *Research in the Teaching of English, 52*(1), 55–76.

Delgado, R., & Stefancic, J. (2012). *Critical race theory: An introduction*. New York, NY: New York University Press.

Dickerson, A. M. (2005). Caught in the trap: Pricing racial housing preferences. *Michigan Law Review, 103*, 1273–1291.

Dixson, A. D., & Rousseau, C. K. (2005). And we are still not saved: Critical race theory in education ten years later. *Race Ethnicity and Education, 8*(1), 7–27. https://doi.org/10.1080/1361332052000340971

Donnor, J. K. (2005). Towards an interest-convergence in the education of African-American football student athletes in major college sports. *Race Ethnicity and Education, 8*(1), 45–67. https://doi.org/10.1080/1361332052000340999

Dumas, M. (2016). Against the dark: Antiblackness in education policy and discourse. *Theory into Practice, 55*(1), 11–19. https://doi.org/10.1080/00405841.2016.1116852

Dumas, M. J., & Ross, K. M. (2016). "Be real black for me" imagining BlackCrit in education. *Urban Education, 51*(4), 415–442. https://doi.org/10.1177/0042085916628611

Evans-Winters, V. E., & Esposito, J. (2010). Other people's daughters: Critical race feminism and Black girls' education. *Journal of Educational Foundations, 24*(1–2), 11–24.

Fasching-Varner, K. J., Mitchell, R. W., Martin, L. L., & Bennett-Haron, K. P. (2014). Beyond school-to-prison pipeline and toward an educational and penal realism. *Equity & Excellence in Education, 47*(4), 410–429. https://doi.org/10.1080/10665684.2014.959285

Flores, N., & Rosa, J. (2015). Undoing appropriateness: Raciolinguistic ideologies and language diversity in education. *Harvard Educational Review, 85*(2), 149–171. https://doi.org/10.17763/0017-8055.85.2.149

Garcia, D. G., Yosso, T. J., & Barajas, F. P. (2012). "A few of the brightest, cleanest Mexican children": School segregation as a form of mundane racism in Oxnard, California, 1900–1940. *Harvard Educational Review, 82*(1), 1–25.

Garcia, N. M., Lopez, N., & Velez, V. N. (2018). QuantCrit: Rectifying quantitative methods through critical race theory. *Race, Ethnicity and Education, 21*(2), 149–157. https://doi.org/10.1080/13613324.2017.1377675

Gillborn, D. (2010). The white working class, racism and respectability: Victims, degenerates and interest-convergence. *British Journal of Educational Studies, 58*(1), 3–25. https://doi.org/10.1080/00071000903516361

Gillborn, D., Warmington, P., & Demack, S. (2018). QuantCrit: Education, policy, 'Big Data' and principles for a critical race theory of statistics. *Race Ethnicity and Education, 21*(2), 158–179. https://doi.org/10.1080/13613324.2017.1377417

Harris, C. I. (1993). Whiteness as property. *Harvard Law Review, 106*(8), 1707.

Hayes, C., & Hartlep, N. D. (2013). Unhooking from whiteness: The key to dismantling racism in the United States. In *Rotterdam*. Dordrecht: Sense Publishers.

Haynes Writer, J. (2008). Unmasking, exposing, and confronting: Critical race theory, tribal critical race theory and multicultural education. *International Journal of Multicultural Education, 10*(2), 1–15.

Hsu, F. (2015). The coloniality of neoliberal English: The enduring structures of American colonial English instruction in the Philippines and Puerto Rico. *L2 Journal, 7*(3), 123–145.

Iftikar, J. S., & Museus, S. D. (in press). On the utility of Asian critical (AsianCrit) theory in the field of education. *International Journal of Qualitative Studies in Education*. https://doi.org/10.1080/09518398.2018.1522008

Johnson, L. L., Jackson, J., Stovall, D. O., & Baszile, D. T. (2017). "Loving blackness to death": (Re) imagining ELA classrooms in a time of racial chaos. *English Journal, 106*(4), 60–66.

Juarez, B. G., & Hayes, C. (2014). On being named a Black supremacist and a race traitor: The problem of white racial domination and domestic terrorism in U.S. teacher education. *The Urban Review, 47*(2), 317–340. https://doi.org/10.1007/s11256-014-0294-5

Ladson-Billings, G. (1998). Just what is critical race theory and what's it doing in a *nice* field like education? *International Journal of Qualitative Studies in Education, 11*(1), 7–24. https://doi.org/10.1080/095183998236863

Ladson-Billings, G., & Tate, W. (1995). Toward a critical race theory of education. *Teachers College Record, 97*(1), 47–68.

Larnell, G. V., Bullock, E. C., & Jett, C. C. (2016). Rethinking teaching and learning mathematics for social justice from a critical race perspective. *Journal of Education, 96*(1), 19–29. https://doi.org/10.1177/002205741619600104

Ledesma, M. C., & Calderón, D. (2015). Critical race theory in education: A review of past literature and a look to the future. *Qualitative Inquiry, 21*(3), 206–222. https://doi.org/10.1177/1077800414557825

Leigh, P. R. (2003). Interest convergence and desegregation in the Ohio Valley. *The Journal of Negro Education, 72*(3), 269–296. https://doi.org/10.2307/3211248

Leonardo, Z. (2009). *Race, whiteness, and education.* New York, NY: Routledge.

Leonardo, Z. (2013). *Race frameworks: A multidimensional theory of racism and education.* New York, NY: Teachers College Press.

Leonardo, Z., & Boas, E. (2013). Other kids' teachers: What children of color learn from white women and what this says about race, whiteness, and gender. In M. Lynn & A. Dixson (Eds.), *The handbook of critical race theory in education* (pp. 313–324). New York, NY: Routledge Press.

Liggett, T. (2014). The mapping of a framework: Critical race theory and TESOL. *Urban Review: Issues and Ideas in Public Education, 46*(1), 112–124. https://doi.org/10.1007/s11256-013-0254-5

Lopez, M. P. (2005). Reflections on educating Latino and Latina undocumented children: Beyond *Plyler v. Doe. Seton Hall Law Review, 35*, 1373–1405.

Lynn, M., & Parker, L. (2006). Critical race studies in education: Examining a decade of research on US schools. *The Urban Review, 38*(4), 257–290. https://doi.org/10.1007/s11256-006-0035-5

Matias, C. E. (2016). *Feeling white: Whiteness, emotionality, and education.* Rotterdam: Sense Publishers. https://doi.org/10.1007/978-94-6300-450-3

Matsuda, M. J., Lawrence, C. R., Delgado, R., & Crenshaw, K. W. (Eds.). (1993). *Words that wound: Critical race theory, assaultive speech, and the first amendment.* Boulder, CO: Westview Press.

Melamed, J. (2011). *Represent and destroy: Rationalizing violence in the new racial capitalism.* Minneapolis, MN: Minnesota University Press.

Milner, H. R. (2008). Critical race theory and interest convergence as analytic tools in teacher education policies and practices. *Journal of Teacher Education, 59*(4), 332–346. https://doi.org/10.1177/0022487108321884

Morrison, D., Annamma, S. A., & Jackson, D. D. (2017). *Critical race spatial analysis: Mapping to understand and address educational inequity.* Sterling, VA: Stylus Publishing.

Museus, S. D., & Iftikar, J. (2014). Asian critical theory (AsianCrit). In M. Y. Danico (Ed.), *Asian American society: An encyclopedia* (pp. 95–98). Thousand Oaks, CA: Sage Publications and Association for Asian American Studies. https://doi.org/10.4135/9781452281889

Omi, M., & Winant, H. (2015). *Racial formation in the United States.* New York, NY: Routledge.

Park, J. J., & Liu, A. (2014). Interest convergence or divergence?: A critical race analysis of Asian Americans, meritocracy, and critical mass in the affirmative action debate. *The Journal of Higher Education, 85*(1), 36–64. https://doi.org/10.1080/00221546.2014.11777318

Parker, L. (2017). Schools and the no-prison phenomenon: Antiblackness and secondary policing in the Black Lives Matter era. *Journal of Educational Controversy, 12*(1), 1–24.

Patel, L. (2014). Countering coloniality in educational research: From ownership to answerability. *Educational Studies, 50*(4), 357–377. https://doi.org/10.1080/00131946.2014.924942

Pérez Huber, L. (2008). Building critical race methodologies in educational research: A research note on critical race testimonio. *FIU Law Review, 4*(1), 159–173.

Pérez Huber, L., & Solórzano, D. (2015). Racial microaggressions as a tool for critical race research. *Race, Ethnicity, and Education, 18*(3), 297–320. https://doi.org/10.1080/13613324.2014.994173

Rosa, J., & Flores, N. (2017). Unsettling race and language: Toward a raciolinguistic perspective. *Language in Society, 46*(5), 621–647.

Sampson, C. (2018). (Im)Possibilities of Latinx school board members' educational leadership toward equity. *Educational Administration Quarterly.* https://doi.org/10.1177/0013161X18799482

Sampson, C. R. (2016). So it "became white activists fighting for integration?" Community organizations, intersectional identities, and education reform. *Urban Review, 49*(1), 72–95. https://doi.org/10.1007/s11256-016-0382-9

Singleton, D. (2007). Interest convergence and the education of African-American boys in Cincinnati: Motivating suburban whites to embrace interdistrict education reform. *Northern Kentucky Law Review, 34*, 663–697. https://doi.org/10.1017/S0047404517000562

Snelgrove, C., Dhamoon, R., & Corntassel, J. (2014). Unsettling settler colonialism: The discourse and politics of settlers, and solidarity with Indigenous nations. *Decolonization: Indigeneity, Education & Society, 3*(2), 1–32.

Solórzano, D. G. (1997). Images and words that wound: Critical race theory, racial stereotyping, and teacher education. *Teacher Education Quarterly, 24*(3), 5–19.

Solórzano, D., Allen, W. R., & Carroll, G. (2002). Keeping race in place: Racial microaggressions and campus racial climate at the University of California, Berkeley. *Chicano/Latino Law Review, 23*, 15–112.

Solórzano, D. G., & Delgado Bernal, D. (2001). Examining transformational resistance through a critical race and LatCrit theory framework: Chicana and Chicano students in an urban context. *Urban Education, 36*(3), 308–342. https://doi.org/10.1177/0042085901363002

Solórzano, D. G., & Velez, V. N. (2016). Using critical race spatial analysis to examine the Du Boisian color-line along the Alameda Corridor in Southern California. *Whittier Law Review, 37*, 423–438.

Solórzano, D. G., & Yosso, T. J. (2002). Critical race methodology: Counter-storytelling as an analytical framework for education research. *Qualitative Inquiry, 8*(1), 23–44. https://doi.org/10.1177/107780040200800103

Stovall, D. O. (2016). *Born out of struggle: Critical race theory, school creation, and the politics of interruption*. Albany, NY: SUNY Press.

Sung, K. (2017). "Accentuate the positive; eliminate the negative": Hegemonic interest convergence, racialization of Latino poverty, and the 1968 Bilingual Education Act. *Peabody Journal of Education, 92*(3), 302–321. https://doi.org/10.1080/0161956X.2017.1324657

Sung, K. (2018). Raciolinguistic ideology of antiblackness: Bilingual education, tracking, and the multiracial imaginary in urban schools. *International Journal of Qualitative Studies in Education, 31*(8), 667–683. https://doi.org/10.1080/09518398.2018.1479047

Terry, C. L. (2011). Mathematical counterstory and African American male students: Urban mathematics education from a critical race theory perspective. *Journal of Urban Mathematics Education, 4*(1), 23–49.

Tuck, E., & Yang, K. W. (2012). Decolonization is not a metaphor. *Decolonization: Indigeneity, Education & Society, 1*(1), 1–40.

Walter, M., & Andersen, C. (2013). *Indigenous statistics: A quantitative research methodology*. New York, NY: Routledge.

Yosso, T. J. (2005). Whose culture has capital? A critical race theory discussion of community cultural wealth. *Race Ethnicity and Education, 8*(1), 69–91.

Yosso, T. (2006). *Critical race counterstories along the Chicana/Chicano educational pipeline*. New York, NY: Routledge.

Zion, S. D., & Blanchett, W. J. (2011). [Re]conceptualizing inclusion: Can critical race theory and interest convergence be utilized to achieve inclusion and equity for African American students? *Teachers College Record, 113*(10), 2186–2205.

Chapter 5
Disentangling the Complexities of Queer Theory and Intersectionality Theory: Research Paradigms and Insights for Social Justice

Christian D. Chan, Sam Steen, Lionel C. Howard, and Arshad I. Ali

Abstract Queer theory and intersectionality theory have emerged as prominent paradigms guiding decisions for research design and methodology in educational research. Despite their increasing prominence and implementation in educational research, applying these paradigms can result in confusion and conflation without understanding their unique distinctions. Additionally, queer theory and intersectionality theory each carry their own legacies, predecessors, and philosophical underpinnings. Queer theory primarily focuses on disrupting the restrictions associated with binaries and identity categories, whereas intersectionality theory involves an examination of social identities (e.g., race, sexuality, gender identity) and intersections to understand power relations and inequities. With an overarching introduction to queer theory and intersectionality theory as two distinct paradigms, this chapter involves the following goals: (a) explain key aspects of queer theory and intersectionality theory as distinct paradigms; (b) identify differences between queer theory and intersectionality theory; and (c) provide recommendations for understanding paradigmatic differences in research.

Queer theory is a paradigm of research focused on the diverse experiences of sexuality, gender identity, and affection; rejecting binaries in identity categories; and using experiences of historically marginalized communities to examine injustices

C. D. Chan (✉)
Idaho State University, Pocatello, ID, USA
e-mail: chanchr2@isu.edu

S. Steen
University of Arizona, Tucson, AZ, USA
e-mail: samsteen@email.arizona.edu

L. C. Howard · A. I. Ali
The George Washington University, Washington, DC, USA
e-mail: lchoward@gwu.edu; arshadali@gwu.edu

© The Author(s) 2019   59
K. K. Strunk, L. A. Locke (eds.), *Research Methods for Social Justice and Equity in Education*, https://doi.org/10.1007/978-3-030-05900-2_5

and barriers (Lugg & Murphy, 2014). In contrast, intersectionality theory is a paradigm of research focused on inequities occurring within interpersonal experiences and systems (e.g., workplace, school, community), connections between social identities (e.g., race, ethnicity, sexuality, gender identity), an understanding of which identities and environments produce power, and an agenda toward social justice by identifying points to implement change (Collins & Bilge, 2016). Using a paradigm of research (e.g., queer theory) involves a preliminary understanding of the history, contributors, and philosophical underpinnings. A paradigm of research, hence, relates to the researchers' personal philosophy and values; fit between research purpose and design; and connection across the entire process of the study (e.g., initial research question formation, tools for data collection, the process of data analysis, writing the report, determination of findings). The paradigm outlining a research study is an approach emerging from theoretical underpinnings to guide the research purpose, decisions for methodology, the lens for data analysis, and the use of the findings.

Queer theory and intersectionality theory are important in their attention to barriers and inequities affecting historically marginalized communities (e.g., LGBTQ+ communities, people of color) by recognizing their identities (Guba & Lincoln, 1994; Kincheloe, McLaren, Steinberg, & Monzó, 2017). For this reason, educational research continues to build upon the work of queer theorists and intersectional theorists while making current contributions. Scholars implementing queer theory or intersectionality theory as paradigms in their research studies can carefully consider how research impacts the communities of interest and mobilizing participants and researchers to institute change in the face of their respective communities. Although some research in education addresses these issues, the majority of educational research still relies on using data accessible to researchers as truth rather than questioning the possibilities giving rise to such data (Detamore, 2010; Patel, 2016; Tuck & Wang, 2018). With a majority of research using empirical evidence to inform their practices, researchers, scholars, and practitioners can exclude historically marginalized communities and pose barriers to scholars attempting to produce change, action, and experiences in the lens of queer theory or intersectionality theory.

Paradigms specifically require an understanding of distinction. For example, queer theory and intersectionality theory result in their own unique underlying principles and tenets to align the purposes and offerings for a research study on social justice (Bilge, 2013; Chan, Erby, & Ford, 2017; Collins, 2015; Cor & Chan, 2017; Hancock, 2016). Nonetheless, scholars and researchers continue to grapple with the conceptualization of the parallels between these theoretical frameworks while elucidating its distinctions to increase accessibility for research methods closely involved in social justice and equity efforts (Duong, 2012; Fotopoulou, 2012). While unifying conceptual and empirical literature to more fluidly interpret queer theory and intersectionality theory, this chapter delves into the following goals: (a) explain key aspects of queer theory and intersectionality theory distinctly; (b) illustrate differences between each paradigm as its own distinct framework; and (c) generate recommendations for use in research.

Distinguishing Between Queer Theory and Intersectionality Theory

Queer theory and intersectionality theory have produced conceptual frameworks and empirical analyses wrestling with the nature of identity categories, organizations of power, historicization, and social location. Due to their critical roots, some areas within their approaches may seem similar. Their approaches and purposes, however, are vastly different as a result of their legacy and theoretical underpinnings.

Queer Theory

Queer theory emerged from a long-standing history as a method to reject identity categories, even with LGBTQ+ communities naming their identities to hold to power (Jagose, 2009; Lugg, 2003; Lugg & Murphy, 2014). Distinctly, queer theory as an analytic framework operates as a poststructuralist approach to disrupt binaries (e.g., cisgender-transgender; gay-heterosexual; male-female) to ultimately question the power instituted by categories (Few-Demo, 2014; Few-Demo, Humble, Curran, & Lloyd, 2016; Fish & Russell, 2018; Mayo, 2017). As a result, its theoretical roots have evolved from the work of several scholars attempting to push the boundaries on sexuality and gender, including Foucault (1980), Rubin (1984, 2011), Butler (1990, 2004), and Sedgwick (1990, 1993). More distinctly, predecessors contributing to the development of queer theory essentially reject identity categories as elements tied to power while noting the cultural, political, historical, and contextual tensions influencing the construction of identity categories (Ahmed, 2006; Butler, 1990, 2004). Thus, the queer theory approach defines queer as a verb as much as a noun, considering the complicated, messy, and political nature of identities in association with the interruption of binaries (McCann, 2016; Misgav, 2016).

As queer theory continues to emerge in scholarly research focused on equity and social justice, the approach notably operates from a generated set of underlying principles core to the heart of its complexity and deconstruction of power and identity (Love, 2017; Lugg & Murphy, 2014). Queer theory is distinct in its approach to be disruptive of identity categories, realities highlighted by the construction of identities, and structures and power relations governed by classifications and identity categories (Goodrich, Luke, & Smith, 2016; Lugg & Murphy, 2014; Rumens, 2016, 2017; Jagose, 2009). For this reason, queer theory analyzes several systemic components, including history and context, to critically examine manifestations of power determined by binaries and identity categories (Gedro & Mizzi, 2014; McCann, 2016).

Other than exclusively problematizing social structures, queer theory focuses on reorienting visibility of marginalized communities through giving voice to unique and complex forms of agency, representation, and identity (Adams & Holman

Jones, 2011; Love, 2017). Given its antiessentialist platform (Lugg, 2003; Lugg & Murphy, 2014) as a defined approach to consider unique, individualized, and authentic experiences divergent across communities (e.g., LGBTQ+ communities), queer theory enacts an empowerment to reify and author narratives unique to the variability by noting fluidity, complexity, and intersections with other social identities (e.g., race, ethnicity; Rumens, 2013, 2017; Lugg & Murphy, 2014). Hence, queer theory takes on the *antiessentialist* value of realizing that not all experiences will represent the same identity or identities, especially as intersections with other dimensions of social identity accentuate divergence (Few-Demo et al., 2016). Thus, rejecting categories and binaries is the crux of the poststructuralist approach by realizing many interpretations and experiences can coexist outside of claimed identities. Tied together with fluidity, refuting binaries is a core component of queer theory approaches through substantiating the connection between binary identity categories as a function for substantiating power (Rumens, 2013).

Intersectionality Theory

Intersectionality theory was born out of collective movements angled toward social action, equity, equality, and human rights, particularly for communities experiencing multiple forms of marginalization (Chan et al., 2017; Cor & Chan, 2017). With implications for scholarly and educational practices, intersectionality emerged from decades of dialogues centered on protections and rights for women of color while resisting restrictions and disenfranchisement from feminist movements (Carbado, Crenshaw, Mays, & Tomlinson, 2013; Cole, 2008, 2009; Grzanka, Santos, & Moradi, 2017; Parent, DeBlaere, & Moradi, 2013). Intersectionality also rose to prominence specifically through the work of Crenshaw (1988, 1989, 1991) as a legal analytic framework to question the protections held by antidiscrimination law. Distinctly, Crenshaw critiqued legal scholarship for examining through the lens of a single axis (e.g., exclusively race; exclusively gender) the possibility that a Black woman would still face inequities. Although intersectionality has been tied closely to the work of Crenshaw (1988, 1989, 1991) and Collins (1986, 1990, 2004), feminist and intersectional scholars trace the history and genealogy of intersectionality to multiple women of color and queer women of color using personal narratives of multiple marginalizations as the basis for collective action (Anzaldúa, 1987; Combahee River Collective, 1977/1995; hooks, 1981, 1984, 1989; Lorde, 1984; Moraga & Anzaldúa, 1983). Attuned to the gravity of their personal experiences with marginalization, predecessors of intersectionality cited the problematic erasure of women of color in feminist movements (Collins, 1986; Crenshaw, 1989, 1991) while subversively interrupting the boundaries on choosing single categories of identity to convey their existence (Anzaldúa, 1987; Lorde, 1984; Moraga & Anzaldúa, 1983). Hence, the evolution of intersectionality carries prominent roots in feminism and, more distinctly, Black feminism (Bilge, 2013; Carbado et al., 2013; Cho, 2013; Cho, Crenshaw, & McCall, 2013).

Notably, intersectionality considers the unique lived experiences inherent in multiple dimensions of social identity (e.g., race, ethnicity, gender identity, sexuality, affection, size, regional identity, spirituality, ability status, generational status, social class) through realizing diversity as a factor within and between identity categories (Bowleg, 2008, 2012; Chan, 2017; Chan et al., 2017, 2018; Cole, 2008, 2009; Corlett & Mavin, 2014; McCall, 2005). Intersectionality institutes an approach dedicated to the experiences of multiply-marginalized individuals and communities rendered invisible by social structures (e.g., environments, communities, policies, advocacy, and human rights movements; Bilge, 2013; Bowleg, 2013; Carastathis, 2016; Cor & Chan, 2017; Crenshaw, 1989, 1991). Intersectional approaches also realize the phenomenon of carrying both privilege and oppression simultaneously (Smooth, 2013) as an outcome of complexities and linkages among social identities (Collins & Bilge, 2016). This particular principle accentuates the complex, unique realities illustrated through multiple overlapping forms of oppression (Cho, 2013; Shields, 2008; Warner, Settles, & Shields, 2016). Connecting immensely with social identities, intersectionality operates with the assumption that social identities are not necessarily mutually exclusive entities, but rather, linkages serve as the analytical lens for understanding inequities and opportunities for social justice (Carastathis, 2016; Corlett & Mavin, 2014; Gopaldas, 2013). Analyses formed with a lens of intersectionality continue to examine how such linkages remain connected to political, contextual, and historical forces sustaining roots of subordination and stratification of power (i.e., specific communities having privilege and power over other groups; Bowleg, 2012; Bowleg & Bauer, 2016; Love, 2017; Smooth, 2013).

The promise of intersectionality, however, does not exclusively rely on a conceptualization of multiple identities (Moradi & Grzanka, 2017). Intersectionality, in particular, does not exist without an interrogation of power and the structures that sustain inequities (Bowleg, 2017; Bowleg & Bauer, 2016; Collins & Bilge, 2016). Consequently, intersectionality critically analyzes the personal experiences of marginalization to reflect relationships with social structures and levels of power responsible for the historical reproduction of subordination (Collins, 1986, 2004). The philosophy of intersectionality is interrogative in this manner to problematize inequitable systems of power, but more so to reform systems for the liberation of multiply-marginalized communities (Chan, 2017; Chan et al., 2017; Cho et al., 2013). Thus, approaches grounded in intersectionality amplify possibilities and sites of change to enact a social justice agenda and to determine systemic change (Collins & Bilge, 2016; Corlett & Mavin, 2014).

Applications for Educational Research on Social Justice and Equity

With the explication of both intersectionality and queer theory as their own distinct paradigms, it is ostensibly important for researchers to understand the distinctions between the two paradigms to ultimately guide their decisions for a research study and research design. They are separate and distinct according to their own underlying principles and histories. The following recommendations provide additional guidelines to understand the comparison and to ascertain a foundation of decisional processes and critical thinking in social justice and equity research.

History and principles. A researcher using queer theory would likely need to examine the work of predecessors, such as Foucault (1980), Butler (1990, 2004), Sedgwick (1990, 1993), and Rubin (1984, 2011). In contrast, researchers using intersectionality would likely reference the works of Crenshaw (1988, 1989, 1991), Anzaldúa (1987), Collins (1986, 1990, 2015), Lorde (1984), hooks (1981, 1984, 1989), and Moraga and Anzaldúa (1983). Researchers using queer theory would likely investigate research questions associated with critiques intended to disrupt binaries and identity categories. In this scope, queer theory operates with a poststructural lens intended to give voice to multiple perspectives and meanings disrupting classifications of binaries and identity categories (Lugg, 2003). Thus, researchers using queer theory assume that identity categories need to be deconstructed as misguided illusory social constructions of power rather than identity markers associating lived experiences with specific communities. To understand power and complexity of social identities (Collins & Bilge, 2016), researchers using intersectionality, in contrast, would likely highlight linkages between social identities or linkages between forms of oppression (e.g., racism, genderism, heterosexism) as the crux of their research questions (Bowleg & Bauer, 2016; Bowleg, 2013, 2017; Warner & Shields, 2013). Thus, intersectionality scholars would still rely on the realities and experiences associated with specific identities by assuming that identities and intersections produce actual realities of marginalization.

The purpose of queer theory would involve a critique of identity categories and binaries, whereas intersectionality theory would involve identity categories to locate power, relationships, and complexity. The outcome of a study using queer theory would be a disruption of binaries and identity categories. The outcome of intersectionality theory carries implications for a systematic agenda toward social action, which highlights key aspects from the research study about action steps to change an inequitable system. This outcome from an intersectionality study would also likely focus on the realization of gaps located as a result of multiple marginalizations. These contrasting features of queer theory and intersectionality theory are important to consider, especially with the type of product offered as a result of the research contribution. Although research contributions using queer theory would involve a critique and disruption of identity categories, research using intersectionality theory would likely involve recommendations for action based on understanding intersecting forms of oppression.

Distinctions of power. Queer theory and intersectionality theory involve their own distinct relationships and assumptions of power. For intersectionality scholars, power is centered specifically in these intersections to illustrate visibility and to determine points to capitalize on social action. When scholars and researchers view through the lens of intersectionality, they examine realities attached to specific social identities (e.g., race, gender, sexuality), forms of oppression (e.g., racism, genderism, heterosexism), and their intersections lead to an understanding of which communities carry power and where inequities of power might exist (Bowleg, 2017).

Queer theory conversely involves a disruption of the boundaries held in identity categories and of binaries (Lugg, 2003; Plummer, 2011). Power is indicative of the boundaries associated with identity categories. Queer theory especially provides an assumption that power was an illusory social construction shown in identity categories and binaries. Thus, queer theory requires its poststructural lens to critique and disrupt binaries and identity categories as problematic social constructions.

Reflexive thinking and reflexivity. Reflexivity statements and reflexive thinking provide a platform to consider how the researchers inform the production of a research study and analysis in education (Plummer, 2011). The critical notions embedded in intersectionality theory and queer theory form the ideology that research, the phenomena of interest, and analyses are not objective processes (Crotty, 1998). Thus, reflexivity statements garner interrogative thinking that keeps researchers accountable to participants and the purpose of a research study. Nonetheless, they are helpful to illustrate researchers' intentionality with decisions in the study. Illustrating complexity and in-depth thinking through interrogating self, social location, and, hence, social conditions, reflexivity is not intended to distance researchers from their participants, but rather, reflexivity functions as an approach to remain conscious of researcher-participant relationships, inequities, and interactions of power and privilege (Fine et al., 2003). To understand reflexivity, researchers can, for instance, participate in journaling to note their experiences, emotions, and perspectives throughout the process of a study. As an additional example to address reflexive thinking, researchers can involve periodic meetings throughout a research study with communities of two to three other scholars to discuss their process, interpretations of data, and approaches within a research study.

Researchers should note the different approaches of reflexivity unique to queer theory and intersectionality theory. Queer theory and intersectionality theory can differ in their perspectives toward reflexivity. Intersectionality theory may prioritize the researchers' privilege, oppression, and power through their own social identities and intersections interacting with entities and individuals in their research. Queer theory may influence the approach toward reflexivity by informing researchers on how they are thinking within the forms of identity categories and binaries. To involve queer theory in reflexivity, researchers can likely think about how their own personal reflections and assumptions may reinforce specific binaries or interpretations in the lens of identity categories. Similarly, researchers can infuse this type of reflexivity in a research study by questioning how their interpretations of data may be consistent with reinforcing classifications of binaries and identity categories. Using the lens of queer theory, researchers can use reflexivity to aim more closely to the goal of disrupting binaries and identities as fixed, associated realities rather than social constructions.

Conclusion

Researchers can note the differences between queer theory and intersectionality theory as their own unique, distinct paradigms. Queer theory and intersectionality theory involve their own unique underlying principles ultimately forming decisions for a research study. Although the evolution of empirical and conceptual research grounded in analytic frameworks of intersectionality theory and queer theory continues to grow exponentially, the provided list of recommended readings captures major luminaries augmenting movements and implementation grounded in both intersectionality theory and queer theory. Similarly, researchers attempting to complicate these frameworks should also examine a variety of recent theoretical frameworks generated by the substantiation of intersectionality and queer theory, such as queer of color critique (see Brockenbrough, 2015; McCready, 2013).

Recommended Readings

Ahmed, S. (2006). *Queer phenomenology: Orientations, objects, others*. Durham, NC: Duke University Press.

This book is useful for deconstructing lived experience influenced by contextual factors within phenomenological approaches and methods rather than associating with realities associated with identities.

Browne, K., & Nash, C. J. (Eds.). (2010). *Queer methods and methodologies: Intersecting queer theories and social science research*. Abingdon, UK: Ashgate Publishing.

This book provides multiple perspectives reflecting the implementation of queer theory in research. Researchers may find the text useful to assist with conceptualizing queer methods in their research design.

Collins, P. H., & Bilge, S. (2016). *Intersectionality*. Malden, MA: Polity Press.

This book offers an accessible description of principles, histories, and philosophies used to understand intersectionality. The text involves practices and movements associated with intersectionality to inform the conceptualization of intersectionality in practice, scholarship, and research.

Crenshaw, K. (1989). Demarginalizing the intersection of race and sex: A Black feminist critique of antidiscrimination doctrine, feminist theory and antiracist politics. *University of Chicago Legal Forum, 1989*(1), 139–167.

This article is a seminal contribution by Crenshaw as a major contributor to intersectionality scholarship. Researchers can use this article to inform historical context surrounding approaches involved in intersectionality.

Grzanka, P. R. (Ed.). (2014). *Intersectionality: A foundations and frontiers reader* (1st ed.). New York, NY: Westview Press.

This book provides several different viewpoints on intersectionality as a paradigm. The text involves discussions surrounding philosophical underpinnings and implementation for specific research methods.

Hancock, A.-M. (2016). *Intersectionality: An intellectual history*. New York, NY: Oxford University Press.

This book contextualizes the history of intersectionality by showcasing an understanding of its principles and key forerunners.

Lugg, C. A., & Murphy, J. P. (2014). Thinking whimsically: Queering the study of educational policy-making and politics. *International Journal of Qualitative Studies in Education, 27*(9), 1183–1204. https://doi.org/10.1080/09518398.2014.916009

This journal article reflects an application of queer theory, including underlying principles, to educational policy. Researchers might find the article useful for their understanding and foundation of principles informing the use of queer theory.

References

Adams, T. E., & Holman Jones, S. (2011). Telling stories: Reflexivity, queer theory, and auto-ethnography. *Cultural Studies ↔ Critical Methodologies, 11*(2), 108–116. https://doi.org/10.1177/1532708611401329

Ahmed, S. (2006). *Queer phenomenology: Orientations, objects, others*. Durham, NC: Duke University Press.

Anzaldúa, G. (1987). *Borderlands/la Frontera*. San Francisco, CA: Aunt Lute Books.

Bilge, S. (2013). Intersectionality undone: Saving intersectionality from feminist intersectionality studies. *Du Bois Review, 10*(2), 405–424. https://doi.org/10.1017/S1742058X13000283

Bowleg, L. (2008). When black + lesbian + woman ≠ black lesbian woman: The methodological challenges of qualitative and quantitative intersectionality research. *Sex Roles, 59*(5–6), 312–325. https://doi.org/10.1007/s11199-008-9400-z

Bowleg, L. (2012). The problem with the phrase *women and minorities:* Intersectionality—An important theoretical framework for public health. *American Journal of Public Health, 102*(7), 1267–1273. https://doi.org/10.2105/AJPH.2012.300750

Bowleg, L. (2013). "Once you've blended the cake, you can't take the parts back to the main ingredients": Black gay and bisexual men's descriptions and experiences of intersectionality. *Sex Roles, 68*(11–12), 754–767. https://doi.org/10.1007/s11199-012-0152-4

Bowleg, L. (2017). Towards a critical health equity research stance: Why epistemology and methodology matter more than qualitative methods. *Health Education & Behavior, 44*(5), 677–684. https://doi.org/10.1177/1090198117728760

Bowleg, L., & Bauer, G. (2016). Invited reflection: Quantifying intersectionality. *Psychology of Women Quarterly, 40*(3), 337–341. https://doi.org/10.1177/0361684316654282

Brockenbrough, E. (2015). Queer of color agency in educational contexts: Analytic frameworks from a queer of color critique. *Educational Studies, 51*(1), 28–44. https://doi.org/10.1080/00131946.2014.979929

Butler, J. (1990). *Gender trouble: Feminism and the subversion of identity*. New York, NY: Routledge.

Butler, J. (2004). *Undoing gender*. New York, NY: Routledge.

Carastathis, A. (2016). *Intersectionality: Origins, contestations, horizons*. Lincoln, NE: University of Nebraska Press.

Carbado, D. W., Crenshaw, K. W., Mays, V. M., & Tomlinson, B. (2013). Intersectionality. *Du Bois Review, 10*(2), 303–312. https://doi.org/10.1017/S1742058X13000349

Chan, C. D. (2017). A critical analysis of systemic influences on spiritual development for LGBTQ+ youth. *Journal of Child and Adolescent Counseling, 3*(3), 146–163. https://doi.org/10.1080/23727810.2017.1341795

Chan, C. D., Erby, A. N., & Ford, D. J. (2017). Intersectionality in practice: Moving a social justice paradigm to action in higher education. In J. M. Johnson & G. C. Javier (Eds.), *Queer people of color in higher education* (pp. 9–29). Charlotte, NC: Information Age Publishing.

Chan, C. D., Cor, D. N., & Band, M. P. (2018). Privilege and oppression in counselor education and supervision: An intersectionality framework. *The Journal of Multicultural Counseling and Development, 46*(1), 58–73. https://doi.org/10.1002/jmcd.12092

Cho, S. (2013). Post-intersectionality: The curious reception of intersectionality in legal scholarship. *Du Bois Review, 10*(2), 385–404. https://doi.org/10.1017/S1742058X13000362

Cho, S., Crenshaw, K. W., & McCall, L. (2013). Toward a field of intersectionality studies: Theory, applications, and praxis. *Signs, 38*(4), 785–810. https://doi.org/10.1086/669608

Cole, E. R. (2008). Coalitions as a model for intersectionality: From practice to theory. *Sex Roles, 59*(5–6), 443–453. https://doi.org/10.1007/s11199-008-9419-1

Cole, E. R. (2009). Intersectionality and research in psychology. *American Psychologist, 64*(3), 170–180. https://doi.org/10.1037/a0014564

Collins, P. H. (1986). Learning from the outsider within: The sociological significance of black feminist thought. *Social Problems, 33*(6), S14–S32. https://doi.org/10.2307/800672

Collins, P. H. (1990). *Black feminist thought: Knowledge, consciousness and the politics of empowerment*. New York, NY and London: Routledge.

Collins, P. H. (2004). Learning from the outsider within: The sociological significance of black feminist thought. In S. Harding (Ed.), *The feminist standpoint theory reader* (pp. 103–126). New York, NY: Routledge.

Collins, P. H. (2015). Intersectionality's definitional dilemmas. *Annual Review of Sociology, 41*(1), 1–20. https://doi.org/10.1146/annurev-soc-073014-112142

Collins, P. H., & Bilge, S. (2016). *Intersectionality*. Malden, MA: Polity Press.

Combahee River Collective. (1995). Combahee River Collective statement. In B. Guy-Sheftall (Ed.), *Words of fire: An anthology of African American feminist thought* (pp. 232–240). New York, NY: New Press.

Cor, D. N., & Chan, C. D. (2017). Intersectionality feminism and LGBTIQQA+ psychology: Understanding our present by exploring our past. In R. Ruth & E. Santacruz (Eds.), *LGBT psychology and mental health: Emerging research and advances* (pp. 109–132). Santa Barbara, CA: Praeger/ABC-CLIO.

Corlett, S., & Mavin, S. (2014). Intersectionality, identity and identity work. *Gender in Management, 29*(5), 258–276. https://doi.org/10.1108/GM-12-2013-0138

Crenshaw, K. (1988). Race, reform, and retrenchment: Transformation and legitimation in antidiscrimination law. *Harvard Law Review, 101*(7), 1331–1387. Retrieved from http://www.jstor.org/stable/pdf/1341398.pdf

Crenshaw, K. (1989). Demarginalizing the intersection of race and sex: A Black feminist critique of antidiscrimination doctrine, feminist theory and antiracist politics. *University of Chicago Legal Forum, 1989*(1), 139–167.

Crenshaw, K. (1991). Mapping the margins: Intersectionality, identity politics, and violence against women of color. *Stanford Law Review, 43*(6), 1241–1299. https://doi.org/10.2307/1229039

Crotty, M. (1998). *The foundations of social research: Meaning and perspective in the research process*. St. Leonards: Allan & Unwin.

Detamore, M. (2010). Queer(y)ing the ethics of research methods: Toward a politics of intimacy in researcher/researched relations. In K. Browne & C. J. Nash (Eds.), *Queer methods and methodologies: Intersecting queer theories and social science research* (pp. 167–182). Burlington, VT: Ashgate.

Duong, K. (2012). What does queer theory teach us about intersectionality? *Politics & Gender, 8*(3), 370–386. https://doi.org/10.1017/S1743923X12000360

Few-Demo, A. L. (2014). Intersectionality as the "new" critical approach in feminist family studies: Evolving racial/ethnic feminisms and critical race theories. *Journal of Family Theory & Review, 6*(2), 169–183. https://doi.org/10.1111/jftr.12039

Few-Demo, A. L., Humble, Á. M., Curran, M. A., & Lloyd, S. A. (2016). Queer theory, intersectionality, and LGBT-parent families: Transformative critical pedagogy in family theory: Queer theory, intersectionality, and LGBT-parent families. *Journal of Family Theory & Review, 8*(1), 74–94. https://doi.org/10.1111/jftr.12127

Fine, M., Weis, L., Weseen, S., & Wong, L. (2003). For whom? Qualitative research, representations, and social responsibilities. In N. K. Denzin & Y. S. Lincoln (Eds.), *The landscape of qualitative research* (2nd ed., pp. 167–207). Thousand Oaks, CA: SAGE Publications.

Fish, J. N., & Russell, S. T. (2018). Queering methodologies to understand queer families. *Family Relations, 67*(1), 12–25. https://doi.org/10.1111/fare.12297

Fotopoulou, A. (2012). Intersectionality queer studies and hybridity: Methodological frameworks for social research. *Journal of International Women's Studies, 13*(2), 19–32.

Foucault, M. (1980). *History of sexuality: Volume one: An introduction.* New York, NY: Vintage.

Gedro, J., & Mizzi, R. C. (2014). Feminist theory and queer theory: Implications for HRD research and practice. *Advances in Developing Human Resources, 16*(4), 445–456. https://doi.org/10.1177/1523422314543820

Goodrich, K. M., Luke, M., & Smith, A. J. (2016). Queer humanism: Toward an epistemology of socially just, culturally responsive change. *Journal of Humanistic Psychology, 56*(6), 612–623. https://doi.org/10.1177/0022167816652534

Gopaldas, A. (2013). Intersectionality 101. *Journal of Public Policy & Marketing, 32*, 90–94. https://doi.org/10.1509/jppm.12.044

Grzanka, P. R., Santos, C. E., & Moradi, B. (2017). Intersectionality research in counseling psychology. *Journal of Counseling Psychology, 64*(5), 453–457. https://doi.org/10.1037/cou0000237

Guba, E. G., & Lincoln, Y. S. (1994). Competing paradigms in qualitative research. In N. Denzin & Y. S. Lincoln (Eds.), *Handbook of qualitative research* (pp. 105–117). Thousand Oaks, CA: Sage.

Hancock, A.-M. (2016). *Intersectionality: An intellectual history.* New York, NY: Oxford University Press.

hooks, b. (1981). *Ain't I a woman: Black women and feminism.* Boston, MA: South End Press.

hooks, b. (1984). *Feminist theory: From margin to center.* Cambridge, MA: South End Press.

hooks, b. (1989). *Talking back: Thinking feminist, thinking black.* Boston, MA: South End Press.

Jagose, A. (2009). Feminism's queer theory. *Feminism & Psychology, 19*(2), 157–174. https://doi.org/10.1177/0959353509102152

Kincheloe, J. L., McLaren, P., Steinberg, S. R., & Monzó, L. (2017). Critical pedagogy and qualitative research: Advancing the bricolage. In N. K. Denzin & Y. S. Lincoln (Eds.), *The SAGE handbook of qualitative research* (5th ed., pp. 235–260). Thousand Oaks, CA: Sage.

Lorde, A. (1984). *Sister outsider: Essays and speeches.* Trumansburg, NY: Crossing Press.

Love, B. L. (2017). A ratchet lens: Black queer youth, agency, hip hop, and the Black ratchet imagination. *Educational Researcher, 46*(9), 539–547. https://doi.org/10.3102/0013189X17736520

Lugg, C. (2003). Sissies, faggots, lezzies, and dykes: Gender, sexual orientation and new politics of education? *Educational Administration Quarterly, 39*(1), 95–134.

Lugg, C. A., & Murphy, J. P. (2014). Thinking whimsically: Queering the study of educational policy-making and politics. *International Journal of Qualitative Studies in Education, 27*(9), 1183–1204. https://doi.org/10.1080/09518398.2014.916009

Mayo, C. (2017). Queer and trans youth, relational subjectivity, and uncertain possibilities: Challenging research in complicated contexts. *Educational Researcher, 46*(9), 530–538. https://doi.org/10.3102/0013189X17738737

McCall, L. (2005). The complexity of intersectionality. *Signs, 30*(3), 1771–1800. https://doi.org/10.1086/426800

McCann, H. (2016). Epistemology of the subject: Queer theory's challenge to feminist sociology. *Women's Studies Quarterly, 44*(3/4), 224–243. https://doi.org/10.1353/wsq.2016.0044

McCready, L. T. (2013). Conclusion to the special issue: Queer of color analysis: Interruptions and pedagogic possibilities. *Curriculum Inquiry, 43*(4), 512–522. https://doi.org/10.1111/curi.12024

Misgav, C. (2016). Some spatial politics of queer-feminist research: Personal reflections from the field. *Journal of Homosexuality, 63*(5), 719–721. https://doi.org/10.1080/00918369.2015.111 2191

Moradi, B., & Grzanka, P. R. (2017). Using intersectionality responsibly: Toward critical epistemology, structural analysis, and social justice activism. *Journal of Counseling Psychology, 64*(5), 500–513. https://doi.org/10.1037/cou0000203

Moraga, C., & Anzaldúa, G. (Eds.). (1983). *This bridge called my back: Writings by radical women of color* (2nd ed.). New York, NY: Kitchen Table/Women of Color Press.

Parent, M. C., DeBlaere, C., & Moradi, B. (2013). Approaches to research on intersectionality: Perspectives on gender, LGBT, and Racial/Ethnic identities. *Sex Roles, 68*(11–12), 639–645. https://doi.org/10.1007/s11199-013-0283-2

Patel, L. (2016). *Decolonizing educational research: From ownership to answerability*. New York, NY: Routledge.

Plummer, K. (2011). Critical humanism and queer theory: Living with the tensions. In N. K. Denzin & Y. S. Lincoln (Eds.), *The SAGE handbook of qualitative research* (4th ed., pp. 195–207). Thousand Oaks, CA: SAGE.

Rubin, G. S. (1984). Thinking sex: Notes for a radical theory of the politics of sexuality. In C. S. Vance (Ed.), *Pleasure and danger: Exploring female sexuality* (pp. 267–293). London: Routledge.

Rubin, G. S. (2011). *Deviations: A Gayle Rubin reader*. Durham and London: Duke University Press.

Rumens, N. (2013). Queering men and masculinities in construction: Towards a research agenda. *Construction Management and Economics, 31*(8), 802–815. https://doi.org/10.1080/01446193. 2013.765021

Rumens, N. (2016). Towards queering the business school: A research agenda for advancing lesbian, gay, bisexual and trans perspectives and issues. *Gender, Work and Organization, 23*(1), 36–51. https://doi.org/10.1111/gwao.12077

Rumens, N. (2017). Queering lesbian, gay, bisexual and transgender identities in human resource development and management education contexts. *Management Learning, 48*(2), 227–242. https://doi.org/10.1177/1350507616672737

Sedgwick, E. K. (1990). *Epistemology of the closet*. Berkeley, CA: University of California Press.

Sedgwick, E. K. (1993). *Tendencies*. Durham, NC: Duke University Press.

Shields, S. A. (2008). Gender: An intersectionality perspective. *Sex Roles, 59*(5–6), 301–311. https://doi.org/10.1007/s11199-008-9501-8

Smooth, W. G. (2013). Intersectionality from theoretical framework to policy intervention. In A. R. Wilson (Ed.), *Situating intersectionality: Politics, policy, and power*. New York, NY: Palgrave Macmillan.

Tuck, E., & Wang, K. W. (2018). Introduction: Born under the rising sign of social justice. In E. Tuck & K. W. Wang (Eds.), *Toward what justice? Describing diverse dreams of justice in education* (pp. 1–18). New York, NY: Routledge.

Warner, L. R., & Shields, S. A. (2013). The intersections of sexuality, gender, and race: Identity research at the crossroads. *Sex Roles, 68*(11–12), 803–810. https://doi.org/10.1007/s11199-013-0281-4

Warner, L., Settles, I., & Shields, S. (2016). Invited reflection: Intersectionality as an epistemological challenge to psychology. *Psychology of Women Quarterly, 40*(2), 171–176. https://doi.org/10.1177/0361684316641384

Chapter 6
Using Critical Theory in Educational Research

Kamden K. Strunk and Jasmine S. Betties

Abstract Critical theory remains a central theoretical framework in research for equity and social justice. In this chapter, we introduce some of the major concepts in critical theory and the educational theory of critical pedagogy. We also attempt to differentiate critical theory from other perspectives like critical race theory, with which it is often conflated. We also suggest ways in which critical theory can be mobilized in educational research. While a short chapter such as this cannot capture the complexity and long history of critical theory and critical pedagogy approaches, we aim to provide a useful introduction and resources for those wishing to go further with this perspective.

Critical theory is a powerful analytic frame for understanding educational disparities and injustice as functions of power, domination, and exploitation. Often confused with other perspectives, critical theory centers economic, financial, and labor issues as central animating forces in oppression and domination. It is easy to hear the phrase 'critical theory' and think of it as a kind of umbrella term for other critical perspectives (critical race theory, critical whiteness, DisCrit, and other perspectives). However, critical theory is a distinct set of theoretical and analytical tools which sometimes overlap with and sometimes diverge from other perspectives.

Key to understanding critical theory and how it differs from other perspectives is the fact that it emerges from Marxist critique (Horkheimer, 1982). That Marxist heritage shapes many of the assumptions and applications of critical theory. This means that critical theory centers class-based struggle and economic oppression. That is, in the clearest sense of critical theory, oppression, domination, and power are

K. K. Strunk (✉)
Educational Psychology and Research Methodologies, Auburn University, Auburn, AL, USA
e-mail: kks0013@auburn.edu

J. S. Betties
Auburn University, Auburn, AL, USA
e-mail: jsb0084@auburn.edu

© The Author(s) 2019
K. K. Strunk, L. A. Locke (eds.), *Research Methods for Social Justice and Equity in Education*, https://doi.org/10.1007/978-3-030-05900-2_6

71

primarily understood through economics, labor, and class struggle. That is not to say that critical theory or critical theorists deny the reality of racism, white supremacy, cisheteropatriarchy, ableism, or any other forms of oppression. To the contrary, those systems are all potent in their subjugation of marginalized groups. However, this approach does view those dynamics as being, at their core, economic systems. Because of that, the central organizing feature of those oppressive systems is, in the US context at least, capitalism (Postone & Galambos, 1995). That said, contemporary uses of critical theory are often a bit removed from a true Marxist analysis but are still informed by that perspective and shaped by that history.

One critique of critical theory and related approaches is a positivist impulse (Gottesman, 2016). That is, because of its roots as a Marxist approach, critical theory tends to envision an ideal society. The envisioning of an ideal carries with it an implicit belief in an absolute truth (a perfect society) which individuals can strive to approximate. Many contemporary critical theorists address that impulse directly and pull from poststructuralist, postcolonial, and other perspectives. However, it remains true that critical theory has some positivist flavor which those using the theory ought to carefully reflect upon and work to reimagine. Another critique of critical theory is that it, in the view of some, insufficiently centers things like race/racism and gender/sexism. Critical theoretical approaches typically reject the material reality of social identities like race, gender, and sexual identity (Leonardo, 2013), and like many other approaches, critical theorists often suggest that those social identities are ideological constructions rather than material realities. That is, race is not 'real' in the sense that there is no actual material state one can adequately describe as 'race'. However, race has been constructed as a category that means a great deal in society. Moreover, race has been constructed in binary ways (white/people of Color) that privilege White people and allow them to accumulate wealth and power at the expense of (and as a product of the labor of) people of Color. In fact, it takes a great deal of sustained effort to elevate the symbolism of skin color variations to the ideological status of binary racial categories (Leonardo, 2013). Similar arguments could be made about other social identities—the identity categories themselves are ideological constructs that have taken on the meanings of a white supremacist cisheteropatriarchal society, and their construction is a way in which those in power justify and extend oppression and dehumanization. In other words, race is not a material reality, but race matters very much and racism is all too real. Denying the material reality of those social identities need not decenter systems of oppression that operate on social identity. Rather, that rejection of static or 'real' social identities can shift the focus away from individual bodies and onto systems that commodify, exploit, and oppress those bodies.

In this short chapter, we attempt to introduce some of the key concepts in critical theory. We use the terms critical theory and critical pedagogy as somewhat interchangeable throughout. While that perhaps shows ideological or theoretical slippage in our own conceptualizations, it is also true that they are often used as if they were interchangeable in the research literature. We do not intend to imply there are no differences—but for the purposes of a text on educational research, the distinctions are muddier as critical pedagogy adopts and expands many of the tenets of critical theory (Giroux, 1997) with specific applications to education, teaching, and schools.

Commodification of Knowledge/Power

One of the key developments in modern educational reform, which has occurred alongside the rise of neoliberalism, is the commodification of knowledge (which critical pedagogy holds is an inseparable concept from power (McLaren, 2002)). Increasingly, discourses around education center on its value in monetary and labor-force terms. While prior eras included an understanding of education as a public good (Bowles & Gintis, 2011) that bestowed benefits on society by producing informed citizens capable of self-governance (Huang, Van den Brink, & Groot, 2009), the neo-liberal turn brought with it an emphasis on education as a private good (Olssen & Peters, 2005) that benefits individuals by improving their economic status (Bourdieu, 2011) or by providing a more skilled pool of laborers for corporate interests (Helliwell & Putnam, 2007). Alongside this turn came objections to public funding of colleges and universities (with logics such as, 'why should I pay for someone else to get a better job?'). There is much to say about this turn, as others have done elsewhere (Strunk, Locke, & McGee, 2015). However, important to this discussion of critical theory is the construction of knowledge (and thus, of schooling and education) as a set of commodities whose value is primarily monetary and labor related.

By commodifying knowledge, in a critical theory analysis, one also commodifies power. Power takes on a monetary value (and thus can be assigned a price), incentivizing those with power to oppress others through educational systems in order to preserve their societal advantage. This point is particularly important—systems of power, domination, and oppression primarily serve to preserve the power and wealth of those in dominant social positions and to ensure that fewer and fewer individuals accumulate more and more power and wealth. In our context, those power and wealth divides fall along racialized, gendered, sexualized, and other identity category lines, such that white supremacist cisheteropatriarchy becomes fused with economic systems of exploitative capitalism. However, critical theory not only observes this commodification and the ways it motivates oppressive systems but also explains how those systems come to be and how they operate to ensure oppressive outcomes.

Dialectical Theory

A central feature of the critical theory approach is dialectical theory—the notion that individuals are created by and simultaneously create social realities (Kemmis & Fitzclarence, 1986). This concept involves a recognition that individuals exist in relationship with a social world that has shaped them and their knowledges, while simultaneously recognizing that individuals also comprise the social context and their actions shape its contours. For example, the institution of schooling creates specific social realities for children (realities which are limited and delimited by oppression, shaping some students to be laborers and others to hold power and wealth). However, schools comprise other people (who, of course, used to be schoolchildren), whose actions, ideologies, and beliefs shape what is taught, how it is taught, and to whom. Moreover, the children attending the school, through their actions, questions, beliefs, and embodied social identities, also shape the process of schooling.

As a result, systems (like schools) are replete with contradictions. Those contradictions open possibilities for making visible the operations of power and for interrupting oppressive cycles. In fact, one apparent contradiction that schools inhabit is that they often serve simultaneously as places of oppression and of empowerment (Giroux, 1981). Because of the tension that exists in the relationship between individuals and their contexts (where both the individual and the context are continually acting to shape one another), such contradictions emerge and require "new constructive thinking and new constructive action… to transcend the contradictory state of affairs" (Carr & Kemmis, 1983, p. 36). Such actions can potentially move systems toward equity and liberation, but more often individuals act to uphold the oppressive status quo, often because those who benefit from the status quo are also those with power.

Ideological Domination

Within this complex system of socially constructed realities, ideological domination takes hold. Because certain ideologies also uphold the privileging of some groups and oppression of others and render that inequitable economic situation both comprehensible and justifiable, those ideologies become dominant, reified as part of the 'common sense' (Giroux, 2011). In the US context (as in most contexts), that dominant ideology is capitalist white supremacist cisheteropatriarchy. This ideology holds that white, straight, cisgender men are inherently better than other groups (people of Color, LGBTQ people, women, etc.) and thus are deserving of a superior social position. It justifies the imposition of oppressive practices and inequitable outcomes as a just and righteous intervention to ensure those worthy of economic gains and of power maintain it. As others have suggested, this dominant ideology is visible in the ways research methods have evolved (Bonilla-Silva & Zuberi, 2008), how economies are structured, and helps explain things like slavery and segregation. That ideology is still present and animates much of contemporary educational discourse, but it is taught in ways that are often subtle, even invisible.

Hidden Curriculum

Dominant ideologies enter the 'common sense' through their presence in the hidden curriculum. Schools have explicit curricula for teaching content areas, creating critical thinking skills, and other topics. However, beyond those formal lessons, schools and teachers impose ideological lessons about what is valued, valuable, and worthy, as well as what knowledges and ways of knowing are valid (Giroux & Purpel, 1983). Those lessons are taught alongside the formal curriculum in ways that are often unnoticed. In a commonly cited example, teachers and schools often insist on standard English, implicitly signaling that other languages, ways of speaking, and ways of representing knowledge are less valid. Because schools teach some ways of knowing, establishing knowledges, or representing knowledges as 'better' than others, they also teach that the ideology aligned with those 'better' ways is superior. Students, then, come to understand whiteness and cisheterosexism as if they were 'natural' and more desirable. In this way, the hidden curriculum results in social reproduction. As a result of their own education in white supremacist cisheteropatriarchy, students go on to impose those same values and ideologies on others. The ideological and social systems currently in place, and which are oppressive, become reproduced in each new class of students unless they are radically interrupted (Kemmis & Fitzclarence, 1986; Giroux, 1981).

Hegemony

As a result of dominant ideologies and the hidden curriculum, social practices are established which seem benign on their face, but they act to reify oppression and domination. Because those social practices are consensual in nature, oppressed groups routinely participate in them, unknowingly contributing to their own oppression (Giroux, 1981). This process of participation in consensual social practices that reify domination is referred to as hegemony. This should not be understood as placing 'blame' for oppression on oppressed groups. Instead, hegemony highlights the pervasiveness of dominant ideologies and their power to structure relations to reinforce existing dominant ideologies. Sometimes referred to as a silent struggle, the powerful seek to gain the consent of those they oppressed, ultimately leading oppressed people to unwittingly participate in their own subordination (Ryan, 1976). The concept of hegemony also helps clarify why violence is not a necessary feature in oppression and domination. Violently oppressive regimes often meet with ferocious resistance. But, by instituting a set of normalized, naturalized social practices in which people voluntarily participate that reify oppressive power relations, no force is necessary, nor is coercion.

Reflecting on the current state of US sociopolitical affairs, hegemony is clear. Individuals likely to be more negatively affected by new policies and regressive laws openly support them. They do so in part because of a socially constructed reality in which participating in those efforts might lead to actual rewards. Hegemony creates a situation where "both rulers and ruled derive psychological and material rewards in the course of confirming and reconfirming their inequality" (Gitlin, 1980, p. 253). This is carried out in part through the standardization of vocabularies and representational symbols (language), which naturally limit what constitutes valid ways of being and knowing. Hegemonic systems are inherited through the systems of signs, expectations, idiomatic expressions, and available tools and technologies (Strunk,

Locke, & Martin, 2017). Researchers using critical theory often attempt to understand how dominant ideologies become infused in hidden curricula, ultimately allowing hegemony to occur.

Anti-oppressive Education and Critical Pedagogy

Although the evolution of critical theory and critical pedagogy is complicated, and scholars have questioned the centrality of Paulo Freire to initiating that move (Gottesman, 2016), he remains a pivotal figure in critical pedagogy. In shifting the attention to schools as sites of oppression and ideological reproduction, Freire (1970) critiqued the usual 'banking model' of education in which, "education becoming an act of depositing, in which the students are the depositories and the teacher is the depositor. Instead of communicating, the teacher issues communiques and makes deposits that the students patiently receive, memorize, and repeat" (p. 72). For Freire, this model of education perpetuates the continuity of oppression and is the 'greatest tool' in the hands of the oppressor. Instead, Freire (1970) urged teachers to adopt a problem-posing approach to education, which is grounded on freedom and emphasizes that teachers must see themselves in a partnership with their students. This approach to education also encourages students to become social agents—challenging ways of being that oppress them and their community (Duncan-Andrade & Morrell, 2008).

Over the years, various critical pedagogues and theorists have explored different approaches to doing the work of liberation in classrooms. These include hooks' (2014) call for transgressive pedagogy, Giroux's body of work on critical pedagogy, Gore's (2003) theoretical work, and recent applications to urban education including that of Duncan-Andrade and Morrell (2008). Critical pedagogy is also a contested terrain, with approaches and their implications hotly debated. However, these various approaches all seek to work with education for liberatory ends. Critical pedagogues are typically most focused on how to improve classroom practices, how to help students develop critical consciousness and analyze their own experiences, and how to make classrooms liberatory and resistive spaces.

Applications for Educational Research

Applying critical theory and critical pedagogy to research requires turning the analytic focus away from individuals and onto systems. It is often all too easy to point to problematic individuals and their oppressive practices, seeking to place blame for inequity on so-called 'bad actors'. One of the contributions of critical theory is the assertion that, even absent any bad actors, in a system where every individual acts from a place of good intentions, their placement in an ideological system that has always centered white supremacist cisheteropatriarchy will ensure they still reproduce inequitable outcomes. In other words—while individual racists, sexists, homophobes, transphobes, ableists, and others are clearly a problem and there is merit in individual anti-bias work—systems, ideologies, and institutions must be the targets of critical inquiry.

Applied carefully, this shift in focus from individual misbehavior to systemic and ideological issues can be extremely generative. It encourages researchers to take a generous approach to participants, recognizing their actions as often a symptom rather than a cause of oppression. Again, this is not to absolve individuals of their responsibilities to act justly, but it does decenter their individual actions as part of a system. Because of that shift, critical theory work often focuses on systems, ideologies, and institutions rather than on individuals. To put this another way, the level of measurement ought not to be individuals but contexts or institutions. While one might collect data from, for example, individual teachers, administrators, or students, the analytic focus would be on the systems in which those individuals operate. The unit of analysis, in other words, ought to be beyond the individual.

Critical theory approaches also recognize the subjectivity of the researcher(s) as a key component in shaping the study. If one accepts dialectical theory, one must also accept that researchers live in relationship with their contexts, simultaneously creating and being created by them. Critical scholars, then, should engage in self-criticism and reflection to understand their own contribution to oppressive systems, the ways in which research itself can be oppressive, and how their interactions with research participants might oppress or liberate. Others in this volume have written more extensively on issues of reflexivity and positionality, but those concepts become important in a critical theory context because of the dialectical nature of lived realities.

As a theoretical framework, critical theory emphasizes the insidious nature of power—that power reinscribes itself, and power relations are reified and reproduced in each new group of individuals. So often, critical researchers will focus on how that reproduction occurs and examine ways in which the power/knowledge reproduction cycle can be interrupted. Critical theory researchers also search out and focus on generative contradictions in education. Those spaces where contradictions emerge often show the cracks in oppressive systems—they offer a point of leverage to more closely understand and also to interrupt oppression.

Limitations of Critical Theory

While many have written about the limits of a critical theory approach grounded in Marxist analysis, here we highlight a few of the concerns. Researchers have commented that, while Marxist analysis is useful in describing and understanding systems, it is often less useful in suggesting approaches to transforming systems (short of the Marxist suggestion of a full revolution). In the US context, this has been particularly true of Marxist approaches to understanding race and racism. Pure Marxist analysis tends to fall short of fully explaining or predicting race-based oppression (Leonardo, 2013). Other analyses of race point to the shortcomings of

Marxist approaches in this regard. By treating race and racism as purely ideological, these approaches are insufficient to explain how race also constrains the actions and ideologies of those constructed as White or to fully describe the ways in which race-based oppression operates. Critical race theorists and critical whiteness theorists have done much to further those explorations. Similarly queer theorists have done much to deepen the exploration of genders and sexualities. That is not to suggest that those theories expand on or grow out of critical theory—though some of those perspectives might be understood as reactions to critical theory.

The most compelling educational research often mobilizes pieces of more than one theory, pulling conceptual tools from more than one framework. In what Lather (2006) describes as paradigm proliferation, researchers can engage with multiple frameworks and ultimately arrive at entirely new theoretical constructs and analytic tools. Among those tools can be elements of critical theory and Marxist analysis. However, we encourage researchers to move beyond dogmatic adherence to a particular frame and instead to think broadly about how the range of theories have variously explored elements of oppression and liberation and how they might inform future thinking and research.

Suggested Readings

Gottesman, I. (2016). *The critical turn in education: From Marxist critique to post-structuralist feminism, to critical theories of race*. New York, NY: Routledge.

This text is extremely useful in understanding how critical approaches to educational research have evolved, responded to one another, and the history of their usage. It is also a very readable text and could probably be completed over a weekend due to its Gottesman's approachable writing style. The text is also useful in positioning various theoretical views and theorists in relationship with one another.

Giroux, H. A. (2011). *On critical pedagogy*. New York, NY: Bloomsbury.

While Giroux's work has been the subject of some criticism, this text is extremely helpful in understanding some of the key concepts in his work on critical pedagogy and is among the more heavily cited critical pedagogy works. This text is also useful in unpacking what it means to examine the ideological construction of education rather than simply examining practices or outcomes.

References

Bonilla-Silva, E., & Zuberi, T. (2008). Toward a definition of white logic and white methods. In E. Bonilla-Silva & T. Zuberi (Eds.), *White logic, white methods: Racism and methodology* (pp. 3–29). Lanham, MD: Rowman and Littlefield.
Bourdieu, P. (2011). The forms of capital. In I. Szeman & T. Kaposy (Eds.), *Cultural theory: An anthology* (pp. 81–93). Malden, MA: Wiley-Blackwell.

Bowles, S., & Gintis, H. (2011). *Schooling in capitalist America: Educational reform and the contradictions of economic life.* Chicago, IL: Haymarket Books.

Carr, W., & Kemmis, S. (1983). *Becoming critical: Knowing through action research.* Victoria, BC: Deakin University Press.

Duncan-Andrade, J. M. R., & Morrell, E. (2008). *The art of critical pedagogy: Possibilities for moving from theory to practice in urban schools.* New York, NY: Peter Lang.

Freire, P. (1970). *Pedagogy of the oppressed.* New York, NY: Continuum Publishing.

Giroux, H. A. (1981). *Ideology, culture, and the process of schooling.* Philadelphia, PA: Temple University Press.

Giroux, H. A. (1997). *Channel surfing.* New York, NY: St. Martin's Press.

Giroux, H. A. (2011). *On critical pedagogy.* New York, NY: Bloomsbury.

Giroux, H. A., & Purpel, D. (Eds.). (1983). *The hidden curriculum and moral education: Deception or discovery?* Berkeley, CA: McCutchen Publishing.

Gitlin, T. (1980). *The whole world is watching: Media in the making and unmaking of the new left.* Berkeley, CA: University of California Press.

Gore, J. (2003). What we can do for you! What can "we" do for "you"?: Struggling over empowerment in critical and feminist pedagogy. In A. Darder, M. Baltodano, & R. D. Torres (Eds.), *The critical pedagogy reader* (pp. 331–348). New York, NY: Routledge and Falmer.

Gottesman, I. (2016). *The critical turn in education: From Marxist critique to poststructuralist feminism, to critical theories of race.* New York, NY: Routledge.

Helliwell, J. F., & Putnam, R. D. (2007). Education and social capital. *Eastern Economic Journal, 33*(1), 1–19. https://doi.org/10.1057/eej.2007.1

hooks, b. (2014). *Teaching to transgress.* New York, NY: Routledge.

Horkheimer, M. (1982). *Critical theory.* New York, NY: Continuum.

Huang, J., Van den Brink, H. M., & Groot, W. (2009). A meta-analysis of the effect of education on social capital. *Economics of Education Review, 28*(4), 454–464. https://doi.org/10.1016/j.econedurev.2008.03.004

Kemmis, S., & Fitzclarence, L. (1986). *Curriculum theorizing: Beyond reproduction theory.* Victoria, BC: Deakin University Press.

Lather, P. (2006). Paradigm proliferation as a good thing to think with: Teaching research in education as a wild profusion. *International Journal of Qualitative Studies in Education, 19*(1), 35–57. https://doi.org/10.1080/09518390500450144

Leonardo, Z. (2013). *Race frameworks: A multidimensional theory of racism and education.* New York, NY: Teachers College Press.

McLaren, P. (2002). Critical pedagogy: A look at the major concepts. In A. Darder, M. Baltodano, & R. D. Torres (Eds.), *The critical pedagogy reader* (pp. 69–96). New York, NY: Routledge and Falmer.

Olssen, M., & Peters, M. A. (2005). Neoliberalism, higher education and the knowledge economy: From the free market to knowledge capitalism. *Journal of Education Policy, 20*(3), 313–345. https://doi.org/10.1080/02680930500108718

Postone, M., & Galambos, L. (1995). *Time, labor, and social domination: A reinterpretation of Marx's critical theory.* Cambridge, UK: Cambridge University Press.

Ryan, W. (1976). *Blaming the victim.* New York, NY: Vintage Books.

Strunk, K. K., Locke, L. A., & Martin, G. L. (2017). *Oppression and resistance in Southern higher and adult education: Mississippi and the dynamics of equity and social justice.* New York, NY: Palgrave Macmillan.

Strunk, K. K., Locke, L. A., & McGee, M. K. (2015). Neoliberalism and contemporary reform efforts in Mississippi's public education system. In M. Abendroth & B. J. Porfilio (Eds.), *Understanding neoliberal rule in K-12 schools: Educational fronts for local and global justice* (pp. 45–59). Charlotte, NC: Information Age Publishing.

Chapter 7
Viewing Research for Social Justice and Equity Through the Lens of Zygmunt Bauman's Theory of Liquid Modernity

Danielle T. Ligocki

Abstract Understanding the power that research holds to advance the need for social justice and equity is a crucial step in making real societal, institutional, and educational change. This chapter seeks to explain Zygmunt Bauman's theory of liquid modernity and engage the reader with a new understanding regarding how this theory works to frame and explain this current historical moment and how all areas of society have been impacted but specifically the work of the researcher.

When working to choose a framework and methodology for a research study, the task can feel daunting and unfamiliar. What am I trying to learn? How do I want to analyze my data? What lenses exist that are appropriate for viewing my data? What are the experiences of my participants? I struggled with the same questions. However, as I worked to frame my initial study and research question a few years ago, I realized that the current state of our world is pushing down the population in ways that are deeply impactful, specifically when studying social phenomena. With this in mind, I settled on the theory of liquid modernity. This theory acts as a guide in understanding how the conditions of our social world are acting upon us as social actors, citizens, and human beings.

Zygmunt Bauman's theory of liquid modernity can aid in conducting research for social justice and equity in education. This theory posits that we are currently living not in a post-modern society, but rather in a liquid modern society, which means that the nature of our lives is fluid and always in flux. This changes the lens through which people may view certain issues, as they are no longer looking for the greater meta-narrative that was once sought out in post-modern times, but rather they are working to understand the ways in which a complete denigration of the line that once separated public lives from private lives now impacts the world.

D. T. Ligocki (✉)
Oakland University, Auburn Hills, MI, USA
e-mail: danielleligocki@oakland.edu

© The Author(s) 2019
K. K. Strunk, L. A. Locke (eds.), *Research Methods for Social Justice and Equity in Education*, https://doi.org/10.1007/978-3-030-05900-2_7

Bauman views this historical moment as one of crisis, and his theory of liquid modernity frames the reasoning for why the world is in this state. When looking at the work of Bauman and specifically at his theory of liquid modernity, one can see an understanding and situating of neoliberalism, as well as Henry Giroux's notions of disposability and Michel Foucault's work on the panopticon running through it. For Bauman, elements of society have shifted so greatly that the rampant individualism of neoliberalism, along with the constant threat and implementation of surveillance, has worked together to construct a new period of time. Layered on top of surveillance and neoliberalism are notions regarding disposability, cultural insensitivity, and the breaking down of social networks, all of which have left Bauman with a theory of liquid modernity as a means of defining this time in history.

What Is Liquid Modernity?

Zygmunt Bauman makes clear in his work that the theory of liquid modernity addresses the characteristics of this current historical moment. Because, as Bauman posits, the world now exists constantly in a liquid state, the fluidity of the world has enabled a complete breakdown of social networks, which has resulted in oversharing of our private lives as a means of public recognition and self-surveillance. Because this type of information moves so quickly and because people move from one bit of information to the next without ever coming to a finishing point, society now sees an overwhelming posture of insensitivity, coupled with a thoughtless disposability of both people and things. The liquid nature of our world then, for Bauman, explains how neoliberalism has taken over society and schools and explains why it is exceedingly difficult to focus work on the need for social justice and equity.

Liquid modernity is a theoretical perspective that explains how we are living in a time that is lacking in solid bonds; a time of oversharing, over-surveillance, and a lack of private lives; a pervasive feeling of disposability; insensitivity; and a world lacking a sense of community. Put more succinctly, this theory explains how "time flows, but no longer marches on. There is constant change, but no finishing point" (Bauman, 2007b, p. 121). This lack of a finishing point has a great impact on lives today, as people are constantly working to have the newest, best, shiniest things, all while quickly working to dispose of anything that does not serve immediate needs.

With this in mind—having no finishing point and always working on moving forward—one can see how these ideals push back against educating for social justice and equity. How can educators and researchers work toward equity and social justice in education for all students, but especially those who are traditionally marginalized, if there is a quickness to dispose of not only things but also people? How is it possible to work toward a practice of transformative education when any feeling of community or solid bonds ceases to exist? While disposability is only one piece of Bauman's theory, it works to undergird why conducting research or teaching for social justice and equity has become strenuous. The theory of liquid modernity explains that people and things are all disposable, so that makes it very difficult to advocate for a population that is often pushed to the margins of society.

A Lack of Social Networks

Bauman (2012) explains that social networks have disintegrated and nothing has taken their place. This, he says, is an unintended effect of the new 'lightness and fluidity' of our world. However, this complete disintegration of social networks has a very tangible effect on the lives of researchers, as well as the lives of those with whom they may be working. This lack of solid bonds has created a void where close-knit, deeply felt relationships with friends, peers, family members, and even teachers were once felt and appreciated. Bauman asserts that the current historical moment is one that is lacking in a feeling of community and connection. Because of this lack of community and connection, everything is viewed now as an individual problem or issue to be addressed. Viewing shortcomings as an individual issue is not new and is at the core of neoliberalism, which has taken over all aspects of society and education. This leads to an obscure situation where people are increasingly connected to other people and places all over the world electronically, but they cannot find that same connection to people and places in their own real lives. Members of society are forever occupied by a screen of some sort but not by the people sitting right next to them. These shifting dynamics and the different emotional climate are having very real effects on relationships everywhere. Without social networks, the idea that "it takes a village" becomes obsolete, and the wrap-around services that are so desperately needed for some students and families are not possible.

Public and Private Lives

While there may be a lack of solid, personal relationships, there appears to be no problem with very public connections and a complete lack of privacy. Once upon a time, we occupied a space in which people held pieces of information so deeply, so closely to their hearts, that a select few were privileged to these thoughts and feelings. In the time of liquid modernity, this information is now shared freely with complete strangers. If it is not shared on the Internet, it did not happen, right? People need an audience. While Michel Foucault (1977) may have once talked about the panopticon as a means of discipline and punishment, we now see a virtual panopticon, a self-imposed permanent visibility with no regard for privacy and no juxtaposition between private and public lives. Foucault warned his readers years ago regarding the threat of constant surveillance from organizations much bigger than the individual, but now Bauman speaks to the ills of taking this surveillance on willingly and without reservation. People now conduct their own surveillance, where the thought of keeping anything private or in personal lives only is completely unheard of. Between Facebook, Snapchat, Instagram, and so many other platforms, people over-surveil themselves to the point of saturation. Where there once existed a clear line between public lives and personal lives, in Bauman's liquid modern theory, this line no longer exists. Instead of private lives, important secrets, and trusted advisors, everything is televised for the world to see and keep a close eye on how many 'likes' private information might garner.

Insensitivity

This lack of private lives and sharing of everything has not led to a greater appreciation for others' lived experiences; instead, liquid modernity explains that society is living in a time that is lacking in sensitivity. Not only is society lacking a feeling of sensitivity, but it also operates under the premise that both people and things are disposable. This disposability is illustrated clearly by the rampant consumerism that envelopes most people, but many are not as willing to see and acknowledge that this notion of disposability extends to people as well. If someone is lacking in buying power, cannot contribute to society in a way that seems viable, is struggling, or in need of extra assistance, they are deemed as disposable and pushed to the fringes of society. Society needs to look no further than the demolishing of social services or the school to prison pipeline to see that this is true. Clearly, the liquid feeling of the world and the fluidity with which everything moves means that there is no room for those who do not measure up in one way or another and no longer is there the sensitivity to even think about this phenomenon.

Disposability

This practice of disposability and ensuing lack of sensitivity can be seen in the lack of community that pervades the liquid modern world. There was a time, not that long ago, where neighborhoods, schools, and even families felt like communities. In liquid modernity, however, this no longer exists. Zygmunt Bauman makes clear that relationships are fragile and fleeting in our current time because people are constantly working to keep on moving. Because of this, relationships simply do not take shape; they are not grounded. The result of this constant movement and lack of relationships is a lack of critical thought and meaning-making in our world. Not only are people lacking in critical thought, but they also do not sit still long enough to realize the people, relationships, or feeling that might be missing from the world. Instead, people look for distractions, in all forms. People choose to focus instead on the mess that is someone else's fluid world, as maybe their own mess will then not seem so bad. Bauman makes clear to his reader, "With moral pain smothered before it becomes truly vexing and worrying, the web of human bonds woven of moral yarn becomes increasingly frail and fragile, falling apart at the seams" (Bauman & Donskis, 2013, p. 16). These bonds are disintegrating and leaving all with a lack of community and solid relationships.

Liquid Modernity in Applied Research

Zygmunt Bauman has used the theory of liquid modernity to describe life as a time when there is no longer a beginning or an end, just an endless cycle of replacing and renewing. This endless cycle applies to both people and things. Bauman also explains that life in the liquid modern world is similar to walking in a minefield—we do not know when something is going to blow, but we know that it will eventually. When educators and researchers think of the world in those terms, it becomes clear what a startling time this is for all people but specifically those who advocate for social justice and equity. How does one push basic human concepts like equity, social justice, and an ethic of care when people are viewed through the lens of disposability, where everyone and everything is replaceable? This is where using liquid modernity as a theoretical framework for research can be valuable when conducting research for social justice and equity in education.

In solid modern times, "'to be modern' meant to chase 'the final state of perfection'—now it means an infinity of improvement, with no 'final state' in sight and none desired" (Bauman, 2012, p. IX). During the times of modernity, the purpose of life was to arrive at one great point, but this is not the case now. The world and all people are always flowing and in motion. This fluidity makes research that much more difficult, as people do not stay focused on one idea or issue long enough to make real, lasting, impactful change. Those who have been in the field of education long enough have seen plenty of initiatives come and go, never having enough time to take root and see if real, meaningful, lasting change has been made. Again, this is because of the lightness and fluidity of the time we are living in—if something does not work, push it aside and try the next best thing. This approach is problematic in most areas of life but certainly in education.

As researchers viewing work through the lens of liquid modernity, the first step is to ensure that people feel a deep attachment to the work that they are doing and that they value and respect the people and places with which they are working. This is especially important when working with human subjects; if researchers want their research subjects to participate in discussions, focus groups, and observations, they must trust that the researcher will not get swept up in the fluidity of their world and instead put in the time that is necessary and appropriate to allow them to tell their stories or share their experiences. When so much of today's world is built on uncertainty, educators need their research participants to feel like the work that they were told was going to happen actually happens in that way. This is especially important when researchers are working with groups who are traditionally marginalized. Eve Tuck (2009) referred specifically to urban and native communities when she wrote that they feel, "over researched yet, ironically, made invisible" (p. 411). If educators and researchers are truly working for equity and social justice when research is being conducted, researchers must be keenly aware of the bonds that need to be made and the ways in which they truly need to both hear and see all research subjects.

"To put it bluntly, under conditions of 'liquidity' everything could happen yet nothing can be done with confidence and certainty" (Bauman, 2012, p. XIV). This is important to consider when one thinks about schooling and students. Professionals like to tell their students and their research subjects and participants that the sky is the limit, they can do anything, but the theory of liquid modernity says that, with few social supports in place and even less empathy, young people in schools are constantly living in a state of fear and uncertainty. This means that, when working to conduct research for education, this must be at the front of the researcher's brain. Researchers should be asking, "How is my work going to impact the lives of the people that I am working with?" If researchers are truly conducting educational research for social justice and equity, it is imperative that they center the voice and agency of their participants, while acknowledging their own privileged place and positionality.

Voice and agency are imperative in the work of all researchers but especially those who are working for social justice and equity. When people think of the manner in which Bauman describes his theory of liquid modernity, it is clear that for folks who are deemed disposable, there is no voice, no agency, and no autonomy. As researchers, all must be acutely aware of the ways in which consequences of the liquid modern world are bearing down on potential participants. Before working with research participants or proposing outcomes from research studies, it is imperative that the voices of those who are so often voiceless are included. In liquid modern times, too many are left without voice and agency, often because they are deemed disposable. Additionally, because of the lack of public and private lives, researchers have to be certain that the stories of participants are told in their own way and in their own words, rather than as a sound bite or headline. If researchers are truly committed to conducting research for social justice and equity in education, the voices of those who are too often 'othered' or pushed to their fringes must be included.

Implications for Researchers

When working with research subjects, it is important to think about the consequences of living in the time that is defined by Bauman's theory of liquid modernity. Researchers must remember that there is no longer a meta-narrative that is driving the lives and experiences of the participants that they work with; rather than working toward one great ending, people instead continue to restart over and over again. Because there is a constant turnover and rate of change in the world, participants' views on ideas such as education, society, and personal relationships, for example, may look different than they did even just ten years ago. Mark Davis (2013) tells his readers that we are currently navigating "a lived experience characterized by a series of seemingly disconnected intensities" (p. 9). These disconnected intensities may be apparent in the research subjects or contexts that researchers work with, and they must be careful not to conflate the characteristics of liquid modernity with the characteristics of their subjects. This is especially important when conducting research in a way that is meant to advocate for social justice and equity in education. If researchers mistakenly conflate the characteristics of this time with the characteristics of the subjects, they run the risk of perpetuating the status quo, which will only derail any attempt at social justice work. While this may be easier said than done, it is critical that researchers work hard to get to know the participants of their work so that a deep understanding and relationship exists before embarking on any research.

Because the world is entrenched in such a disconnected time, Bauman (2011a, 2011b) asserts that not only is society devoid of meaningful human interactions but that people avoid them at all costs, finding them inconvenient and tedious. This lack of human interactions and deep relationships will likely manifest themselves in research, specifically in research regarding education for social justice and equity. In this time when there is an enormous lack of social supports and basic human kindness, trying to tease out a person's perspective or the context of a classroom interaction can become increasingly more difficult. Because of this, it is important that research methods—specifically critical, qualitative research methods—center the voice of the participants and spend a significant amount of time not only looking at how to analyze discourse and speech acts but also looking at how to critically analyze non-verbal cues and body language. This attention to centering the words and actions of participants has always been critical to the work of social justice scholars, but it has become even more of an imperative in a time that is characterized by the theory of liquid modernity. With face-to-face interactions and human contact occurring less and less frequently, the nuances of working with people have changed and researchers must possess a sensitivity in their work that acknowledges the ways in which the traits of a liquid modern world have influenced what basic conversation may look like.

Not only have the ways in which people interact with each other changed, but the ways in which people present themselves have changed as well. The lack of public and private lives in liquid modernity means that most people—both young and old—have begun to craft a 'media self.' Nick Couldry (2009) explains that a "media self" is the version of ourselves that we share publicly. It may be wildly different from what we would consider our 'real self,' or it may just be a slightly polished version of who we are behind closed doors. However, confusion may result here, as the lines between public and private lives are blurred in liquid modern time. If this is the case—that we do not know where the line is between who we are publicly and who we are privately—research participants may have a difficult time being their 'real selves' with the researchers who would like to work with them. Encouraging participants to present a raw version of themselves can be a difficult thing for researchers to contend with, but this circles back to what was mentioned earlier in this chapter about building relationships with participants. If researchers are truly advocates for equity and social justice in education, then they should not be conducting research with human subjects if they are not fully invested in their lives and experiences. Additionally, after working with participants, it is important to spend a good deal of time with the data, really working to understand what the participants said and apply a lens of critical thought if there appears to be disparities between what they said one day versus what they said on another day. Again, this has always been true, but this is even more apparent in the time of liquid modernity.

Conclusion

As researchers and educators for social justice, the theory of liquid modernity must be considered before working with human subjects and trying to apply data and expertise. This chapter has provided a vision for how researchers can view critical, qualitative, social science research through the lens of liquid modernity and how to approach subjects and data with this framework in mind. Specifically, researchers need to consider the experiences of human subjects with the time of liquid modernity in mind, in order to give greater context and recognize the ways in which our current lived experience is markedly different from what it was during the modern and post-modern times.

In liquid modernity, society is sorely lacking in deep, solid bonds and human interactions. Bauman explains that there is no line between public and private lives, a feeling of community is nearly nonexistent, both people and things are disposable, and a good part of this disposability is due to the ever-increasing lack of sensitivity in the human race. This lack of sensitivity and a pervasive sense of disposability have contributed mightily to a disintegration of social networks, where too many people continue to float through the fluid world without deep roots. All of these issues must be considered when conducting research for social justice and equity in education. Researchers must be mindful of the ways in which societal shifts are weighing down on research participants and ensure that they do whatever they can to combat these issues, both when working with participants and when coding data. When mindful of these issues, researchers can strive to form bonds with their participants that they work with in order help them present their authentic selves. Researchers can also deeply commit to the work that they are doing, so that it does not become just one more thing in which they flow back and forth. Additionally, when working with both data and participants, researchers must be intentional about centering participant voice and attempt to ensure agency. Finally, if researchers understand that our current moment in history is one that is framed by the theory of liquid modernity, then they will have a nuanced enough view to understand when participants seem to contradict themselves or appear unclear during the time spent together.

Research needs to act as a tool of empowerment, not as another way to oppress those who are already marginalized and pushed to the fringes. If researchers and educators can work to gain a deeper understanding of liquid modernity and the ways in which this theory is pressing on everyone's lives, people can work to ensure that research in education works toward social justice and equity, rather than as another tool of oppression or, worse yet, another tool that comes and goes.

Suggestions for Additional Reading

Bauman, Z. (2017). *A chronicle of crisis: 2011–2016*. London, UK: Social Europe.

In *A Chronicle of Crisis: 2011–2016*, Bauman uses 24 chapters to explicate different situations that are specific to liquid modernity and the ways in which these issues are playing out across the globe.

Giroux, H. (2009). *Youth in a suspect society: Democracy or disposability?* New York, NY: Palgrave Macmillan.

Giroux spells out a compelling argument in this text regarding the current state of young people and the ways in which they are viewed and treated in today's society. He speaks clearly about disposability and consumerism, grounding these concepts strongly in theory.

Monahan, T. (2009). The surveillance curriculum. In A. Darder, M. Baltodano, & R. Torres (Eds.), *The critical pedagogy reader*. New York, NY: Routledge.

This chapter takes an interesting look at surveillance in public schools and how these heightened levels of surveillance are working to view young people as either victims or criminals who need to be controlled.

Noddings, N. (2003). *Caring: A feminine approach to ethics & moral education*. Berkeley, CA: University of California Press.

Noddings looks at care for others through the lens of a mother's care for her child. She questions whether organizations can truly be ethical when operating outside of caring relationships and suggests a need to realign education.

References

Bauman, Z. (2007b). Liquid arts. *Theory, Culture and Society, 24*(1), 117–126. https://doi.org/10.1177/0263276407071579

Bauman, Z. (2011a). *Culture in a liquid modern world*. Cambridge, UK: Polity Press.

Bauman, Z. (2011b). Privacy, secrecy, intimacy, human bonds, and other collateral casualties of liquid modernity. *The Hedgehog Review, 13*(1), 20–29. https://doi.org/10.1057/9780230290679_2

Bauman, Z. (2012). *Liquid modernity*. Cambridge, UK: Polity Press.

Bauman, Z., & Donskis, L. (2013). *Moral blindness: The loss of sensitivity in liquid modernity*. Cambridge, UK: Polity Press.

Couldry, N. (2009). Teaching us to fake it: The ritualized norms of television's "reality" games. In S. Murray & L. Ouellette (Eds.), *Reality TV: Remaking television culture*. New York, NY: New York University Press.

Davis, M. (2013). Hurried lives: Dialectics of time and technology in liquid modernity. *Thesis Eleven, 118*(1), 7–18. https://doi.org/10.1177/0725513613500268

Foucault, M. (1977). *Discipline and punish*. New York, NY: Pantheon Books.

Tuck, E. (2009). Suspending damage: A letter to communities. *Harvard Educational Review, 79*(3), 409–428. https://doi.org/10.17763/haer.79.3.n0016675661t3n15

Chapter 8
Thinking Critically About "Social Justice Methods": Methods as "Contingent Foundations"

Lucy E. Bailey

Abstract This chapter offers reflections on emancipatory research methods and examples of maneuvers in feminist qualitative methodology that are oriented toward social justice, crystallizing in the specific space, time, and moment of inquiry. In the spirit of Lather's (*Getting lost: Feminist efforts toward a double(d) science*. Albany: SUNY Press, 2007) advocacy to keep methodology "alive" and "loose" (p. 27), I argue that inquiries with emancipatory aims, and that conceptualize, conduct, and represent research aligned with those aims, must work against defining and freezing any method, tool, approach, theory, or representation at the outset of a study as inherently just. Casting a critical eye on "social justice methods," I argue that all researchers are subject to shifting forms of normalization and that we should work toward keeping methods as contingent and dynamic, to serve educational projects with varied allegiances and aims.

This chapter offers some reflections on socially just research methods as well as examples of maneuvers in qualitative methodology that are oriented toward social justice but are project specific, crystallizing in the space, time, moment, and trajectory of inquiry. As part of this larger collection of papers that recount journeys of *becoming* justice-oriented researchers—a project that to me always seems in process, never complete—and exploring what socially just methods might look like, I describe elements of my thinking over the years grounded in my feminist commitments to poststructuralist approaches in educational research (e.g., Lather, 1993; Richardson, 1997; St. Pierre & Pillow, 2000) and over a decade of teaching diverse qualitative methodology courses to graduate students. My purpose is to draw from feminist theorizing to emphasize the importance of keeping methodologies "open, alive [and] loose" (Lather, 2007, p. x; see Bailey & Fonow, 2015).

L. E. Bailey (✉)
Oklahoma State University, Stillwater, OK, USA
e-mail: lucy.bailey@okstate.edu

© The Author(s) 2019
K. K. Strunk, L. A. Locke (eds.), *Research Methods for Social Justice and Equity in Education*, https://doi.org/10.1007/978-3-030-05900-2_8

91

I begin by discussing the shifting norms shaping the horizons of research, thought, and practice in our post-truth era, including those shaping the practices that might constitute socially just inquiries. As many have argued (see *Qualitative Inquiry*, 2004, Vol. 10, Nos. 1–2), the broader context of politics and power influences research terrain, methodological possibilities, and researcher choices. Being aware of the norms and debates governing research practices and methods courses are important aspects of inquiry. I then turn to a foundational premise in my thinking about research endeavors that has crystallized over the years: that inquiries with justice-oriented aims and that conceptualize, conduct, and represent research aligned with such aims must work against what I call the "methodological taxidermy" (Bailey, 2016, 2017) of conceptualizing and freezing any given method, approach, or representation at the outset of a study as inherently just. In other words, a certain interviewing practice, the use of one theory or another, or enacting a method such as auto/ethnography or photovoice often associated with emancipatory inquiries, does not ensure emancipatory aims, processes, or outcomes. A variety of forces shape what "justice" or "equity" might look like in a given context. As forms of power constantly shift, emancipatory practices must remain dynamic and supple. This stance includes keeping open the vision of practices aligned with such inquiries, from considering the context of production, the research imaginary, the micropractices and decisions researchers make during the inquiry, to the analytic processes and final re-presentation. In fact, as I've noted elsewhere (e.g., Bailey & Fonow, 2015), choosing not to proceed with an inquiry may be the most fitting ethical choice. Third, I fold into this discussion a variety of inquiry examples, writing primarily from a feminist and qualitative perspective. In the spirit of Lather (1986a, 1986b, 2007), researchers seeking more humanizing and emancipatory approaches—those that work *with* rather than *on* people—are always working within/against contemporary discourses and practices toward the horizons of the not-yet.

Horizons of Research Thought

Decades of development in methodology have expanded the horizons of researchers' imaginaries for "producing different knowledge and producing knowledge differently" (St. Pierre, 1997, p. 175). This productive proliferation has emerged in the wake of critiques of, and resistance to, positivism and other theoretical perspectives as onto-epistemologies have expanded and flourished. Those who consider positivist framings limiting, even authoritarian and hegemonic, have developed a range of feminist, critical, and decolonizing participatory, arts-based, visual, and auto/ethnographic approaches for exploring social and material phenomenon, that significantly are intended to create more "liveable" (Lather, 1993) and "bearable worlds" (Ahmed, 2017). In its diversity, this body of work shifts away from seeking "knowledge for knowledge's sake" toward embracing inquiry as a vehicle for connection, disruption, change, and resistance. In this vision, inquiry practices should reflect and further those justice aims.

These shifts reflect some common characteristics associated with this "eighth moment" of qualitative inquiry (Denzin & Lincoln, 2015) that are well known among qualitative researchers oriented to inquiries that have emerged within contemporary "paradigm proliferation" (Lather, 2006). For the purposes of this essay, I mention several here. First, contemporary methodology is a dynamic, rich field of thought and practice constituted by diverse and contested allegiances and expressions; second, researchers have many options for undertaking their inquiries emerging from their diverse ontological, epistemological, and axiological grounding and aims; third, power relations shape the orchestrations of inquiries on any topic, with any approach, which makes the researcher's work in contemplating and interrogating the methods they choose constitutive of the knowledge they produce; and fourth, researchers' historical, contextual, and personal positionings are always implicated in inquiry. Feminist emancipatory research aiming to disrupt gendered = racialized = classed (and other) norms and relations of power thus takes many forms depending on the researcher's epistemological, ontological grounding and focus of inquiry. For decades, scholars have worked to unsettle entrenched norms and assumptions, to reflect and critique, to build community, to resist injustice, and to enact change (Denzin, 2010; Denzin & Giardina, 2018; Lather, 1986a, b).

Central to the art and science of emancipatory research projects is the context in which issues and methods arise and the awareness that, like the justice issues they take on, research methods, paradigms, and choices are situated in power relations. No inquiry space or tool transcends its context and time. Lincoln and Cannella (2004) detailed the "dangerous" discourses that have recurred to champion a limited set of evidence-based practices for conducting inquiry. As part of a broader collection of essays interrogating the power dynamics that legitimize some research approaches over others (grounded at the time in the National Research Council report issued in 2002, see *Qualitative Inquiry*, 2004, Vol. 10 (1–2)), Lincoln and Cannella argued that championing a rigid set of "gold standard" methods reflects dangerous epistemologies shaping academic discourse. These rigid norms—what they called "methodological conservativism" at the time—have profound implications for research, including which methods are taught and supported, which research imaginaries are cultivated, which projects are valued, which are funded, and which understandings of the world are nourished. They note a key danger that is worthwhile to consider in a methods collection because of its salience to researchers' very identities. Lincoln and Cannella (2004) argue that researchers immersed in such discourses of "good research" can become disciplined as good subjects in ways that shape their/our embodied sense of researcher competence. We absorb messages about the standards of "good research" and the behavior of "good researchers," and then discipline ourselves to those practices that can direct and constrain the trajectories of our knowing and doing. In this sense, learning methods is tied to cultivating a vision of a "possible self" (Marcus & Nurius, 1986) a future version of ourselves we might imagine becoming, a good researcher in formation.

I regularly observe the power of such discourses in my work with graduate students as they learn the terms, tools, concepts, and skills necessary to conduct research "well," to do it "right." Developing a sense of competence as "good researchers" can manifest in compliance to dominant approaches that saturate almost all fields in research, including education, rather than exploring context-based questions and experimenting with diverse approaches to keep possibilities open. Methodology courses, in general, are designed for this very purpose. All researchers are vulnerable to shifting forms of normalization and prescription, to discourses that champion hegemonic standards, or even "new" and "better" methods, including those oriented toward social justice. Claims about any methods can become prescriptive, associated with a "right" and "good" identity to embrace as a researcher, whether through dominant or feminist and critical approaches. These forces necessitate that researchers continually analyze research norms as part of their methodological practice.

Yet, recently, Cannella (2014) and many others (e.g., Davies, 2005; Denzin & Giardina, 2018) have written with a degree of urgency to highlight how renewed neoliberal dangers are shaping every fiber of the contemporary academy and threatening the successes of emancipatory research developments over the last three decades. As one field opens, another can become threatened. These shifts are accompanied by sustained attacks on science and higher education. Cannella writes:

> [F]orms of backlash …are …impacting life in academia, from patriarchal challenges to diverse perspectives such as feminism, to the construction of hegemonic discourses that co-opt and reinscribe such as mixed methods and evidence-based practices. Underlying all of this are both local and global neoliberalism that locks one into forms of governmentality through which all aspects of human functioning are interpreted as related to capital. (Cannella, 2014, p. xvi)

Institutional pressures toward accountability and privatization shape the way academics can use our time and, accordingly, engage in research. To paraphrase Rhoades (1998), academics in some ways have "become managed professionals under the control of professional managers" (quoted in Denzin & Giardina, 2018, p. 3). Codifying "gold standards" of research risks directing scholars away from a broad, flexible base of theoretical and methodological approaches that serve emancipatory ends in compliance to dominant forces. Others suggest working within the contemporary academy itself reproduces hegemonic power relations antithetical to justice projects because even the act of producing scholarship in the amounts, genres, and forms demanded to sustain our institutional roles in present circumstances often have little purchase outside the academy, which few—including academics—have time to read or access.[1] Denzin and Giardina (2018) detail the creeping presence of the "research marketplace" in which all scholarship can become products in a colonizing, competitive, corporatized, and privatized system. In a post-truth, violent, politically troubled time, they recommend that researchers take seriously how to serve the public sphere, "beyond the boundaries of the research marketplace" (Denzin & Giardina, 2018, p. 7). Brown's (2014) "disruptive" theatrical work with black girls celebrates that very goal. She writes, "wreckless theatrics means the new ideas and meanings we perform about black girlhood circulate beyond traditional academic sites of the classroom, beyond the printed word and go much further than a small group of elites" (p. 48). Turning a critical eye to the paradigms governing academic practices (as Dillard's, 2006, 2012 demonstrates) to nourish black feminist spiritual epistemologies aligns with that call.

Cumulatively, that these external forces shape the horizons of inquiry serves as a reminder for researchers engaged in emancipatory projects to consider power and politics in the orchestrations and transformations of research terrain as *central* to the practice of methods. This is a broader sense of methods than choosing a theory, who and how to interview, and whether and how to conduct member checks. This sense of methods includes cultivating the spaces and conditions in which emancipatory projects might flourish and fostering dialogue about the broad shifts and ideals that shape research thought and practice. It necessitates resisting instrumentalist discourse and efficiency mandates to support diverse questions, onto-epistemologies, and methodologies. It involves nourishing an open stance to what emancipatory inquiries might look like as forms of power shift and morph, including the entrenchment of new discourses in education that curtail research imaginaries and support conventions that police the boundaries of what is possible. It also means cultivating collective support for embodied researchers who take up this work. Researchers are of course not simply efficient instruments of methodology but embodied actors in a network of intra-acting relations, materialities, contexts, and responsibilities that constitute methodological practice. For example, Dillard's (2006, 2012) work interrogates the politics of inclusion and exclusion of scholars of color in discussions of research paradigms and methodologies. She offers a rich framing borne of her lived experience and reflections that she terms "endarkened transnational feminist epistemologies," emphasizing spirituality of global black feminist inquiries as acts of "responsibility and reciprocity" rather than quests to fix research "problems" (2012, p. 59).

Cannella (2014) reminds readers that emancipatory practices can have embodied costs. In her foreword to the edited collection, *Disrupting Qualitative Inquiry*, Cannella (2014) expresses that there are "intellectual, emotional, and bodily struggles and pressures of being a critical researcher who wants to survive in, while transforming, a society (and institution) that has, despite the work of the previous generation of scholars remained patriarchal, oppressive, capitalist, and competitive" (p. xvi). Considering the researcher's embodied, emotional labor and their logistical struggles are personal and methodological necessities for justice work (see Blee, 2018; Brown, 2014, p. 48). That means that emancipatory research is much more than using the right methods, terms, or theoretical frameworks; from a feminist perspective, the embodied labor of the researcher is always part of the "body" of approaches for social justice and equity in education. Self-care and care with our research communities are justice-oriented acts that resist patriarchal corporate academic cultures that demand more and more from embodied scholars. Feminist scholars of color have long framed self-care as a necessary, radical act in their political work. As African American feminist poet Audre Lorde wrote decades ago in *Burst of Light* (1988), "Caring for myself is not self-indulgence, it is self-preservation, and that is an act of political warfare" (p. 131). She wrote these words in the context of caring for herself while living with cancer and continuing her activist writing work in hostile conditions for women of color. Her powerful words have broad resonance in post-truth times, suggestive for considering radical self-care and reflection as fundamental—and just—aspects of the work of inquiry.

Resisting "Methodological Taxidermy" (Bailey, 2016, 2017)

All norms have power to fix thinking, to occlude and foreclose conceptual possibilities, and to reproduce hegemonic power relations. In that spirit, what constitutes a justice-oriented approach cannot be decontextualized, fixed, or prescribed, but it must remain dynamic, supple, and project specific. No tools or methodologies can bear stable meanings or inherently emancipatory uses. To mobilize any such tool or concept as fixed in meaning or potential enacts a form of what I call "methodological taxidermy," stuffing once dynamic entities into fixed forms that hang glassy-eyed on a researcher's wall; frozen in meaning; decontextualized from their animated, embodied, pulsing context of production; or potential creative use (Bailey, 2016, 2017). Instead, questions, tools, approaches pulse with potential in relation and context. The forms and systems of class, gender, and racial power, among others, that justice-oriented scholarship addresses are supple, dynamic, and diffuse. For example, in Alexander's (2012) incisive text, *The New Jim Crow*, she underscores that racism is a "highly adaptable" force (p. 21), taking different forms at different historical moments. In contemporary feminist work, it is thus vital to keep questions and approaches productive, "promiscuous" (Childers, Rhee, & Daza, 2013), "alive," and "loose" (Lather, 2007, p. X) for responding to supple and shifting forms of power.

As many have noted, "social justice," "emancipatory," and "decolonizing" concepts appearing in literature for decades are at times so common and ambiguous that their meaning and power is lost. What does one mean by social justice? For whom and for what purpose? How does intent, design, twists and turns in the field, or representation matter in enacting justice-oriented projects? Must a researcher identify his/her project as a social justice inquiry to be so? How does one "measure" or assess the effects of one's research in terms of accomplishing justice aims? Does a project need to effect critical consciousness with participants or produce change in a targeted group or an audience? Must it thus enact "catalytic validity" (Lather, 1993) moving beyond traditional correspondence theories of truth in validity claims to assess a project based on whether it enacts the change or affects the participants in the ways the research intended? Must a project produce a product at all (see MacLure, 2013)? Or is the dynamic created through the human, animal, material research entanglements—even shifts in the researcher's awareness, connections with others, and belief systems—enough? Responses to these questions are ever-shifting and project specific.

A set of processes have become common for researchers to use in emancipatory projects. Such tools and stances include careful attention to power dynamics in conducting, analyzing, and representing research, including researcher reflexivity, peer dialogue, peer analysis, and member checks among many others. Yet, in the case of member checks and collaborative analysis, for example, the very tools scholars have posed to disrupt researcher authority and increase equity in the research process can also burden participants with more tasks than they care to have. Numerous students have shared over the years that their quests for member checks from busy people—all undertaken for the laudable and ethical reason to ensure participants have a "voice" in checking and expanding the data they shared—have met with little interest, even dismissal, as a way they want to spend their time. Scholars have noted how validity processes such as inter-rater reliability and peer analysis reflect reductive and homogenizing impulses (Kvale, 1996): the analytic hunt for common themes and researcher consensus of any kind can tyrannically impose a kind of interpretive violence as it directs researchers' attention to common denominators and homogeneity rather than difference as signifiers of valid findings and sound analysis. The point here is not that researchers should discard member checks or peer analysis, or that transparency and participant choice are not ethical orientations; rather, homogenized prescriptions associated with any method and under-theorized extractions of techniques from one ontological or epistemological field to another are not inherently "emancipatory." Such approaches can fix and reproduce rather than unsettle power relations in research.

Recent turns to arts-based approaches, auto/ethnography, and photovoice, among others, reflect researchers' excitement about the "new" as more promising approaches to undertaking their work. Yet, neither dominant experimental design reflecting one side of the epistemological continuum nor photovoice and auto/ethnography, on the other, can be frozen as either inherently problematic or adequate emancipatory approaches. Methodological potential is context specific. For instance, in an educational initiative undertaken in Afghanistan to expand women's visibility in an agricultural high school curriculum, a focus group with stakeholders involved in the project, women and men alike, objected to even the most modest changes to make curriculum more inclusive and representative of family labor. They objected to including photographs of any women of child-bearing age in the textbook pages and felt uncomfortable with the term "gender" because of its Western connotations. Using photographs of working women for the laudable purpose of representing women as agricultural workers and agents in the curriculum was not possible because they rendered women too visible and subject to the scrutiny of unknown others (Salm, Mukhlid, & Tokhi, 2018). However emancipatory visual data and photography might become as a curricular choice, as a site of analysis (see Tavares, 2016), as a critical, decolonizing method, or as a research outcome in a range of contexts, a project that includes women's visual representation as a vehicle for equity could actually be antithetical to emancipatory aims, even dehumanizing, because of the cultural and gendered meaning photographs can accrue in a given space and time.

Pillow's (2003, 2015) ongoing critique of the use of "reflexivity" in research provides another example of resisting methodological taxidermy (Bailey, 2016, 2017) in research practice and keeping approaches open and dynamic. The concept of "reflexivity" has varied expressions (e.g., reflexivity on audience, data, researcher positionality, see Fonow & Cook, 1991; as discomfort, interpretation, and genealogy, see Pillow, 2003, 2015), but for decades has been recognized as one necessary analytic practice to signal "good" (generally non-positivist) qualitative work. When I teach any form of qualitative methodology, I provide varied examples of the productivity of reflexivity as a stance in research. Indeed, in their early work, Fonow and Cook (1991) described the practice of reflexivity as a key tenet of feminist inquiry. In the wake of this important feminist move and the diverse analytic layers and trajectories it has inspired (Bailey & Fonow, 2015), researchers have fueled an incitement to "reflexivity" that suggests the importance, even urgency, for researchers to work the research hyphen (Fine, 1994), to reflect on their subject position in relation to the people, topic, and/or circumstances of inquiry, and to acknowledge and explore researcher investments. Such reflexivity is oriented to rendering researchers' subject positions visible and transparent as gendered, racialized, and otherwise historically situated producers of knowledge in contrast to the "omniscient" researcher position expected and championed with positivist epistemologies of detachment and objectivity. The approach embraces a researcher's responsibility to critically reflect on all aspects of the inquiry (Bailey & Fonow, 2015; Fonow & Cook, 1991).

Yet, despite the productivity of reflexivity as a stance, there is nothing inherently justice-oriented about reflecting on one's subject position in relation to a given project. It depends on a variety of issues, including one's view of oneself, one's view of the subject, one's focus in research, one's political allegiances, and the work such reflexivity enables. Pillow (2003) details the sense of "catharsis" and "cure" that "confessional" reflexivity practices can produce—the sense for the researcher that she or he has accomplished or resolved something tangible through reflecting on and "confessing" one's investments. We are always positioned in networks of power in which our reflexive labor may be limited, perfunctory, or personally cathartic rather than transformative for the project. Considered in relation to Lincoln and Cannella's discussion of "dangerous discourses," of the subtle ways in which research norms become inscribed, engaging in reflexivity can similarly fuel the researcher's sense that she/he is doing "good" justice work. Pillow (2015) theorizes additional ways of putting reflexivity to work, working against its conceptual stasis and taken-for-granted understandings.

All concepts and approaches such as reflexivity, voice (Jackson & Mazzei, 2008), empowerment, or others widely accepted and even cherished in the practice of emancipatory research are produced at a given historical moment in conversation with other concepts and forces (Bailey & Fonow, 2015). Such practices can become static and coopted, part of a perfunctory validity checklist, rather than transformative and nourishing analytically. Many of these techniques have invited productive critique, underscoring the importance of continual revisiting and unsettling taken-for-granted practices in methodology rather than codifying them as inherently emancipatory. Concepts and approaches in any research endeavor, including those commonly oriented toward social justice, might best be thought of as "contingent foundations"; always temporary, shifting, and contestable "authorizing grounds"; and conceptual springboards (Butler, 1992, p. 7). Butler used the phrase "contingent foundations" in considering how to imagine a feminist politics in the wake of postmodernism that doesn't rely on the concept of "woman," or other stable conceptual platforms for action. Similarly, researchers can consider engaging in diverse projects for their justice potential, however defined, and consider methods as unstable "authorizing grounds," that are always subject to dismissal, dismantling, revision, and new understandings in new contexts.

Embracing a justice-oriented stance in research practice may, in fact, mean choosing not to use a set of methods typically associated with emancipatory practices. It may mean engaging with long-standing positivist-imbued quantitative approaches to accomplish research aims. Some feminist researchers, for example, freely use quantitative methods and experimental designs to explore a range of phenomena (see Reinharz, 1992). They might not articulate a "social justice" purpose or detail practices commonly associated with emancipatory approaches such as reflexivity, member checking, participant collaboration, or creative methodologies. For such studies to be intelligible to funding agencies and in policy circles, in fact, might necessitate that researchers use conventional methods and reporting styles. An auto/ethnography would not have the same purchase for readers in those contexts.

A researcher might decide the most socially just path would be to discontinue a given research project, limit the material shared, or experiment with various re-presentational styles, recognizing the (im)possibilities of re-presentation. Choosing what to represent in research is fraught with political implications. For instance, in Blee's (2002, 2018) important anti-racist work on white supremacist groups, she recognized the women she interviewed often wanted to use her research to promote the mission of their groups. They believed her publications would provide them greater visibility. As a result, Blee chose to use pseudonyms for the groups in her research reports so as not to fuel their racist missions. Similarly, Richardson's (1997) impetus to shift from traditional sociological methods in the 1990s to embrace poetry and narrative emerged from her perception that traditional research representation might enact a form of violence on her participants. She describes abandoning conventional sociological methods to use poetic analysis and representation as a feminist style most aligned with her data and her work. Dillard's ongoing work theorizing endarkened feminist epistemologies relies on ineffable concepts of the sacred and spiritual and the practice of (re)membering to "create a world that does not yet exist for African ascendant people" (2012, p. 115). She writes with a questioning, poetic, narrative voice that resists fixed notions of identity or methodology (p. 111).

For Lather and Smithies (1997), they hurried to publish an early version of their book on women living with HIV/AIDS to ensure its speedy availability for the participants and their families. Recognizing the complexities of the women's embodied condition and their temporal vulnerability, the authors' push to publish allowed the community members to see their stories in print quickly while the researchers finished the final version of the book for the academic community. For Brown (2014), some experiences she has working with girls in "wreckless theatrics" never made it to a broad audience; she noted that those details were kept only for the girls' own pleasure. As a final example tied to images, feminist science scholar Anne Fausto-Sterling (1995) considered how best to represent her critical analysis on the eighteenth- and nineteenth-century scientific practices of exploiting Saartjie Sarah Baartman's body. Baartman was a South African woman whose body was exhibited publicly on the stage during her short life and, later after death, in museums. In Fausto-Sterling's published analysis of the scientific racism fueling Baartman's treatment, she chose not to re-present any images of Baartman to resist sustaining in scholarship into the twenty-first century the racist and sexist objectification to which the medical community subjected her in the nineteenth century. Each of these feminist decisions is project specific, grounded in the unique topic, purpose, participants, and field of representation the project enters.

Thinking Contextually About Emancipatory Practices

My comments in this essay are musings rather than manifestos, emerging from my interest in working against the freezing of research practice that codifies norms, hierarchies, and prescriptive inquiry practices. When one fixes a methodology as inherently emancipatory, a kind of "method-fetishism" results, a potentially decontextualized championing of a given method, tool, or approach. Bartolome's (1994) use of the term "method-fetishism" in the context of teaching is productive. She critiques the broad quest in education for the "right" methods to "fix" and improve academic achievement for struggling students. She sees this fixation on the right methods as illusory and "myopic" (p. 174). Similarly, we need a range of methods that emerge through intersections among field, participants/researcher, purpose, and questions.

Here, I turn to varied examples in research practice focused on embodiment as another way to keep methods "alive and loose." I see these practices as "contingent foundations" rather than prescriptions as I, like others, grapple with how to enact work that remains committed to unsettling norms while pursuing questions arising from my specific context and endeavors. Varied practices have emerged in contemporary methodology from the growing calls to focus research on neoliberal threats to the academy and the "dangers" and struggles for critical researchers detailed earlier (e.g., Cannella, 2014). As one example, I've been concerned about the erasure of the embodied aspects of faculty labor from contemporary discussions: that thinking and writing and teaching and research are not simply intellectual acts but always of and through the body. These concerns led me to consider how to better foreground embodiment in research practice focused on higher education.

Collaborative Auto/Ethnography

One important expression of this feminist commitment to embodied inquiry emerged through working with a friend and colleague on a collaborative auto/ethnography (considering self-in-culture through writing) that explored her experiences with postpartum depression. This narrative gradually unfolded to focus on the production of academic-vulnerable-gendered-selves-in culture. The methods unfolded utterly in context and collaboration. We used data from our emails, journal reflections, and unsettling memories to detail the emotional aspects of negotiating the pressure and culture of higher education with a gendered, misunderstood, and vulnerable condition (Kearney & Bailey, 2012). We worked in partnership to make visible the felt effects of an intense, neoliberal, masculinist culture for her body and life, and we did not label the work methodologically until close to its completion. Looking back, I'm still not sure the category of "collaborative auto/ethnography" fully fits the work, and I'm not sure it matters. The piece had several transformative effects, all of which were modest and contextual: first, the process was emotionally cathartic for her and for us, deepening our understanding of the events; second, the process of thinking, writing, and revising together deepened our relationship as critical colleagues and friends; third, even though the essay focused on "her" experience, the piece relied on creatively narrating a collaborative "I" voice to blur boundaries and to render visible shared gendered politics affecting women in our context more broadly; and, finally, the essay became part of a body of work on academic mothering salient for other women negotiating gendered vulnerabilities in higher education.

Embodied Data Analysis

In another project, I began envisioning interview data as embodied to disrupt my normative engagements with "data" and heighten sensitivity in analysis. This project emerged organically. How researchers imagine their interview data matters fundamentally in how they approach analysis and what they believe it can tell them about the phenomenon of interest (if it can tell them anything at all, see Lather & St. Pierre, 2013). Researchers may see transcripts as vehicles for capturing individual voice, as co-constructed narrations, as identity performances, as signals of broader discourses, or as material that intra-acts with the researcher, place, time, and other aspects of the inquiry, among other possibilities. For one project focused on embodiment, I adopted Kvale's (1996) warning to "beware" of transcripts. While his caution was not rooted in an emancipatory orientation, I put the warning to work with that spirit. Kvale argues that transcription is a form of re-presentation, an act of transferring a person's spoken words through a recording, then a taped/digital representation, and then to a textual page for extraction and use. Rather than simply a mechanical process, the work of transcription transforms, decontextualizes, and flattens the original utterances. It does not represent the real; to Kvale, it is a translation and "co-authored" construction (p. 281). Other scholars theorize transcription in complex ways as well; for example, see Poindexter (2002).

With this caution in mind, rather than typing transcripts of some "data" I had gathered, which is a standard validity practice in qualitative inquiry, I tuned in to the breath, pauses, and subtleties of movement I could hear as I listened to audio tapes of interviews. I imagined the data as embodied, pulsing, alive, as extensions of the participants' physical being when we had talked in place. My interest in enacting this stance was less to divest myself of the responsibility to represent or to convey that such a stance would provide a better, more authentic representation. Rather, the process helped me engage with the data differently, considering the location of its heart or soul and breath, and which parts of the data I should slough off lightly, like skin, or sever entirely, for the health of the body as a whole. Listening *with* participants to the co-authored (Kvale, 1996) "data" as a form of member checking and collaborative meaning-making opens additional possibilities as well (Bailey, 2012).

This engagement expanded as I added context and movement to the analysis process. As Ellingson (2017) has explored recently, researchers' embodied experiences and context can enrich meaning-making in data analysis. In my work, I organically moved in different places to listen to and read the data—playing tapes in my car as I commuted between campuses, slumping over transcripts on bus rides home, underlining, listening, reading and rereading—this approach entangles my embodied labor and subjectivities in the encounters with the text or the sound, foregrounding place and space, where I sit, how I experience the "data." I have listened to the data as I have traveled through space; its contours different in a classroom than riding on a bus in the dark late at night after teaching. In a study situated in Oklahoma, I listened to participants' voices as I drove on Oklahoma highways, long stretches of pitted pavement between cattle ranches, amber plains, and skies dotted with glistening white windmills. The process heightened my awareness of how place shaped the original material I called "data," expanding to include the place/space where it was produced, experienced, and processed, helping me think differently about what mattered to me and to participants.

Negotiating Representation

Exploring the experiences of underrepresented groups in Oklahoma required other methods (Bailey, 2012), including long-term incubation and immersion with the data as I grappled with the politics of representation. A diverse and complex state (Joyce, 1998; Joyce & Harris, 2007), the indigenous territory now referred to as Oklahoma is suffused with a history of colonialism and resistance and an economic base of oil, natural gas, aviation, and agriculture. While the state's dominant racial/ethnic group is non-Hispanic whites, the land is home to over 60 Native American tribes, who constitute about 10% of the demographics of the state, in addition to African Americans (8%), people of Latino, Hispanic and/or Spanish descent (8%), and a small percentage (around 1%) of people who identify as Asian in census categories. The area is known for its socially and politically conservative views and voting patterns. It is also a state with representatives who have garnered national attention in recent years for, among other issues, their reductive conflations of Muslims and gays with terrorism (see Mason, 2015). The politics in this state have in fact, as Mason (2015) explores, energized the LGBTQ movement at the national level. In one project, I intended to contribute a small offering to more geographically-grounded analyses and more complex representations of the experiences of minoritized groups in education. Geographically grounded and diverse representations, I hoped, would contribute to unsettling further the "controlling images" (Collins, 2000) in which many groups are constituted.

Yet, the project has periodically stalled in its complexity for me as a researcher. It has crawled along, transforming only my own thinking at this stage, the hope of meeting "catalytic validity" criteria merely a faint goal in the distance as I figure out how to analyze and frame data so saturated with constructions of, for example, people of color as "outsiders" in science, technology, education and mathematics (STEM) fields and sexual minorities as sinners, terrorists, diagnosable, or simply, victims, that my own representations will likely do little to unsettle them, or worse, because of the slippages of language and the data participants have shared, might only solidify and thicken existing problematic constructions. Pausing to ponder and reflect has been imperative.

I blur over details of the data here to emphasize the central message: the traumatic or complex events of people's lives can easily map on to constructions of vulnerable subjects as damaged, and their life experiences reduced to narratives of victimization rather than layers in a structurally shaped multidimensional life. Researchers in relation and in context must take time to consider how to represent their work and its implications. I've also been aware that peeling these layers away from the body of data I am responsible for "transforming into findings" (Patton, 2002) and shedding it in a discarded data pile may silence experiences that, for some participants, were transformative in the telling and inextricably woven with other aspects of identity. Accordingly, like Richardson's (1997) turn to poetic representation, Fausto-Sterling's (1995) careful parsing of her representations, and Wilson's (2004) decision on how to represent sex tourism in Thailand in a voyeuristic and overdeveloped field of representation, I believe that a just choice regarding some data I have collected might be not to represent those experiences at all. The telling may be enough. In such a case, bearing witness (Lather & Smithies, 1997) in the research *process* and the relationships we formed *through inquiry*, rather than representation in a broader field might be the just choice. Narrating one's experiences, as Lewis (2018) underscores, can be thought of as far more than static data to extract from context. In Indigenous inquiries, stories are utterly ontological—they are sites and methods of being, existence, critique, and resistance.

Historical Research

Historical research provides other contexts for keeping embodied methodological questions and practices in motion in feminist research. A long-held feminist argument has been that "history is written by the victors," which has often oriented feminist historical research to recovering the stories of people less visible in dominant accounts. Those sites and voices, in turn, function to nourish and reshape the historical record. The very existence of material artifacts is tied to politics and power—who could write, who could preserve objects that mattered to them, which materials represent legitimate sites of history—as well as the inevitable losses, erasure, and deterioration that shape which archival materials survive over time. Archival materials connote a fixity that differs from contemporary interview data and yet necessitate similar onto-epistemological and ethical questions. What do feminist inquiries look like with historical work? What is a humanizing method in a historical study? What are the conceptions of history with which we are working? What is our purpose? Conventional emancipatory tools are not a fit: no member checks are possible in historical work; there is no embodied access to historical context in which the data was produced.

Feminist scholars have used a variety of methods to engage in histories that stretch or disrupt those written by victors. Jennifer Terry's work on "deviant" historiography has provided a crucial method for engaging in feminist archival research. Because Terry's subjects had left no known archival materials to make sense of their lives, Terry turned her attention to dominant accounts to look for traces of marginalized subjects through those accounts. Terry (1991) sought glimmers of resistance female sexual minorities demonstrated historically through some of the only records available—dominant medical accounts that sought to photograph, measure, and scrutinize their bodies to locate the exact site of their presumed "deviance." This practice of looking to the body to find and fix the site of human character has recurred historically in varied forms (see Terry & Urla, 1995). While the scientific accounts Terry analyzed essentially objectified the embodied subjects under study, she sought through those dominant accounts to mark and interpret resistance from the women who were subjected to the scrutiny. Such work brings different theories to bear on archival materials to open interpretation in layers.

What constitutes feminist methods is produced in the dynamics, relationships, and context of a given study, all shaped by broader methodological forces and conditions. Social justice methods must remain "contingent foundations." These practices might involve an array of new questions about existing paradigms governing inquiry, new methodologies, new onto-epistemologies, new tools that open dominant practices to fluidity and creativity oriented toward change. These practices might involve conventional methods and academic products in forms that will be recognizable and intelligible in dominant practices. They might involve moving outside the academy to engage directly with local, collaborative endeavors (Denzin & Giardina, 2018) that are never published in academic journals. They might involve projects in which people engage in arts-based and visual methods focused more *on process* and relationships than *product*. They might involve displacing the human subject entirely as the central site of inquiry to consider intra-actions with non-human beings, environments, and material entities (see Lather & St. Pierre, 2013; Taylor & Hughes, 2016). As this volume of essays shows, the practices are diverse, contested, and always unfolding—and it serves feminist emancipatory ends to keep them that way.

Suggested Readings

Dillard, C. (2012). *Learning to (re) member the things we've learned to forget: Endarkened feminisms, spirituality, & the sacred nature of research and teaching.* New York, NY: Peter Lang.

Lather, P. (1986). Research as Praxis. *Harvard Educational Review, 56*(3), 257–278.

This essay brings a critical perspective to social justice research methods by underscoring the importance of researchers' awareness of broad political and academic discourses shaping inquiry, of keeping methods varied and flexible, and offers examples to demonstrate these points in action.

Note

1. For example, one article noting the proliferation of journals and scholarly outlets cites 1.8 million articles produced yearly, an impossible mass to read, conceptualize or grapple with, while academic demands continue to rise. See Eveleth, R. (2014). "Academics write papers arguing over how many people read (and cite) their papers." Smithsonian.com. https://www.smithsonianmag.com/smart-news/half-academic-studies-are-never-read-more-three-people-180950222/. Retrieved July 31, 2018.

References

Ahmed, S. (2017). *Living a feminist life.* Durham, NC: Duke University Press.

Alexander, M. (2012). *The new Jim crow: Mass incarceration in the age of colorblindness.* New York, NY: The New Press.

Bailey, L. (2012, May). *'Oklahoma processing.' Data analysis processes that serve social justice agendas.* Paper at the International Congress of Qualitative Inquiry, Champaign-Urbana, IL.

Bailey, L. (2016, May). *Thinking with taxidermy: Tracking and troubling readings of Patti Lather.* Paper at the International Congress of Qualitative Inquiry, Champaign-Urbana, IL.

Bailey, L. (2017, April). *Methodological taxidermy: Working with/against the scholarship of Patti Lather.* Presentation at the American Educational Research Association Annual Meeting, San Antonio, TX.

Bailey, L. E., & Fonow, M. M. (2015). Foundational commitments, intergenerational knowledge production, and new trajectories: Feminist methodologies. In G. Cannella, M. S. Perez, & P. Pasque (Eds.), *Critical qualitative inquiry: Foundations and futures* (pp. 51–76). Walnut Creek, CA: Left Coast Press.

Bartolome, L. (1994). Beyond the methods fetish: Toward a humanizing pedagogy. *Harvard Educational Review, 64*(2), 173–194.

Blee, K. (2002). *Inside organized racism: Women in the hate movement.* Oakland, CA: University of California Press.

Blee, K. (2018). *Understanding racist activism: Theory, methods, and research*. New York, NY: Routledge.

Brown, R. N. (2014). "She came at me wreckless!": Wreckless theatrics as disruptive methodology. In N. R. Brown, R. Carducci, & C. R. Kuby (Eds.), *Disrupting qualitative inquiry: Possibilities and tensions in educational research* (pp. 35–52). New York, NY: Peter Lang.

Butler, J. (1992). Contingent foundations: Feminism and the question of "postmodernism". In J. Butler & J. Scott (Eds.), *Feminists theorize the political* (pp. 3–21). New York, NY: Routledge.

Cannella, G. (2014). Foreword. In N. R. Brown, R. Carducci, & C. R. Kuby (Eds.), *Disrupting Qualitative inquiry: Possibilities and tensions in educational research* (pp. xv–xvi). New York, NY: Peter Lang.

Childers, S., Rhee, J., & Daza, S. L. (2013). *Promiscuous feminist methodologies in education*. New York, NY: Routledge.

Collins, P. H. (2000). *Black feminist thought*. New York, NY: Routledge.

Ellingson, L. (2017). *Embodiment in qualitative research*. New York: Routledge.

Davies, B. (2005). The (im)possibility of intellectual work in neoliberal regimes. *Discourse: Studies in the Cultural Politics of Education, 26*(1), 1–14.

Denzin, N. (2010). *A qualitative manifesto: A call to arms*. Walnut Creek, CA: Left Coast Press.

Denzin, N., & Lincoln, Y. (Eds.). (2015). *The SAGE handbook of qualitative research*. Thousand Oaks, CA: SAGE.

Denzin, N. K., & Giardina, M. D. (Eds.). (2018). *Qualitative inquiry in the public sphere*. New York, NY: Routledge.

Dillard, C. B. (2006). *On spiritual strivings: Transforming an African-American woman's academic life*. Albany: State University New York Press.

Dillard, C. (2012). *Learning to (re) member the things we've learned to forget: Endarkened feminisms, spirituality, & the sacred nature of research and teaching*. New York, NY: Peter Lang.

Fausto-Sterling, A. (1995). Gender, race, and nation: The comparative anatomy of 'hottentot' women in Europe, 1815–1817. In J. Terry & J. Urla (Eds.), *Deviant bodies: Critical perspectives in science and popular culture* (pp. 19–48). Bloomington, IN: Indiana University Press.

Fine, M. (1994). Working the hyphens: Reinventing the self and other in qualitative research. In N. Denzin & Y. S. Lincoln (Eds.), *Handbook of qualitative research* (pp. 70–82). Thousand Oaks, CA: Sage.

Fonow, M. M., & Cook, J. (Eds.). (1991). *Beyond methodology: Feminist scholarship as lived research*. Bloomington, IN: Indiana University Press.

Jackson, A. Y., & Mazzei, L. A. (Eds.). (2008). *Voice in qualitative inquiry: Challenging conventional, interpretive, and critical approaches*. London, UK: Routledge.

Joyce, D. D. (Ed.). (1998). *'An Oklahoma I had never seen before': Alternative views of Oklahoma history*. Norman, OK: University of Oklahoma Press.

Joyce, D. D., & Harris, F. L. (Eds.). (2007). *Alternative Oklahoma: Contrarian views of the sooner state*. Norman, OK: University of Oklahoma Press.

Kearney, K. S., & Bailey, L. E. (2012). "We shoot our wounded": Pregnancy, mothering and PPD on the tenure track. In A. O'Reilly & L. O. Hallstein (Eds.), *Academic motherhood in a post-second wave context: Problems, strategies, and possibilities*. Bradford, ON: Demeter Press.

Kvale, S. (1996). The 1,000 page question. *Qualitative Inquiry, 2*(3), 275–284. https://doi.org/10.1177/107780049600200302

Lather, P. (1986a). Issues of validity in openly ideological research: Between a rock and a soft place. *Interchange, 17*(4), 63–84. https://doi.org/10.1007/BF01807017

Lather, P. (1986b). Research as Praxis. *Harvard Educational Review, 56*(3), 257–278. https://doi.org/10.17763/haer.56.3.bj2h231877069482

Lather, P. (1993). Fertile obsession: Validity after poststructuralism. *The Sociological Quarterly, 34*(4), 673–693. https://doi.org/10.1111/j.1533-8525.1993.tb00112.x

Lather, P. (2006). Paradigm proliferation as a good thing to think with: Teaching research in education as a wild profusion. *International Journal of Qualitative Studies in Education, 19*(1). https://doi.org/10.1080/09518390500450144

Lather, P. (2007). *Getting lost: Feminist efforts toward a double(d) science*. Albany: SUNY Press.

Lather, P., & Smithies, C. (1997). *Troubling the Angels: Living with HIV/AIDS*. Boulder, CO: Westview Press.

Lather, P., & St. Pierre, E. (2013). Introduction: Post qualitative research. *International Journal of Qualitative Studies in Education, 26*(6), 629–633. https://doi.org/10.1080/09518398.2013.788752

Lewis, P. (2018). Indigenous qualitative research in the neoliberal public sphere. In N. Denzin & M. D. Giardina (Eds.), *Qualitative inquiry in the public sphere* (pp. 66–77). New York, NY: Routledge.

Lincoln, Y., & Cannella, G. (2004). Dangerous discourses: Methodological conservativism and governmental regimes of truth. *Qualitative Inquiry, 10*(1), 5–14. https://doi.org/10.1177/1077800403259717

Lorde, A. (1988). *A burst of light, essays*. London, UK: Sheba Feminist Publishers.

MacLure, M. (2013). Researching without representation? Language and materiality in post-qualitative methodology. *International Journal of Qualitative Studies in Education, 26*(6), 658–667. https://doi.org/10.1080/09518398.2013.788755

Marcus, H., & Nurius, P. (1986). *American Psychologist, 41*(9), 954–969.

Mason, C. A. (2015). *Oklahomo: Lessons in unqueering America*. New York, NY: SUNY Press.

Patton, M. Q. (2002). *Qualitative research and evaluation methods*. Thousand Oaks, CA: SAGE.

Pillow, W. (2003). Confession, catharsis or cure? Rethinking the uses of reflexivity as methodological power in qualitative research. *International Journal of Qualitative Studies in Education, 16*(2), 175–196. https://doi.org/10.1080/0951839032000060635

Pillow, W. S. (2015). Reflexivity as interpretation and genealogy in research. *Cultural Studies ↔ Critical Methodologies, 15*(6), 419–434. https://doi.org/10.1177/1532708615615605

Poindexter, C. (2002). Meaning from methods: Re-presenting narratives of an HIV-affected caregiver. *Qualitative Social Work, 1*(1), 59–78. https://doi.org/10.1177/147332500200100105

Qualitative Inquiry. (2004). Vol. 10 (1–2).

Reinharz, S. (1992). *Feminist methods in social research*. New York, NY: Oxford University Press.

Rhoades, G. (1998). *Managed professionals: Unionized faculty and restructuring academic labor*. New York: SUNY Press.

Richardson, L. (1997). *Fields of play: Constructing an academic life*. New Brunswick, NJ: Rutgers University Press.

Salm, M., Mukhlid, K., & Tokhi, H. (2018). Inclusive education in a fragile context: Redesigning the agricultural high school curriculum in Afghanistan with gender in mind. *Gender and Education, 30*. https://doi.org/10.1080/09540253.2018.1496230

St. Pierre, E. A. (1997). Methodology in the fold and the irruption of transgressive data. *International Journal of Qualitative Studies in Education, 10*(2), 175–189.

St. Pierre, E. A., & Pillow, W. (2000). *Working the ruins: Feminist poststructuralist theory and methods in education*. New York, NY: Routledge Press.

Tavares, H. M. (2016). *Pedagogies of the image: Photo-archives, cultural histories, and postfoundational inquiry*. New York, NY: Springer Press.

Taylor, C., & Hughes, C. (Eds.). (2016). *Posthuman research practices in education*. London, UK: Palgrave Macmillan.

Terry, J. (1991). Theorizing deviant historiography. *Differences: A Journal of Feminist Cultural Studies, 3*(2), 55–74.

Terry, J., & Urla, J. (1995). *Deviant bodies: Critical perspectives on difference in science and popular culture*. Bloomington, IN: Indiana University Press.

Wilson, A. (2004). *The intimate economies of Bangkok: Tomboys, tycoons, and Avon ladies in the world city*. Berkeley, CA: University of California Press.

Chapter 9
Institutional Review Boards: Purposes and Applications for Students

Leslie Ann Locke

Abstract The objective of this chapter is to introduce students to the processes involved with applying for institutional review board (IRB) approval. I discuss what human subjects review is and its purpose, then move on to a discussion of the potential make-up of an IRB and the related roles of the members. Lastly, I describe some of the processes associated with applying for IRB approval and some of the main elements necessary for an application.

The objective of this chapter is to introduce students who will be working with human subjects for their dissertation work or otherwise to the processes involved with applying for institutional review board (IRB) approval. First in this chapter I discuss what human subjects review is and its purpose. I then move on to a discussion of what an IRB might look like and the roles of the board. Later, I discuss some of the processes associated with applying for IRB approval and some of the main elements necessary for an IRB application.

University-Sponsored Research with Human Subjects: Purpose

An IRB or a committee is charged with performing an ethical review of proposed research. It does so by examining the methods of a proposed study with the intent to ensure that they are ethical and do not "harm" participants. That is, the researchers who designed the study did so in ways that ensure the rights and welfare of human

L. A. Locke (✉)
Educational Policy and Leadership Studies, University of Iowa,
Iowa City, IA, USA
e-mail: leslie-locke@uiowa.edu

© The Author(s) 2019
K. K. Strunk, L. A. Locke (eds.), *Research Methods for Social Justice and Equity in Education*, https://doi.org/10.1007/978-3-030-05900-2_9

subjects or participants who will take part in the study. The board's review is a means of safeguarding ethical conduct of research and the protection of participants.

An IRB at a university may consist of faculty, staff, and community members. However, all university IRBs are steered by federal guidelines and the Department of Health and Human Services. In addition and depending on the study, research may be further advised by the Office for Civil Rights, National Institutes of Health, the Food and Drug Administration, and/or the National Science Foundation. You can find the federal guidelines here: https://www.hhs.gov/ohrp/regulations-and-policy/guidance/faq/45-cfr-46/index.html

Why Is IRB Approval for Research Necessary?

It wasn't always the case that universities required IRB approval for research with human subjects. After World War II when a variety of events were discovered, committed by the Nazis, the Nuremberg Military Tribunal developed the Nuremberg Code, which was used to judge the Nazis in court. Significantly, the Nuremberg Code initiated the official consent process whereby participants of research studies must be presented with information about the study such that they understand their contribution and they must voluntarily consent to participate. Further, the researcher is responsible for obtaining consent. You can read more about the Nuremberg Code here: https://www.ushmm.org/information/exhibitions/online-exhibitions/special-focus/doctors-trial/nuremberg-code

Since the establishment of the Nuremberg Code, similar principles for research have been institutionalized such as the Declaration of Helsinki, which created the means for the approval and monitoring of research by independent committees. Additionally, the "Tuskegee Study" or the 40-year-long US Public Health Service Syphilis Study at Tuskegee (you can learn more about the Tuskegee Study here: https://www.cdc.gov/tuskegee/index.html) encouraged legislation to further protect research participants and provide informed consent, including the risks and benefits associated with a study. The Tuskegee Study also resulted in the creation of a National Commission for the Protection of Human Subjects of Biomedical and Behavioral Research. This Commission published the Belmont Report, which called for three basic and ethical principles that researchers must employ when conducting research with human participants. These principles include respect for persons, beneficence, and justice. You can read the Belmont Report here: https://www.hhs.gov/ohrp/regulations-and-policy/belmont-report/read-the-belmont-report/index.html

What we now know as "IRB" was created in 1974 through the National Research Act. The Act called for a system to regulate research involving human participants. Later, in 1991, federal agencies adopted the primary regulations in a common Federal Policy for the Protection of Human Subjects or the "Common Rule."

The Federal Policy for the Protection of Human Subjects or the "Common Rule" was codified in separate regulations by 15 federal departments and agencies. It

... outlines the basic provisions for IRBs, informed consent, and Assurances of Compliance. Human subject research conducted or supported by each federal department/agency is governed by the regulations of that department/agency. The head of that department/agency retains final judgment as to whether a particular activity it conducts or supports is covered by the Common Rule. (U.S. Department of Health and Human Services, n.d., n.p.)

A human subject or participant, according to the Common Rule, is a living individual who will participate in a study (data will be collected from/about them). Within the Common Rule are additional protections for vulnerable populations including human fetuses, neonates, prisoners, children, the financially vulnerable, and the elderly. There are also extra protections for those who are cognitively impaired. If you wish to work with individuals from these groups, you will be required by IRB to attain additional information, that is, assent (agreement to participate in a study, from, for example, a parent or guardian, who is able to provide legal consent).

IRBs are particularly concerned about "risk" and particularly for members of the previously mentioned groups, that is, what are the risks to the human subject related to participating in a study. Importantly, there is no such thing as a study with no risk. Risk is determined by the potential harms that may be experienced by a participant as a result of partaking in a research study. Factors associated with risk may include the procedures involved in a study, the setting or context in which the study takes place, the equipment associated with the study, the researcher(s') level of training and/or experiences, and the health or age of the participant. Many studies are considered "minimal risk," which indicates that "The probability and magnitude of harm or discomfort anticipated in the research are not greater than those ordinarily encountered in daily life or during the performance of routine physical or psychological examinations or tests" (U.S. Government Printing Office, n.d., p. 135).

What Students Can Anticipate with an IRB Application

If a student is intending to work with human subjects directly in their study, then they should count on some form of required IRB review. The IRB application and process can vary across institutions, but there will be certain items necessary for the application to ensure that it gets reviewed. However, IRB approval is required before any research activities begin. Students typically need a faculty advisor on their projects.

As noted previously, IRB applications and processes vary across institutions; therefore, it is difficult to expand on what exactly the process might look like. Some institutions will ask the researcher to decide which type of review they want, exempt, expedited, or full. Whichever type you choose or are assigned by an IRB, the type is not related to time, that is, expedited does not equate to "quick." Rather, the type of review refers to how many folks will review the application. A full board review indicates there is greater than minimal risk to participants and there may be seven to ten individuals who review the application. Expedited refers to not more than minimal risk to participants and the application may be reviewed by one person. And finally, exempt does not mean that it is exempt from review. It means that according to the federal regulations, the project describes one of six categories of research that is exempt from some of the requirements of human subjects research, including continued review by IRB or all of the required elements of consent.

Your IRB may have a "determinations" process where they will take a preliminary review of your study and decide on the level of review required. At the University of Iowa, for example, researchers can complete a Human Subjects Determination Form, where before completing and submitting the IRB application, researchers are asked a few key questions regarding the study and then the IRB advises whether or not the study is or is not human subjects research.

What Will You Need for Your IRB Application?

IRB applications require multiple elements. First, each researcher involved in the study will need to complete the required human subjects training though the Collaborative Intuitional Training Initiative (CITI). Depending on the area of research (biomedical, social-behavioral), there are separate online trainings available. Educational institutions have subscriptions to CITI, and the training is free for those associated with the institution. You can learn more about CITI training here: https://about.citiprogram.org/en/homepage/

If you are conducting a study in a school or school district, it is likely that you will need permission from the superintendent(s) and/or the principal(s) of the districts and/ or schools. Likewise, if you are working with individuals at an institution of higher education, you may need permission from particular offices at the relative institutions. Note that these letters of permission may be required/requested from IRB.

If you are planning to conduct research outside of the USA, you should plan on obtaining IRB approval from your home institution *and* from the local context. For example, if you are working with an institution of higher education you should work with their IRB office or equivalent. If an in-country IRB is not available, the researcher should identify a local expert who is willing to evaluate the proposed study in terms of local and contextual standards. Most universities have a form or a template for the expert to complete regarding the study and the local context. Gaining this local permission may take considerable time.

The IRB will also want to know that you have done some preliminary investigation into the scholarship as it relates to your study—such that your study will be an original and necessary contribution to the field. Thus, there may be a space in the application where you are to provide a short review of the literature and a list of related references.

Moreover, you should be prepared to explain and justify to the IRB the number of participants that will be included in the study and how you will protect their identities (if applicable). Further, you will need to supply the research questions guiding the study and the main ambitions of the investigation.

Additionally, you should have your ideas for participant consent clearly articulated. If you want to waive the consent process, that must be clearly articulated and justified. If you ask participants to read and sign a consent form, you must provide that form with your application. Most IRBs have exemplars and/or templates of such forms.

Next, you should have your data collection instruments ready. This may include interview protocol(s) (list of questions) that you will use in your interviews or the survey(s) or questionnaire(s) you plan to distribute to the participants. The IRB will also be interested in knowing about the research methodologies you plan to apply in the study.

Finally, the IRB will want to know who else, outside of your research team, will be interacting with the data. For example, if you will have your interviews transcribed by a person or company outside of your research team, they will want to know who that person is and may require some additional information from them. IRB will also want to know how you will store and transport the data related to the study.

It is not uncommon for IRB to request more information on an initial application. However, eventually most IRB applications are approved. IRB applications may seem cumbersome; however, they are there to make sure all the necessary precautions have been addressed in order to best protect the interests of the participants in a study. Students should consult with their IRB office early about the application process and requirements. Doing so will save time and energy.

Final Thoughts

It is possible to make changes to an IRB application after initial approval. For example, if the number of participants increases or if you see that now you should, for example, distribute a survey in addition to conducting interviews, you can make those "modifications." Incorporation of any measures or techniques that were not addressed in the initial application should be handled through a modification process through the same IRB office.

Lastly, once IRB approval has been obtained, it has an expiration date. Typically, IRBs approve a research project for one year. If all aspects of the study are not completed within one year, the researcher(s) may ask for the approval to be extended.

References

U.S. Department of Health and Human Services. (n.d.). Federal policy for the protection of human subjects ('Common Rule'). Retrieved from https://www.hhs.gov/ohrp/regulations-and-policy/regulations/common-rule/index.html

U.S. Government Publishing Office. (n.d.). 45 CFR § 46.102—Definitions. Retrieved from https://www.gpo.gov/fdsys/search/searchresults.action?st=45+C.F.R.+%C2%A7+46.102%28i%29

Part II
Approaches to Data Collection and Analysis

Chapter 10
Typical Areas of Confusion for Students New to Qualitative Research

Leslie Ann Locke

Abstract Students who are new to qualitative research methods tend to struggle with a handful of key concepts. This chapter consists of some of my reflections regarding teaching introductory qualitative research methods courses for graduate students from a variety of fields. I detail the major challenges I have seen students struggle with in these classes, namely truth and objectivity, generalizability or lack thereof, positionality, and ambiguity. I interweave my perspectives about these challenges and hopefully provide some useful wisdom for students to take away.

This chapter consists of some of my reflections regarding teaching introductory qualitative research methods courses for graduate students from a variety of fields. My intent in this chapter is to detail the major challenges I have seen students struggle with in these classes or the aspects of qualitative research that students find most confusing. There are four areas that seem to give students the most discomfort, namely truth and objectivity, generalizability or lack thereof, positionality, and finally, the ambiguity seeming inherent in qualitative research. Throughout the chapter, I include my perspectives about these aspects and hopefully provide some useful wisdom for students taking such classes so that both they find it useful and it serves as a means to reduce their challenges and discomfort.

A note regarding social justice and equity before I get into the challenges for beginning students of qualitative methods. Many students in my qualitative courses intend to focus their dissertation work within areas of social justice and equity in education. Thus, with regard to teaching qualitative methods, it is important for me that students learn to struggle with the challenges they confront in the methodology in order to best and authentically reflect the perceptions and experiences of the participants in their

L. A. Locke (✉)
Educational Policy and Leadership Studies, University of Iowa,
Iowa City, IA, USA
e-mail: leslie-locke@uiowa.edu

K. K. Strunk, L. A. Locke (eds.), *Research Methods for Social Justice and Equity in Education*, https://doi.org/10.1007/978-3-030-05900-2_10

future studies. Thus, knowing the literature thoroughly, understanding that multiple (even exponential) truths exist, and realizing that their positionality and identities are important to both the research process and the expression and representation of the findings are all relevant. I feel a particular responsibility to my students, the participants in their future studies, and the field, when I teach qualitative methods. That is, social justice and equity are important aspects of how and why I teach qualitative methods.

And now, on to the challenges. The issues I have seen students struggle with most in my qualitative classes are truth and objectivity, generalizability or lack thereof, positionality, and finally, the ambiguity seeming inherent in qualitative research. These areas seem to cause the students the most discomfort throughout the course. I detail each below.

Additionally, although I use a variety of texts and readings in my qualitative courses, I am relying heavily on the most recently adopted and main textbook from my courses, Merriam and Tisdell (2015), to support my claims here. I find this text to be very readable and students have found it to be an approachable source.

"Objectivity," Truth, and Multiple Realities

Every semester I have students who struggle with concepts related to epistemology, ontology, and axiology—the nature of knowledge, reality, and beliefs and values. And relatedly, when I ask them questions like "How do you know what you know?" and "How do you know what you know is true?" and "Is what is true for you also always true for me?" their responses go from relatively confident to not confident at all. I use this exercise to then discuss "truth" and "objectivity" in research. Many students, particularly those who have been exposed to more quantitative ideas about "research," have difficulty with this concept. "Objectivity," as they have been taught, is something—perhaps if not wholly attainable—is always a thing to strive for.

As a critical scholar and a qualitative researcher, my approach to "objectivity" is often unlike approaches of other faculty many of my introductory qualitative students have encountered or have studied under. Because we begin with a history (and within a present) of marginalization, that is, a structure of inequality—where individuals and groups have been and continue to be denied access to and the opportunity to contribute to "official knowledge" as we think of it through "research"—attaining "objectivity" is not possible. Even striving for such a goal seems not only improbable but unjust in a variety of ways, in my opinion. This does not mean that we should not adhere to principles of sound research—that is, we should do whatever we like without regard to established practices for ethical research. It does mean though that participants' realities are impacted by social, economic, political, and educational structures that have historically and presently limit access and opportunity. That is, the powerful exist, as do the disempowered. If we reflect on our history, the powerful have had access and opportunity to conduct research and create "knowledge." Thus, truth is relative, and a single truth is not attainable. What is true for one participant or group may not be true for another participant or group. Regardless of the approach to research—critical or not—the realities of power, and relatedly, access and opportunity, remain.

Qualitative researchers understand that reality is "holistic, multidimensional, and ever-changing; it is not a single, fixed, objective phenomenon waiting to be discovered, observed, and measured as in quantitative research" (Merriam & Tisdell, 2015, p. 242). That under study in qualitative research, people's realities through their perceptions and experiences, is also not fixed or objective. Specific to this notion, Merriam and Tisdell (2015) note "what is being investigated are people's constructions of reality—how they understand the world. And just as there will be multiple accounts of eyewitnesses to a crime, so too there will be multiple constructions of how people have experienced a particular phenomenon, how they have made meaning of their lives, or how they have come to understand certain processes" (p. 243).

The goals of qualitative approaches include to understand, to describe, to interpret, to empower, to deconstruct, to problematize, to question, to interrupt (Merriam & Tisdell, 2015). Thus, instead of a "capital T," objective truth—and predicting, testing, and controlling—qualitative researchers are after something else. And that something else, according to Wolcott (as cited in Merriam & Tisdell, 2015), "is understanding" (p. 240). That is, we are after the multiple "lower case ts" with all of their messiness and pluralities.

Generalizability

Another concept that introductory qualitative students struggle with is generalizability. They often come to class with ideas that suggest that the only research that is worth conducting is research that can be generalized to people outside of the sample. When I tell them that the intent of qualitative research is to better understand the particular, and that qualitative work is not meant to be generalizable—they often ask, "Well, then, why would anyone conduct a qualitative study?"

This is a tough one both for me to explain and for students to understand. I ask them—"Have you read any quantitative studies that suggested that the findings are true for everyone?" Really, in my opinion, with any approach to research, one can only generalize to their own data—which is exactly what qualitative studies do. That is, as researchers, we can only discuss, interrogate, and project ideas from the data that we have collected and analyzed. With a qualitative study, however, researchers typically articulate the context and participant sample such that if a reader were to believe they had a similar problem, context, and population, they may well apply similar techniques and ask similar research questions. This then, would be one study that can be added to the literature to better inform our understanding of the whole. To illustrate this point about generalizability, I like to use a couple of analogies. Think of a stone mason building a brick wall, or puzzle that has yet to be assembled. Each study, whether it is qualitative or quantitative or mixed methods, participatory action research, or something else, is one brick—and the wall the bricks create is our understanding of a particular topic. Likewise, each study is a separate, individual puzzle piece, which helps to complete the puzzle. The puzzle and the picture it creates represent our understanding of a particular topic. Any study, whatever the method, is just one piece of a larger body of knowledge—it is not *the* knowledge.

Merriam and Tisdell (2015) note that the challenges that students new to qualitative methods experience around generalizability are nothing new. They go on to note that "part of the difficulty lies in thinking of generalizability in the same way as do investigators using experimental or correlational designs" (p. 253). And, as I noted above, even in these types of approaches to research, "generalizations are made within specified levels of confidence" (Merriam & Tisdell, 2015, p. 253).

With a goal of "understanding" and not "generalizing," there is much to be learned from qualitative research. Whether or not the findings from a qualitative study could also apply to another similar context is up to the reader to decide. Citing Lincoln and Guba, Merriam and Tisdell (2015) state:

> the notion of "transferability," in which "the burden of proof lies less with the original investigator than with the person seeking to make an application elsewhere. The original inquirer cannot know the sites to which transferability might be sought, but the appliers can and do." The investigator needs to provide "sufficient descriptive data" to make transferability possible. (p. 254)

Thus, "validity" has traditionally been understood by qualitative researchers as "credibility." Because qualitative researchers will "never capture an objective 'truth' or 'reality,' the field has established a variety of strategies to increase the credibility or the "correspondence between research and the real world" (Wolcott as cited in Merriam & Tisdell, 2015, p. 244). These include, but are not limited to, triangulation, member checks, peer debriefing, examining positionality, creating an audit trail, and prolonged engagement in the setting or research context. (See Merriam & Tisdell, 2015, chapter 9 for a detailed examination of strategies to bolster credibility in qualitative research.)

The matter of generalizability in qualitative research, whether "the extent to which a study's findings apply to other situations" (Merriam & Tisdell, 2015, p. 256) is up to the reader and the people in those other situations. However, it is the researcher's responsibility to articulate the context, participants, and methods in sufficient detail such that another researcher may apply similar methods in a similar context. This is what is referred to as rich, thick description—or "a highly descriptive, detailed presentation of the setting and in particular, the findings of the study" (Merriam & Tisdell, 2015, p. 257).

Positionality

Another area where students struggle is with "positionality," or how one, as the researcher, is positioned and how they are drawn to their research interests. For many students, they have never been asked to think deeply about why they want to study what they want to study. This can be an emotional process. Regardless, these interests should be interrogated. It is not as though we pick up research interests from the super market or that they drop from the sky. They come from somewhere, and that somewhere is connected to our identities, histories, and experiences.

Positionality is not just a list of the identities that define us but a reflection of those identities, the power dynamics that have helped to shape those identities, as well as a consideration of why is this the right study for me? Why do I want to study this? Why is now the right time to conduct this study? (e.g., Why this? Why me? Why now?) (see Patel, 2015). Other critical questions students should attend to when thinking about how they personally connect to their research interests are What am I going to do with this research? Who benefits? How does who I am influence the claims I make on the data? How does who I am influence the research process? What changes will come about from the research?

With all of this come questions about qualitative research processes, the researcher as instrument, and about bias. Merriam and Tisdell (2015) offer a list of questions, including the following, which I am asked some version of every semester: "If the researcher is the primary instrument for data collection and analysis, how can we be sure the researcher is a valid and reliable instrument? Isn't the researcher biased and just finding out what he or she expects to find? Don't people often lie to field researchers? If somebody else did this study, would they get the same results?" (p. 241).

Qualitative researchers attend to bias in several ways; a solid first step is articulating their positionality as this helps to get at the questions above about validity and reliability and expectations. To the questions about the truthfulness of a participant's responses, it is not our place as researchers to judge a participant's responses. After all, one person's truth is different from the next person's truth. And yes, two researchers will have different results. This is the nature of qualitative work.

Ambiguity

Another area that I find where students struggle is with the ambiguity that is inherent in qualitative research, that is, the lack of clear delineations between approaches and the overlap in the types of analytic strategies used in different approaches. Students' struggles with this seems to stem from two primary areas. The first is that of the researcher as the human instrument—and that as such, the researcher is in charge of how they design and conduct the work. The second is the overlap between the different approaches (or "traditions" as Cresswell refers to them). That is, students find it challenging to decipher between a phenomenological study and an interpretivist study—particularly as a researcher may use similar or identical data collection methods and analytic procedures in either approach.

The researcher as instrument is an important component of qualitative research and one that amplifies the importance of a researcher's positionality. Because the researcher is responsible for analyzing/coding the data, those data will undoubtedly be analyzed through the researcher's "lenses," that is, the ways the researcher views and understands the world, the ways they interpret experiences, as well as their histories and identities. This causes students to ask questions about bias and how this will surely impact the data. Yes. It will. However, there are many ways in qualitative research that the researcher can work to establish the "validity" of the data (not objectivity) and ensure, as much as it is possible, that they take all necessary steps to reflect the participants' authentic experiences and perceptions. These steps may include a variety of techniques including bracketing, memoing, and reflexive journaling, as well as other strategies to establish trustworthiness such as member checking and peer debriefing. Merriam and Tisdell (2015) provide a useful list of ways to reinforce "validity" and "reliability" in qualitative research, see p. 259.

Students also get frustrated with the overlap of the methodological approaches in the various "traditions" in qualitative research. Specifically, one may use similar coding techniques in a case study and in an interpretivist study, as they might use in a phenomenological study. In their efforts to do it "right," students want to see distinct lines between the "traditions," and they simply do not exist. Rather, it is up to the researcher to clearly articulate why their study is phenomenological, a case study, an interpretivist study, or something else. The coding strategies, the means of establishing trustworthiness, and the means of increasing rigor and validity may be very similar in any of those studies. Embrace the ambiguity, I say. And convince your readers that the finding of your study are "worth paying attention to" (Lincoln & Guba, 1985, p. 290) with the proper criteria for such an approach.

Final Thoughts

Qualitative research can be difficult for students who have been exposed only to quantitative research to fully embrace, especially in the beginning. However, I do believe that most of the students in my classes come away with a different and broader understanding of research, and appreciate the value of qualitative work. One of the things I say in my classes is "If you learn nothing else from me, learn this. Your research questions will guide your methodology, not the other way around." So, if qualitative research methods speak to you and you think you might want to apply them in your dissertation work, be sure to ask appropriate research questions.

A final note about qualitative software. Students typically want to know about coding software—and how it can lighten their load in terms of analysis. Qualitative analyses are inductive and are based on the researcher's knowledge of the field and the context. Moreover, as analyses are individualistic (e.g., different researchers will see different things in the data), it is impossible for a computer program to "code" the data intuitively. These programs, such as NVivo, ATLAS.ti, Dedoose, and others, are good storage facilities for your data—which may make it easier to keep track of and organize. Further, if a researcher is after understanding how many times a word or phrase is said, these programs can calculate that and create some related graphics. However, the researcher is still responsible for "coding" the data.

References

Lincoln, Y. S., & Guba, E. G. (1985). *Naturalistic inquiry*. New York, NY: Sage.

Merriam, S. B., & Tisdell, E. J. (2015). *Qualitative research: A guide to design and implementation*. Hoboken, NJ: John Wiley & Sons.

Patel, L. (2015). *Decolonizing educational research: From ownership to answerability*. New York, NY: Routledge.

Chapter 11
Youth Participatory Action Research: The Nuts and Bolts as well as the Roses and Thorns

Shiv R. Desai

Abstract Youth Participatory Action Research (YPAR) challenges traditional social science research because it teaches young people how to inquire about complex power relations, histories of struggle, and the consequences of oppression directly related to their lives. More significantly, YPAR provides marginalized youth with an opportunity to exercise their agency by being civically engaged, developing their critical consciousness, and learning how to advocate for oppressed communities. The purpose of this chapter is to do the following: (1) discuss the historical origins of YPAR and demonstrate how it is part of Indigenous/decolonizing methodological traditions, (2) provide key characteristics of YPAR and how it has been utilized in the field, (3) explain the central critiques of YPAR, and (4) provide key significant insights and challenges from my own YPAR study with system-involved youth.

Introduction

Caraballo, Lozenski, Lyiscott, and Morrell (2017) explain how Youth Participatory Action Research (YPAR) is "a critical research methodology that carries specific epistemological commitments toward reframing who is 'allowed' to conduct and disseminate education research with/about youth in actionable ways" (p. 313). Put simply, YPAR challenges traditional social science research because it teaches young people how to inquire about complex power relations, histories of struggle, and the consequences of oppression directly related to their lives (Cammarota & Fine, 2010; Rodríguez & Brown, 2009). Youth are involved in all aspects of the

S. R. Desai (✉)
University of New Mexico, Albuquerque, NM, USA
e-mail: sdesai@unm.edu

© The Author(s) 2019
K. K. Strunk, L. A. Locke (eds.), *Research Methods for Social Justice and Equity in Education*, https://doi.org/10.1007/978-3-030-05900-2_11

research cycle: from formulating research questions to collecting and analyzing data to presenting findings and offering key recommendations that lead to social action and meaningful change (Mirra, Garcia, & Morrell, 2016). More significantly, YPAR provides marginalized youth with an opportunity to exercise their agency by being civically engaged, developing their critical consciousness, and learning how to advocate for oppressed communities (Dolan, Lin, & Christens, 2005; Irizarry, 2011; Johnson et al., 2017).

In this chapter, I first discuss the historical origins of YPAR and how it is part of Indigenous/decolonizing methodological traditions. Next, I provide key characteristics of YPAR. Third, I discuss how YPAR has been utilized in the field. Afterward, I discuss central critiques of YPAR. I conclude by providing some significant insights and challenges from my own YPAR study with system-involved youth.

Historical Context of YPAR

YPAR can be described as an ethnographically based inquiry process to challenge and transform traditional power structures that has its roots in Participatory Action Research (PAR) (Fals Borda & Rahman, 1991). Since the 1970s, PAR has been employed in Latin America. Fals Borda and Rahman (1991) define PAR as an "experiential methodology" because it countervails power for the "poor, oppressed and exploited groups and social classes" (p. 121). More importantly, from the very beginning, there is grassroots participation on the design and implementation of research. PAR is explicit and unapologetic in its goal of social justice and social transformation.

Conversely, PAR can also be traced to Paulo Freire's pivotal work on praxis, critical pedagogy, and critical consciousness (Cammarota & Fine, 2010; McIntyre, 2000; Morrell, 2004), which raised important questions concerning how to empower the poor. Lastly, other scholars trace the origins of PAR to various Indigenous communities in Africa, Asia, Latin America, and South Pacific (Caraballo et al., 2017; Mirra et al., 2016). In this fashion, PAR acknowledges and celebrates Indigenous knowledge as well as a process that engages in decolonization.

YPAR builds on PAR in that it seeks to empower the oppressed, challenge social injustices, and helps young people connect to decolonial knowledge(s). Furthermore, PAR and YPAR forefront the voices of participants throughout the research investigation and engage in social justice-oriented group work by prioritizing the well-being of youth and their communities (Bautista, Bertrand, Morrell, Scorza, & Matthews, 2003). Additionally, both help participants interrogate essential issues that are impacting their lives and teach them how to advocate for change. Thus, both PAR and YPAR help "to demystify and deconstruct power structures, [and] then transform them in order to construct a new reality, [wherein] critical agency is fostered" (Caraballo et al., 2017, p. 316). Fundamentally, PAR and YPAR provide the necessary tools for the oppressed to engage in social action and create social change within their communities.

Decolonizing Methodology

YPAR embraces and advocates for a *methodology of the oppressed* (Sandoval, 2000) where research serves the marginalized and allows them to tell their stories in their own words. In addition, YPAR complements Indigenous/decolonizing methodologies (Denzin & Lincoln, 2008; Smith, 1999) because it is concerned with presenting alternative knowledges, highlighting subjugated knowledge, and concerns itself with liberatory practices by empowering those who have been denigrated by Western research. More importantly, researchers who utilize YPAR are well aware of how Western research has been utilized to dehumanize colonized communities.

As a result, YPAR researchers are interested in creating innovative approaches to methodology that presents youth participants in authentic ways that preserve their ways of being and demonstrate how their epistemologies actually help to sustain them in the face of oppression. Moreover, this novel form of research is similar to Indigenous/decolonizing methodologies in that it assists in correcting past wrongs, directly challenges colonization, and forefronts the lived experiences of the oppressed. Furthermore, this revolutionary approach speaks to oppressed/colonized people because it is explicitly political, offers a reflexive discourse, and stresses subversive, multivoiced participatory methodology (Denzin & Lincoln, 2011). Last but not least, it is committed to liberatory and emancipatory inquiry for social justice purposes.

Key Principles of YPAR

McIntyre (2000) and Rodríguez and Brown (2009) have developed the following three principles of YPAR: (1) the collective investigation of a problem that directly addresses the needs of youth involved, (2) the reliance on marginalized youth knowledge that validates and incorporates their lived experiences, and (3) the desire to take collective action to improve the lives of oppressed youth. Caraballo et al. (2017) add that YPAR has four distinct entry points: (1) academic learning and literacies, (2) cultural and critical epistemological research, (3) youth development and leadership, and (4) youth organizing and civic engagement.

Academic learning and literacies focus on how YPAR has been utilized to foster academic literacies, disciplines, and learning in a way that is transformative and leads to academic enrichment (Bautista et al., 2003; Mirra, Filipiak, & Garcia, 2015; Morrell, 2004). Cultural and critical epistemological research demonstrates how YPAR helps youth to connect with cultural knowledge, cultural identity, and reclaiming lost knowledge (Alberto, Cerecer, Cahill, & Bradley, 2011; Cammarota & Romero, 2009; Johnston-Goodstar, 2013; Torre, 2009). Youth development and leadership articulate how YPAR supports youth to develop socially and emotionally through their research as well as become leaders within their community or school

(Grace & Langhout, 2014; Kirshner & Ginwright, 2012). Lastly, youth organizing and civic engagement illustrate how YPAR assists in community organizing, helps influence policy, and fosters youth advocacy (Foster-Fishman, Law, Lichty, & Aoun, 2010; Ginwright & Cammarota, 2007; Kornbluh, Ozer, Allen, & Kirshner, 2015).

YPAR in the Field

One of the first studies to document YPAR was conducted in conjunction with photovoice to examine the violence youth experienced within their communities (McIntyre, 2000). Furthermore, McIntyre contends that one of the chief benefits of YPAR is the power of "engaging in a process that positions youth as agents of inquiry and as 'experts' about their own lives" (p. 126). Henceforth, it is not surprising that several scholars have employed YPAR to assist youth, both in and out of school, in order to address a variety of issues such as community violence, school segregation, the prison-industrial complex, juvenile justice, and educational inequity (Akom, Cammarota, & Ginwright, 2008; Alberto et al., 2011; Cammarota & Romero, 2009; Desai & Abeita, 2017; Fine, 2009; Ginwright, 2007; Grace & Langhout, 2014; Yang, 2009). Cammarota and Romero (2009) present three student cases that demonstrate how YPAR can be used as a bridge between the classroom and students' realities. Cerecer, Cahill, and Bradley (2013) had youth conduct interviews, create a video-docudrama, and utilize social media such as a blog to disseminate their findings on undocumented immigrants. Yang (2009) notes how his YPAR study helped high school students gain mathematical knowledge and concepts by deconstructing school accountability report cards. Other scholars have utilized youth culture such as hip-hop and spoken word poetry to help youth articulate the problems they see in their communities (Rodríguez & Brown, 2009). Furthermore, YPAR has also been utilized to reclaim cultural knowledge and revitalize lost traditions (Conrad, 2015; Foster-Fishman et al., 2010; Irizarry, 2011). Lastly, in all of these studies, youth present their findings to various public and academic communities in the hopes of affecting and creating more socially just policies.

Tensions Within YPAR

Caraballo et al. (2017) have identified several tensions in YPAR, such as the following: projects being co-opted by mandates, a lack of continuity, internal politics, scheduling issues, and conflicting values among facilitators. The politics and complexity of maintaining relationships with community members and organizations are of particular concern due to turnover (Irizarry, 2009). Other YPAR researchers have noted the tensions associated with facilitators and youth in regard to knowing when to "step in" versus "step out" (Winn & Winn, 2016, p. 116). On the one hand, YPAR is youth driven, and youth voice should be privileged; on the other hand, youth still need guidance and assistance in the completion of projects and maintaining project goals. In addition, the tedious process of "grinding" (i.e., data analysis and data interpretation) (Mirra et al., 2016) is not always fun and can be taxing. Consequently, youth may not always be engaged in this process. Lastly, scholars warn that YPAR's liberatory framework, which has "the power to support meaningful social and political change, often lose their radical capacity as they are co-opted or absorbed into the mainstream" (Caraballo et al., 2017, p. 329). This idea translates to how researchers must maintain fidelity to the principles of YPAR.

Leaders Organizing 2 Unite & Decriminalize

Now that I have provided the history of YPAR and how it has been utilized in the field, I will now describe the YPAR project I have conducted. This example serves as a case study of the successes and challenges of maintaining an ongoing YPAR project.

Over the last three years, I have worked with Leaders Organizing 2 Unite & Decriminalize (LOUD) members—who comprise both formerly incarcerated and youth on probation and allies—who have worked toward creating a more socially just and humanizing criminal justice system through YPAR. Throughout this process, youth have found their voice and have been able to speak out and raise awareness on critical issues that needed reform within the juvenile justice system (JJS) by speaking directly with key decision-makers and shaping public policy.

Located in a major urban city in the Southwest, LOUD is a partnership between a local grassroots community organization and the local Juvenile Detention Alternative Initiative (JDAI), which is housed within the local JJS. The former helps youth mobilize regarding issues such as racial justice, health, economic, and education equity. It also provides a platform to engage these issues through civic engagement. The latter is a model site for JDAI, which is sponsored by the Annie E. Casey Foundation. As a model site, other JJS sites from the nation and around the world visit to learn how to reduce juvenile incarceration rates.

At the time of this study, I was working with six Latinas and three Latinos, one African American male, and one Diné female. Additionally, half of the members self-identified as queer. The ages of the LOUD members ranged from 15 to 20 years, and educationally, they ranged from a high school freshman to a first-year college student. Overall, members joined LOUD because they were interested in sharing their experiences of being incarcerated in order to advocate for change and reform within the JJS.

It is important to note that for formerly incarcerated youth, their freedom hovers on a tightrope. Over the course of three years, we had members placed in residential treatment programs for alleged drug violations, who were then isolated from the outside world. We had some members who went on the "run" (absconding from their probation) because of home instability, not having shelter, or alleged violations. Fortunately, no member has had to go to a youth prison, but a few did have detention holds (placed in the detention center) on them (from two days to two weeks). These were strong, painful reminders of how easily freedom can be taken away, and how members may be removed from their families, their communities, their schools, and of course from this study at any time. New members were welcome to join anytime during the course of the study.

Major Successes of LOUD

Conceivably, the greatest success of LOUD has been the ability to help youth become system free and find their voice, which ultimately enabled them to become the best advocates for juvenile justice reform since they had firsthand knowledge. Part of this advocacy came via the partnership with the local JDAI that wanted system-involved youth to participate in their various steering committees such as Reducing Racial and Ethnic Disparities (RRED). They also were invited to help reshape the state Probation Agreement. As a result of LOUD youth participation, the revised state Probation Agreement moved away from a punitive instrument to a more individualized instrument that focuses on positive youth development. More importantly, LOUD youth conducted approximately 120 surveys that were given to system-involved youth, which examined their experiences at different points in the JJS: court hearings, detention center, prison, residential treatment programs, and/or probation. Lastly, LOUD youth conducted four focus group interviews inside the detention center and three focus group interviews with Specialty Court programs. This research is unparalleled because I am not aware of youth being allowed to conduct research in incarceration facilities. While I assisted LOUD youth in each step along with another facilitator, what is important to highlight is the fact that LOUD youth were responsible for developing the survey and focus group questions, analyzing the data, and providing recommendations.

These findings were shared with the local JDAI and their various steering committees. In addition, LOUD youth presented our research during various national site visits to the local JDAI. LOUD youth even spoke at the state capital to lobby for juvenile justice reform; two of them spoke directly with the Lieutenant Governor on the issues youth face in the state. Additionally, they have presented our work at national education conferences. Furthermore, LOUD youth have also demonstrated academic success. Nearly 95 percent of LOUD youth graduated from high school or obtained their General Education Development (GED). Thus, LOUD has underscored the findings in the field: (1) developing cultural identity, critical consciousness, and (re)connecting to cultural knowledge; (2) developing youth advocacy, activism, and civic engagement; (3) developing positive youth development and leadership; and (4) developing academic and college-going skills.

Key Challenges in LOUD

While LOUD has enjoyed tremendous success, there have also been some tough challenges. The first challenge was developing trust. Given the makeup of LOUD, youth were apprehensive of the adult facilitators at first. For many system-involved youths, they have witnessed adults abuse their power and violate their trust. Therefore, "brokering relationships" (Mirra et al., 2015, p. 50) was especially important as LOUD first got started. YPAR was secondary to youth getting to know adult facilitators and solidifying the culture of the group, which was learning how to advocate, how to communicate during steering committee meetings, and teasing out the various issues of the JJS. Similar to L. T. Winn and Winn (2016), in the first and second years, the adult facilitators were constantly trying to find a balance of when to "step in" versus "step out." YPAR was a novel approach to the youth, and they were also trying to figure out what it meant. The third challenge was the transiency of the participants. Since we were working with system-involved youth, over the years, we had youth not able to attend or continue with the program because they were placed on detention holds, they were sent to residential treatment programs for drug treatment, and other youth stopped participating because they were absconding. However, we were fortunate that youth always came back, even if briefly. The next main challenge was getting youth to engage in the "grind" (Mirra et al., 2016), which meant having youth analyze the data and find key themes. They were always excited and ready to take the lead when time came to perform the focus group interviews. However, they were less enthusiastic when time came to analyze the data since coding data can be tedious.

Sustainability was one of the most significant challenges. After the second year of LOUD, we found out that the community organization where LOUD was housed was shutting down due to financial reasons. This issue caused a major rupture because for a few months we struggled to find a new community organization that would sponsor us. Once we found a new community partner, new roles had to be adjusted. Moreover, it was difficult to obtain support for LOUD because the community organization had their own set of programs. Simultaneously, the community-based co-facilitator was leaving to pursue a graduate degree. This news was devastating to LOUD members who had bonded with her. She was an outstanding, incredible advocate for them and worked tirelessly to ensure they had opportunities to influence JJS policies. As all of this was occurring, we also found out that funding for her position would be cut. This update was damaging because the community-based facilitator served as a pseudosocial worker. She would help youth find resources such as shelter, food assistance, attend probation meetings and/or court hearings, and help youth navigate different life obstacles. I was able to perform many of these duties, but after the second year, I was fortunate to have a new addition to my family—a baby girl who was born a micro-preemie. Since she was born so early, she faced health challenges, and my priorities shifted. Life-changing events are something that needs to be added to the literature as an important issue that contributes to YPAR success or not.

Finally, the last key issue missing from the literature that must be considered is how group dynamics might change. While LOUD members had co-constructed community agreements, it did not always mean they were followed. Therefore, it is important to continue to revisit community expectations and remind youth of the culture that is being established and nurtured. Additionally, one issue that we did not take into account was how social media can impact group dynamics. For instance, sometimes what members posted affected the group and led to serious disagreements. In other cases, an argument escalated on social media, which resulted in youth saying hurtful words to each other. Ultimately, these arguments would infiltrate the group, and adult facilitators would have to settle the disputes, which at times, impacted the group and project goals. Therefore, it is vital for adult facilitators to be aware of group dynamics and have in place protocols on how to handle youth conflict.

Conclusion

Throughout this chapter, I have discussed the emancipatory framework of YPAR, which is summarized as follows:

> Grounded in its catalytic nature, we propose that a YPAR critical-epistemological approach leads to the coconstruction of critical knowledges that can, in turn, reframe the question of what counts as knowledge and research, and what constitutes action, in education research and scholarship. Such a critical-epistemological framework must be grounded in the contexts of inequality in which it is to be employed, and developed in juxtaposition to the theoretical and methodological shifts of our time. (Caraballo et al., 2017, p. 330)

As stated above, YPAR fundamentally changes the paradigm of what counts as knowledge and research, how to utilize research to create social action or change, and how research should be a co-endeavor between researchers and facilitators. Furthermore, I have discussed how YPAR projects have demonstrated great promise in promoting youth activism and civic engagement, leadership, critical consciousness, and academic achievement. Most importantly, I have shown how regardless of activities with students or research topics addressed in YPAR, what unites YPAR scholars is a strong commitment to marginalized students and empowering them to seek solutions on the issues that most impact their daily lives. Furthermore, there is a deep commitment to developing authentic, caring relationships with participants so that YPAR scholars are as much mentors as they are educators. Finally, YPAR researchers understand the gravity of developing and fostering youth agency. Youth are well-respected collaborators in this process and are given the responsibility to help create social change. Perhaps, the most important aspect of YPAR "is the realization of the full humanity of young people" and embracing the "potential in all students by offering them opportunities to name, explore, and analyze their experiences...[and they are the] experts of their own lives" (Mirra et al., 2016, p. 5).

Suggested Readings

Caraballo, L., Lozenski, B. D., Lyiscott, J. J., & Morrell, E. (2017). YPAR and criti-cal epistemologies: Rethinking education research. *Review of Research in Education, 41*(1), 311–336.

This article is the most recent literature of YPAR in the field of education. It dis-cusses the key elements of YPAR and how it can be utilized to fundamentally change research paradigms.

Cammarota, J., & Fine, M. (2010). *Revolutionizing education: Youth participatory action research in motion* (J. Cammarota & M. Fine, Eds.). New York, NY: Routledge; Taylor and Francis Group.

This edited book provides a unique overview of several YPAR projects found throughout the country. It offers different frameworks utilized within YPAR and bridges theory and practice by bringing together youth participants and scholars in the field.

Mirra, N., Garcia, A., & Morrell, E. (2016). *Doing participatory action research: Transforming inquiry with researchers, educators and students*. New York, NY: Routledge; Taylor and Francis Group.

This book offers an unprecedented, in-depth exploration of the Council of Youth Research, which is one of the longest running YPAR programs. The book also pro-vides a step-by-step guidance on how to successfully create a YPAR project.

References

Akom, A. A., Cammarota, J., & Ginwright, S. A. (2008). Youthtopias: Towards a new paradigm of critical youth studies. *Youth Media Reporter, 2*(1), 108–129.

Alberto, D., Cerecer, Q., Cahill, C., & Bradley, M. (2011). Resist this! Embodying the contradic-tory positions and collective possibilities of transformative resistance. *International Journal of Qualitative Studies in Education, 24*(5), 587–593. https://doi.org/10.1080/09518398.2011.600269

Bautista, M. A., Bertrand, M., Morrell, E., Scorza, D., & Matthews, C. (2003). Participatory action research and city youth: Methodological insights from the Council of Youth Research. *Teachers College Record, 115*(10), 1–23.

Cammarota, J., & Fine, M. (Eds.). (2010). *Revolutionizing education: Youth participatory action research in motion*. New York, NY: Routledge.

Cammarota, J., & Romero, A. F. (2009). A social justice epistemology and pedagogy for Latina/o students: Transforming public education with participatory action research. *New Directions for Youth Development, 2009*(123), 53–65. https://doi.org/10.1002/yd.314

Caraballo, L., Lozenski, B. D., Lyiscott, J. J., & Morrell, E. (2017). YPAR and critical epistemolo-gies: Rethinking education research. *Review of Research in Education, 41*(1), 311–336. https://doi.org/10.3102/0091732X16686948

Cerecer, D. A., Cahill, C., & Bradley, M. (2013). Toward a critical youth policy praxis: Critical youth studies and participatory action research. *Theory Into Practice, 52*(3), 216–223. https://doi.org/10.1080/00405841.2013.804316

Conrad, D. (2015). Education and social innovation: The youth uncensored project—A case study of youth participatory research and cultural democracy in action. *Canadian Journal of Education, 38*(1), 1–25.

Denzin, N. K., & Lincoln, Y. S. (2008). Introduction: Critical methodologies and indigenous inquiry. In L. T. Denzin, K. Norman, & Y. S. Lincoln (Eds.), *Handbook of critical and indigenous methodologies* (pp. 1–20). Thousand Oaks, CA: SAGE Publications. https://doi.org/10.1177/0741713609350411

Denzin, N. K., & Lincoln, Y. S. (2011). *The SAGE handbook of qualitative research* (4th ed.). Thousand Oaks, CA: SAGE Publications.

Desai, S. R., & Abeita, A. (2017). Breaking the cycle of incarceration: A young black male's journey from probation to self-advocacy. *Journal of Urban Learning, Teaching & Research, 13*, 45–52.

Dolan, T., Lin, C., & Christens, B. D. (2005). Combining youth organizing and youth participatory action research to strengthen student voice in education reform. *National Society for the Study of Education, 114*(1), 153–170.

Fals Borda, O., & Rahman, M. A. (1991). *Action and knowledge: Breaking the monopoly with participatory action research*. New York, NY: Apex.

Fine, M. (2009). Postcards from metro America: Reflections on youth participatory action research for urban justice. *Urban Review, 41*(1), 1–6. https://doi.org/10.1007/s11256-008-0099-5

Foster-Fishman, P. G., Law, K. M., Lichty, L. F., & Aoun, C. (2010). Youth ReACT for social change: A method for youth participatory action research. *American Journal of Community Psychology, 46*(1), 67–83. https://doi.org/10.1007/s10464-010-9316-y

Ginwright, S. A. (2007). Black youth activism and the role of critical social capital in Black community organizations. *American Behavioral Scientist, 51*(3), 403–418. https://doi.org/10.1177/0002764207306068

Ginwright, S. A., & Cammarota, J. (2007). Youth activism in the urban community: Learning critical civic praxis within community organizations. *International Journal of Qualitative Studies in Education, 20*(6), 693–710. https://doi.org/10.1080/09518390701630833

Grace, S., & Langhout, R. D. (2014). Questioning our questions: Assessing question asking practices to evaluate a yPAR Program. *Urban Review, 46*(4), 703–724. https://doi.org/10.1007/s11256-014-0279-4

Irizarry, J. G. (2009). Reinvigorating multicultural education through youth participatory action research. *Multicultural Perspectives, 11*(4), 194–199. https://doi.org/10.1080/15210960903445905

Irizarry, J. G. (2011). Buscando la libertad: Latino youths in search of freedom in school. *Democracy & Education, 19*(1), 1–10.

Johnson, K. C., Drew, C., Lin, J., Dobbins, S., Ozer, E., & Auerswald, C. (2017). "I learned that we matter"—Reflections on strategies to engage formerly homeless young adults in youth participatory action research. *Journal of Adolescent Health, 60*(2), S29–S30. https://doi.org/10.1016/j.jadohealth.2016.10.075

Johnston-Goodstar, K. (2013). Indigenous youth participatory action research: Re-visioning social justice for social work with indigenous youths. *Social Work, 58*(4), 314–320. https://doi.org/10.1093/sw/swt036

Kirshner, B., & Ginwright, S. A. (2012). Youth organizing as a developmental context for African American and Latino adolescents. *Child Development Perspectives, 6*(3), 288–294. https://doi.org/10.1111/j.1750-8606.2012.00243.x

Kornbluh, M., Ozer, E. J., Allen, C. D., & Kirshner, B. (2015). Youth participatory action research as an approach to sociopolitical development and the new academic standards: Considerations for educators. *Urban Review, 47*(5), 868–892. https://doi.org/10.1007/s11256-015-0337-6

McIntyre, A. (2000). Constructing meaning about violence, school, and community: Participatory action research with urban youth. *The Urban Review, 32*(2), 123–154. https://doi.org/10.102 3/A:1005181731698

Mirra, N., Filipiak, D., & Garcia, A. (2015). Revolutionizing inquiry in urban English classrooms: Pursuing voice and justice through youth participatory action research. *English Journal, 105*(2), 49–57.

Mirra, N., Garcia, A., & Morrell, E. (2016). *Doing participatory action research: Transforming inquiry with researchers, educators and students.* New York, NY: Routledge.

Morrell, E. (2004). *Becoming critical researchers: Literacy and empowerment for urban youth.* New York, NY: Peter Lang Publishing.

Rodríguez, L. F., & Brown, T. M. (2009). From voice to agency: Guiding principles for participatory action research with youth. *New Directions for Youth Development, 2009*(123), 19–34. https://doi.org/10.1002/yd.312

Sandoval, C. (2000). *Methodology of the oppressed.* Minneapolis, MN: University of Minneapolis Press.

Smith, L. T. (1999). *Decolonizing methodologies: Research and indigenous peoples.* London, UK: Zed Books.

Torre, M. E. (2009). Participatory action research and critical race theory: Fueling spaces for nos-otras to research. *The Urban Review, 41*(1), 106–120. https://doi.org/10.1007/s11256-008-0097-7

Winn, L. T., & Winn, M. T. (2016). "We want this to be owned by you": The promise and perils of youth participatory action research. In S. Greene, K. J. Burke, & M. K. McKenna (Eds.), *Youth voices, public spaces, and civic engagement* (pp. 111–130). New York: Routledge.

Yang, K. W. (2009). Mathematics, critical literacy, and youth participatory action research. *New Directions for Youth Development, 2009*(123), 99–118. https://doi.org/10.1002/yd.317

Chapter 12
Advancing Social Justice with Policy Discourse Analysis

Elizabeth J. Allan and Aaron R. Tolbert

Abstract Policy discourse analysis (PDA) draws from critical and poststructural theories to provide researchers with an approach to identifying dominant discourses shaping policy problems and solutions. Such analyses reveal how discourse contributes to shaping subject positions, or roles, with implications for practice. This chapter defines PDA, describes the conceptual principles of the approach, and details the research methods for the implementation of a PDA study. Examples of studies employing PDA are shared to illustrate the utility of the approach.

Policy analysis offers an avenue for understanding the intractability of some equity and social justice challenges. However, conventional methods of policy analysis may be limited by dominant discourses that shape policy problems and may even reinforce the very problems they seek to alleviate. For example, it has been many decades since the passage of key civil rights laws and gender equity policy (e.g., Title IX) with implications for educational institutions. While progress has been made since these landmark decisions, the pace of change can seem slow considering what is at stake. Attaining socially just and equitable practices and inclusive climates in schools, colleges, and universities is paramount to their missions, yet this goal remains elusive, and efforts to roll back current gains continue to be a reality. Drawing on understandings of discourse and power, alternate approaches to policy analysis emerge providing insights that have the potential to impact practice. In this chapter, we review a methodology and methods that provide tools for rethinking and unthinking policy problems and policy solutions in the pursuit of social justice.

E. J. Allan (✉)
University of Maine, Orono, ME, USA
e-mail: elizabeth.allan@maine.edu

A. R. Tolbert
SUNY Schenectady County Community College, Schenectady, NY, USA
e-mail: tolberar@sunysccc.edu

© The Author(s) 2019
K. K. Strunk, L. A. Locke (eds.), *Research Methods for Social Justice and Equity in Education*, https://doi.org/10.1007/978-3-030-05900-2_12

Discourse

Discourse is a term often used but without a simple definition. Considered broadly, discourse refers to both spoken and written language use, and the study of discourse (discourse analysis) includes the examination of both talk and text and its relationship to the social context in which it is produced. For our purposes, discourses are socially constructed constellations of words and images that both reflect and contribute to shaping particular realities.

Rather than understanding language and discourse as static entities that can stand in isolation and be investigated as such (e.g., a stretch of text or collection of words on paper), poststructuralist thinkers contend that language and discourses are dynamic sites for the construction of meaning (Välimaa & Hoffman, 2008; van Dijk, 2008). Discourses are contingent upon historical context and power dynamics shaping the sociopolitical landscape. Yet, from a poststructural perspective, discourses not only reflect culture, they also actively produce it. However, as individual actors take up discourses to interpret the world around them, dominant discourses are most likely to be drawn upon because they tend to eclipse counter-discourses that can provide alternate views or perspectives. For instance, if a focus on reducing sexual assault on campus is undergirded by a dominant discourse of femininity, the problem of campus safety is often articulated as a "woman's issue" where women are framed as "vulnerable to assault" and in need of protection. In this framing, blue light systems, self-defense training, and "cover your cup" stories may be the predominant policy responses by postsecondary institutions. By drawing on a dominant discourse of femininity, even well-intentioned leaders may only focus on policy solutions that may help women feel more safe but rarely address root causes or conditions producing the violence. In contrast, if policy problems and solutions are framed through a counter-discourse that highlights the social construction of violent masculinity, the proposed solutions would more likely focus on strategies to help students critically analyze gender norms, build skills for clear communication about consent, and develop skills for bystander intervention in potential sexual assault scenarios that involve acquaintances. A counter-discourse that focuses on answering how good young men grow to become young adult assailants may never surface when the problem of campus safety is framed within dominant discourses.

Thus, from a poststructural perspective, discourse produces the ideological and epistemic framing of issues and therefore shapes the thinking and action of actors; thus, this productive power, not a Marxian hegemonic power, is the focus. This occurs as dominant discourses are taken up in the construction of new ideas, practices, and policies. Further, and especially important to thinking about policy issues, poststructural theory contends that discourse is the place "where our sense of ourselves, our subjectivity, is *constructed*" (Weedon, 1997, p. 21).

It is this productive property of discourse (i.e., discourse *produces* reality rather than simply reflecting it) that shapes the development of particular kinds of research questions. For example, researchers who employ policy discourse analysis (PDA) ask, "What is being produced or constructed through a particular policy or practice?"

and "What are the discourses shaping particular perspectives, images, and cultural practices?" Instead of focusing solely on the efficacy of intended policy outcomes, this form of analysis can be used to identify issues in the framing of policy "problems" or "solutions."

The concept of dominant discourses is also vital for understanding the utility of discourse analysis for examining policy. Typically, dominant discourses embedded in policy are normalized to such an extent that they are rarely called into question. That is, dominant discourses often eclipse other potential ways of making sense of the world and one's experience in it. For example, framed from a neoliberal marketplace discourse, schooling can be understood as a cornerstone of a democratic society, a necessity for job training, workforce development, and a thriving middle class. Yet, a counter-discourse might contend that compulsory schooling was developed and remains, in many respects today, a mechanism for creating obedient citizens who participate in reproducing the capitalist status quo.

Scholars have investigated dominant discourses of "excellence" in shaping college student experience and research university practice (Hotchkins & Dancy, 2015; Iverson, 2012) and dominant discourses of gender and sexuality in shaping understandings of school safety and teen pregnancy and campus sexual assault policies (Iverson, 2015; Pillow, 2004, 2006). Likewise, scholars have shown that access to higher education is shaped by policy discourses affecting opportunity programs (Hinsdale, 2012) and undocumented students (Gildersleeve & Hernandez, 2012). We turn next to a brief overview of the larger field of policy analysis as a contextual backdrop for a more detailed description of PDA theory and methods to follow.

Policy and Policy Analysis

Within the context of developing or developed societies, it is commonly understood that social policies serve as frameworks for decision-making in response to societal problems. The adoption of new policies, or a revision of old policies, is a complex process shaped by the larger sociopolitical landscape and policy actors within it. As such, human values play a role because many policies allocate resources for a collective course of action in response to a societal problem. Public policy, defined by Larson and Lovell (2010), is "a collection of policies embodied in constitutions, statutes, rules, and regulations, and enacted by various governments at some level" (p. 3).

Regardless of the particular policy reach, the study of policy can involve analyses of policy environments including power, demographic trends, political culture, ethics, values, and discourse (Fowler, 2012). The field of policy studies includes a range of different analytic approaches. In general, key differences among these approaches can be understood by the extent to which human values are acknowledged and by how policy problems are framed. For instance, the *rational scientific* model of policy analysis generally treats problems according to a step-by-step process of examining facts to arrive at the best policy solutions for any given problem. Proponents of the rational scientific approach advocate an apolitical and objective process that involves policy analysis, implementation, and evaluation. Other models of policy analysis move away from an expertise-based, formulaic, and objective process and propose a more flexible analytic process where the complexities of human values are taken into account, and a wide range of stakeholders are included in the policy process. In general, these theorists are referred to as *political rationalists* because they apply a rational approach to dealing with values inherent in the policy process.

For example, in response to the need to enhance racial and socioeconomic diversity at baccalaureate degree-granting institutions, a rational scientific approach might lead policy analysts to examine demographic trends in enrollment numbers and pinpoint access to higher education as a key policy problem. Given this framing, enhancing affordability and increasing the number of qualified students applying to college would likely become proposed policy solutions. In taking a more flexible approach that acknowledges the role of human values, a political rationalist approach might be more apt to move beyond the issue of access to consider issues of campus climate when analyzing policy solutions for increasing the racial and socioeconomic diversity of students.

As a whole, however, many established approaches to policy analysis are criticized for their failure to acknowledge *assumptions* undergirding the articulation of policy. For example, the very "problem" that a policy may be designed to solve may only be a problem for a particular group (Bertrand, Perez, & Roger, 2015; Suspitsyna, 2012). A simple noise ordinance in a neighborhood is a hypothetical example. For some, neighbors' music may be a nuisance, but for others, loud outdoor music may indicate social engagement. Typically, these critiques assert that traditional policy approaches are embedded in a modernist frame that implicitly advances particular perspectives about efficiency, productivity, and personhood, and furthermore that these approaches often assume a common understanding of the very meaning of the term "policy." Adding to this, other scholars have asserted that conventional approaches to policymaking and policy analysis are constructed through a lens that privileges rational/scientific logic, which often results in policy perspectives that are narrow, linear, and managerial in focus.

As noted by Allan (2010), policy researchers and analysts are frequently called upon for expertise in assessing the effectiveness of policy and making recommendations for improvement. Yet, despite the implementation and refinements of policy based on the analysis of gathered data, some problems—such as those associated with access, equity, and social justice—continue to challenge educational institutions and systems. The seemingly glacial pace of change toward social justice, despite committed efforts of practitioners and analysts alike, has prompted scholars to explore the utility of discourse analysis for the study of policy.

Policy Discourse Analysis

In contrast to previously established forms of policy analysis, PDA is a hybrid methodology drawing from critical, poststructural, and feminist theories to inform an approach to policy analysis that foregrounds the discursive shaping of policy problems as a mechanism for advancing social justice. Traditional approaches to policy analysis do not typically consider subject positions as central to the analysis, nor do they specifically focus on the role of policy in the promotion of emancipatory goals. Subject positions are similar to identities, but instead of a construct produced in the mind of the individual, a subject position is an identity that others produce by drawing upon dominant discourses. In contrast to traditional policy approaches, PDA is a framework to guide policy analysts to include examination of (1) the process by which policy problems are defined, (2) the influence of identity differences in the shaping of policy problems and solutions, and (3) the ways in which policy as discourse not only reflects but also contributes to producing subjectivities and sociopolitical realities (Allan, 2010; Bacchi, 1999; Marshall, 2000). As such, this approach to policy analysis supports policy research questions that seek to understand and disrupt systems of oppression and assumptions guiding inequitable practices.

In some academic circles with expressed commitments to social justice, poststructuralism may be critiqued for being too esoteric to be of much practical use. Given the strong influence of poststructuralism in PDA, this assertion merits further elaboration. In her extensive treatment of this subject, Mills (1997) responded to the critique noting that theories of discourse acknowledge material conditions in our daily lives. In other words, conditions like poverty and discrimination are not simply discursive or linguistic effects—they are real conditions with real and damaging consequences for human beings. Nonetheless, such conditions are produced by, and understood through, a particular confluence of discourses and power relations that create "conditions of possibility" (Foucault, 1979). Certainly, a range of theories exists to offer lenses through which to understand conditions like poverty. For example, Marxism offers a distinct perspective from a capitalist or meritocratic approach. However, a distinguishing feature of a poststructural lens from other explanatory lenses is the foregrounding of discourse and the contention that we come to understand material aspects of our daily lives through discourse (Mills, 1997; St. Pierre, 2000; Weedon, 1997). In other words, "realities" are produced through the discursive shaping of materiality.

An example of recent policy scholarship employing discourse analysis is Bertrand et al. (2015), who analyzed how political leaders in separate political parties discuss educational attainment gaps between racially and economically diverse peoples. Their work showed that some policymakers explained these gaps through structural inequality while other policymakers drew on deficit discourses and placed responsibility for low educational outcomes on lower socioeconomic status families or racially minority families. Showing the value of PDA, Bertrand et al. (2015) found that those policymakers who drew on deficit discourses made the low educational outcomes "appear natural through the use of several sub-strategies, including obscuring the identity of those harmed by inequality" (p. 2). In direct relation to this, alternate scholarship has shown that students entering college who are deemed "underprepared" and in need of developmental education are often placed in pejorative subject positions, as either encumbering society with additional educational costs or being maligned by failing higher educational institutions (Tolbert, 2017).

In other recent work, scholars using PDA have found that access to higher education is shaped by policy discourses affecting opportunity programs (Hinsdale, 2012), undocumented students (Gildersleeve & Hernandez, 2012), and university diversity plans (Iverson, 2012). Moreover, Suspitsyna (2012), through an analysis of 163 US Department of Education speeches, found that dominant discourses shaping higher education are focused primarily on the economy and economic contributions of postsecondary institutions as opposed to intellectual or social contributions.

To summarize, key introductory concepts for understanding PDA include the following: (1) discourses are more than words on paper—they are constellations of words and images that produce meaning, (2) discourses (and language) are dynamic and not only reflect but also produce culture, and (3) it is through discourse that we gain a sense of ourselves (subjectivities) and come to interpret the physical and social aspects of the world in which we live. PDA illuminates these discourses to examine persistent policy problems in new ways with implications for unthinking and rethinking policy solutions (Allan, 2008, 2010).

Policy Discourse Analysis Methods

Similar to other forms of inquiry, PDA begins with carefully crafted research questions to frame an investigation. These research questions, informed by the hybrid methodology previously described, are guided by overarching questions linked to identifying how a particular policy, a set of policies, and/or policy process draw on discourses to construct policy problems, solutions, and images—and how the identified discourses shape and re/produce particular subject positions. For example, a PDA investigation of the Every Student Succeeds Act (ESSA) could be anchored by research questions that ask: what does ESSA describe as problems and solutions for schools and students? What are the predominant images of students, teachers, and staff that emerge from this policy? What discourses are employed to shape these problems, solutions, and images? What subject positions are re/produced through these discourses?

While policies alone cannot fully capture discourses that are fluid and contextual, they can provide perspectives about the ways in which discourses are drawn upon to construct policy, shape subject positions while also articulate policy problems and recommended actions to resolve those problems. Guided by the research questions, careful data gathering and data analysis for PDA are vital to the credibility of the study.

One criticism of many forms of discourse analysis (as compared to PDA) is poor reporting of data sampling, incomplete descriptions of the tools and methods of analysis, and a dearth of examples of how discrete data lead to particular results. While not all scholars employing PDA are explicit about these foundational research steps, we contend that clear and well-articulated methods of analysis are crucial to building the legitimacy of PDA.

Gathering data. In choosing samples for data analysis, PDA scholars often identify a period from which to gather documents or artifacts because of the inherent assumption that discourses are fluid and contextually based. For example, a five-year range of documents might be considered depending on when the policy issue gained traction in a given context. Decisions about the type of policy artifacts and the sources of them are also important because the scope of analysis, and its limitations, is linked to the sample. In 2012, Gildersleeve and Hernandez (2012) sampled 12 In-State Resident Tuition (ISRT) policies because the simple fact was that only 12 states in the USA had ISRT policies at the time. Similarly, Suspitsyna (2012) chose a three-year range and analyzed 164 speeches from the US Department of Education looking at the specific level of federal (as opposed to state) economic discourses in educational policy. Allan (2010) employed PDA to examine 21 women's commission policy reports produced at four research universities over a period of three decades, and Iverson (2012) analyzed 21 diversity action plans and policy reports produced at 20 land-grant universities over a five-year period.

Once a given focus is established, it is important for the researcher to describe the extent to which the documents or artifacts are widely consumed by a given audience and how they reflect a given population or focus. PDA scholars often summarize the search engines or other mechanisms used to identify source documents, the number of documents retrieved, and the criteria for identifying primary or secondary documents. Primary documents undergo a multi-phase analysis process while secondary documents act as reflexive points to calibrate and test the credibility of the primary document analyses.

Analyzing and interpreting the data. Data analysis for PDA scholars can vary but often takes the form of multiple, explicitly articulated stages or phases. Drawing from our own work and others, we advocate a rigorous process that includes the following five phases. In phase one, documents are sorted and the texts are deductively coded based on the research questions. In phase two, inductive and deductive coding allows for in-depth analysis of data sorted in phase one. A key tenet is that codes are not produced first and then applied to documents because in that model, a researcher's preconceived ideas and biases are more likely to be applied to the data set. This would then be no different from a "close reading" of the front page of major newspapers on a given day and then proclaiming insights from the reading. In contrast, PDA is a grounded methodology where the codes are generated through the systematic process, not in advance, of data analysis.

A third phase of data analysis is similar to theme building in basic interpretive qualitative research or grounded theory methodology. In PDA, the codes generated in phases one and two are then examined apart from their original sources and grouped in category maps informed by the study's theoretical frameworks and research questions. A fourth phase of analysis is a careful reading of the category maps to identify predominant themes as well as potential policy silences. Finally, a fifth phase allows for dominant discourses to be identified and subject positions to emerge from these dominant discourses.

An example of policy silences can illuminate this concept. First, using PDA, Bertrand et al. (2015) found that the educational attainment gaps between Whites and students from minoritized groups (percentage of graduates at postsecondary institutions) are shaped by deficit discourses that "assert[…] that those most negatively impacted by inequality *cause* inequality" (p. 2). This means, drawing upon dominant discourses, minorities are blamed for their own lack of college degree attainment. The silence identified was a lack of focus on structural inequality, built through the history of slavery and segregation that produced the inequitable K-12 systems of education today. Throughout PDA, it is recommended that scholars engage in established practices that enhance research credibility including an audit trail that documents a researcher's analytic decisions; logs of reflexive notes beginning with foregrounding researcher assumptions prior to the analysis; working with one or more peer reviewers to help check potential biases and challenge assumptions; and triangulation through a layered analytic approach that includes secondary documents. Being explicit about a scholar's positionality, both in advance of the study and in reflection after the analysis is complete, is key to the credibility of the findings.

In contrast to other discourse approaches, PDA does not rely solely on a word count of particular words in an identified sample of documents because the simple presence or absence of a particular word, in the density of a single or many policy documents, is not indicative of dominant discourses, nor can a count of words reflect on the use of the word in analyses. Likewise, PDA does not follow lines of many discourse analysis approaches that provide exact guides on document sampling without accounting for the methods of coding or phases of analysis. Articulating that "multiple rounds of coding were used" as the full summary of analysis is not sufficient to identify how the analysis moves beyond a close reading. Thus PDA creates rigor and indicated credibility by having clearly articulated stages of document sampling and data analyses.

Writing it up. The writing of PDA findings can be quite different from other forms of summarizing research results. PDA scholars strive to articulate findings without oversimplification or generalization (especially beyond the scope of the sample of documents) while also not staying too granular or detailed such that only those who have analyzed the data can understand the findings. The development of terminology to name dominant discourses and subject positions clearly is an important initial step, and building on the work of established PDA scholarship can be a helpful starting point. Sometimes, scholars create visual maps of the discourses to indicate how policy documents follow narrative chains (Allan, Gordon, & Iverson, 2006; Tolbert, 2017). Another feature of PDA is to illustrate dominant discourses and subject positions with thick, rich description that includes data excerpts representative of the range of sources examined. Discussions of PDA studies connect back to the literature review such that contextual history of a dominant discourse can also be illuminated. Finally, as the goals of PDA are grounded in emancipatory principles, articulating some initial implications for policy and policy studies is an essential part of PDA. Yet, given the poststructural influences of PDA, it is also vital for researchers to be cautious of contributing to a new regime of truth, asserting the certainty of their findings by articulating a commitment to dismantling the very findings they have produced.

Policy Discourse Analysis: Implications for Practice

An example of how a PDA study yields findings to inform social justice practice can be seen in Tolbert's (2017) study, where five dominant discourses were traced relative to developmental education policy. A narrative chain pervaded the documents shaped by dominant discourses of crisis, accountability, efficacy, standardization, and policy fiat. Critically, these dominant discourses were seen as working through interdiscursivity, with the effect of producing pejorative subject positions for both students and faculty involved with developmental education. Developmental students were positioned either as encumbering society with the cost of their education for a second time, implicitly wasting taxpayer dollars, or as maligned, as harmed by an ineffective and broken developmental education system. Likewise, faculty were framed as "prosaic" through dominant policy discourses where their outdated teaching philosophies and pedagogies were to blame for poor student outcomes with the implication that faculty needed to be managed by college administrators or policymakers themselves. These findings are supported by the work of Parker, Barrett, and Bustillos, 2014.

Tolbert's (2017) study revealed that dominant discourses framed developmental education as a broken system that was harming students and keeping them from attaining their college degrees. The dominant discourses in the policy briefs can be said to have, in part, *produced* problems with developmental education by simplifying the issues. The dominant discourses tended to oversimplify and thus eclipse highly contested and complex debates about the potential merits and drawbacks of development education (Goudas & Boylan, 2012).

The idea that developmental students "encumber" society has moved throughout discursive landscapes since the 1990s when blaming students for the cost of remediation was prominent in policy debates (Soliday, 2002). Against the backdrop of this discursive landscape, the CUNY system implemented a policy mandating that developmental education would be limited to two-year institutions (Soliday, 2002), thereby creating a tiered system as a greater proportion of racially minoritized students were identified as needing developmental education (Parker & Richardson, 2005) and thus funneled to associate granting institutions. Analysis of policy silences reveals another impact of this discursive history where cultural capital or community cultural wealth (Yosso, 2005) of minoritized students is overlooked when dominant discourses frame developmental students as deficient.

Numerous other applications of PDA exist in scholarly literature. For example, Bertrand et al. (2015) used PDA to understand policy insiders' discursive strategies for engaging with racism and class when discussing education, finding that in relationship to deficit discourses, "naturalization" occurred "which Bonilla-Silva (2014) described as the practice of explaining away systemic racism as a natural occurrence" (Bertrand et al., 2015, p. 21). In a study of diversity action plans, Iverson (2012) described how dominant discourses of access shape these policy documents and points to the need to "resist and contest dominant conceptions of diversity" (p. 168) that tend to homogenize difference and reinforce the status quo. Allan's (2008) study of university women's commission reports underscored how dominant discourses of gender reinscribe images of women as vulnerable outsiders to the institution and how policy solutions were shaped in response to these images.

In a study of transgender policy efforts at research universities, Dirks (2016) employed PDA to explore dominant discourses framing recommendations for inclusivity efforts. Finding that many such recommendations were predicated upon a discourse of trans-vulnerability, Dirks asks readers to consider if well-intended efforts might be reinscribing genderism in the guise of gender inclusivity. In another study, Iverson (2015) revealed potential unintended consequences of sexual assault policies by examining their discursive framing, and Hoffman (2010) explored ways in which dominant discourses shaping Title IX can reinforce a gendered system of power that promotes the commercial interests of men's sports and relegates women's sports to fulfill developmental goals.

In sum, PDA is a methodological approach that guides scholars in analyzing how discourses shape and produce realities that frame policy problems, the modality of solutions, and the interpretations of policy results. As described in this chapter, PDA also features rigorous methods along with theoretical underpinnings that make it well suited for advancing social justice through emancipatory inquiry.

Suggested Readings

Allan, E. J. (2010). Feminist poststructuralism meets policy analysis: An overview. In E. J. Allan, S. Iverson, & R. Ropers-Huilman (Eds.), *Reconstructing policy in higher education: Feminist poststructural perspectives* (pp. 11–35). New York, NY: Routledge.

This chapter provides a more detailed introduction to the theoretical and conceptual underpinnings helpful to understanding policy as discourse.

Dirks, D. A. (2016). Transgender people at four Big Ten campuses: A policy discourse analysis. *Review of Higher Education, 39*(3), 371–393. https://doi.org/10.1353/rhe.2016.0020

This article provides a powerful illustration of a recent PDA study revealing how the policy discourses may actually undermine the outcomes of the policies intended to support trans-individuals.

Foucault, M. (2001). From "Truth and Power". In V. B. Leitch (Ed.), *The Norton anthology of theory and criticism* (pp. 1667–1670). New York, NY: W.W. Norton and Company.

Though brief, this passage may provide the most critical definition of "power" for poststructuralist thinking. Understanding how power is defined, especially in contrast to Marxian or positivist forms of power, is a conceptual key to poststructuralist work.

Gildersleeve, R. E., & Hernandez, S. (2012). Producing (im)possible peoples: Policy discourse analysis, in-state resident tuition and undocumented students in American higher education. *International Journal of Multicultural Education, 14*(2), 1–19. https://doi.org/10.18251/ijme.v14i2.517

In this study, researchers detail a PDA study of state laws to powerfully illuminate how tuition policy discourses shape understandings of identity relative to undocumented students in US higher education.

Iverson, S. V. (2012). Constructing outsiders: The discursive framing of access in university diversity policies. *Review of Higher Education, 35*(2), 149–177. https://doi.org/10.1353/rhe.2012.0013

This article provides a compelling illustration of a PDA study examining diversity action plans at US land-grant universities finding that well-intended policy efforts to enhance diversity and inclusivity may unwittingly reinforce inequitable practices.

Mills, S. (2011). *Discourse: The new critical idiom* (2nd ed.). New York, NY: Routledge.

This text provides a helpful introduction to the term "discourse" and how the term is used in the many varied sub-fields within scholarly work. The text introduces the history and language of debates and development of the idea of discourse for an audience not familiar or acquainted with the birth of the study of semiotics and structuralism under Saussure and Lacan. It also helps distinguish some of the fault lines between critical and poststructural thinking on discourse.

van Dijk, T. A. (Ed.). (2011). *Discourse studies: A multidisciplinary introduction* (2nd ed.). Thousand Oaks, CA: SAGE Publications.

While vast in its scope, and more focused on critical discourse analysis rather than policy discourse analysis, this text is a series of collected essays that provides multiple competing and interwoven definitions of power and discourse. It also includes relevant examples of the applications of discourse theory in research.

References

Allan, E. J. (2008). *Policy discourses, gender, and education: Constructing women's status.* New York, NY: Routledge.

Allan, E. J. (2010). Feminist poststructuralism meets policy analysis: An overview. In E. J. Allan, S. Iverson, & R. Ropers-Huilman (Eds.), *Reconstructing policy in higher education: Feminist poststructural perspectives* (pp. 11–35). New York, NY: Routledge.

Allan, E. J., Gordon, S., & Iverson, S. (2006). Re/thinking practices of power: The discursive framing of leadership in postsecondary education. *The Review of Higher Education, 30*(1), 41–68. https://doi.org/10.1353/rhe.2006.0045

Bacchi, C. L. (1999). *Women, policy, and politics: The construction of policy problems.* Thousand Oaks, CA: Sage.

Bertrand, M., Perez, W., & Rogers, J. (2015). Unmasking policy insiders' discourses and discursive in upholding and challenging racism and classism in education. *Education Policy Analysis Archives, 23*(93), 1–30. https://doi.org/10.14507/epaa.v23.2068

Dirks, D. A. (2016). Transgender people at four Big Ten campuses: A policy discourse analysis. *Review of Higher Education, 39*(3), 371–393. https://doi.org/10.1353/rhe.2016.0020

Foucault, M. (1979). *Discipline and punish: The birth of the prison.* New York, NY: Vintage Books.

Fowler, F. C. (2012). *Policy studies for educational leaders: An introduction.* New York, NY: Pearson.

Gildersleeve, R. E., & Hernandez, S. (2012). Producing (im)possible peoples: Policy discourse analysis, in-state resident tuition and undocumented students in American higher education. *International Journal of Multicultural Education, 14*(2), 1–19. https://doi.org/10.18251/ijme.v14i2.517

Goudas, A. M., & Boylan, H. R. (2012). Addressing flawed research in developmental education. *Journal of Developmental Education, 36*(1), 2–13.

Hinsdale, M. J. (2012). Opportunity reconsidered. *Journal of Student Affairs Research and Practice, 49*(4), 415–428. https://doi.org/10.1515/jsarp-2012-6471

Hoffman, J. (2010). The dilemma of the senior woman administrator role in intercollegiate athletics. *Journal of Issues in Intercollegiate Athletics, 3*(5), 53–75.

Hotchkins, B., & Dancy, E. (2015). Rethinking success: Black male values in higher education. *Spectrum: A Journal on Black Men, 4*(1), 73–98. https://doi.org/10.2979/spectrum.4.1.05

Iverson, S. V. (2012). Constructing outsiders: The discursive framing of access in university diversity policies. *Review of Higher Education, 35*(2), 149–177. https://doi.org/10.1353/rhe.2012.0013

Iverson, S. V. (2015). The risky subject: A policy discourse analysis of sexual assault policies in higher education. In S. C. Wooten & R. W. Mitchell (Eds.), *The crisis of campus sexual violence: Critical perspectives on prevention and response* (pp. 15–32). New York, NY: Routledge.

Larson, T. E., & Lovell, C. D. (2010). The integration of higher education and public policy: A complex and often misunderstood nexus. In C. D. Lovell, T. E. Larson, D. R. Dean, & D. L. Longanecker (Eds.), *Public policy and higher education* (2nd ed., pp. 3–9). Boston, MA: Pearson.

Marshall, C. (2000). Policy discourse analysis: Negotiating gender equity. *Journal of Education Policy, 15*(2), 125–156. https://doi.org/10.1080/026809300285863

Mills, S. (1997). *Discourse.* London, UK: Routledge.

Parker, T. L., & Richardson Jr., R. C. (2005). Ending remediation at CUNY: Implications for access and excellence. *Journal of Educational Research & Policy Studies, 5*(2), 1–22.

Parker, T. L., Barrett, M. S., & Bustillos, L. T. (2014). *The state of developmental education: Higher education and public policy priorities.* New York, NY: Palgrave Macmillan.

Pillow, W. S. (2004). *Unfit subjects: Educational policy and the teen mother.* New York, NY: Routledge.

Pillow, W. S. (2006). Teen pregnancy and education politics of knowledge, research, and practice. *Educational Policy, 20*(1), 59–84. https://doi.org/10.1177/0895904805285289

Soliday, M. (2002). *The politics of remediation*. Pittsburgh, PA: University of Pittsburgh Press.

St. Pierre, E. (2000). Poststructural feminism in education: An overview. *International Journal of Qualitative Studies in Education, 13*(5), 477–515. https://doi.org/10.1080/09518390050156422

Suspitsyna, T. (2012). Higher education for economic advancement and engaged citizenship: An analysis of the U.S. Department of Education discourse. *Journal of Higher Education, 83*(1), 49–72. https://doi.org/10.1353/jhe.2012.0003

Tolbert, A. R. (2017). *Discourses of developmental English education: Reframing policy debates*. Retrieved from: DigitalCommons@UMaine *Electronic Theses and Dissertations*. 2659. https://digitalcommons.library.umaine.edu/etd/2659

van Dijk, T. A. (2008). *Discourse and power*. New York, NY: Palgrave Macmillan.

Välimaa, J., & Hoffman, D. (2008). Knowledge society discourse and higher education. *Higher Education, 56*(3), 265–285. https://doi.org/10.1007/s10734-008-9123-7

Weedon, C. (1997). *Feminist practice and poststructuralist theory* (3rd ed.). Cambridge, MA: Blackwell.

Yosso, T. J. (2005). Whose culture has capital? A critical race theory discussion of community cultural wealth. *Race Ethnicity and Education, 8*(1), 69–91. https://doi.org/10.1080/1361332052000341006

Chapter 13
Through Their Eyes, in Their Words: Using Photo-Elicitation to Amplify Student Voice in Policy and School Improvement Research

Jeff Walls and Samantha E. Holquist

Abstract Although various measures of student success are often used as data points in scholarly and policy debates about how to improve schools, the policy and school-level changes that stem from these discussions are presumed to be taken on *behalf* of students without very much effort to meaningfully include students' perspectives on the proposed changes. The purpose of this chapter is to highlight the promise of photo-elicitation-based data collection to authentically leverage student voice in research on policy and school improvement in ways that promote equity and critical social justice. Photo-elicitation, in its simplest form, involves inviting research participants to take photographs of a space (e.g., a school) under a broad prompt (e.g., places where you like to have fun) (Harper, *Visual Studies, 17*, 13–26, 2002; Torre & Murphy, *Education Policy Analysis Archives, 23*, 2015). This chapter highlights methodological choices researchers must make in utilizing photo-elicitation and how these choices bear on the equity implications of this method.

In this chapter, we hope to highlight the potential of a data collection method known as photo-elicitation for better incorporating student voice into both education research and school and policy change efforts. Photo-elicitation, in its simplest form, involves either inviting research participants to take photographs of a space (e.g., a school) under a broad prompt (e.g., places where you like to have fun) or researchers selecting photographs and asking participants to respond (Harper, 2002; Torre & Murphy, 2015). Researchers then ask additional questions to elucidate participants' experiences fully.

J. Walls (✉)
University of Louisiana at Lafayette, Lafayette, LA, USA
e-mail: jeffrey.walls@louisiana.edu

S. E. Holquist
University of Minnesota, Minneapolis, MN, USA

© The Author(s) 2019
K. K. Strunk, L. A. Locke (eds.), *Research Methods for Social Justice and Equity in Education*, https://doi.org/10.1007/978-3-030-05900-2_13

151

Although various measures of student success are often used as data points in scholarly and policy debates about how to improve schools, the policy and school-level changes that stem from these discussions are presumed to be taken on *behalf* of students without very much effort to meaningfully include students' perspectives on the proposed changes. Recently, scholars have been more attentive to the potential of incorporating "student voice" into school change efforts in order to generate more authentic and inclusive reform initiatives (Jones & Yonezawa, 2002; Mitra, 2014; Mitra & Gross, 2009; Rudduck & Fielding, 2006).

We argue that greater incorporation of student voice holds promise for producing greater social justice in education because it helps researchers, educators, and policymakers "recognize that relations of unequal power are constantly being enacted"—particularly between adults and students—and asks educational stakeholders to "think critically about knowledge; what [they] know and how[they] know it"—particularly with respect to meeting the needs of all students (Sensoy & DiAngelo, 2017, pp. 20–21). However, several obstacles remain to fully incorporating student voice into educational reform and research efforts. First, there has been little effort to incorporate student voice into policy initiatives. Second, efforts to incorporate student voice often leads to "surface compliance" rather than a deeper commitment to understanding and using students' input (Rudduck & Fielding, 2006, p. 219). Third, some of the ways that researchers and practitioners elicit students' input have the effect of narrowing or prejudicing the scope of students' responses. Surveys and semi-structured interviews may pre-define the topics of responses in a way that does not fully capture students' experiences.

In the present study, we first offer a brief synopsis on how a researcher's choice of method may implicate issues of educational equity and social justice. Then, we thoroughly explore photo-elicitation methodology and its variants. Next, we highlight the ways photo-elicitation creates more room for meaningful student voice in school improvement and policy research. We briefly sketch the use of photo-elicitation in school improvement and policy research conducted by the authors and conclude by appraising the benefits and shortcomings of photo-elicitation and potential alterations to the method based on emerging video and social media technologies.

Relationship Between Method and Educational Equity

A researcher's choice of method is inextricably tied up with questions of how the research will be interpreted and how it may be used by stakeholders. Some educational researchers claim to be neutral analysts, while others hope that their research will produce a fairer or more ethical society. What, then, does it mean for a researcher to center social justice in the researcher's choice of method? We believe Charmaz (2008) offers some important insight:

> An interest in social justice means attentiveness to ideas and actions concerning fairness, equity, equality, democratic process, status, and hierarchy, and individual and collective

rights and obligations. It signifies thinking about creating good societies and a better world and being human, national and world citizens. It means exploring tensions between complicity and consciousness, choice and constraint, indifference and compassion, inclusion and exclusion, poverty and privilege, and barriers and opportunities. It also means taking a critical stance toward actions, organizations, and social institutions. Social justice studies require looking at both realities and ideals. Thus, contested meanings of "shoulds" and "oughts" come into play. And, unlike positivists of the past, these researchers openly bring their shoulds and oughts into the discourse of inquiry. (p. 207)

One broad heading of research that is closely tied to questions of social justice and equity is participatory action research. Participatory action research is a community-based research method that emphasizes action and broad participation and seeks to co-create new knowledge between researchers and participants by attempting to produce change in the community (Chevalier & Buckles, 2013). Many participatory action research projects have made use of visual methods such as reflexive photo-elicitation or a variant known as photovoice (see, e.g., Jurkowski, 2008; Wang & Burris, 1997).

One particular branch of participatory action research, known as Youth Participatory Action Research (YPAR), focuses on teaching youth to confront and resist the forces that reproduce inequities (Cammarota & Fine, 2008). YPAR provides youth with an opportunity to engage in their social context and acquire the knowledge necessary to broaden their personal perspectives (Cammarota & Romero, 2010). It encourages youth to participate in research practices, such as reflexive photo-elicitation (which we describe in greater detail later), aimed at understanding current community injustices and creating safe, vibrant neighborhoods that lead to healthy, positive youth identities. Ultimately, YPAR can help youth develop skills to become active civic participants and confront social justice concerns (Rodriquez & Brown, 2009).

We believe that reflexive photo-elicitation (as well as photovoice, a technique explored in the next chapter in this volume) is an important research method for facilitating students' participation in both school improvement and the policy arena, and thus an important approach to foreground issues of social justice and equity and ensure that students can have a meaningful voice in these settings. In the next section, we explain photo-elicitation in greater detail.

Understanding the Photo-Elicitation Methodology

In this section, we detail the history of photo-elicitation briefly, important decisions to be made by researchers employing photo-elicitation techniques, and briefly survey some of the variants of photo-elicitation. It is important to note that the later variants on the original method have greater application to social justice and equity than do the earlier uses. At the conclusion of the section, we briefly discuss the relationship between photo-elicitation and student voice.

Brief History of Photo-Elicitation Research

Using photographs in research is not a new practice, the anthropologists Margaret Mead and Gregory Bateson used photographs in their study of Balinese culture in the 1940s (Bateson & Mead, 1942). Before that, anthropologists used photographs in field studies dating back to the early twentieth century (Harper, 1998). However, photo-elicitation in its most basic sense (using photographs *in the interview process*) was first employed by John Collier (1957) in mental health research. In a later text, Collier described photo-elicitation as a form of open-ended interviewing. In Collier's description, and in traditional photo-elicitation research generally, photographs are selected by the researcher and interpreted by the research subject. Harper (1998) describes how photo-elicitation can help researchers to "see" cultural knowledge that they may have otherwise missed: "a shocking thing happens in this interview format; the photographer, who knows his or her photograph as its maker... suddenly confronts the realization that she or he knows little or nothing about the cultural information contained in the image" (p. 35).

Since Collier's original explication of photo-elicitation, the method has gained popularity and also produced a number of variants. However, in 2002, Harper found only 53 academic studies using photo-elicitation. Looking at the field of education, in particular, Torre and Murphy (2015) found only 35 peer-reviewed studies utilizing photo-elicitation as of 2015.

Choices About Data Collection and Data Analysis

Epstein, Stevens, McKeever, and Baruchel (2006) highlight several important considerations about photo-elicitation research methods: who will take the photographs, what will appear in the photographs, and how will the photographs be used in the interview setting. In the sections later, we address each of these questions in turn and conclude by examining ties between photo-elicitation research and student voice.

Who takes the photographs? In traditional photo-elicitation interviews, photographs are either taken by a researcher or selected by the researcher from pre-existing photographs (e.g., from historical archives or photo albums) (Lapenta, 2012). This approach has practical benefits, such as allowing the researcher to focus interviewees' attention on particular spaces or places within their setting and allowing researchers to gather multiple viewpoints about a particular image. Furthermore, to the extent that photo-elicitation is intended largely as a rapport-building technique, having a common set of photographs for interviewees to react to is likely to help the researcher build relationships.

Harper (1998) points out that differences in how researchers use photo-elicitation techniques often stem from the different ways that researchers think about knowledge and what we can know about the world (also known as epistemology).

Researchers who believe that there are objective truths about the world and that the purpose of research is to uncover these truths (also known as post-positivist researchers) are more likely to use a form of photo-elicitation where the researcher selects the photographs. Post-positivist researchers are likely to be relatively comfortable establishing categories of analysis (Crotty, 1998). Other researchers, who believe that reality is socially constructed and depends on lived experience (interpretivist researchers), or researchers who believe that unequal power relations is the social force that most animates how people experience the world (critical researchers) are more likely to use photo-elicitation techniques where participants generate photographs. Interpretivist and critical researchers are likely to believe that categories of analysis generated by participants, or in a partnership between researchers and participants, are a better way to understand the social world than categories of analysis generated only by the researcher. We believe that forms of photo-elicitation where participants take the photos that guide the interview are more useful to researchers committed to producing greater equity and social justice in education, for reasons that we detail later.

There are two main variants of photo-elicitation that involve photographs taken by participants: reflexive photo-elicitation and photovoice. Reflexive photo-elicitation is similar to the traditional form of photo-elicitation described earlier, except that the photographs are taken by participants rather than researchers. Lapenta (2012) identifies two advantages of reflexive photo-elicitation. First, it allows participants "to have increased voice and authority in interpreting their own… social contexts" and reduces "researcher bias in the selection of specific images" (Lapenta, 2012, p. 205). Second, reflexive photo-elicitation can contextualize other sources of data (i.e., surveys, etc.) by allowing participants to give a rich local rendering of their experiences (Lapenta, 2012, p. 205).

Photovoice extends reflexive photo-elicitation techniques into the realm of participatory action research (Wang, 1999). According to the originators of the technique, photovoice has three goals: "(1) to enable people to record and reflect their community's strengths and concerns, (2) to promote critical dialogue and knowledge about important community issues through large and small group discussion of photographs, and (3) to reach policymakers" (Wang & Burris, 1997, p. 370). Because photovoice is a participatory research method, it involves initial training on the power dynamics and ethics involved in capturing images, followed by extensive large and small group discussions on which participant-generated images best capture the story (or stories) of the community (Lapenta, 2012, p. 6). Finally, participants describe "issues, themes, or theories" exemplified by the photos they have selected, which helps researchers to "hear and understand how people make meaning themselves, or construct what matters to them" (Wang & Burris, 1997, pp. 381–382).

Traditional photo-elicitation, reflexive photo-elicitation, and photovoice can be conceived of along a spectrum based on whether they are researcher driven or participant driven. Traditional photo-elicitation is more or less fully driven by the researcher, while photovoice is driven primarily by participants. Reflexive photo-elicitation involves a negotiation about meaning between the researcher and the participant.

Another way in which photovoice differs from both traditional photo-elicitation and reflexive photo-elicitation is that it highlights the assets and issues of a community, rather than foregrounding a researcher-defined problem or question: the community itself is the object of analysis. Once researchers have decided on who will take the pictures, they must decide what the photographs will contain.

What appears in the photographs? The question of who will take the pictures bears on what ultimately appears in the photographs. If researchers select the images, they have complete discretion about what the photographs contain. In this case, researchers may choose photographs to help them understand the context of physical or social spaces or may select photographs of a local phenomenon that researchers hope participants can help them better understand. Harper (2002) suggests that photographs should appear from an "unusual angle" in order to help participants think about their everyday experiences in a novel way.

In the case of reflexive photo-elicitation, or photovoice, researchers have considerably less discretion about the content of images. Researchers may choose to prompt participants based on topic (e.g., "a place where you feel you don't belong") or spatial or temporal issues (e.g., "the places where you spend the most time"). Researchers may also choose to limit the number of pictures they ask participants to take or ask them to take pictures in ways that are ethically bound (e.g., limiting the amount of time disrupting daily school activities) (Torre & Murphy, 2015). In photovoice, because prompts are more likely to be participant driven, training on the ethics of camera use and image capture is especially important (Wang & Burris, 1997).

How are photographs used in the interview and analysis? Torre and Murphy (2015) note that photo-elicitation interviews may "proceed much like a typical qualitative interview, except that researchers are able to prompt participants to give deeper explanations by referring to particular pictures" (p. 10). Researchers may make a number of choices about how to use the pictures in the interview, including who will decide what order to talk about the pictures in, what criteria to use to decide which pictures to talk about (e.g., the most important), and whether participants will be asked to manipulate or sort pictures (e.g., to put them in chronological order). If the photographs are selected by the researcher, the researcher may choose to present pictures to participants in the same order each time or to change the order across interviews.

One reason why photo-elicitation interviews are useful for exposing and challenging extant power structures is that talking about photographs breaks the natural question-answer turn-taking system of a research interview (Lapenta, 2012). Because participants are encouraged to grapple with the images on their own terms, their descriptions of the images are not directed as answers to particular research questions. Thus, researchers should take care during interviews to leave space for photos to remain uncategorized.

Researchers operating from a variety of qualitative analysis methods use photo-elicitation techniques, including action research, grounded theory, and ethnography. One important decision for researchers to make about data analysis of photo-elicitation interviews is whether the photos themselves will be analyzed (Torre &

Murphy, 2015). Some researchers elect to simply analyze the transcripts of the interviews, while other researchers make the photos an integral part of their analysis; for example, some researchers analyze the differences in photographs between those who occupy different social positions (Clark-Ibanez, 2004). Researchers thus have a variety of research design decisions to make about how photographs will shape the reader's understanding of what happened in the research.

Relationship between photo-elicitation and student voice. Photo-elicitation is an important method to bring authentic student voice into the research process. Broadly, student voice is defined as the ways in which all students have opportunities to participate in and influence the decisions that will shape their lives and the lives of their peers (Mitra & Gross, 2009). Student voice is often seen as a more equitable and social justice-oriented approach to impacting reforms in school communities as students' experiences, particularly those of underrepresented youth, are brought to the forefront (Rudduck & Fielding, 2006). Both participatory action research and photo-elicitation, through reflexive photo-elicitation and photovoice, offer opportunities for students to deeply engage in the research process and take ownership over the experiences shared (Cammarota & Romero, 2010; Torre & Murphy, 2015). Surveys and traditional interviews may have the effect of delimiting the topics to which participants respond, resulting in responses that do not fully capture students' experiences. The inclusion of research methods that promote student voice is likely to result in more equitable and socially just research outcomes as researchers gain a fuller and more authentic understanding of students' lived experiences.

Using Photo-Elicitation in Data Collection: Two Case Study Examples

As noted, photo-elicitation is an important method for facilitating the inclusion of students' experiences in school improvement and the policy arena and thus an important approach to foreground issues of social justice and equity and ensure that students can have a meaningful voice in these settings. In this section, we examine how photo-elicitation was used as a data collection method to highlight student voices and promote equity in two studies performed by the authors: one focused on school improvement and the other focused on education policy. While each study utilized a different approach to photo-elicitation, they both empowered students to discuss their experiences as well as challenge researchers' understanding of how students understand educational environments.

Photo-Elicitation in School Improvement Research

The school improvement study explored how adults collaborate to produce socially supportive school environments and how students experience those efforts. The researchers decided to utilize photo-elicitation in order to explore tensions in how school adults use their positional and relational power in their efforts to care for students. The study took place at two middle schools and involved participant observation and semi-structured interviews of school personnel, as well as photo-elicitation interviews of students where students took photos and discussed them with the interviewer.

In this study, photo-elicitation was especially useful at highlighting students' experience of school as continuous and highly social, rather than discrete and based on academic content (e.g., students don't take pictures of individual classes; they are much more likely to highlight social spaces or to think about classes in terms of relationships). Students' photos often highlight the "gray zones" of life in schools, places where rules and relationships are unsettled (e.g., hallways, times before and after school). Student photos frequently challenge adults' notions of acting on behalf of students' interests and highlight environments that are comfortable for students but not adults (e.g., conflicts over lunchroom seating arrangements and lunchroom volume). Student photos often highlight power structures in terms of what activities and behaviors are recognized and what is less valued (e.g., the well-maintained athletics display cases vs. the defaced student art projects). Without the use of photo-elicitation with students, the author may not have been able to capture how students experience their school environment or dig deeper into the inequitable power structures present within the school.

Photo-Elicitation in Education Policy Research

The education policy study explored how students, through intentional efforts to advance student voice, collectively participate in and influence the policymaking process for state-level K-12 educational decision-making. The study examined how members of two state-wide student voice efforts impacted policy and involved participant observation and semi-structured interviews of high school student members and adults. During interviews, students discussed how they utilized social media and photos to influence policymakers. Students selected and examined photos posted on social media (taken and posted by student members) that they believed were important to how they experienced and influenced the policy process.

Students' photos of the policy process highlight whom they believe to be the education decision-makers (e.g., legislators), where decisions are made in the process (e.g., the state capitol), and how they see themselves in the process (e.g., testifying or writing policy briefs before meetings). In discussing the photos, students explain how some photos felt empowering (e.g., a picture in the capitol after an important meeting with a legislator), while others felt *tokenizing* (e.g., when legislators wanted to take photos with them instead of discussing policy priorities). Students assert that the empowering photos pushed them to keep working on the policy changes they were seeking, particularly after receiving positive feedback through comments on social media, while the tokenizing photos helped them establish relationships with key legislators and enabled them to get first meetings. Students demonstrated a sophisticated understanding of the hierarchical power relationship between their peers and legislators and used photos to leverage this relationship for future policy reforms. Via the use of photo-elicitation, the author was able to deeply explore how students experienced the policymaking process, and particularly how they perceived and responded to power structures between students and decision-makers.

Future Directions

Photo-elicitation is a data collection method with the potential to authentically leverage student voice in research on policy and school improvement in ways that promote equity and critical social justice. Photo-elicitation provides researchers and students with an opportunity to dig deeper into their experiences in education environments and uncover the ways in which they may be inequitable. While there are many opportunities in photo-elicitation for deeper understandings of student experiences, there are also limitations. Photo-elicitation is unusually dependent on a researcher's ability to build meaningful rapport with students, although the technique may also facilitate rapport building. It also requires that researchers create an environment where students feel comfortable sharing their social world. Furthermore, photo-elicitation can be misapplied to reinforce researchers' preconceived notions about schools and student voice in education policymaking.

Nevertheless, as social media lowers the barriers to meaningful student participation in the policymaking arena (e.g., Marjory Stoneman Douglas High School students following the February 14, 2018, school shooting), researchers need to utilize innovative methods to capture students' experiences. Interview techniques that leverage students' photographs and other media are critical to understanding their social world. Moreover, students are increasingly engaging in social justice efforts via social media and other electronic platforms. Research techniques that allow students to both speak about the ways that schools and policies intersect their lives and engage via mediums they are accustomed to using are important for authentically incorporating student voice in school improvement and policy change efforts.

Suggested Readings

Lapenta, F. (2012). Some theoretical and methodological views on photo-elicitation. In E. Margolis & L. Pauwels (Eds.), *The SAGE handbook of visual research methods* (pp. 201–213). London, UK: SAGE Publications. https://doi. org/10.4135/9781446268278.n11

Lapenta's chapter offers a good overview on the methodological variants of photo-elicitation research. Additionally, Lapenta discusses some of the ethical considerations of photo-elicitation research.

Wang, C. C., & Burris, M. A. (1997). Photovoice: Concept, methodology, and use for participatory needs assessment. *Health Education & Behavior, 24*(3), 369–387. https://doi.org/10.1177/109019819702400309

Wang and Burris provide an overview of photovoice and photovoice's potential as a participatory action research method. The article includes a discussion of the full arc of the photovoice process.

Cammarota, J., & Romero, A. (2010). Participatory action research for high school students: Transforming policy, practice, and the personal with social justice education. *Education Policy, 25*(3), 488–506. https://doi.org/10.1177/0895904810361722

Cammarota and Romero offer a discussion on how to enmesh youth in participatory action research to achieve social justice aims.

References

Bateson, G., & Mead, M. (1942). *Balinese character: A photographic analysis.* New York, NY: Academy of Sciences. https://doi.org/10.1525/aa.1943.45.4.02a00120

Cammarota, J., & Fine, M. (2008). Youth participatory action research: A pedagogy for transformational resistance. In *Revolutionizing education: Youth participatory action research in motion* (pp. 1–11). London, UK: Routledge Taylor & Francis Group. https://doi.org/10.1080/09518398.2016.1201609

Cammarota, J., & Romero, A. (2010). Participatory action research for high school students: Transforming policy, practice, and the personal with social justice education. *Education Policy, 25*(3), 488–506. https://doi.org/10.1177/0895904810361722

Charmaz, K. (2008). Grounded theory in the 21st century: Applications for advancing social justice studies. In N. K. Denzin & Y. E. Lincoln (Eds.), *Handbook of qualitative research* (3rd ed., pp. 507–535). Thousand Oaks, CA: SAGE Publications.

Chevalier, J. M., & Buckles, D. J. (2013). *Handbook for participatory action research, planning, and evaluation.* Ottawa, ON: SES2 Dialogue.

Clark-Ibanez, M. (2004). Framing the social world with photo-elicitation interviews. *American Behavioral Scientist, 47*(12), 1507–1527. https://doi.org/10.1177/0002764204266236

Collier, J. (1957). Photography in anthropology: A report on two experiments. *American Anthropologist, 59*, 843–859. https://doi.org/10.1525/aa.1957.59.5.02a00100

Crotty, M. (1998). *The foundations of social research.* Thousand Oaks, CA: SAGE Publications.

Epstein, I., Stevens, B., McKeever, P., & Baruchel, S. (2006). Photo-elicitation interview (PEI): Using photos to elicit children's perspectives. *International Journal of Qualitative Methods, 5*(3), 1–11. https://doi.org/10.1177/160940690600500301

Harper, D. (1998). An argument for visual sociology. In J. Prosser (Ed.), *Image-based research: A sourcebook for qualitative researchers* (pp. 24–41). London, UK: Psychology Press.

Harper, D. (2002). Talking about pictures: A case for photo-elicitation. *Visual Studies, 17*(1), 13–26. https://doi.org/10.1080/14725860220137345

Jones, M., & Yonezawa, S. (2002). Student voice, cultural change: Using inquiry in school reform. *Equity & Excellence in Education, 35*(3), 245–254. https://doi.org/10.1080/10665680290175257

Jurkowski, J. M. (2008). Photovoice as participatory action research tool for engaging people with intellectual disabilities in research and program development. *Intellectual and Developmental Disabilities, 46*(1), 1–11. https://doi.org/10.1352/0047-6765(2008)46[1:PAPART]2.0.CO;2

Lapenta, F. (2012). Some theoretical and methodological views on photo-elicitation. In E. Margolis & L. Pauwels (Eds.), *The SAGE handbook of visual research methods* (pp. 201–213). London, UK: Sage Publications. https://doi.org/10.4135/9781446268278

Mitra, D. L. (2014). *Student voice in school reform: Building youth-adult partnerships that strengthen schools and empower youth.* Albany, NY: SUNY Press.

Mitra, D. L., & Gross, S. J. (2009). Increasing student voice in high school reform: Building partnerships, improving outcomes. *Educational Management Administration & Leadership, 37*(4), 522–543. https://doi.org/10.1177/1741143209334577

Rodriquez, L. F., & Brown, T. M. (2009). From voice to agency: Guiding principles for participatory action research with youth. *New Directions for Youth Development, 123*, 19–34. https://doi.org/10.1002/yd.312

Rudduck, J., & Fielding, M. (2006). Student voice and the perils of popularity. *Educational Review, 58*(2), 219–231. https://doi.org/10.1080/00131910600584207

Sensoy, Ö., & DiAngelo, R. (2017). *Is everyone really equal?: An introduction to key concepts in social justice education.* New York, NY: Teachers College Press.

Torre, D., & Murphy, J. (2015). A different lens: Using photo-elicitation interviews in education research. Education Policy Analysis Archives, 23, Article 111. https://doi.org/10.1080/14725860220137345

Wang, C. C. (1999). Photovoice: A participatory action research strategy applied to women's health. *Journal of Women's Health, 8*(2), 185–192. https://doi.org/10.1089/jwh.1999.8.185

Wang, C. C., & Burris, M. A. (1997). Photovoice: Concept, methodology, and use for participatory needs assessment. *Health Education & Behavior, 24*(3), 369–387. https://doi.org/10.1177/109019819702400309

Chapter 14
Using Photovoice to Resist Colonial Research Paradigms

Susan Cridland-Hughes, McKenzie Brittain, and S. Megan Che

Abstract In this chapter, we explore a critical version of photovoice to describe a study of single-sex middle school classrooms in a small school in the Southeast (single-sex is the term used by the school district so we preserve its use here while acknowledging the term is inaccurately conflated with gender by the district). Photovoice is the use of photo documentation by community participants to investigate a particular aspect of a community (Wang & Burris, *Health Education & Behavior, 24*, 369–387, 1997). Students were asked to document their experiences in middle school, single-sex classrooms through photos and captions, and the submitted photos were coded for themes. We share now a critical analysis of the implementation of photovoice and our imperfect research process. This analysis is guided by recommendations by members of historically marginalized communities for reframing research to be collaborative and responsive to the needs of the community (Bishop, *The SAGE handbook of qualitative research*. Thousand Oaks, CA: SAGE, 2005).

Why do researchers engage in research? Ary, Jacobs, and Razavieh (2002) argue that research reflects the desire to "discover general principles or interpretations of behavior that people can use to explain, predict, and control events in educational situations" (p. 17). This goal is important—we can answer important and socially relevant questions such as the patterns and trends of social patterns and access and denial to resources by looking at large-scale, quantitative data. However, this is by no means the only reason that we as researchers engage in research. Bogdan and Biklen (2003) establish the goal of qualitative research as "better understand[ing] human behavior and experiences…because it is with concrete incidents of human behavior that investigators can think more clearly and deeply about the human condition" (p. 38). This desire to explore both specific instances and broad analyses

S. Cridland-Hughes (✉) · M. Brittain · S. M. Che
Clemson University, Clemson, SC, USA
e-mail: scridla@clemson.edu; mhoxit@g.clemson.edu; sche@clemson.edu

© The Author(s) 2019
K. K. Strunk, L. A. Locke (eds.), *Research Methods for Social Justice and Equity in Education*, https://doi.org/10.1007/978-3-030-05900-2_14

163

highlights multiple ways of knowing and being in the world, and the range of methods within the research tradition helps us probe not only ways of knowing but also ways of engaging in research.

Qualitative research specifically emerged from a desire to understand the lived experiences of individuals and communities, exploring the nuances that undergird the more commonly reported statistics and analysis of the behavior of people across large groups (Erickson, 2011). Qualitative studies ask questions and record answers that offer the potential for community members to take a central role in interpreting the norms and expectations that affect decision-making both as an individual and as a member of a group.

This description of qualitative research is a simplified version of a more complex discussion: calling something qualitative research does not immediately absolve the research of positivist notions of expertise and authority. Critiques of quantitative research reflect how study participants become discrete data points, rather than complex individuals within communities with perspectives and interpretations of what has value (Denzin & Lincoln, 2005). Smith (1999) reminds us that "ways in which scientific research is implicated in the worst excesses of colonialism remains a powerful remembered history for many of the world's colonized peoples" (p. 5). The goal of this chapter is to explore the necessary conditions for facilitating social justice research with individual communities through qualitative research and specifically through the use of photovoice as a research method. Our hope is that examples of where these attempts have succeeded and failed will help researchers consider how they enter a space guided by the participants, where the researcher-participant relationship adjusts to achieve balance, "flattening" power dynamics in the co-negotiation of meaning.

Entering the Space: Acknowledging and Resisting the Colonizing Nature of Research

For qualitative research specifically, researchers draw boundaries around a place and space in order to understand how a group or community "make[s] sense of their world and the experiences they have in the world" (Merriam, 1998, p. 6). Researchers draw boundaries when we determine research questions, when we decide we will examine women in mathematics rather than men, and when we choose a theoretical lens through which to explore our research questions. In the most respectful examples of qualitative research, the work helps us understand people across a broad array of experiences and spaces. For example, as ethnographers, it may help us understand why a particular group chooses to do things in a particular way. While in some perspectives even this is colonizing, it simultaneously recognizes that there is no one location of knowledge but rather many locations and many types of knowledge.

While qualitative research often highlights issues of power, it does not inherently resist the colonizing impulse. In many cases, the drawing of research boundaries often originates far away from the community and the members who interact in that community. As we make choices about inclusion and exclusion, we colonize the space of research that "serves as a metaphor for colonial knowledge, for power, for truth" (Denzin & Lincoln, 2005, p. 1). By the time research is presented to the participants, we have mapped the space of analysis such that the community itself is no longer allowed to negotiate boundaries and meaning. In this chapter, already we have bounded the analysis such that the reader is limited to the scholars and goals that we have included, even though the reader has knowledge of his or her own goals that may add to or challenge the goals presented here.

Paris and Winn (2014) criticize:

> a history of qualitative inquiry seeking to, at worst, pathologize, exoticize, objectify, and name as deficient communities of color and other marginalized populations in the U.S. and beyond, and at best, to take and gain through research but not to give back. (p. xvi)

Decolonizing qualitative research resists colonial research paradigms, opening up, as Smith (1999) articulates, "different approaches and methodologies… to ensure that research with indigenous peoples can be more respectful, ethical, sympathetic and useful" (p. 9). The idea of decolonizing raises questions about how much a research relationship can be decolonized. Although qualitative researchers may develop rich relationships with community members, and, in many cases, even create shared spaces where both negotiate and examine meaning, there is often a separation between the observational lens of the researcher and the lived experiences of a community.

This understanding that researchers inherently colonize space has led qualitative researchers to explore ways to decolonize research and assume responsibility for the colonizing nature of the researcher gaze (Smith, 1999). Members of historically marginalized communities have offered suggestions for reframing research to be collaborative and responsive to the needs of the community so that there is bidirectional sharing of knowledge and resources. Bishop (2005) describes how, in research conducted with Maori communities, the Maori have highlighted five key questions: who initiates research, who benefits from the research, who determines the representation of the community, is the research legitimate, and who is accountable for the researchers entering into the space and publishing about the community. These questions are not questions that are specific to this one community but rather are questions that govern every study done by a researcher seeking to engage a community in dialogue.

The Theoretical and Philosophical Underpinning for Choosing Photovoice

The five questions provided by Bishop offer a useful frame for assessing the balance of power in research, a balance particularly important when engaging in qualitative research. In our study, we attempted to flatten the research relationship by using photovoice methodology to explore the experiences of youth in single-sex class-rooms. We use the term single-sex because that is the language of the district, but we discuss later how the choice of terms challenged our attempt to locate research power with the participants.

Photovoice is a community-based participatory research methodology with three goals: (1) record and reflect community strengths and concerns, (2) promote critical dialogue and knowledge about important issues, and (3) reach policymakers (Wang & Burris, 1997). Photovoice draws on similar epistemological orientations to photo-elicitation, as described in Chap. 13 by Walls and Holmquist (2019); however, pho-tovoice requires that the photos used are generated and provided by community members. While photo-elicitation can use any image, photovoice sees the images created by participants as the researcher lens. A research orientation focused on dialogue with the community about issues of concern to the community shifts the theoretical considerations of the role of the researcher and the research participant, as well as the negotiations necessary for building a non-hierarchical relationship between all people interested in making sense of research questions. It is important to note that there is also a well-established tradition of critical research within youth-led participatory action research (YPAR) that cedes responsibility for research to youth (Mirra, Garcia, & Morrell, 2016). The YPAR orientation emphasizes pro-viding support to youth asking questions about their own communities and helping youth explore how educational decision-making interacts with their communities in problematic ways. Additionally, design-based research methods such as social design experiments (Gutiérrez & Jurow, 2016) operate from the frame that the research space can be one that dismantles existing hierarchies and structures in search of new, more socially just interactions between stakeholders. These evolving research methodologies, including photovoice, reflect the need to include members of communities in the design of research and in the interpretation that occurs both before entering a community and while engaging in data collection and analysis. Photovoice offers one way of structurally privileging the voices and analyses of community members, but it is not the only way to approach the responsibility of ceding space for meaning-making.

One primary reason that researchers in education employ a photovoice methodol-ogy is to understand and center student perspectives (in contrast to teacher, parent, or school leader perspectives). For instance, Whitfield and Meyer (2005) use photovoice to establish a relationship between the teacher and students to understand students' ideas about science and about connecting the classroom to students' lives. Cook and Quigley (2013) use photovoice as a pedagogical tool to investigate ways university students connect with science. The researchers use photovoice to reveal students' inter-est in an inquiry project, reflecting on science embedded in the community around them. Cook and Quigley (2013) additionally examine relationships between the par-ticipant, the image, and the way the image was produced. The theme in these educa-tional photovoice studies is that they each center and explore student perspectives.

Another purpose for the use of photovoice in educational studies is to illuminate realities in diverse and often marginalized contexts in ways that privilege participant voice, knowledge, and perspective. In Graziano's (2011) study of educational realities of 16 Hispanic[1] English Language Learner (ELL) students in an urban elementary school, she found that student participation in photovoice was connected with those students' opportunities for developing verbal, written, reading, and listening language skills. Simmonds, Roux, and Avest (2015) incorporate a narrative-photovoice methodology in a study with South African schoolgirls to capture and understand these students' lived experiences, particularly of gender (in)equity. The activity of capturing photos provided opportunities for participants to critically reflect on their lives as girl students in their particular context. Similarly, Shah (2015) utilized a photovoice methodology with adolescent-aged girls in Western India, specifically attending to power-sharing and production of each girl's "voice."

Our photovoice study also employs a critical version of photovoice because the aim of our study was connected to concerns for power dynamics and reification of traditional gendered norms and expectations. We were wondering (and, to some extent, concerned about) how the act of separating students into two apparently distinct genders might influence the ways in which students went about the complicated process of constructing their identities. We asked students about their experiences in these gendered classrooms, and we share now a critical analysis of our imperfect research processes.

Designing a Photovoice Study

Our photovoice study asked the following questions: how is being in a single-sex classroom different from being in a coeducational public academic classroom and does this differ across content areas? We recruited youth from a rural middle school in the Southeastern United States that assigned students to single-sex academic classes for grades 6–8. We had 12 participants in all, across grades 6–8, 6 male and 6 female, enrolled in a combination of single-sex and coeducational academic classes. Each student participated in five interviews over the academic year including these topics: what it is like for the students to be in single-sex and coeducational settings, what are their perspectives of single-sex and coeducational settings, do they have preferences for one class type over the other (and why), why did they decide to participate in single-sex settings, and what connections, if any, do the students see between class type and their learning.

In addition to semi-structured individual interviews, students were asked to document their experiences in single-sex and coeducational settings with photographs that capture the essence of what it means, from their perspective, to be in a single-sex or coeducational classroom. Students were asked to provide 10 photographic images that convey an aspect or aspects of their experiences in single-sex and coeducational classrooms at the rate of approximately 1–2 images per month and to construct a brief caption for the images they provide to the research team. We have included some data from those images and captions to demonstrate how youth participants (referenced in the text by pseudonyms) used the photo as a lens into their worlds.

Applying the Five Questions to Our Photovoice Study

Initiation of research. This research reflected questions and study design established by the external researchers. Additionally, our participants were still within a very traditionally hierarchical middle school environment. Initial access to the school came primarily through administration, then teachers, then parents, and then through the students themselves. While this is understandable given the strict scrutiny provided to research done with students, this also changed our access to the community as a whole. Although one researcher had a long-standing relationship with school administrators who were interested in how the single-sex education structure was functioning in their school, our focus on the students as a community could have been perceived by the youth as imposed from outside. However, using photovoice allowed youth the opportunity to guide both the focus of the study and the follow-up questions.

Who benefited? Students involved in the study benefited financially from participation because they received incentives. In some cases, they also seemed to benefit from the opportunity to reflect on their experiences. The data youth participants submit will benefit the research team as it is incorporated into presentations and publications. Adult members at the school receive very little in the way of benefits.

Representation. If we are moving through gatekeepers to recruit participants, then how can we know when we have reached a representative group of participants and collection of images? At one point, the teacher helping us reach out to students for participation expressed concerns about whether one student was a "good" student for the study. Her internal assumptions about what would make a good student affected the recruitment she did for participation.

Legitimacy. We asked youth participants to submit photos and captions so that our interpretation of the caption was connected with their own understanding of what the individual student was capturing. As we analyzed the data, we refined the semi-structured interviewing protocol to reflect data from the specific images from the individual student—Brooke's questions would be tied to the previous images and captions that Brooke submitted. The generic nature of the questioning, then, gave way to dialogue about individual ideas and perspectives.

Accountability. Our study revealed that we had limited accountability within the larger community. We privileged the voices of students to the exclusion of the story that the leaders wanted to tell. The lines we drew about whom to include and whom to exclude in the image collection process meant that we protected space for students but were more vocal in our resistance to adult members of the school. Much as in Cushman's study, we had to choose a side.

Tensions and Tradeoffs with Photovoice as a Methodology

Navigating Power Dynamics Between School, Students, and Researchers

One of the first tensions we encountered as we began the study was how best to support students as they started to explore the images they wanted to capture. The research team continuously discussed how to navigate freedom and to value participant perspectives while also giving guidance to students who did not necessarily know what to look for when taking photos. We questioned how to balance structure with agency, particularly in photovoice where the primary goal of the research study is allowing participants to guide the interpretation through their own lenses.

We also questioned how and whether to isolate the goals of the students from the goals of the adults in the space. It may be that when photovoice is done in communities that do not have bureaucratic barriers to participation, the interaction and negotiation with individual members of the community reflect a flattened hierarchy. In a schooled setting, researchers were constantly negotiating access from adults while students were operating within pre-established norms.

One of the other tensions that emerged was around the use of incentives for student participation. Our study was funded through an internal grant; students were using their own devices to capture images, so we provided Amazon gift cards rather than providing individual cameras. We did not notify students that they would receive Amazon gift cards for their participation until after they agreed to participate in the study; however, once they began the study, they knew that the submission of images and captions would result in a form of compensation for their time. One student started late, but none of our youth participants dropped out of the study, and all of them submitted the target number of images and captions. Additionally, they all participated in the follow-up interviews. In one way, this appears to be a success of the study: we had a complete data set for students allowing us to follow the trajectory of their perspectives when asked about their experiences in single-sex education. However, the depth of the captioning and the images recorded varied greatly across participants. This led to many conversations among the research team members about the motivation for students to continue to participate in the study. For example, at one point, a student submitted the following photo and caption (Fig. 14.1).

This image does not appear to have any immediately discernible connection to the student's experiences in the single-sex educational environment; however, the caption does offer some thought regarding the student's understanding of the environment. Our research team chose to code and analyze all data that were submitted without attempting to judge the motivation of the student.

Fig. 14.1 "Discipline from
the teachers can be difficult
because sometimes the
guys (or girls) in the class
don't want to listen"

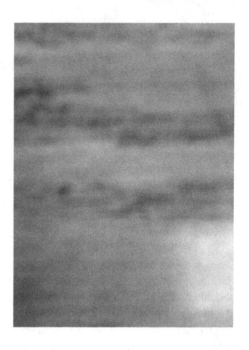

Identifying Filters and Their Contributions to Dehumanizing Research Practices

While the previous section focuses on the power dynamics of the study, there were other tensions connected with how filters contributed to dehumanizing research practices. One of the filters we did not anticipate was the sorting process that occurs at a single-sex school when students are placed into classes and classified as male and female. The research team used the linguistic boundaries drawn by the school to choose students for the study, recruiting "a total of 12 students (six female, six male) who are concurrently enrolled in at least one single-sex academic class and one coeducational academic class" (Recruiting Script, Single-Sex Education Study, 2015). We recruited 11 students, and our study attempted to privilege student perspectives and specifically looked for student perspectives from boys and girls. However, there is an implicit assumption that students selected for this study agreed with the school-level determination based on sex, and there was no space for students to determine whether their gender matched the assigned placement. We accepted existing boundaries based on the comfort level of the school community around terminology; while we could have responded by removing sex- and gender-connected pronouns as we asked students to record their experiences, we continued to operate within colonizing language and structures. In our debriefing conversations, we reflected on the challenge of access being predicated on administrative comfort and how the students operating in these colonizing structures were also not served if we were unable to ask critical questions about those structures.

There was also a filtering process in place when students were recruited for the study. That filtering process was both technological (did students have access to a device) and attitudinal (did students possess habits of interaction valued by the school such that they were recommended for the study). This filtering process may have resulted in students who were recognized as "doing school well" and thus good representatives for the school as a whole. While students who worked with us did identify problems, those most likely to identify the problems with single-sex education might be those students who were least likely to be identified as good students.

Practical Affordances for a More Humanized Approach to Research

After reading about the challenges and limitations we experienced, you may be wondering whether the process of transferring power to community members and equalizing power is worth it. Our use of photovoice, however, revealed that even with the challenges of filtering and motivation, there were successes for data collection and data analysis.

With regard to data collection, we were able to hold space for students to guide the questions connected with their daily lived experiences. Photo submissions from the students did not go through the administration of the school but were submitted directly to a member of the research team. In a research team memo dated November 6, 2016, the following clarifications were made:

1. (School contact) will be present to ensure that cell phones are used in a responsible manner by students solely to transmit study data to the research phone number.
2. Students are solely responsible for the content of the caption and the selection of images.

This flattened research centered youth voices about their experiences in data collection. The administration of the school did not have a role in determining the value of the images and captions submitted, and the research team did not overlay on their observations of the experience their own assumptions about value and merit. Instead, we limited our analysis to the images and asking questions about the text that students provided.

In some cases, the process of taking photos and creating captions helped youth participants critically explore the structures that surrounded them. Over the course of the data collection year, some students created captions questioning the value of using sex assignments to delineate classes. For example, Brooke started with the following image that seemed to accept that single-sex classes were positive for students (Fig. 14.2).

Her final image and caption, however, reflected an analysis that was critical of the single-sex environment, emphasizing the competition between peers (Fig. 14.3).

Fig. 14.2 "Students seem
more focused and on-task"

Fig. 14.3 "In a unisex
class, we always thought
that we were bigger than
each other. Our egos were
high"

Additionally, students in the older grades were able to reflect on their previous
experiences in single-sex classes and the transition back to integrated classrooms.
The photovoice methodology allowed them to direct the research to both current
experiences and how those experiences compared with their previous experiences.

The self-directed nature of photovoice as a methodology allowed students to control what they chose to share as well as how they wished to process their experience of this single-sex middle school environment.

Questions to Consider when Doing Photovoice

Embarking on a photovoice study requires a particular philosophical and practical orientation to the planning and design of research, and we recommend that you ask yourself the following questions as you design and engage in the research process:

Philosophical Questions

1. How does this research study resist notions of researcher primacy in the critical process?
2. How does this research directly benefit the community to whom I have reached out and position community members as equal partners in the research space?
3. What safeguards can I put in place to ensure that there is constant attention to the negotiated relationship that privileges community knowledge and community insight?
4. What are the existing structural filters that make it difficult for individual community members to reflect honestly on their experiences (e.g., oppressive discourse or hierarchical structures)?

Implementation Questions

1. How can this research study respond to a community need?
2. When working with participants who require additional protections, how can we add those protections without limiting participants' opportunities to critique and evaluate the community?
3. How will members of the community be involved in the interpretation of the images and captions submitted?

Understanding the ways researchers colonize can help us understand methods for avoiding colonizing processes within a perpetually asymmetric power structure that undergirds society. As researchers, we can and should intentionally plan for humanizing and socially just research.

Suggested Readings

Delgado, M. (2015). *Urban youth and photovoice: Visual ethnography in action.* Oxford, UK: Oxford University Press.

Delgado explores photovoice in urban communities with young people, highlighting how photovoice incorporates skills from youth who have grown up with easy access to phones and photographic technology.

Edwards, M., Perry, B., Janzen, K., & Menzies, C. (2012). Using the artistic pedagogical technology of photovoice to promote interaction in the online post-secondary classroom: The students' perspective. *Electronic Journal of e-Learning, 10*(1), 32–43.

Edwards, Perry, Janzen, and Menzies used photovoice to promote interactions in online post-secondary classrooms, focusing on students' perspectives regarding the effect of photovoice on interactions in the courses.

Smith, L. T. (1999). *Decolonizing methodologies: Research and indigenous peoples.* New York, NY: ZED Books, Ltd.

This text is particularly important for understanding the historical and contemporary implications of research with historically marginalized communities and to understand the responses by indigenous communities to outsider representations of their communities and culture.

Note

1. The term Hispanic is preserved from the original study.

References

Ary, D., Jacobs, L., & Razavieh, A. (2002). *Introduction to research in education* (6th ed.). Belmont, CA: Wadsworth/Thomson Learning.

Bishop, R. (2005). Freeing ourselves from neocolonial domination in research: A Kaupapa Maori approach to creating knowledge. In N. Denzen & Y. Lincoln (Eds.), *The SAGE handbook of qualitative research* (3rd ed., pp. 109–138). Thousand Oaks, CA: SAGE.

Bogdan, R., & Biklen, S. (2003). *Qualitative research for education: An introduction to theories and methods* (4th ed.). Boston, MA: Allyn and Bacon.

Cook, K., & Quigley, C. (2013). Connecting to our community: Utilizing photovoice as a pedagogical tool to connect college students to science. *International Journal of Environmental and Science Education., 8*(2), 339–357.

Denzin, N., & Lincoln, Y. (2005). The discipline and practice of qualitative research. In N. Denzen & Y. Lincoln (Eds.), *The SAGE handbook of qualitative Research* (3rd ed., pp. 1–32). Thousand Oaks, CA: SAGE.

Erickson, F. (2011). A history of qualitative inquiry in social and educational research. In N. Denzen & Y. Lincoln (Eds.), *The SAGE handbook of qualitative research* (4th ed., pp. 18–43). Thousand Oaks, CA: SAGE.

Graziano, K. J. (2011). Working with English language learners: Preservice teachers and photovoice. *International Journal of Multicultural Education, 13*(1), 1–19. https://doi.org/10.18251/ijme.v13i1.354

Gutiérrez, K., & Jurow, A. (2016). Social design experiments: Toward equity by design. *Journal of the Learning Sciences, 25*(4), 565–598. https://doi.org/10.1080/10508406.2016.1204548

Merriam, S. (1998). *Qualitative research and case study applications in education.* San Francisco, CA: Jossey-Bass.

Mirra, N., Garcia, A., & Morrell, E. (2016). *Doing youth participatory action research: Transforming inquiry with researchers, educators, and students*. New York, NY: Routledge.

Paris, D., & Winn, M. T. (Eds.). (2014). *Humanizing research: Decolonizing qualitative inquiry with youth and communities*. Los Angeles, CA: SAGE.

Shah, P. (2015). Spaces to speak: Photovoice and the reimagination of girls' education in India. *Comparative Education Review, 59*(1), 50–74. https://doi.org/10.1086/678699

Simmonds, S., Roux, C., & Avest, I. (2015). Blurring the boundaries between photovoice and narrative inquiry: A narrative-photovoice methodology for gender-based research. *International Journal of Qualitative Methods, 14*(3), 33–49. https://doi.org/10.1177/160940691501400303

Smith, L. T. (1999). *Decolonizing methodologies: Research and indigenous peoples*. New York, NY: ZED Books, Ltd.

Walls, A., & Holmquist, S. (2019). Through their eyes, in their words: Using photo-elicitation to amplify study voice in policy and school improvement research. In K. Strunk & L. Locke (Eds.), *Research methods for social justice and equity in education*. Palgrave Macmillan.

Wang, C., & Burris, M. (1997). Photovoice: Concept, methodology, and use for participatory needs assessment. *Health Education & Behavior, 24*(3), 369–387. https://doi.org/10.1177/109019819702400309

Whitfield, D., & Meyer, H. (2005). Learning from our students: Photovoice and classroom action research. *The Science Education Review, 4*(4), 97–103.

Chapter 15
Re-introducing Life History Methodology: An Equitable Social Justice Approach to Research in Education

James S. Wright

Abstract Educational researchers who are mindful of social justice are suggested to consider contemporary research methodologies' historical alignment with colonization: Expansion and the ensuing epistemicide. This chapter argues that life history methodology can be used as a counter to traditional research methodologies and provides space to collect and analyze data in a way that counters past traditions. Contemporary educational research methodologies and methods are replete with historical baggage so pronounced that social justice advocates can, unwittingly, engage in research methods that reify the harms that they seek to counter. Life history provides real opportunities for educational researchers to develop new knowledge by listening to and validating the experiences of the most vulnerable populations. Life history challenges the idea of a universal truth—stemming from Eurocentric positionalities.

Research Methodologies and Hegemony

In my social justice approach to research I am mindful of contemporary research methodologies' historical impact in the establishment of colonization. This chapter talks about European expansion and the various entanglements it wrought, displacement, violence, and death, in pursuit of conquests. Contemporary research methodologies are aligned with this history. Discursively, contemporary research methodologies in education impose, violate, and censure the epistemologies and cultures of dominated and minoritized Black and Brown communities and students (Battiste, 2013; Sharp, 2008; Smith, 1999; Willinsky, 2000). In my attempt to sidestep these educational research landmines, I am cautious of this history and its

J. S. Wright (✉)
San Diego State University, San Diego, CA, USA

© The Author(s) 2019
K. K. Strunk, L. A. Locke (eds.), *Research Methods for Social Justice and Equity in Education*, https://doi.org/10.1007/978-3-030-05900-2_15

177

contemporary effects. I argue that life history methodology has the potential to off-set the entanglements of violence, marginalization, and imposition embedded in research methodologies. Life history research as a methodology consists of a collective of life stories that comprise the main data source. Life history methodology consists of a theoretical analysis of the method—life stories and the socio-cultural, socio-economic, and political aspects and assumptions related to these methods. My application of life history seeks to counter the problematic elements found in the culture of educational research.

Life History as a Counterculture

I utilize the life history methodology as an antithesis to traditional educational research methods. Some scholars call life history methodology a counterculture—a divergence from traditional educational research methods—the ways we come to know including the strategies, paradigms, research models, grammars, and theories in educational research (Dhunpath, 2000; Goodson & Sikes, 2001). Life history as a counterculture is complementary to the necessitated cultural insurgency and resistance to the culture of education policy (Stein, 2004) discourses and practices that deficitizes policy beneficiaries often identified as minoritized communities (Black and Brown students).

Life historians re-present life stories as told to them and are mindful of their own frames of reference. I utilize life history to help highlight cultural elements of educational discourses and practices. A life story is a rendition of a lived experience, an interpretive layer, but moving to life history needs additional stories, theories, context, and further interpretations, which adds richness. Goodson and Sikes (2001) argue for life stories as the starting point for life history work. The life stories of research participants, as well as researchers, can be central to a life history study, as part of the life history methodology (Wright, 2017). Goodson and Sikes (2001), in following many eminent sociologists, suggest that life history methodology is the perfect method to study any aspect of social life. Although being a community member is not required in life history, I argue that life history methodology, while not without potential for abuse and misuse, is effective at explaining the lived experiences and perspectives of the community under study. The abuse and misuse that can occur have a long history, some of which have been referenced in this chapter, such as misinterpretations from outsiders that often lead to violence. However, abuse and misuse can occur from within as alluded to in Khalifa's (2015) *Can Blacks Be Racists?* I conducted my dissertation as well as other research in communities where I was born and raised. I share similar histories and culture, and I understand the local discourses, idioms, and practices found in those communities. In my utilization of life history methodology, I situate myself in the study as part of the greater life history project.

Life History Research: Stories from an Urban District

> Speaking in and through stories then becomes a way to engage self-transformation a kind
> of rite of passage…I am aware of the value of story and its ability to transform my research,
> and resist the Eurocentric frameworks that privileged other peoples' stories and analyses…
> (Battiste, 2013, p. 17)

I utilize the life history methodology as a collection of stories, including my own, from current or former residents of an urban Connecticut school district. I was born and raised within the communities that comprise the school district under study. The life stories add *culturally responsive* information to the study of educational studies. My approach to the life history methodology is to humanize the experiences of African Americans, Latinxs, and others in the urban communities, by chronicling samples from their lived experiences. Moreover, the recording of these narratives works to fill gaps in educational history and in research on Black and Latinx/urban education in the United States in general and in urban communities in Connecticut more specifically.

Historiography and Life History Methodology

Life history methodology is used throughout qualitative, quantitative, and mixed-methods studies. Life historians work from the language individuals use to express and define their lives (Goodson & Sikes, 2001). Jones (1983) called upon a qualitative approach to social analysis using life history and regarded it as a unique tool used to examine and analyze the subjective experience of individuals and their construction of the social world. Life historians examine how individuals narrate their experiences and perceptions of their lived social context (Goodson & Sikes, 2001). Jones (1983) noted that "of all research methods, it [life history methodology] perhaps comes closest to allowing the researcher access to how individuals create and portray the social world around them" (p. 147). Rubby Dhunpath (2000) suggests that the life history methodology "approach is probably the only authentic means of understanding how motives and practices reflect the intimate intersection of institutional and individual experience in the postmodern world" (p. 544). Life history methodology is interpretive and epistemologically grounded in the everyday, commonsense world (common to those who reside in their worlds) and is ontologically rooted within the constructions and explanations members of those worlds ascribe to their reality and actions (Denzin, 1983; Jones, 1983).

Life History: Stories and Coping

Gramling and Carr (2004) outlined the various dimensions and methodological considerations of life history, including coping. They pointed out that life history was "a holistic, qualitative account of life that emphasizes the experiences of the individual and how the person copes. It links experiences to subsequent actions and theoretical perspectives with personal experiences" (Gramling & Carr, 2004, p. 208). There is a growing body of interdisciplinary literature—psychology, philosophy, and the natural sciences—acknowledging the value of narratives (Dhunpath, 2000; McAdams, 2008).

Coping and time encapsulated. In the historiographical research literature, research methods such as biographies, oral histories, and life stories are distinguished from life history methodology. Oral history is a method in which memory and experience can be captured for future generations, which can be a component of life history methodology. Life history methodology is broader in scope and consists of a theoretical analysis of life stories. Also, life history is more holistic; it seeks to capture how individuals cope. It links these actions (coping) and personal experiences with theoretical perspectives. Life history is also distinguished by a framework of time (Gramling & Carr, 2004). For example, my life history encapsulates the timeframe from 2010 to 2016.

The life stories in my work (Wright, 2017) illustrated how we—my family and others from the urban community that I was raised in—coped—under the socio-cultural/socio-economic climate, which included deindustrialization, well-documented political malfeasance, mass incarceration, failed schools and schooling practices, and ambivalent educators (Wright, 2017). These life stories, which underscored and evidenced these ills, were removed from life experiences, interpreted, and made into text. A life story is a rendition of a lived experience, an interpretive layer, but the move to life history needs additional stories and context and further interpretations, such as interviews, documents, and theory, which add richness.

Life stories and life history as creating identity. Goodson and Sikes (2001) asserted "life history research provides [opportunity] to tell your life story, to craft a narrative that links together events, experiences, and perceptions, [it] is the explicit opportunity to create an identity" (p. 41). This happens in all social situations, not just in the context of research. People tell their stories in a certain way for a certain purpose, guided by their environments, which helps construct the identity that they wish to re-present (Goodson & Sikes, 2001).

Identifying urban life in Connecticut. The construction of life history is a joint creation between the life historian and the storytellers. Life history methodology is appropriate for equitable social justice educational research and praxis. I conducted a study in Connecticut, a state often thought of for its affluence and wealth. Rarely do people associate Connecticut, its cities, and neighborhoods with impoverished Black and Brown families and failing schools. These life stories of people living in the shadows of Connecticut's affluence are brought to the center and amplified (Wright, 2017).

According to Goodson and Sikes (2001), life historians are creating and crafting stories when they design and write their research. But it is not only life historians who are implicated in creating/crafting stories in their research. No matter their approach or method, all researchers—quantitative, qualitative, or historical—are engaged in storytelling. Scholars, Clough (1992) and Goodson and Sikes (2001), have posited that all representations of reality, even statistical representations, are narrative constructs and as a result creative constructs. Similar to scholars engaged in other methodological approaches, life historians re-present life stories as told to them within the context of their own frames of reference.

Life stories and life history as pedagogy. Some scholars advocate for life history as a pedagogical tool, asserting that it can be a cathartic and liberating research tool (Dhunpath, 2000; Witherell & Noddings, 1991). Life histories provide stories of people (idioms, authenticated definitions, and interpretations), struggling through real problems and other situations. They offer liberation from indifferent and disengaged researchers and research generated by samples, and faceless subjects without histories and social context.

Humans in general, and researchers and educators in particular, are fallible humans with vulnerabilities that constantly resurface. Curriculum historian Ivor Goodson (1992) argued that because teaching is personal, it is critical to know the type of person the teacher is. I argue that it is equally critical to know educators and researchers—who they are, their politics, and their inclinations. Educators and researchers are humans shaped by histories, politics, values, morals, and a worldview (Dhunpath, 2000; Goodson, 1992).

Interpretive Framework

The epistemological position of life history is interpretive as opposed to normative. An interpretive lens seeks to understand the phenomena from within (emic) as opposed to a normative style of inquiry, which seeks to study phenomena from without (etic) (Jones, 1983). *Emic* researchers are sometimes referred to as insiders. An insider starts from the perspectives of the research participants: The concepts and categories deemed meaningful and appropriate by members of the culture whose beliefs and actions are a part of the analysis (President & Fellows Harvard University, 2008; Smith, 1999). Etic researchers are sometimes referred to as outsiders. An outsider uses theories and perspectives from outside of the setting being analyzed. The words emic and etic, according to linguistics and anthropologists in the 1950s and 1960s, refer to two different approaches toward researching human beings. Since the 1950s and 1960s, the concepts have evolved and have been adopted by various researchers across disciplines including education (President & Fellows Harvard University, 2008).

Insider-Outsider Perspectives: Emic and Etic Approaches to Research

The interpretive lens offered by life history informs us that knowledge and under-standing are bound by context. Jones (1983) contends that context is the result of a socially constructed world of patterns and frames. Interpretive inquiry seeks to address questions asked, along with the historical and social context that they are asked from "within" social phenomena. This context emerging from within social phenomena brings "to the surface the essential dimensions of a social process or social context" (Jones, 1983, p. 150). This means that context should always be according to the lived perspectives of the research participants and less an interpre-tation of those lived experiences by an outsider, who may exhibit little care that the interpretations are representative and authentic.

A normative inquiry, or studying phenomena from without, gives the researcher "ontological control." Jones (1983) argued that a study done from without "is inclined to impose a definition on the subject of inquiry and to postulate relation-ships of a hypothetical kind" (p. 150). This outsider control exercised by the researcher is a common research protocol. This *ontological control* often leads to misinterpretation, misunderstanding, and, to varying degrees, replicating the vio-lence of research that was central to colonization.

Between an Emic Rock and Etic Hard Place

While some methodologies rely more heavily on one approach over the other, "many researchers live in the tension between these two extremes" (President & Fellows Harvard University, 2008, p. 1). A completely etic approach to research risks overlooking potentially new and/or groundbreaking concepts and perspec-tives. And at the same time, all researchers come into a research project with previ-ous concepts, perspectives, and lenses through which they see the world (President & Fellows Harvard University, 2008). Emic and etic research methods are academic concepts introduced in the mid-twentieth century by anthropologists and linguists to study humans and as such are engulfed in ethnocentric (Eurocentric) and political controversy (President & Fellows Harvard University, 2008; Sharp, 2008; Smith, 1999). Nonetheless, insider and outsider, emic and etic, perspectives are used in my engagement with life history.

Critiques of Life History

One of the challenges of doing life history research is the transformation of the life stories of individuals into a life history. This transformation requires the inclusion of historical context and an acknowledgment of subjectivity (Goodson & Sikes,

2001). Goodson and Sikes (2001) warned that this was "a dangerous move, for it offers the researcher considerable 'colonizing' power to 'locate' the life story with all its inevitable selections, shifts and silences" (p. 17). The colonizing danger of moving from life stories to life history is a real concern that the life historian must contend with.

Outsider from Within: Inside and Out

I use my own life story as part of my life history research. Stories from my life indicate familiarity with urban Black and Brown discourses in the city, idioms, and taken-for-granted knowledge. In many ways, I am an *insider* in the study. My connection makes me accessible to the circumstances of my study as a person both within and outside of the phenomena. I have personal connections with many of the people whose stories I included in my life history study. I am honest about these connections, and I attempt to be reflective about my own place in the life history (Wright, 2017). However, as an academic, I am a part of a larger institution and academic community with different discourses, idioms, and taken-for-granted knowledge, which also makes me an *outsider*. Juggling these two worlds as both an insider and an outsider is a primary task for the life historian. My insider connections do not guarantee that I will not misrepresent these communities. An insider is still capable of imposing and inflicting violence upon the community under study with an intentionally or otherwise skewed collection and analysis processes.

According to Rubby Dhunpath (2000), there are three possible responses to critiques of life history research. The first possibility is not to respond at all. But avoidance is inappropriate, and "would smack of the same kind of intellectual arrogance often exhibited by empiricists" (Dhunpath, 2000, p. 543). However, in answering the question, the life historian should be mindful of her/his engagement in the paradigm wars: The socially constructed dichotomy between empirical research designs and other research designs—the quantitative versus qualitative/humanities versus social science debates (Gage, 1989; Howe, 2009; Tadajewski, 2009). The second possibility according to Dhunpath is to aggressively defend the virtues of the life history research approach at the risk of becoming an apologist for its legitimacy, thereby reaffirming the dominance espoused by empiricists. A third possibility is to stake a claim of life history as a counterculture to traditional research methodologies (Dhunpath, 2000). To position life history as a counterculture provides leverage toward an intervention into Westernization (Mignolo, 2011, 2012), its method—White supremacy (Khalifa, 2015)—and it's racist discourses, rhetoric, and practices located in the culture of educational praxis as indicated in Stein's (2004) culture of education policy thesis and others. The culture of education policy frames policy beneficiaries as culturally deficient and blames their historical, socio-cultural, and socio-economic predicament on a lack of, and a need for, *standard American values* (Stein, 2004).

Interdisciplinary Confusion

When it is done well, life story methods and the life history research methodology crosses disciplinary boundaries. This allows the convergence of multiple disciplines while maintaining the integrity of each. However, some scholars raise concerns and cite confusion associated with this approach. Scholars have argued that the plurality of voices could cause harsh discord and fragmented perspectives, which could lead to a culture of misunderstanding and miscommunication (Dhunpath, 2000; Hargreaves, 2011).

Identifying importance and representation. The relationship between the researcher and the researched and the act of deeming someone or a situation as important is further complicated by the researcher's veneration or disdain for the participants in the study. Such a situation is potentially dysfunctional. Furthermore, how is life history positioned outside of the oppressive conditions, specifically in regard to research traditions, that have silenced individuals? Close attention must be paid to matters of representation and retelling of stories (Dhunpath, 2000; Goodson, 1992).

The nuance of representation. Gayatri Chakravorty Spivak (1988) wrote, what many consider, a classic essay on the problem of speaking for cultural others—*Can the subaltern speak?* According to Sharp (2008), Spivak's complex article has been interpreted in various ways. The premise of the article, according to Sharp (2008), was to discuss the problem of speaking for those whose cultural background is profoundly different from one's own. Spivak (1988) is critical of the self-assured, scientific method used by Western scholars' way of knowing the *other* (read non-Western). Scholars refer to the Westerner speaking for non-Westerners as epistemic violence or epistemicide, the damage done to the ways of knowing and understanding indigenous and non-Western cultures with regard to religion, science, philosophy, architecture, and governance (de Sousa Santos, 2014; Spivak, 1988).

As a result, Westerners—with profoundly different cultural backgrounds—have been purveyors of epistemicide, resulting in the marginalization and death of the subaltern voice and culture. As it pertains to educational research and praxis, I argue, epistemological imposition—epistemicide—is found across the educational landscape. Attempts to recover the subaltern voice by cultural outsiders and cultural insiders are not equivalent. Furthermore, cultural insiders should be mindful of the inevitability and dangers of essentialism. Such dangers highlight the difficulty of recovering "a voice for the subaltern without negating its heterogeneity" (Sharp, 2008, p. 114).

The challenges of representation. Representation has its limits. These limits include, and are not limited to, determining what information is relevant to include as a person's story. de Sousa Santos (2014) contends that once relevancy is established the phenomenon must be identified, detected, and recognized. Detection is the process by which traits or features in a phenomenon are defined. Recognition is the delineation of the parameters that guide the specific system of explanation or interpretation that the detected phenomena will be classified through (de Sousa

Santos, 2014). These strategies and processes are predisposed and inclined with the potential for abuse. In other words, researchers and historians chose to center specific aspects of their research, perhaps leaving out more valuable aspects, at least more valuable to its research participants. This inevitability occurs for various reasons, oftentimes partisan reasons such as adherence to political ideologies and discourses as well as racial, ethnic, and other alignments/misalignments.

The value of representation. Robert J. C. Young (2004) argued that "it was never the case that the subaltern could not speak: rather that the dominant would not listen" (p. 5). In spite of the complexities, nuances, and potential challenges of representation, Spivak (1988) acknowledges the value in speaking for the other by cultural *insiders*. This can be done with mutual boundary setting between cultural insiders and those they represent. In this way validity becomes built in. Temporary alliances and "strategic essentialism" with a clear image of identity as politics of opposition to fight for the rights of minoritized groups are appropriate (Sharp, 2008). In my experience, representation is common and welcomed in African American cultures and communities (we rep[1] where we are from, and we support those who rep us as well). This occurs in other minoritized communities experiencing and enduring Westernized Patriarchal paradigms. Linda Tuhiwai Smith (1999) argued, similarly, that many artists, musicians, and filmmakers try to capture moments of their people and employ representation as both a political concept and a form of expression. Also, Smith suggests that representation was a form of resistance to what has been imposed upon marginalized communities by those engaged in their epistemicide.

Theory, Methodology, and the V Word

Tommy J. Curry (2017) provokes and challenges existing academic frameworks, theories, and research protocols that frame Black men and boys as historically and contemporarily equivalent to and striving toward Westernized models of Patriarchy. These academic frameworks persist in spite of a historical record of succumbing to and resisting Westernized Patriarchal violence and domination imposed upon Black men and boys. Furthermore, Curry argues that Black males' and boys' vulnerability, and struggles to navigate the paradigm of Westernized Patriarchal violence and White supremacy, is misaligned with the ways in which Black men and boys are framed in academic discourse and theory. Curry argues that Black men and boys, the pariahs of American society, rank at the bottom of every socio-economic, socio-political, and statistical category, including criminal justice, health care, and education. Curry's analysis opposes academic framings and research methods related to Black males and boys and decries these as justification for Black male studies.

Gloria Anzaldúa (1990) urges developing new theories—theorizing methodologies—to understand those on the margins of society better. Anzaldúa (1990) argued for "theories that overlap many 'worlds'" theorizing methods whose categories of analysis include race, class, gender, and ethnicity. These are theories "that will point out ways to maneuver between our particular experiences and the necessity of forming our own categories and theoretical models for patterns we uncover" (pp. xxv–xxvi). Similar to concerns raised by Curry (2017) and Anzaldúa (1990), I position life history methodology toward countering marginalization and deficit frameworks.

The Question of Validity

What about validity? Many qualitative theorists have abandoned the concept of validity altogether due to its problematic assumption of a real world that can be judged by standards of objectivity (Dhunpath, 2000; Maxwell, 2013). Some, however, use the term "validity" without its implications of "objective truth" (Maxwell, 2013). Maxwell (2013) thought of validity in a "fairly straightforward, common-sense way, to refer to the correctness or credibility of a description, conclusion, explanation, interpretation or other sort of account" (p. 122). Life history "challenges the notion of there being no 'truth,' but instead asserts that there exists a series of subjective views" (Dhunpath, 2000, p. 547).

In life history, the researcher's own experience is a valid part of her/his own knowledge as long as it is subject to public and critical appraisal (Dhunpath, 2000). Linda Tuhiwai Smith (1999) argues that researchers who are also members of that community have to live and interact with those they study "on a day-to-day basis" (p. 137). Due to the level of collaboration between the researcher and participants, "seeking meaning and explanations together, respondent validation may well be built into the research design" (Goodson & Sikes, 2001, p. 36). "Validity is established by demonstrating that sociological explanation is congruent with the meanings through which members construct their realities and accomplish their everyday practical activities" (Jones, 1983, p. 152). As a member of the community under study, I am open to public criticism.

Conclusion

Life history methodology is a worthy alternative for educational researchers concerned with social justice and equity. Life history provides researchers the space to collect and analyze data in a way that counters much of the traditional methodologies and methods in research. Contemporary educational research methodologies and methods are replete with historical baggage related to colonization and expansion, along with the violence and marginalization that those entailed. This history of colonization and marginalization is so pronounced that perhaps even social justice advocates, unknowingly, engage in research methods that reproduce the harms that they seek to disrupt.

For social justice advocates, life history methodology mandates that the insights, perspectives, and experiences of those experiencing injustice are the main sources of data. Life history provides real opportunities for educational researchers to develop new knowledge by listening to and validating the experiences of the most vulnerable populations. Life history challenges the idea of a universal truth—stemming from Eurocentric positionalities. Life history's position as a counterculture leverages interventions into Westernization and White supremacy's methodologies, theories, and discourses located throughout the educational landscape.

Suggested Readings

Battiste, M. (2013). *Decolonizing education: Nourishing the learning spirit.* Saskatoon, Canada: Purich Publishing.

Marie Battiste is an Indigenous woman tuned in to the plight of her ancestors. She is also Western educated and as such speaks with an authoritative *double consciousness*. As an educational administrator trying to improve educational opportunity for native students, Battiste provides important empirical perspectives aligning Western educational systems with coloniality.

Dhunpath, R. (2000). Life history methodology: "Narradigm" regained. *International Journal of Qualitative Studies in Education, 13*(5), 543–551. https://doi.org/10.1080/09518390050156459

Rubby Dhunpath discusses the increasing popularity of narratives/biographies in educational research. Yet, narratives/biographies are still delegitimized by the positivist/empiricist tradition and its artificial dichotomy between qualitative and quantitative approaches to research. This article proposes narrative/biographical research methodology and methods as a counterculture to *traditional* methods and examines the potential of narratives/biographies in understanding the lives of educators.

Gage, N. (1989). The paradigm wars and their aftermath a "historical" sketch of research on teaching since 1989. *Educational Researcher, 18*(7), 4–10. https://doi.org/10.3102/0013189X018007004

Goodson, I., & Sikes, P. (2001). *Life history research in educational settings: Learning from lives* (1st ed.). Buckingham, UK and Philadelphia, PA: Open University Press.

Life history methodology has emerged in popularity with a variety of educational researchers and topics. This book explores and considers various reasons for this popularity and argues that life history methodology has a major and unique contribution in understanding schools, schooling, and educational experiences. The book uses examples of life history research to illustrate theoretical, methodological, ethical, and practical issues in education and in educational contexts.

Howe, K. R. (2008). Isolating science from the humanities: The third dogma of educational research. *Qualitative Inquiry*. https://doi.org/10.1177/1077800408318302

This article criticizes the quantitative/qualitative *dogmas* of educational research and the incompatibility, fact-value dichotomy premise. The author contends that no epistemological divide can be determined between the empirical sciences and the humanities. Furthermore, empirical research in education and the humanities' focus on values should not be disconnected.

Note

1. Rep is shorthand for represent. A common discourse in Black, African American, and other minoritized communities.

References

Anzaldúa, G. (Ed.). (1990). *Making face, making soul/haciendo caras: Creative and critical perspectives by feminists of color* (1st ed.). San Francisco, CA: Aunt Lute Books.

Battiste, M. (2013). *Decolonizing education: Nourishing the learning spirit*. Saskatoon, Canada: Purich Publishing.

Clough, P. T. (1992). *The end(s) of ethnography: From realism to social criticism*. Newbury Park, CA: SAGE Publications.

Curry, T. J. (2017). *The man-not: Race, class, genre, and the dilemmas of black manhood*. Philadelphia, PA: Temple University Press.

Denzin, N. K. (1983). *Beyond method: Strategies for social research: 1st (first) edition* (G. Morgan, Ed.). SAGE Publications.

Dhunpath, R. (2000). Life history methodology: "Narradigm" regained. *International Journal of Qualitative Studies in Education, 13*(5), 543–551. https://doi.org/10.1080/09518390050156459

Gage, N. (1989). The Paradigm wars and their aftermath: A "historical" sketch of research on teaching since 1989. *Educational Researcher, 18*(7), 4–10. https://doi.org/10.3102/0013189X018007004

Goodson, I. (1992). *Studying teachers' lives* (Reprint ed.). New York, NY: Routledge.

Goodson, I., & Sikes, P. (2001). *Life history research in educational settings: Learning from lives* (1st ed.). Philadelphia, PA: Open University Press.

Gramling, L., & Carr, R. (2004). Lifelines: A life history methodology. *Nursing Research, 53*(3), 207–210.

Hargreaves, D. H. (2011). *Reconstructing teacher education* (J. Elliott, Ed.). Routledge.

Howe, K. R. (2009). Isolating science from the humanities: The third dogma of educational research. *Qualitative Inquiry, 15*(4), 766–784. https://doi.org/10.1177/1077800408318302

Jones, G. R. (1983). *Beyond method: Strategies for social research* (1st ed.). Thousand Oaks, CA: SAGE Publications.

Khalifa, M. (2015). Can Blacks be racists? Black-on-Black principal abuse in an urban school setting. *International Journal of Qualitative Studies in Education, 28*(2), 259–282. https://doi.org/10.1080/09518398.2014.916002

Maxwell, J. A. (2013). *Qualitative research design: An interactive approach* (3rd ed.). Thousand Oaks, CA: SAGE Publications.

McAdams, D. (2008). The life story interview: Foley Center: Northwestern University [The Foley Center: School of Education and Social Policy Northwestern University]. Retrieved April 25, 2016, from http://www.sesp.northwestern.edu/foley/instruments/interview/

Mignolo, W. (2011). *The darker side of western modernity: Global futures, decolonial options.* Durham, NC: Duke University Press Books.

Mignolo, W. (2012). *Local histories/global designs: Coloniality, subaltern knowledges, and border thinking.* Princeton, NJ: Princeton University Press.

President & Fellows Harvard University. (2008). Emic & etic § Q: Foundations of qualitative research in education [Harvard Education]. Retrieved April 28, 2016, from http://isites.harvard.edu/icb/icb.do?keyword=qualitative&pageid=icb.page340911

Sharp, J. (2008). *Geographies of postcolonialism.* Los Angeles, CA: SAGE Publications.

Smith, L. T. (1999). *Decolonizing methodologies: Research and indigenous peoples.* New York, NY: Zed Books.

de Sousa Santos, B. (2014). *Epistemologies of the South: Justice against epistemicide.* New York, NY: Routledge.

Spivak, G. C. (1988). *Spivak CanTheSubalternSpeak.pdf.* Retrieved from http://jan.ucc.nau.edu/~sj6/Spivak%20CanTheSubalternSpeak.pdf

Stein, S. J. (2004). *The culture of education policy.* New York, NY: Teachers College Press.

Tadajewski, M. (2009). The debate that won't die? Values incommensurability, antagonism and theory choice. *Organization, 16*(4), 467–485. https://doi.org/10.1177/1350508409104504

Willinsky, J. (2000). *Learning to divide the world: Education at empire's end* (1st ed.). Minneapolis, MN: University of Minnesota Press.

Witherell, C., & Noddings, N. (1991). *Stories lives tell: Narrative and dialogue in education.* New York, NY: Teachers College Press.

Wright, J. (2017). *School leadership in dirty water: Black and Minoritized perspectives on mayoral control and turnaround in Waterbury, CT 2011–2016.* PhD thesis, Michigan State University, East Lansing, MI. Retrieved from ProQuest LLC.

Young, R. (2004). *White mythologies: Writing history and the west* (2nd ed.). London, UK: Routledge.

Chapter 16
Quantitative Methods for Social Justice and Equity: Theoretical and Practical Considerations

Kamden K. Strunk and Payton D. Hoover

Abstract Quantitative methods, in both their historical and contemporary use, have been mobilized from hegemonic, positivist perspectives with implicit assumptions of whiteness and cisheteropatriarchy. Often, quantitative approaches are dehumanizing, totalizing, and homogenizing. However, there is growing interest in and efforts toward using quantitative methods for more equitable aims. In this chapter, we highlight some of the historical, theoretical, and practical challenges in using quantitative methods in equity-oriented scholarship and suggest practical ways to humanize those methods.

Even a superficial review of the research cited in policy briefs, produced by and for US federal agencies, and referred to in public discourse would reveal that the vast majority of that research is quantitative. In fact, some federal agencies have gone so far as to specify that quantitative methods, and especially experimental methods, are the gold standard in social and educational research (Institute for Education Sciences, 2003). In other words—those with power in policy, funding, and large-scale education initiatives have made explicit their belief that quantitative methods are better, more objective, more trustworthy, and more meritorious than other methodologies.

Visible in the national and public discourses around educational research is the naturalization of quantitative methods, with other methods rendered as exotic or unusual. In this system, quantitative methods take on the tone of objectivity, as if the statistical tests and theories are some sort of natural law or absolute truth. This is in spite of the fact that quantitative methods have at least as much subjectivity and rocky history as other methodologies. But because they are treated as if they were objective

K. K. Strunk (✉)
Educational Psychology and Research Methodologies, Auburn University, Auburn, AL, USA
e-mail: kks0013@auburn.edu

P. D. Hoover
Auburn University, Auburn, AL, USA
e-mail: pdh0009@auburn.edu

© The Author(s) 2019   191
K. K. Strunk, L. A. Locke (eds.), *Research Methods for Social Justice and Equity in Education*, https://doi.org/10.1007/978-3-030-05900-2_16

and without history, quantitative methods have a normalizing power, especially in policy discourse. In part because of that normalization, quantitative methods are also promising for use in research for social justice and equity. The assumption that these methods are superior, more objective, or more trustworthy than qualitative and other methodologies can be a leverage point for those working to move educational systems toward equity. Several chapters in this volume illustrate specific approaches to and applications of quantitative methods for social justice and equity, but our purpose in this chapter is to more broadly review the practical and theoretical considerations in using quantitative methods for equitable purposes. We begin by exploring the ways in which quantitative methods are not, in fact, neutral given their history and contemporary uses. We then describe the ways that quantitative methods operate in hegemonic ways in schools and broader research contexts. Next, we examine the potential for dehumanization in quantitative methods and how researchers can avoid those patterns. We then offer practical considerations for doing equitable quantitative research and highlight the promise of quantitative work in social justice and equity research.

Quantitative Methods Are Neither Neutral nor Objective

Although in contemporary discourse quantitative methods are often presented as if they are neutral, objective, and dispassionate, their history reveals they are anything but. One of the earliest and most prominent uses of quantitative methods was as a means of social stratification, classification, and tracking. In one such example, early advances in psychometric testing were in the area of intelligence testing. Those efforts were explicitly to determine 'ability' levels among candidates for military service and officer corps (Bonilla-Silva & Zuberi, 2008). In other words, the earliest psychometric tests helped to determine who was fit to fight and die, and who was fit to lead and decide.

Those same tests were used to legitimate systems of white supremacy and racial stratification. Efforts such as *The Bell Curve* (Herrnstein & Murray, 1994) used intelligence tests as evidence of the inferiority of people of color and thus justified their marginalized place in society. That book became highly influential, though contested, in psychological and educational research. Of course, since its publication, *The Bell Curve* has been criticized and debunked by numerous scholars (Richardson, 1995), as have intelligence tests in general (Steele & Aronson, 1995). In addition to demonstrating the flawed logic and problematic methods in *The Bell Curve*, others have also demonstrated that intelligence tests as a whole are racially biased, culturally embedded, and the scores are affected by a large range of outside factors (Valencia & Suzuki, 2001). Still, the work in intelligence testing, a key early use of quantitative methods, continues to animate white supremacist discourses and oppressive practices (Kincheloe, Steinberg, & Gresson, 1997). Meanwhile, as a whole, quantitative methodologists have not engaged in critical reflection on the history of our field and have instead argued for incremental changes, ethical standards, or methodological tweaks to mitigate documented biases in our tests and methods (DeCuir & Dixson, 2004).

We here use intelligence testing as one example of the ways quantitative methods have served oppressive ends. However, there are many more examples. Statistical comparisons have been used to 'track' children into various educational pathways (e.g., college prep, vocational education, homemaking) in ways that are gendered, racialized, and classed (Leonardo & Grubb, 2018). At one point, quantitative methods were used to justify the 'super-predator' rhetoric that vastly accelerated the mass incarceration epidemic in the USA (Nolan, 2014). Randomized controlled trials (the Institute of Education Sciences' 'gold standard' method) have contributed to the continued de-professionalization of teachers and a disregard for context and societal factors in education (IES, 2003). It would be nearly impossible to engage in any review of the ways quantitative methods have been used in the US context that would not lead to the conclusion that they have exacerbated, enabled, and accelerated white supremacist cisheteropatriarchy as the dominant ideology.

Beyond these specific examples is the larger ideological nature of quantitative methods. These methods come embedded with hidden assumptions about epistemology, knowledges, and action. As we describe later, though, quantitative methods are often cleansed of ideological contestation in ways that render those assumptions and beliefs invisible, with researchers regarding their quantitative work as objective truth (Davidson, 2018). Yet even in areas often treated as generic or universal, like motivation theory, quantitative work often embeds assumptions of whiteness in the theoretical and empirical models (Usher, 2018). Quantitative methods, then, are caught up in ideological hegemony in ways that are both hidden and powerful.

Quantitative Methods and the Cultural Hegemony of Positivism

Giroux (2011) describes a culture of positivism that pervades US education and which is linked with quantitative methods. Positivism is a default position—the 'objective' and 'absolute' nature of reality are treated as taken for granted, leaving any other position as exotic, abnormal, and othered. Simultaneously, the culture of positivism acts to remove a sense of historicity from teaching and learning (Giroux, 2011). Students learn, via the hidden curriculum, that the current mode of thinking and validating knowledge is universal and has not shifted meaningfully. Of course, that is simply not true, and vast changes in knowledge generation and legitimization have occurred rapidly. But, in part through this lost historicity, positivistic thought is stripped of any sense of contestation. There might be 'alternative' views presented, but the notions of positivism are presented as without any true contention.

Within that dynamic, and embedded in a culture of positivism, quantitative methods, too, are stripped of any sense of controversy. Other methods exist, and we can learn about them but as an alternative to quantitative methods. Statistical truths are presented as the best truths and as truths that can only be countered with some other, superior, quantitative finding. In fact, they have become so enmeshed with the culture of positivism that quantitative methods instructors routinely suggest that their work is without any epistemological tone at all—it is simply 'normal' work.

That claim does not hold up to any amount of scrutiny, though. The statistical models themselves are infused with positivism throughout. Take the most popular statistical model—the General Linear Model (GLM). GLM tests have assumptions that must be met for the test to be properly applied, and those assumptions belie the positivist and postpositivist nature of the model. Assuming random assignment not only assumes experimental methods but elevates those methods as 'ideal' or 'better' than other methods. Assuming predictors are measured without error implies that any such thing as error-free observations exists and centers the concern over error and measurement (a central feature of postpositivist thinking). The assumption of independent observation directly stems from a positivist approach and suggests that more interpretivist or constructivist approaches lack adequate rigor. Also, all of these models position explanation, prediction, and control as the goals of research, goals that critical scholars often critique. While much more can be said about deconstructing the GLM assumptions (Strunk, in press) and the assumptions of other approaches, it is clear that those models are invested in the culture of positivism. That investment represents a substantial challenge for the use of quantitative methods in critical research for social justice and equity.

Dehumanization and Reimagination in Quantitative Methods

Relatedly, much of the work on topics of equity and justice, like research on race, sexuality, gender identity, income, indigeneity, ability, and other factors, proceeds in quantitative work from a deficit perspective. By comparing marginalized group outcomes (as is often done) to privileged group outcomes, the analysis often serves to frame marginalized groups as deficient in one way or another. While such comparisons can be useful in documenting inequitable outcomes, the results also highlight disparities that are already well documented and that can serve oppressive purposes. In fact, the ethical standards for tests and measurement include mention of the fact that tests that put marginalized groups in an unfavorable light should be reconsidered (American Educational Research Association et al., 2014).

Another trend in quantitative work that studies inequity and inequality is to focus on resiliency or strengths (Ungar & Liebenberg, 2011). The motive in those approaches is admirable. Such researchers seek to shift the focus from deficits to assets, highlighting the ways in which marginalized communities create opportunities and generate thriving (Reed & Miller, 2016). However, those approaches have pitfalls, too. The danger is that, by suggesting ways in which marginalized groups can build resiliency or capitalize on their strengths, researchers are again re-centering the 'problem' as residing with marginalized groups. To put it another way—one might ask who is required to have resiliency, and who can succeed without it. Members of marginalized groups and individuals in oppressive systems require much more resiliency than individuals those systems were created to benefit. Because of that, the push for resiliency and assets research actually has the potential to further oppress by placing the burden of 'success' on people for whom our society was designed to create failure. Instead, researchers can focus their attention on the systems, discourses, and practices that create marginality and how those systems can be re-created.

Researchers, though, can reimagine the purposes and possibilities of quantitative methods research. Quantitative methods can serve equitable aims and can move toward social justice. Doing so is difficult work: the very process of turning human beings into numbers is inherently dehumanizing. However, approaching quantitative methods from critical theoretical perspectives (such as those included in this book), and being thoughtful, reflexive, and critical about how the methods are used, the methodological literature, and the positionality of the researchers themselves, can generate more humanizing possibilities.

Practical Considerations for Quantitative Methods

How, then, can quantitative researchers better position their work to achieve social justice and equity aims? We here highlight several practical considerations for researchers to consider in their use of quantitative methods. We do not suggest ideal or 'right' answers but hope that reflecting carefully on some of these questions can lead to more equitable quantitative work. These considerations have to do with the meaning of GLM statistics, issues of measurement, issues of research design, and questions about inferences and conclusions.

Measurement Issues and Demographic Data

Measurement issues are one area that present challenges for equitable quantitative work. The mere act of quantification can be dehumanizing. Reducing human lives and the richness of experiences to numbers, quantities, and scales distances researchers from participants and the inferences from their experiences. Moreover, researchers must make difficult decisions about the creation of categorical variables. While many students and established scholars alike default to federally defined categories (like the five federally defined racial categories—white, non-Hispanic; Black, non-Hispanic; Hispanic; Asian; and Native American), those categories are rarely sufficient or appropriate. Researchers, such as Teranishi (2007), have pointed out the problems created by these overly simplistic categories and the practice of 'collapsing' small categories together. When categories are not expansive enough, or when they are combined into more generic categories for data analysis, much of the variation is lost. Moreover, asking participants to select identity categories with which they do not identify can, in and of itself, be oppressive. Thinking carefully about the identities of research participants and how to present survey options is an important step in humanizing quantitative research.

Many times, researchers simply throw demographic items on the end of a survey without much consideration for how those items might be perceived or even how they might use the data. We suggest that researchers only ask for demographic data when those data are central to their analysis. In other words, if the research questions and planned analyses do not make use of demographic items, researchers should consider leaving them out completely. If those items are necessary, researchers should carefully consider the wording of those items. One promising practice is to simply leave response options open, allowing participants to type in the identity category of their choice. For example, rather than providing stock options for gender, researchers can simply ask participants their gender and allow them to type in a freeform response. One issue with that approach is that it requires more labor from researchers to code those responses into categories. However, that labor is worthwhile in an effort to present more humanizing work. Researchers might also find that categories they did not consider are important to participants, enriching the analysis.

In some cases, it is impractical to hand code responses. This is particularly true in large-scale data collection where there might be thousands of participants. It might also be difficult when the study is required to align with institutional, sponsor, or governmental data. For example, it is common for commissioned studies to be asked to determine 'representativeness' by comparing sample demographics to institutional or regional statistics. In such cases, a strategy that might be useful is to allow the open-response demographic item, followed by a forced choice item with the narrower options. In our work, we have used the phrasing, 'If you had to choose one of the following options, which one most closely matches your [identity]?' Doing so allows for meeting the requirements of the study, while also allowing more expansive options for use in subsequent analyses.

As one example, we provide below a sample of decisions researchers might make around collecting data on gender and sexual identities. Similar thinking could inform data collection on a number of demographic factors, as we illustrate in the Appendix found at the end of this chapter.

Other Practical Considerations

One of the primary issues, as we have noted earlier, with using quantitative methods for critical purposes is that those methods were not designed for such work. They were imagined within a postpositivist framework and often fall a bit flat outside of that epistemological perspective. Part of that, as we discussed earlier, is related to the assumptions of statistical models like the GLM, which make a number of postpositivist assumptions about the nature of research and the data. A practical struggle for researchers using those methods, then, is to work against those postpositivist impulses. One way that researchers can do this is by openly writing about their assumptions, their epistemology, their theoretical framework, and how they approach the tests. That type of writing is atypical in quantitative methods but useful.

One important step in using quantitative methods for social justice and equity is to reject the notion that these tests are somehow objective. All research is informed by researcher and participant subjectivities. As others have suggested, the very selection of research questions, hypotheses, measurement approaches, and statistical tests are all ideological and subjective choices. While quantitative work is often presented as if it was devoid of values, political action, and subjectivity, such work is inherently political, unquestionably ideological, and always subjective. A small but important step is acknowledging that subjectivity, the researcher's positionality, and the theoretical and ideological stakes. It is also important for researchers to acknowledge when their subjectivities diverge from the communities they study. As Bonilla-Silva and Zuberi (2008) convincingly argue, these methods were created through the logics of whiteness and, unless researchers work against that tendency, will center whiteness at the expense of all other perspectives and knowledges.

Another practical strategy is to approach the data, and the statistical tests, more reflexively. One of the problems with quantitative work is that, by quantifying individuals, researchers inherently dehumanize their participants. Researchers using quantitative methods must actively work to be more reflexive and to engage with the communities from which their data are drawn in more continuous and purposeful ways. There are statistics that are more person centered than variable centered (like cluster analysis and multidimensional scaling), but even in those approaches, people are still reduced to numbers. As a result, writing up those results requires work to rehumanize the participants and their experiences.

One way in which this plays out is in how researchers conceptualize 'error.' Most quantitative models evidence an obsession with error. In fact, advances in quantitative methods over the past half century have almost entirely centered around the reduction of and accounting for 'error,' sometimes to the point of ridiculousness. Lost in the quest to reduce 'error' is the fact that what we calculate as 'error' or 'noise' is often deeply meaningful. For example, when statistical tests of curriculum models treat variation among teachers as 'error' or even 'noncompliance,' they obscure the real work that teachers do of modifying curricula to be more culturally responsive and appropriate for their individual students. When randomly assigning students to receive different kinds of treatments or instructions, researchers treat within-group variation as 'error' when it might actually be attributable to differences in subject positioning and intersubjectivity. Quantitative methods might not ever be capable of fully accounting for the richness of human experiences that get categorized as 'error,' but researchers can work to conceptualize 'error' differently and write about it in ways that open possibilities rather than dismiss that variation.

Possibilities for Equitable Quantitative Research

Various researchers have already imagined new uses for quantitative methods that accomplish social justice and equity aims. Researchers have used large-scale quantitative data to document the impact of policies and policy changes on expanding or closing gaps. Such evidence is often particularly useful in convincing stakeholders (such as policymakers or legislators) that the injustices marginalized communities voice are 'real' and demand their attention. While it is a sad commentary that the voices of marginalized communities are not sufficient to move policymakers to action, the naturalized sense of quantitative methods as 'objective' or 'neutral' can be useful in shifting those policy conversations.

Others have attempted to integrate various critical theoretical frameworks with quantitative methods. One such approach is QuantCrit, which attempts to merge critical race theory (CRT) and quantitative methods. Much has been written elsewhere about this approach, but it has been used in research on higher education to challenge whiteness in college environments (Teranishi, 2007). Similarly, experimental methods have been used to document the presence of things like implicit bias, the collective toll of microaggressions, and the attempt to map the psychological processes of bias and discrimination (Koonce, 2018; Strunk & Bailey, 2015).

Other possibilities are documented in the following chapters of this text. They include the use of campus-mapping techniques to understand campus climate for equity and justice. Also highlighted is the use of advanced quantitative methods like propensity score matching for documenting racial disparities. Another author describes the use of large-scale data sets for measuring educational inequity. Finally, this text also includes a description of how mixed methods research can further some of these promising features of quantitative methods by marrying them with qualitative approaches.

Appendix: Choosing Demographic Items for Gender and Sexual Identity

First, to decide what demographic information you might collect, answer these questions:

1. Is participant sex/gender central to the research questions and planned analyses? Will you analyze or report based on gender? Is there a gender reporting requirement for your study or the outlets you plan to publish in?

    • Are you writing about gender or sex?

        – Sex is a biological factor, having to do with genital and genetic markers. In most cases, collecting data on gender is the more appropriate and sufficient option. If you need to collect this information, consider:

        An open-response box in which participants can type their sex as assigned at birth.
        Sex as assigned at birth:

            Male
            Female
            Intersex
            Prefer not to respond

- Gender is a social construct, having to do with identity, gender presentation, physical and emotional characteristics, and the internal sense of self participants hold. If you need to collect this information, consider:

  An open-response box in which participants can type their gender identity. An example might look like:

  What is your gender identity? (e.g., man, woman, genderqueer)

  Gender identity (for adults):

  Agender
  Man
  Woman
  Nonbinary/Genderqueer/Genderfluid
  Two spirit
  Another identity not listed here

  Gender identity (for children):

  Boy
  Girl
  Nonbinary/Genderqueer
  Two spirit
  Gender expansive
  Another identity not listed here

- Do you need to collect information about whether participants are transgender?

  - The term 'transgender' typically refers to individuals for whom their gender identity and sex as assigned at birth are not aligned. If you need to collect this information, consider:

    Which do you most closely identify as?

    Cisgender (your gender identity and sex as assigned at birth are the same)
    Transgender (your gender identity and sex as assigned at birth are different)

2. Is participant sexual identity (sometimes called sexual orientation) central to the research questions and planned analyses? Will you analyze based on sexual identity, or is there a reporting requirement for sexual identity in your intended publication outlet?

   - If so, consider:

     - An open-response box in which participants can type their sexual orientation. An example might look like:

       What is your sexual identity? (e.g., straight, gay, lesbian, bisexual, pansexual, asexual)

- Sexual identity:

  Straight/heterosexual
  Gay or lesbian
  Bisexual
  Pansexual
  Queer
  Asexual
  Another identity not listed here

Suggested Readings

Garcia, N. M., Lopez, N., & Velez, V. N. (2017). QuantCrit: Rectifying quantitative methods through critical race theory [Special issue]. *Race and Ethnicity in Education, 21*(2).

This special issue contains multiple pieces exploring the use of QuantCrit, which integrates critical race theory and quantitative methods.

Teranishi, R. T. (2007). Race, ethnicity, and higher education policy: The use of critical quantitative research. *New Directions for Institutional Research, 2007*(133), 37–49. https://doi.org/10.1002/ir.203

This piece is an extremely useful exploration of the problems inherent in quantifying things like race and ethnicity, and it offers specific examples of how those issues play out and how they might be addressed.

Zuberi, T., & Bonilla-Silva, E. (2008). *White logic, white methods: Racism and methodology.* Lanham, MD: Rowman & Littlefield.

This book is written from the perspective of sociology but is an extended exploration of the ways in which quantitative methods have been implicated in racism and eugenics. It also offers explorations of ways forward in research methodology to conduct antiracist work.

References

American Educational Research Association, American Psychological Association, and National Council on Measurement in Education. (2014). *Standards for educational and psychological testing.* Washington, DC: Authors.

Bonilla-Silva, E., & Zuberi, T. (2008). Toward a definition of white logic and white methods. In E. Bonilla-Silva & T. Zuberi (Eds.), *White logic, white methods: Racism and methodology* (pp. 3–29). Lanham, MD: Rowman & Littlefield.

Davidson, I. J. (2018). The ouroboros of psychological methodology: The case of effect sizes (mechanical objectivity vs expertise). *Review of General Psychology.* https://doi.org/10.1037/gpr0000154

DeCuir, J. T., & Dixson, A. D. (2004). "So when it comes out, they aren't surprised that it is there": Using critical race theory as a tool of analysis of race and racism in education. *Educational Researcher, 33*(5), 26–31.

Giroux, H. A. (2011). *On critical pedagogy*. New York, NY: Bloomsbury.

Herrnstein, R. J., & Murray, C. (1994). *The bell curve: Intelligence and class structure in American life*. New York, NY: Free Press.

Institute for Education Sciences. (2003, December). *Identifying and implementing educational practices supported by rigorous evidence: A user friendly guide*. National Center for Education Evaluation and Regional Assistance. Retrieved from https://ies.ed.gov/ncee/pubs/evidence_based/randomized.asp

Kincheloe, J. L., Steinberg, S. R., & Gresson, A. D. (1997). *Measured lies: The bell curve examined*. New York, NY: St. Martin's Press.

Koonce, J. B. (2018). Critical race theory and caring as channels for transcending borders between an African American Professor and her Latina/o students. *International Journal of Multicultural Education, 20*(2), 101–116.

Leonardo, Z., & Grubb, W. N. (2018). *Education and racism: A primer on issues and dilemmas*. New York, NY: Routledge.

Nolan, K. (2014). Neoliberal common sense and race-neutral discourses: A critique of "evidence-based" policy-making in school policing. *Discourse: Studies in the Cultural Politics of Education, 36*(6), 894–907. https://doi.org/10.1080/01596306.2014.905457

Reed, S. J., & Miller, R. L. (2016). Thriving and adapting: Resilience, sense of community, and syndemics among young Black gay and bisexual men. *American Journal of Community Psychology, 57*(1–2), 129–143. https://doi-org.spot.lib.auburn.edu/10.1002/ajcp.12028

Richardson, T. Q. (1995). The window dressing behind The Bell Curve. *School Psychology Review, 24*(1), 42–44.

Steele, C. M., & Aronson, J. (1995). Stereotype threat and the intellectual test performance of African Americans. *Journal of Personality and Social Psychology, 69*(5), 797–811.

Strunk, K. K. (in press). A critical theory approach to LGBTQ studies in quantitative methods courses. In N. M. Rodriguez (Ed.), *Teaching LGBTQ+ studies: Theoretical perspectives*. New York, NY: Palgrave.

Strunk, K. K., & Bailey, L. E. (2015). The difference one word makes: Imagining sexual orientation in graduate school application essays. *Psychology of Sexual Orientation and Gender Diversity, 2*(4), 456–462. https://doi.org/10.1037/sgd0000136

Teranishi, R. T. (2007). Race, ethnicity, and higher education policy: The use of critical quantitative research. *New Directions for Institutional Research, 2007*(133), 37–49. https://doi.org/10.1002/ir.203

Ungar, M., & Liebenberg, L. (2011). Assessing resilience across cultures using mixed methods: Construction of the Child and Youth Resilience Measure. *Journal of Mixed Methods Research, 5*(2), 126–149.

Usher, E. L. (2018). Acknowledging the whiteness of motivation research: Seeking cultural relevance. *Educational Psychologist, 53*(2), 131–144. https://doi.org/10.1080/00461520.2018.1442220

Valencia, R. R., & Suzuki, L. A. (2001). *Intelligence testing and minority students: Foundations, performance factors, and assessment issues*. Thousand Oaks, CA: Sage Publications.

Chapter 17
Large-Scale Datasets and Social Justice: Measuring Inequality in Opportunities to Learn

Heather E. Price

Abstract Large-scale datasets allow for the tracking of persistent patterns of inequality and inequity in education. This chapter demonstrates how inequality in students' learning opportunities compounds in high schools. This chapter uses the Civil Rights Data Collection (CRDC) of Advanced Placement (AP) and International Baccalaureate (IB) curricula to demonstrate how a four-part chain of events in curriculum opportunities exacerbate inequality of education in the US. This census dataset allows for small numbers of historically marginalized voices to be heard among the many. With these voices, researchers can begin to listen to the social injustices that undertow our society and begin to enact change through educational policy. These findings move forward the educational opportunity and tracking discussions in the twenty-first century to understand the nested spaces of opportunity along curricular pipelines.

History repeatedly shows that people are not very good at noticing their biases, and a conglomerate of biases creates social norms with dire consequences for people who are not in power positions. Fortunately, social science and its systematic scientific thinking and analysis provide a venue to question social norms and the impacts on people. But social science is not a silver bullet. Social scientists are also people steeped in the same social norms which can unknowingly frame research—whether qualitative or quantitative. This chapter discusses how large-scale datasets can be used to investigate patterns of social injustice in education and demonstrates these procedures using a case of high school curricula opportunities.

H. E. Price (✉)
Marian University, Fond du Lac, WI, USA
e-mail: hprice@alumni.nd.edu

© The Author(s) 2019
K. K. Strunk, L. A. Locke (eds.), *Research Methods for Social Justice and Equity in Education*, https://doi.org/10.1007/978-3-030-05900-2_17

Large-Scale Data: Risks and Advantages

It was only in 1994 that a book was widely distributed under the auspice of social science which misinterpreted results to conclude that American students of Anglo-Saxon ancestry were biologically predisposed to be more intelligent than students of African ancestry (Herrnstein & Murray, 1994). The authors based these conclusions on large-scale data on achievement patterns among US students. What the authors failed to recognize were their own biases steeped in a history of white supremacy, failing to recognize the generations of US laws making it illegal for entire groups of Americans to read or go to school (Fisher et al., 1996; Jencks & Phillips, 1998). The failure to incorporate these contextual factors created a "false-positive" error when they only looked at differences by racial identity at the individual level on achievement outcomes. Racial and ethnic identities are not to be assessed at the individual level since it is not an individual psychological factor or static attribute, but rather a measure used to reflect dynamic social norms (Bonilla-Silva, 2001). Fortunately, an esteemed group of social scientists gathered their collective talents to point out the major statistical errors in the book and retested the same data with context included to clearly show that racial differences in achievement were artifacts of context and nothing about biology (Fisher et al., 1996).

One of the advantages of large-scale quantitative work is that it can be rerun and replicated. With replication, researchers, like those in University of California at Berkeley (i.e., Fisher et al., 1996), can check others' results and test how omitted variable bias may sway results and explain how the omitted variables provide a lens in which to interpret the results. It is in the interpretation that education policies are developed, so it is the responsibility of researchers to test these biases.

Large-scale datasets can also reveal patterns that are not easily seen with a naked eye. In the earlier example, while complexion can be thought to be observed (although this is steeped in its own set of context and misperceptions), historical racism is not observable. To test the impact of such conceptual ideas, researchers think deeply about which observable variables can be used to represent hard-to-observe social facts. In the earlier case, it was the inclusion of a constellation of measures of unemployment, parents' education level, neighborhood locale, and the like that provided the context in which to test the cumulative impact of generations of historical racism on students' achievement (Fisher et al., 1996; Jencks & Phillips, 1998).

Large-scale studies provide generalizable results and are large enough to disaggregate into subgroup populations. With subgroup clusters, such social justice ideas of equality, equity, and differential treatments and applications can be measured and tested over time and between contexts. These aspects increase the external validity of the analyses and reduce cynics' criticisms that the observed differences are subjective. Instead, the abundance of data points used in large-scale quantitative analyses can provide an avenue for researchers to shelf their preconceived notions of how things appear to operate and instead focus squarely on the patterns in the historical, structural, institutional, and organizational data. With these aspects, the interpretation can be less ridiculed for being prone to interpretation in the eyes of the beholder and instead can be revered as providing the 20/20 lens to clearly see the patterns that undertow our social systems.

Large-Scale Data for Social Justice in Education

In the twenty-first century, large-scale data on students, teachers, school leaders, and school organizations pervade US education. The rhetoric of "data-driven decision-making" abounds (Gummer, Hamilton, Miller, Penuel, & Shepard, 2018), yet school leaders and teachers feel underprepared and lack the time to answer questions with the data (Honig & Coburn, 2008). Shepard discusses how the lack of clear training in research design and questioning risks the misuse and misinterpretation of data where data users do not have the skills to critically assess the quality of the measures, such as whether the measures match the conceptual core of their research questions or whether there were errors in the data collection, input, or coding, or training to test for the assumptions and biases that undergird the data. These problems exist in all data, and thus an undisciplined use of the data can develop into harmful policies for children, their learning, and the democratic education ideal (Gummer et al., 2018). Penuel emphasizes that "evidence-based decision-making" has yet to take shape in our educational organizations and the lack of clear questions to ask of the data, large-scale data become an exercise in reporting numbers without meaning (Gummer et al., 2018). Thus, learning by and training of educational practitioners to ask questions about social justice can shape the type of data that are collected, define the analyses to perform, and develop policies rooted in evidence aimed to ameliorate the injustices among children's learning opportunities.

Defining Educational Opportunities

When considering large-scale data in addressing educational equity and equality, definitions become central to correctly identifying how to measure these attributes. Equity is the penultimate goal where opportunities are not differentiated by birth or ability, and ability to achieve goals is not relegated to a privileged few (Coleman, 1990; Espinoza, 2007; Secada, 1989). Equity thus has two parts: access to opportunities (resource inputs) and achievement successes (outcome outputs). Access to opportunities is rooted in equality. Equality requires the basic tenant of equal access no matter the sociodemographics of the individuals (Coleman, 1990; Espinoza, 2007; Secada, 1989). This can have inputs from community to schooling factors. For schooling, which is the focus of this chapter, this means that "inequality may be defined in terms of consequences of the school for individuals" (Coleman, 1990, p. 25). Essentially, equity aims to the goal of social justice where there would need to be corrective measures to adjust for historical social inequalities. Equity cannot exist without first assessing inequality in order to consider how to appropriately adjust resources.

There are a host of inequality measures to use, from Gini coefficient, mean relative deviation, Theil, and squared coefficient of variation (Reardon & Firebaugh, 2002). These measures capture the amount of proportional distributions of occupants across one space, such as students in schools, counties, or neighborhoods, compared to the general population distribution (for an extensive discussion on this, see Reardon & Firebaugh, 2002). These types of measures can answer questions such as are students who are suspended representative of all the students in the district? In the case of a curricular pipeline where there are multiple nested spaces of (1) students (1a) attending schools with or (1b) without access and if 1a, then (2) students who (2a) are enrolled in the courses or (2b) not and if 2a, then (3) who (3a) takes course exams or (3b) not and finally, if 3a, (4) who passes the exams. A measure thus needs to be comparable across this compound clustering and concentration that moves from one space to define the next space in the pipeline.

Most inequality measures cannot produce comparable gauges of inequality across an interdependent and moving denominator (since there is compounding loss of students at each stage of space). The Herfindahl-Hirschman Index (HHI), used mostly by economists, can do this using a comparable approach to gauge market concentration (Taagepera & Lee Ray, 1977). The HHI assumes that all firms have a 1:1 chance to enter the market (one firm, one chance). Conceptually, groups of students act as "firms" who occupy different spaces of the curriculum market. Since schools have varying distributions of student populations, the formula needs to adjust the 1:1 assumption. The HHI estimate presented in Eq. 17.1 shows the denominator addition that adjusts for the varied proportional representation of students.

The calculations for this normalized HHI inequality measures are:

$$HHI = \sum_{d=1}^{D}\sum_{j=1}^{J} \frac{\left(N_{js} - n_{js}\right)^2}{N_{js}}, \tag{17.1}$$

where N is the proportion in the population, n is the proportion in the pipeline space, j is the subgroup designation, and s is the school.

Equal representation of the groups in the market produces an HHI = 0. The higher the value, the greater a group monopolizes the asset in the market. Unlike many traditional segregation indices of Gini, Theil, and others that restrict to bi-group analyses (white-to-non-white, white-to-Hispanic), the HHI allows for multiple groups to be assessed together. With the HHI, the seven different racial and ethnic group identities[1] cited in the data can be compared as a whole rather than a series of pairs which otherwise would be a set of 21 combination pairs for analyses.

Declaring Data Collections

Another consideration important when researching social justice in education is the type of data collection: census or sample. Census data collect information from an entire population, while sample data collect from a subset of the population (Knoke, Bohrnstedt, & Potter Mee, 2002). Census data include the universe of all cases in the population and thus has no error in the estimations, while sample data collections include a selection of data that can be mathematically transformed to represent the whole population with an estimated tolerance for error (Knoke et al., 2002). In the US, the decennial US Census asks questions of all US households, while the Current Population Survey occurs every month to keep a pulse on the changes in US households using data from a sample of households. For US education, the Common Core of Data from the National Center for Education Statistics (NCES) and the Civil Rights Data Collection (CRDC) from the US Department of Education are two examples of census datasets. The "study" or "survey" named datasets from NCES, such as the Early Childhood Longitudinal Study (ECLS) or the Crime and Safety Surveys datasets, use sample data.

The type of data collection to use depends on the research question. If the core idea is to discuss patterns across the general population of students, teachers, schools, or the like, then datasets using samples do just fine. An advantage of sample datasets is that it is often the case that more nuanced survey questions are asked on particular topics. For example, the ECLS survey can show individual students' waxing and waning through their educational years since it follows the same students and asks the same questions over many years of schooling. With this type of dataset, questions such as the average learning growth patterns over time can be deeply tested, and questions about impacts of teacher qualifications or discipline on student learning can be estimated.

If the research or policy question seeks to understand the differences between student, teacher, or school subgroups, sample or census data oftentimes both can work. However, if the subgroup counts are small, the census data are more reliable because census data are not prone to sampling error. To illustrate this idea, imagine a map of all the homes with students in the US. Now imagine that a representative sample of students by grade level is drawn across the country. If the idea is to ask questions about differences in educational opportunities between boys and girls, then this type of sample would suffice since the laws of statistics would show the high probability that a random sample selected would have nearly an equal representation of boys and girls. If the counts were off by a little bit, weights could be applied to tilt the scales to get the 51/49 girl/boy split found in the population. The models would also want to adjust for transgender student representation as the grade levels got higher since, before teenage years, very few students identify as transgender, but by the teen years, about 0.7 percent of the student population does identify as such (Blad, 2017).

If the goal of the research is to understand the differences in educational opportunities between transgender boys and transgender girls, then data from a general NCES sample-based database would not suffice since it would be highly unlikely that even one transgender student would be selected from that selected sample of households. Even if there were a few transgender students who were sampled by random chance, the information on a few transgender students would be susceptible to much error (i.e., large sampling error) since a handful of students' data could not be relied upon to represent the general patterns among the transgender gender subgroup. To gather data on this group of students, a very particular sampling would need to be designed, or census data could be used since it already has the universe of all students in the database (that is, if there was a more than a binary gender identifier option on the census questionnaire).

All students represent their own voice in census data, whereas sample data allow a selection of students to represent the variation among the unsampled voices. Given the Central Limit Theorem of statistics, the sampled variation is often plenty close to what is needed to test most research questions (Knoke et al., 2002). However, the Central Limit Theorem does not suffice when there are only a few voices to speak within a subgroup.

Illustrating Inequality Using Large-Scale Data

This chapter uses an example of disparities in high school learning opportunities to illustrate these ideas of inequality in US high school curriculum resources. This example uses census data regarding Advanced Placement (AP) opportunities among high school students. In designing this study, a general representative sample of students' high school transcripts could provide enough information on the enrollment rates of students in these courses compared to other courses. However, the question is about more than the general differences between all students. Instead, this question seeks to drill down into the magnitude of differences experienced by students of varying racial or ethnic identities.[2] Given this orientation, the sample numbers would become too small to represent some students' voices. For instance, students who identify as indigenous to the Americas comprise 1 percent of the US school-age population (Musu-Gillette et al., 2016). Even if a transcript data collection was a large representative sample of 10,000 high school students, only approximately 100 of the sample would identify as American Indian[3] across each of the 9th, 10th, 11th, and 12th grades. Of these students, there would only likely be about a dozen American Indian students in college prep courses since these courses are not available to all students and are typically only offered in the upper high school grades. Given these conditions, a study on racial or ethnic inequality in curriculum opportunities is more reliable using a census dataset. Fortunately, the CRDC collects a biannual census from all public schools on the enrollment of students in AP since the 2011–12 school year.

A Brief Background on the Social Injustice of Opportunities to Learn

Since desegregation, education policy has focused on access to curriculum no matter a students' school or district (Orfield & Lee, 2006). Research on tracking provides ample examples of how to measure course enrollment patterns by gauging inequality of representation by students' ascriptive characteristics (Gamoran, 1987;

Hallinan, 1991; Kelly, 2004; Kelly & Price, 2011; Rosenbaum, 1976). Most of the research on differences in quality of delivery and course credentialing comes from qualitative comparative work (Cisneros et al., 2014; Gagnon & Mattingly, 2016; Klugman, 2012; Lareau, 2000; Oakes, 2005; Palmer, 2016). Most quantitative research uses the attainment of students (equity)—high school graduation, college admission—as distal signals of schools' overall curricular rigor. For particular courses, the use of grades and course descriptions from administrative transcript records from nationally representative sample-based datasets of the National Education Longitudinal Study (NELS) and the Education Longitudinal Study (ELS) have been the best proxies to compare across the state-based education system in the US (Gamoran, 1987; Gamoran & Mare, 1989; Lucas & Berends, 2002). However, these quantitative operationalizations of quality or credentialing do not directly link to the *course* curriculum and instead assume that students' grades or attainment are absolute to some external criteria when they are in fact relative to the school standards.

Equality in Learning Opportunities

In the discussion of equality of opportunity, there exists a four-part chain of events that fuels the curricular pipeline. The four-part chain is operationalized for this analysis under the following parameters:

1. *Access*: whether or not students are enrolled in schools with rigorous curriculum offerings.
2. *Treatment*: who in the school with the curriculum participates in those particular courses.
3. *Quality*: whether the courses meet the external expectations of quality. For AP courses, quality is defined as whether or not students had access to taking the AP course exam which can be exchanged for college credit because it is assumed that if the school thought the course was of high quality, then it would offer the test to their students.
4. *Credentialing*: whether students acquire the credential to demonstrate that they learned the expected material in quality courses. For AP courses, the credential in the pipeline is defined as whether or not students who took the exam indeed passed with a mark high enough to gain college credit (for an AP course, this is typically an exam score of 3, 4, or 5.

This sequence of events compounds spaces of learning opportunities along the pipeline.

Evidencing inequality. Figure 17.1 shows the proportion of students within their own racial or ethnic subgroup who have access, are enrolled, take an exam, and pass at least one exam in AP courses. It shows the general clustering patterns along the pipeline for each of the seven racial or ethnic identity subgroups. Each turn in the line shows the places where the valves shut off flow to students along the pipeline.

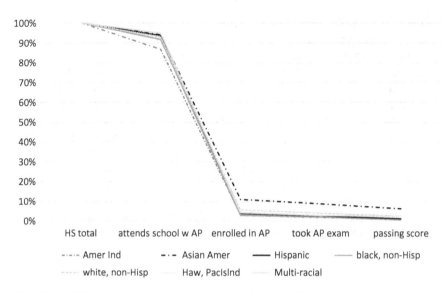

Fig. 17.1 Within-group student shutoff along the Advanced Placement curriculum pipeline. Source: Civil Rights Data Collection, pooled school years of 2011–12 and 2013–14

Access. Although four-in-five high school students attend schools that offer some AP curriculum, three times fewer American Indian students attend these schools. Every other group of students appears to have wide access to AP curriculum in their schools.[4]

Treatment. Figure 17.1 also shows that enrollment in AP courses is selective— only about 1 in 20 students are enrolled in at least one AP course. Between access and treatment, the lines representing white, non-Hispanic, and Asian American students drop less than the others which indicates that these student subgroups are experiencing higher college prep course enrollments compared to their peers.

Quality. Unequal chances to take an AP exam are more extreme for Asian American students than others.

Credential. In the final stage of the pipeline, Hispanic, African American, and Asian American students experience a greater proportion of failing scores on their AP exams compared to their peers who made it through the pipeline with them. Asian American students, on the whole, leave the pipeline with more credentials. By the end of this four-part compounding opportunities to learn, Asian American students earn the college prep credential of a passing score at a rate more than two times greater than their white, non-Hispanic, and multi-racial peers; three times greater than their Hispanic, Hawaiian, and Pacific Islander peers; and nearly five times greater than their African American and American Indian peers who reach the end of the AP pipeline.

Although Asian American students persist at the highest rate in the pipeline among their own identity groups, it is simultaneously the fact that Asian American students only consist of 5 percent of the school-age population (Musu-Gillette et al.,

Table 17.1 HHI scores along the Advanced Placement curriculum pipeline

	Average school HHI	Percent of schools with HHI = 0	Percent of schools with 0 < HHI < 0.25	Percent of schools with 0.25 ≤ HHI < 1	Percent of schools with HHI ≥ 1
Access HHI	0.009	36.9	62.3	0.7	0.1
Treatment HHI	0.395	0.6	61.6	26.6	11.2
Some AP exam HHI	0.245	33.4	52.8	3.9	9.9
Passing score HHI	1.268	43.7	27.6	9.6	19.1
No AP exam HHI	0.240	40.4	38.2	14.2	7.2
Failing score HHI	0.163	60.6	21.0	11.7	6.7

Source: Civil Rights Data Collection, pooled school years of 2011–12 and 2013–14

2016). In the same line of thought, it would be helpful to be able to dig more deeply into the between-group differences. This points to the need for a discussion on market share: where is the inequality in the market along the AP pipeline? What can market share indices like the HHI demonstrate regarding whether certain groups monopolize the AP resources in high schools?

Table 17.1 shows the HHI scores for the schools along the different spaces in the pipeline. Of initial note is the result that more than one in three high schools in the US do not have disparities in three of the four spaces along the pipeline (HHI = 0). Enrollment is the one place in the pipeline where disparities accumulate.

In particular, inequality in access exists, but it is the least monopolized of all the spaces since more than 99 percent of schools have HHI scores less than 1. Enrollment in AP courses has a moderately high rate of monopoly within schools, alluding to the idea that some groups of students "own the AP market" in their schools. Unequal AP exam test-taking is moderate for most schools, but 10 percent of schools show extremely high monopolies over the market (HHI > 1) of who takes AP exams. Inequality scores in regard to obtaining the passing score of 3, 4, or 5 shows that 43.7 percent of schools have no inequality by racial or ethnic identity subgroups, but the flip side is that 19.1 percent of schools show extremely high disparities in market concentrations on passing exam scores.

As a check on the data and the assumptions of who is excluded from the moving denominator, calculations were also made regarding disparities in who does not take the exam or who fails the exam, as is shown below the horizontal line in Table 17.1. With these measures of inequality on full exclusion from opportunity, the results show that there is less chance of subgroup monopolies over these "lack of opportunity" markets (HHI = 0 for 40 percent and 60 percent of students who do not have the opportunity to take an AP exam or earn a passing score, respectively).

Interpreting Evidence

The HHI information, together with Fig. 17.1 information, provides a more complete picture of the inequality issues in high school AP curriculum. The AP treatment HHI points to the continuation of decades of within-school tracking issues where a group of students "own the AP market" in their schools. Whether this happens as a result of school policies on closed-track systems or de facto tracking cannot be determined with these data, but these results do point to questions for further study. The notable proportions of schools with no inequality along the pipeline point to schools that seem to be achieving some equal opportunities in curricula resources for their students, regardless of racial or ethnic identity.[5]

This example shows how to use large-scale data to understand how historically marginalized students are shut out of the pipeline at rates higher than advantaged students. There are distinct racial and ethnic patterns regarding the timing of when students get shut out of the pipeline. These findings complement studies on within-school tracking inequality by moving the discussion forward to understand the nested spaces of opportunity along the curricular pipeline. This study can adjust the policy light on the new twenty-first-century racial inequality emerging in education.

Conclusions

Large-scale datasets allow for persistent patterns of inequality and inequity to be demonstrated. Whether over time or between subgroups, disparities in educational opportunities are hard to disregard when the evidence is clear and consistent. To achieve this level of rigor, education research must clearly define terms related to learning opportunities and injustice. Although the use of equality and equity terms is often conflated, the ideas are importantly distinct. Equality—as in the *Equality of Educational Opportunity* (Coleman et al., 1966)—involves the notion of the absence (compared to the presence) of resources between student groups. That is, if people are in a place where they can get at the same pieces of curricula, and still have unequal outcomes, that's a way of thinking of inequity that goes beyond equality of access.

Large-scale datasets, especially census data collections, allow for small numbers of voices to be heard among the many. It is with these voices that researchers can begin to listen to the social injustices that undertow our society and begin to enact change in educational policy.

Suggested Readings

Espinoza, O. (2007). Solving the equity–equality conceptual dilemma: A new model for analysis of the educational process. *Educational Research, 49*(4), 343–363. https://doi.org/10.1080/00131880701717198

This article reviews the literature on the "meaning, goals, and assumptions of the concepts 'equity' and 'equality', and their implications for social and public policy" (p. 343). It then develops an equality-equity model and provides some ideas about "how 'equity' (i.e. 'equity for equal needs', 'equity for equal potential' and 'equity for equal achievement') and 'equality' (i.e. 'equality of opportunity', 'equality for all' and 'equality on average across social groups') could be treated and measured in future research in relation to different features of the educational process (availability of resources, access, survival, output and outcome)" (p. 343).

Orfield, G., & Eaton, S. E. (1996). *Dismantling desegregation. The quiet reversal of Brown v. Board of Education*. New York, NY: The New Press.

This book speaks to the steady resegregation of American schools. The issue of equality and equity are discussed through the lens of legal rulings on school segregation and integration. It discusses the impact of community on equal access due to residential segregation, white flight, and gentrification. Lastly, the impact of school choice and education politics on the framing of equality and equity in the public sphere is considered.

Secada, W. G. (Ed.). (1989). *Equity and education*. New York, NY: Falmer.

This book takes a critical stance on the formulation of the terms of equality and equity. It reviews how the terms have been redefined not by educators, but by politicians. It provides alternative ways to think of the terms and imagines the impact that the different conceptual definitions might have on students, schooling, and educational outcomes.

Reardon, S. F., & Firebaugh, G. (2002). Measures of multigroup segregation. *Sociological Methodology, 32*(1), 33–67.

Using the example of segregation, this article shows the formulaic differences in measures of inequality. It demonstrates how the metrics produced from different measures can alter the findings of inequality and thus change the implications from the research. It emphasizes the importance of clear concepts in research when choosing a measure to represent inequality. Although technical, the article can be used as a reference guide for choosing measures of inequality.

Notes

1. There are inherent social justice issues related to the forced categorization of persons into a handful of racial or ethnic categories. This discussion holds much merit but is beyond the scope of this chapter. For a good discussion, see Zuberi and Bonilla-Silva (2008).
2. The Civil Rights Data Collection (CRDC) reports at the school-level regarding each school's student body population. Students who identify with more than one racial or ethnic heritage are recorded at the school-level as "multi-racial/ethnic" students. Thus, any counts reported for a racial or ethnic group other than "multi-racial/ethnic" are restricted to students who self-declare heritage to a single racial or ethnic identity.

3. This chapter uses the term "American Indian" whenever the reference is a National Center for Education Statistics (NCES) database since that is the descriptor used in those databases.
4. Since these are census data, there is no need for statistical tests of significance because there is no sampling error or confidence interval to estimate (Knoke et al., 2002).
5. It is not the case that these schools are simply homogenous schools with only one racial or ethnic student body population (for an in-depth analysis, see Price, forthcoming).

References

Blad, E. (2017, March 8). How many transgender children are there? *Education Week.* Retrieved from https://www.edweek.org/ew/articles/2017/03/08/how-many-transgender-children-are-there.html

Bonilla-Silva, E. (2001). *White supremacy and racism in the post-civil rights era.* Boulder, CO: Lynne Rienner Publishers.

Cisneros, J., Gomez, L. M., Corley, K. M., & Powers, J. M. (2014). The Advanced Placement opportunity gap in Arizona: Access, participation, and success. *AASA Journal of Scholarship and Practice, 11*(2), 20–28.

Coleman, J. S. (1990). *Equality and achievement in education.* Boulder, CO: Westview Press.

Coleman, J. S., Campbell, E. Q., Hobson, C. J., McPartland, J., Mood, A. M., Weinfeld, F. D., et al. (1966). *Equality of educational opportunity.* Washington, DC: National Center for Educational Statistics.

Espinoza, O. (2007). Solving the equity–equality conceptual dilemma: A new model for analysis of the educational process. *Educational Research, 49*(4), 343–363. https://doi.org/10.1080/00131880701717198

Fisher, C. S., Hout, M., Sanchez Jankowski, M., Lucas, S. R., Swidler, A., & Voss, K. (1996). *Inequality by design: Cracking the bell curve myth.* Princeton: Princeton University Press.

Gagnon, D. J., & Mattingly, M. J. (2016). Advanced placement and rural schools. *Journal of Advanced Academics, 27*(4), 266–284. https://doi.org/10.1177/1932202x16656390

Gamoran, A. (1987). The stratification of high school learning opportunities. *Sociology of Education, 60*(3), 135–155. https://doi.org/10.2307/2112271

Gamoran, A., & Mare, R. D. (1989). Secondary school tracking and educational inequality: Compensation, reinforcement, or neutrality? *The American Journal of Sociology, 94*(5), 1146. https://doi.org/10.1086/229114

Gummer, E., Hamilton, L. S., Miller, S. R., Penuel, W. R., & Shepard, L. A. (2018, April). *Data-driven decision making: Does it lack a theory of learning to inform research and practice? Fireside Chat* panel discussion presented at the annual meeting of the American Educational Research Association, New York, NY.

Hallinan, M. T. (1991). School differences in tracking structures and track assignments. *Journal of Research on Adolescence, 1*(3), 251–275. https://doi.org/10.1207/s15327795jra0103_4

Herrnstein, R. J., & Murray, C. (1994). *The bell curve: Intelligence and class structure in American life.* New York, NY: Free Press.

Honig, M. I., & Coburn, C. (2008). Evidence-based decision making in school district central offices: Toward a policy and research agenda. *Educational Policy, 22*(4), 578–608. https://doi.org/10.1177/0895904807307067

Jencks, C., & Phillips, M. (Eds.). (1998). *The Black-White test score gap.* Washington, DC: Brookings Institute Press.

Kelly, S. (2004). Do increased levels of parental involvement account for social class differences in track placement? *Social Science Research, 33*(4), 626–659. https://doi.org/10.1016/j.ssresearch.2003.11.002

Kelly, S., & Price, H. (2011). The correlates of tracking policy: Opportunity hoarding, status competition, or a technical-functional explanation? *American Educational Research Journal, 48*(3), 560–585. https://doi.org/10.3102/0002831210395927

Klugman, J. (2012). How resource inequalities among high schools reproduce class advantages in college destinations. *Research in Higher Education, 53*(8), 803–830. https://doi.org/10.1007/s11162-012-9261-8

Knoke, D., Bohrnstedt, G. W., & Potter Mee, A. (2002). *Statistics for social data analysis* (Vol. 4). Itasca, IL: Wadsworth/Thomson Learning.

Lareau, A. (2000). *Home advantage: Social class and parental intervention in elementary education*. New York: Rowman & Littlefield Publishers.

Lucas, S. R., & Berends, M. (2002). Sociodemographic diversity, correlated achievement, and de facto tracking. *Sociology of Education, 75*, 328–348.

Musu-Gillette, L., Robinson, J., McFarland, J., KewalRamani, A., Zhang, A., & Wilkinson-Flicker, S. (2016). Status and trends in the education of racial and ethnic groups 2016 (NCES 2016-007). Washington, DC: National Center for Education Statistics.

Oakes, J. (2005). *Keeping track*. New Haven: Yale University Press.

Orfield, G., & Eaton, S. E. (1996). *Dismantling desegregation. The quiet reversal of Brown v. Board of Education*. New York, NY: The New Press.

Orfield, G., & Lee, C. (2006). *Racial transformation and the changing nature of segregation*. Civil Rights Project at Harvard University. Cambridge, MA: Harvard University Press.

Palmer, J. (2016). Parts of state high-level math, science 'deserts'. *Oklahoma Watch*. Retrieved from http://search.ebscohost.com/login.aspx?direct=true&db=edsnbk&AN=161928E0FA05B2E0&site=eds-live

Reardon, S. F., & Firebaugh, G. (2002). Measures of multigroup segregation. *Sociological Methodology, 32*(1), 33–67. https://doi.org/10.1111/1467-9531.00110

Rosenbaum, J. E. (1976). *Making inequality: The hidden curriculum of high school tracking*. New York, NY: Wiley & Sons.

Secada, W. G. (1989). Educational equity versus equality of education: An alternative conception. In W. G. Secada (Ed.), *Equity and education* (pp. 68–88). New York, NY: Falmer.

Taagepera, R., & Lee Ray, J. (1977). A generalized index of concentration. *Sociological Methods & Research, 5*(3), 367–384. https://doi.org/10.1177/004912417700500306

Zuberi, T., & Bonilla-Silva, E. (Eds.). (2008). *White logic, white methods: Racism and methodology*. Lanham, MD: Rowman & Littlefield Publishers.

Chapter 18
X Marks the Spot: Engaging Campus Maps to Explore Sense of Belonging Experiences of Student Activists

Carli Rosati, David J. Nguyen, and Rose M. Troyer

Abstract Campus maps are common features on college campuses. While these maps tend to illustrate places and spaces, they also hold stories and experiences that may alienate students. In this chapter, the authors share how pairing campus maps with a semi-structured interview protocol can yield new insights into campus life. The chapter begins with a discussion on campus maps and how they've been used to foster exclusion in history. We then provide the readership with insight into our planning process and how we approach the mapping exercise. We conclude with lessons learned and considerations for conducting this type of research.

Maps are parts of our daily lives. People use applications, such as Google Maps, for directions to move from one place to another. Fictional stories about pirates and explorers have often depicted the "X" on a map as the location where treasure can be found. These tales often regard the map as a key for unlocking the secret location. What these stories usually fail to depict is how maps have also been used as exclusionary tools. Countries often fight over how maps depict boundaries across contested spaces. In recent years, US citizens and policymakers have used maps to demonstrate redlining and gerrymandering behaviors that tend to privilege wealthier individuals. In short, maps are consequential tools that also symbolize meaning to others.

C. Rosati
Rice University, Houston, TX, USA
e-mail: cmr14@rice.edu

D. J. Nguyen (✉)
Ohio University, Athens, OH, USA
e-mail: nguyend4@ohio.edu

R. M. Troyer
Denison University, Granville, OH, USA
e-mail: troyerr@denison.edu

In this chapter, we discuss a research application using campus maps for determining places and spaces where student activists perceive belongingness on campus. Researchers using spatial analytical techniques have found inequitable outcomes for individuals depending on where they are located in relation to postsecondary educational institutions (Dache-Gerbino, 2018; Dache-Gerbino & White, 2016; Canché, 2018; Hillman, 2016, 2017). The role of place and space provides an interesting challenge, given that these places are often steeped in a historical lineage that supports the white supremacist tendencies of early founders of colleges and universities. Previous studies have documented that many spaces on campus are not particularly affirming for students holding marginalized and minoritized identities (Strayhorn, 2012; Vaccaro & Newman, 2016). In short, the geography of a campus can shape the educational outcomes and belongingness for many students (Hillman, 2017).

While methods of visual researchers have been increasing in popularity across a range of academic disciplines, higher education researchers have not frequently adopted these methods. Visual methods can "offer a different glimpse into human sense-making than written or spoken texts do because they can express that which is not easily put into words: the ineffable, the elusive, the not-yet-thought-through, the subconscious" (Weber & Mitchell, 1995, p. 34). Visual research methods can "challenge spoken or written texts by offering uniquely rich vantage points" or nuance existing understandings of a particular phenomenon (Nguyen, 2018, p. 44). For example, Nguyen (2018) utilized participant-generated photos to understand better how college students conceptualized the term "success." Participant renderings departed significantly from the institutionally normative ways (e.g., graduation, retention) in which higher education administrators and policymakers have conceptualized this term (Kuh, Kinzie, Schuh, & Whitt, 2010; Lumina Foundation, 2012). Indeed, visual methods paired with traditional qualitative methods can yield new insights.

In this chapter, we discuss how pairing a visual tool—campus maps—with traditional qualitative (e.g., interview) methods can offer a more robust understanding of how student activists experience belongingness and support on campus. This chapter combines multiple modes of data together to enhance practitioners' and scholars' understandings of the collegiate landscape through studying location. We discuss the methodological approach and considerations for using this particular tool. The chapter concludes with a discussion of lessons learned and future directions for researchers.

The Role of Maps

Maps are tools that have been used for centuries. These tools are designed to represent or depict a particular space. Some maps show land contours and features, while others provide information about national and international boundaries. People use maps as a form of navigation over short or long distances, and maps can often be interpreted without knowing a specific language. They visually represent space for people. For example, population density maps illustrate how many people live in a particular area by the font size of the location.

Campus maps are common features on many college campuses. Students use these maps to navigate their way to classroom buildings or to locate the closest dining hall. These maps may be internalized and become an integral part of a student's daily life. In addition to the administratively created map, there is a "hidden curriculum" map that represents an unofficial understanding of campus life. The hidden curriculum map relies on students' perceptions to draw and renegotiate its boundaries. The student-perceived maps are riddled with lore and anecdote about campus life. For example, Beverly Tatum's (1992) *Why Are All the Black Kids Sitting Together in the Cafeteria* explains why some Black students perceived the cafeteria as a space for comfort and belongingness. Studies with sexually minoritized students found students tended to gravitate toward LGBTQ+ centers for a sense of community that they did not receive in academic spaces or residence halls (Fine, 2012). These types of studies begin to illustrate that while institutions frequently spend significant dollars in creating spaces on campus for students, they are not always the most welcoming.

Sense of belonging plays a prominent role in places where a person perceives belongingness. Belongingness fulfills a basic "human need" (Maslow, 1962) that is a foundational building block needed for advanced consideration and development. Within higher education research, sense of belonging emerged as a critique of Tinto's (1993) scholarship on academic and social integration. Initially, Tinto argued that being immersed socially (with peers and campus) and academically (with faculty) led to better student outcomes (e.g., persistence, retention).

Several scholars have offered different perspectives on sense of belonging (Hurtado & Carter, 1997; Samura, 2016; Strayhorn, 2012). Within this particular study, we draw from Strayhorn's (2012) conceptualization of sense of belonging, which describes sense of belonging for students as

> perceived social support on campus, a feeling or sensation of connectedness, the experience of mattering or feeling cared about, accepted, respected, valued by, and important to the group (e.g., campus community) or others on campus (e.g., faculty, peers). (p. 3)

Sense of belonging has been studied with different majoritized and minoritized groups (Means & Pyne, 2017; Samura, 2016; Strayhorn, 2012; Vaccaro & Newman, 2016). These studies have shown that having a sense of belonging positively contributed to academic performance in the classroom. The studies have also highlighted the role of having space and place on campus as a way of promoting sense of belonging for minoritized groups.

In reviewing the literature, we identified one study similarly exploring perceptions of a facet of campus life using campus maps. Hites et al. (2013) used a heat-mapping exercise to explore perceptions of campus safety. Heat maps show the density of responses. Instead of focusing on a particular point, or place, heat maps capture the frequency through which people indicate a certain location on a map. The density is often visually represented using a choropleth approach, which shades a location more and more deeply as the frequency (or density of responses) tends to increase. The more times a location is selected, the richer the color will become. For researchers, these density spots become important sites of understanding as they communicate that something unique is occurring at a particular locale. The researchers used a concurrent triangulation design with ten semi-structured interviews where they asked participants to place dots on a campus map to indicate "hotspots" where they had concerns about their safety. The integration of the campus map data with interview data highlighted the boundaries of campus and remote locations as being places where students felt particularly unsafe. The pairing of the data together provided powerful evidence to the campus community about how best to allocate resources to protect student safety.

Similarly, we explore the integration of campus maps into semi-structured interviews with campus activists. We had a particular interest in exploring the role of space within a college ecology that affects student perceptions of belonging. We used campus maps as a tool for depicting places where student activists felt alienated or perceived a sense of belonging on campus. In the next section, we discuss a specific example of how we used campus maps.

Example

Context

This study occurred at a research, public institution located in the Midwestern US. What makes this site particularly useful for studying equity in interactions is that this institution has a rich history of students engaging in activist-related activities. In this example, we sought to explore the concept of belonging using two research approaches—interviews and heat-mapping—that individually would be insufficient for understanding student experiences. In the remainder of this example, we focus on the steps we took to better understand how campus maps nuanced the data collection procedures. As a reminder, the purpose of the study was to explore *how* and *where* student activists felt like they belonged on campus. Strayhorn's (2012) sense of belonging conceptualization informed the creation of the study's interview protocol and offered an opportunity to take a closer look at social justice and equity on campus from the student activists' point of view.

Data Collection Procedures

The specific technique we used with our campus maps was called heat-mapping where we considered the density of responses. Earlier, we have established how other researchers have used heat-mapping and how this visual method can be especially useful in critically considering belonging, equity, and inclusion on college campuses. The following contains more detailed steps to create a heat-mapping technique of your own that is tailored to what you want to learn about your campus and specific student populations. These steps are suggested and are malleable in nature to best fit your research questions and the student population you are studying. Examples of the study described earlier are integrated into the following steps to help situate the data collection procedures.

Study conceptualization. The first step in this process required the researchers to establish the study's aims. This process required that we consider what previous researchers have done to study the experiences of student activists and their relationships with this specific campus. In our example, we cataloged our annotated bibliography of the study in a spreadsheet that allowed us to look more closely at the topic and the research approach others have taken. What we noticed during our systematic investigation was that researchers had relied primarily on interviews to interpret the experiences of student activists. As a research team, we also talked about experiences common to students at this institution. This discussion led us to consider how place and space matter to students. Our team agreed that we should explore how activists perceive spaces across campus, which led us to pair campus maps in our qualitative interview protocol.

Develop an interview protocol. The interview protocol was developed, discussed, and agreed upon by the researchers. To generate the initial draft of the interview protocol, we returned to scholarly literatures on student activists, belongingness, and space. The most time was dedicated to developing interview questions that mapped to the study's framing. These questions were developed based on a review of the extant literature about student activism and sense of belonging. After constructing the interview questions, we considered different ways to understand better how space influenced the sense of belonging for student activists. Much of our discussion focused on how we could visually depict and understand how place affects belongingness. We thought about common ways people think about college campuses, so we decided to use campus maps as a way of exploring student activists' experiences. As we considered the flow of the interview protocol, we had to consider where might we integrate the campus mapping exercise as a way of adding value and not detracting from the information collected.

Develop the map. Cartography was incorporated into the interview process as a multimethod tool that can be used to triangulate data on students' feelings of belongingness. Early in the interview protocol, the researchers asked activists about places where they organized on campus and why those spaces were selected. This part of the protocol was intended to establish what made some spaces comfortable and fitting in.

Near the end of the interview protocol, our procedures about heat-mapping occurred. To do this, we researched the maps different offices provided on campus and selected the map with the most detail and up-to-date buildings. It is a point of consideration as to whether you will include off-campus spaces that tend to be frequented by students at the university. Once we had the current map of the campus, we utilized Qualtrics, an online survey software, to import the campus map image. Within Qualtrics, the map was able to be sectioned by buildings and different regions on campus. We separated the map into 80 different sections so that we could take a sharper focus on specific areas of campus. After importing the map, we cross-referenced our survey content with the map that was presented on the campus website to ensure validity and reliability. This online tool is optional and was chosen for its ability to quickly interpret data. Alternatively, physical printed versions of campus maps can be used with colored markers for each designated question. This version of the map may make it easier for participants to understand the map and could be more interactive. Our suggested approach is a combination of these two ideas, which is described in the research design considerations later.

Since our process involved an interview protocol to complement the map, we asked participants to describe up to five locations on the map where they felt supported and did not feel supported. As participants described locations on the campus maps, interviewers followed up with in-depth questioning and examples as to why they observed such a perception.

Test the tool. An important consideration for using an online tool, such as Qualtrics, is ensuring the data are captured properly. For example, every researcher tested each section of the map to verify that each of the 80 sections were coded correctly and operated as effectively as designed. The goal of this step was to conduct an internal launch that would effectively function as a stress test. This stress test was utilized to identify any future limitations or bugs that might be able to be caught early in the map importation process.

Following the first round of testing, there were some locations that needed to be recoded. Once the locations on the map were recoded there was a test done with a group of student activists that met the study's criteria, but were excluded so that we could ensure the accuracy of the tools. Each member of the organization tried using the heat map while responding to the interview prompts. These test participants offered us a chance to conduct cognitive interviews with people similar to our participant pool. We used this opportunity as a way to understand the nuances student activists felt when it came to discussing supportiveness and belongingness on campus. When we initially developed the interview protocol, the questions using the map were too general and did not elicit detail. What the cognitive interviews allowed us to do was to develop a set of follow-up questions in the event that participants responded to the interview questions without providing subsequent details. We used this experience as an opportunity to revise our interview protocol.

An early segment of the interview protocol focused on interactions with campus administrators. Representative questions included "How do you feel administrators at [INSTITUTION] view activism? What are some challenges and successes you (or your student organization) face in regards to activism on campus?"

Nearing the end of the interview, we asked activists the following set of questions: "I'm going to give you a map of campus (via Qualtrics). (1) Could you please mark spaces in orange (if any) that you feel safe, welcome, and supported? (2) Could you please mark spaces in blue (if any) that you feel unsafe, unwelcome, or perhaps unsupported? (3) Can you tell us a little about why you feel this way about this particular spaces?" As participants marked the locations, an interviewer was on hand to answer any specific questions that the participant had or if they would like one of us to repeat a question. While interviewers were physically present during this exercise, we did not intervene in any way. We wanted participants to respond openly and honestly.

The heat-mapping process produced an important realization for the researchers. This exercise illustrated the places where students felt like they belonged on campus. We also learned that students have tenuous relationships with specific spaces on campuses. For example, the student center served a beacon of support for nearly all students while doubling as a place where they did not feel like they belonged. One key consideration in interpreting this specific result is that a large number of students had been recently arrested in the student center for protesting around the time of the interviews. This liminal moment provides a nuanced snapshot into the activists' thinking. Without pairing the data with interview information, we would not have been able to capture the depth and the tension students experienced with a specific location. The heat-mapping tool will produce the most meaningful data for researchers if the method is paired with qualitative interview questions that ask for participant rationale of their selections on the map.

Research Design Considerations and Lessons Learned

The heat-mapping component of our qualitative interviews helped us to understand spaces of belonging on campus visually. Themes in relation to power, gender, and geography emerged, allowing researchers to consider how the active and passive coding of public spaces on college campuses influence the students' feelings of belongingness. As a result, we were able to begin to discern whether campus spaces are, in fact, inclusive. This Qualtrics mapping data, paired with open-ended interview questions that allowed participants to verbalize their choices, contributed to a more robust understanding of the emotional burden of navigating public spaces of campus, while allowing researchers to more readily understand what belonging looks like on a physical and geographical scale. In future studies, particularly surrounding student belonging on campus, we encourage researchers to use similar multimethod visual approaches. The following includes reservations and suggestions for modification to the procedures used to implement the graphical method.

Limitations to the data collection included students' difficulty reading the digital map of campus. To incorporate and replicate the heat-mapping methods, researchers should consider explaining the layout of the map, highlighting major/central buildings—such as the student center—to help students visualize what the map is depicting and orient the user. Another helpful suggestion would be to provide an additional enlarged, hard copy of the campus map with a key. This physical version of the map would allow students to rotate the map, mark the map to keep track of their surroundings, and allow for more time regarding what the marked spaces mean to them in their day-to-day lives instead of focusing large amounts of time to locating buildings or spaces. At the conclusion of the exercise, the researcher could photograph the marked spaces.

Another barrier to understanding spaces where students felt supported versus spaces that students' felt unsupported was the multipart roles that many buildings on campus serve. An example from the study discussed earlier was the student center. The student center at this university includes offices for diversity and inclusion, administrative student affairs personnel, a student-run coffeehouse, centralized advising, campus involvement, and rooms available for reservation. All students in our study discussed the student center as a place that they consider both supportive and unsupportive. For this reason, it was absolutely imperative that this map distribution was paired with open-ended questions about their choices. This allowed students the space to explain why they felt this seemingly contradictory way about this building on campus. Without the verbal explanation of feeling supported in the diversity centers, but unsupported in the administrative offices, the map data would have appeared inconsistent and ambiguous. We recommend this open-ended approach to future researchers. We would also consider looking at singular buildings on a campus—such as a student center—to better understand students' complex interactions with their campus environment.

Another modification to the barrier of multipart roles of campus buildings could include walking through the physical spaces with students. Not only would this help the student and researcher better understand the spaces where students have significant emotional responses, but it could also lead to deeper conversation surrounding the physical spaces. We believe that this approach would allow the interview location to be in a space where students felt supported. In turn, this could prompt more raw, personal stories of their history with the space. It may allow researchers, who may not be familiar with every building on campus, to see the organization of a space and ask questions about the functionality of it. If there are comfortable chairs, researchers could inquire if students often go there between classes. If it is a small space without room to sit, the researcher might consider asking if it is the people in the office who cultivate feelings of mattering and belongingness. While heatmapping allows for the simplification of data to understand complex physical spaces across a number of participants, we know that encouraging the power of personal narrative in these open-ended interviews can lead to deeper understandings, findings, and implications for working with students.

Finally, it may be helpful to consider theories of geography and identity when interpreting datasets. An example from our data collection included maps explaining feelings of marginalization in walkways on campus, which are paired with stories regarding poorly lit spaces near the residence halls, fear of sexual assault, and cat-calling. While these walkways are seemingly gender-neutral, used to move passerby from location to location, and impossible to avoid unless you avoid public spaces altogether, the walkways take on gendered components. Women who share stories of restricting their behavior, such as walking only in the daytime with a group of friends, are alluding to normalized practices of public spaces being inherently coded as masculine. In this case, it may be helpful to researchers to unpack theories of geography of gender in relation to college campuses.

Conclusion

In this chapter, we have argued for researchers to consider using visual tools, such as campus maps, to better understand the interconnectedness between sense of belonging and place. Traditional qualitative methods and visual methods elucidate important insights; however, these methods alone are insufficient for providing a robust portrait of campus life. Together, multimodal approaches can begin to address and shift conversations about inequities on campus.

Suggestions for Further Reading

Dache-Gerbino, A. (2018). College desert and oasis: A critical geographic analysis of local college access. *Journal of Diversity in Higher Education, 11*(2), 97–116.

This study uses Geographic Information Systems (GIS) to explore how educational deserts (e.g., institutional availability) exist in highly populated areas, whereas suburban locales tend to have a higher concentration of concentrated institutions.

Canché, M. S. G. (2018). Geographical network analysis and spatial econometrics as tools to enhance our understanding of student migration patterns and benefits in the US higher education network. *The Review of Higher Education, 41*(2), 169–216.

This study employs geographical network analysis and spatial econometrics to view student migration patterns.

Hillman, N. (2017). Geospatial analysis in higher education research. In M.B. Paulsen (Ed.), *Higher education: Handbook of theory and research* (pp. 529–576). New York, NY: Springer.

This handbook chapter reviews literature related to how researchers have been using different geospatial techniques to understand student behaviors and outcomes.

Hites, L. S., Fifolt, M., Beck, H., Su, W., Kerbawy, S., Wakelee, J., & Nassel, A. (2013). A geospatial mixed methods approach to assessing campus safety. *Evaluation Review, 37*(5), 347–369.

This article discusses the use of heat-mapping and focus group data together to better understand student perceptions of safety.

References

Canché, M. S. G. (2018). Geographical network analysis and spatial econometrics as tools to enhance our understanding of student migration patterns and benefits in the US higher education network. *The Review of Higher Education, 41*(2), 169–216.

Dache-Gerbino, A. (2018). College desert and oasis: A critical geographic analysis of local college access. *Journal of Diversity in Higher Education, 11*(2), 97–116. https://doi.org/10.1037/dhe000005

Dache-Gerbino, A., & White, J. A. (2016). College students or criminals? A postcolonial geographic analysis of the social field of whiteness at an urban community college branch campus and suburban main campus. *Community College Review, 44*(1), 49–69. https://doi.org/10.1177/0091552115616677

Fine, L. E. (2012). The context of creating space: Assessing the likelihood of college LGBT center presence. *Journal of College Student Development, 53*(2), 285–299.

Hillman, N. (2016). Geography of college opportunity: The case of education deserts. *American Educational Research Journal, 53*(4), 987–1021. https://doi.org/10.3102/0002831216653204

Hillman, N. (2017). Geospatial analysis in higher education research. In M. B. Paulsen (Ed.), *Higher education: Handbook of theory and research* (pp. 529–576). New York, NY: Springer.

Hites, L. S., Fifolt, M., Beck, H., Su, W., Kerbawy, S., Wakelee, J., et al. (2013). A geospatial mixed methods approach to assessing campus safety. *Evaluation Review, 37*(5), 347–369.

Hurtado, S., & Carter, D. F. (1997). Effects of college transition and perceptions of the campus racial climate on Latino college students' sense of belonging. *Sociology of Education, 70*(4), 324–345.

Kuh, G. D., Kinzie, J., Schuh, J. H., & Whitt, E. J. (2010). *Student success in college: Creating conditions that matter.* San Francisco, CA: Jossey-Bass.

Lumina Foundation. (2012). *Special report: A stronger nation through higher education.* Indianapolis, IN: Author. Retrieved from http://www.luminafoundation.org/publications/A_Stronger_Nation-2012.pdf

Maslow, A. H. (1962). *Towards a psychology of being.* Princeton, NJ: D. Van Nostrand Company.

Means, D. R., & Pyne, K. B. (2017). Finding my way: Perceptions of institutional support and belonging in low-income, first-generation, first-year college students. *Journal of College Student Development, 58*(6), 907–924.

Nguyen, D. J. (2018). Using visual research methods to unlock new understandings of student success. In B. Kelly & C. Kortegast (Eds.), *Engaging images for research, pedagogy, and practice: Utilizing visual methods to understand and promote college student development.* Sterling, VA: Stylus Publishing.

Samura, M. (2016). Remaking selves, repositioning selves, or remaking space: An examination of Asian American college students' processes of "belonging". *Journal of College Student Development, 57*(2), 135–150.

Strayhorn, T. L. (2012). *College students' sense of belonging: A key to educational success for all students.* New York, NY: Routledge.

Tatum, B. D. (1992/2017). *Why are all the Black kids sitting together in the cafeteria?: And other conversations about race.* New York, NY: Basic Books.

Tinto, V. (1993). *Leaving college: Rethinking the causes and curses of student learning.* Chicago, IL: University of Chicago Press.

Vaccaro, A., & Newman, B. M. (2016). Development of a sense of belonging for privileged and minoritized students: An emergent model. *Journal of College Student Development, 57*(8), 925–942. https://doi.org/10.1353/csd.2016.0091

Weber, S., & Mitchell, C. (1995). *"That's funny, you don't look like a teacher!" Interrogating images and identity in popular culture.* New York, NY: Routledge.

Chapter 19
Propensity Score Methodology in the Study of Student Classification: The Case of Racial/Ethnic Disproportionality in Mild Disability Identification and Labeling

Argun Saatcioglu and Thomas M. Skrtic

Abstract Without experimental data, quantitative studies of equity often rely on conventional regression models where potentially conflated measures are specified as competing predictors. We illustrate a "propensity score" (PS) procedure as a novel alternative. This approximates an experiment with observational data. We focus on disproportionate racial/ethnic representation in mild disability labeling, using a large federal dataset. In our procedure, student of color status is empirically specified as a "treatment condition," assignment to which is a function of class measures and related behavior and achievement indicators. This helps align students of color and White students with similar empirical propensity to be students of color. We then test labeling differences and find evidence of strong racial/ethnic disproportionality, which varies by grade and disability type. Other potential applications of our approach are highlighted.

Schools are a paradoxical institution in the United States. On the one hand, they are viewed as the "great equalizer," promoting equity, making them an instrument of welfare policy. On the other hand, schools often distribute opportunity unequally, as advantaged groups benefit from a greater share of educational funds, high-quality teachers and instructional settings, and desirable curricular and extracurricular options (Hochschild & Skovronick, 2003). Schools' contradictory institutional tendencies are a source of enduring debate on virtues and outcomes of educational policy and practice. A central issue is the categorization of students.

Schools categorize students by ability, behavior, and interest. This is partly driven by educators' quest to respond to different student needs and motivations, but it is also influenced by power and privilege. Advantaged groups not only demand differentiated services but also strive to dominate more prestigious and lucrative

A. Saatcioglu (✉) · T. M. Skrtic
University of Kanas, Lawrence, KS, USA
e-mail: argun@ku.edu; tms@ku.edu

© The Author(s) 2019
K. K. Strunk, L. A. Locke (eds.), *Research Methods for Social Justice and Equity in Education*, https://doi.org/10.1007/978-3-030-05900-2_19

categories. Thus, whether schools discriminate in categorizing students is a central question in contemporary research on educational inequality. For instance, historically underserved racial/ethnic groups such as Black and Latinx communities (henceforth, people of color) are underrepresented in advanced academic tracks (Quinton, 2014), and girls are underrepresented in science and mathematics courses (Strauss, 2005). Some view these patterns as stemming from differences in preparation, talent, and motivation (Murray, 2009), while others offer evidence of discrimination in how students are steered into different tracks (Oakes, 2005). Participation in extracurricular activities also is demographically patterned where predominantly White affluent students are overrepresented in prestigious activities, such as debate teams (Wong, 2015). While some see this as a reflection of differences in choice or norms (Murray, 2009), others raise questions of racial/ethnic and social class discrimination (Clotfelter, 2002). Discipline is a particularly racialized and gendered domain of categorization, as students of color and boys are overrepresented in referrals and often subject to more severe punishment (Loveless, 2017). As Heilburn, Cornell, and Lovegrove (2015) report, some educators and administrators are at risk of viewing such patterns as an outcome of group differences in behavior in the contemporary "zero-tolerance" environment. But there is also considerable evidence that schools may discriminate against marginalized students, low-income students, and boys in identifying and judging the severity of disciplinary infractions and determining punishments (Skiba, Michael, Nardo, & Peterson, 2002).

Another contentious domain of categorization is special education, where students of color tend to be disproportionately represented in mild disability labels such as intellectual disability (ID), learning disability (LD), and emotional disturbance (ED) (Skiba et al., 2008). On one side of the debate are those who view the pattern as related to the disproportionately lower-class position of students of color. They argue that higher rates of and more persistent exposure to poverty and related adversities for Black and Latinx students increase their risk of intellectual and behavioral problems, resulting in greater identification and labeling in schools (MacMillan & Reschly, 1998; Wagner, 1995). Thus, disproportionality in mild disability categories is seen as an outcome of schools' efforts to meet student needs (Hosp & Reschly, 2004). The competing view suggests that class position alone is an insufficient explanation for disproportionality and that discrimination also plays a role (Artiles, Kozleski, Trent, Osher, & Ortiz, 2010; Klingner & Harry, 2006). This view emphasizes implicit biases in teachers' attitudes and assumptions about the behavior and ability of students of color, as well as biases embedded in assessment methods and procedures (Skiba et al., 2008).

Quantitative work persistently falls short in settling debates on discrimination. Lack of reliable experimental data has been a common problem. In the absence of rigorous experimental data, quantitative work typically utilizes conventional regression designs to estimate how different categories in schools are associated with race/ethnicity, social class, and gender net of relevant controls (e.g., academic achievement and school context). But, as we shall argue, this approach can be inherently inappropriate, primarily due to unspecified and, in some cases, unobserved relationships between covariates and the demographic traits that are of interest. We address this problem in the context of racial/ethnic disproportionality in mild disability categorization. In what follows, we first explain how the use of conventional regression models perpetuates the debate on such racial/ethnic disproportionality irrespective of opposing views in the debate. We then discuss propensity score (PS) analysis as an alternative approach that approximates an experimental design using observational data. This approach is *not* equivalent to an ideal experimental design, but it is far more effective than conventional approaches in examining the role of race/ethnicity in disproportionality in mild disability categorization. We illustrate the utility of the PS method by analyzing a large federal dataset.

Existing Research on Disproportionality in Mild Disability Categorization

Alternative views on racial/ethnic disproportionality in mild disability categories—racial/ethnic bias versus social class disadvantage—have resulted in the construal of race/ethnicity and poverty as empirically competing predictors of risk of identification and labeling. Quantitative studies on both sides of the debate rely on conventional regression designs where race/ethnicity effects are adjusted to social class and related covariate effects (for reviews, see Skiba et al., 2008). These models generally have the following stepwise form:

$$D_i = \alpha + \beta R_i + \varepsilon_i,$$ (19.1a)

$$D_i = \lambda + \gamma R_i + \Phi C_i + \upsilon_i,$$ (19.1b)

where D is a disability indicator for student i, R is an indicator for racial/ethnic background, and C is a vector of class measures and related covariates (e.g., socioeconomic status [SES], household characteristics, school and district features, academic achievement, family structure). The test of racial/ethnic bias involves a comparison of associated coefficients in Eqs. (19.1a) and (19.1b), namely β and γ. Broadly, if γ is considerably smaller than β (and non-significant), this is interpreted as evidence that class effects (Φ) are primary drivers of mild disability categorization, which is consistent with the view that schools respond to class-related developmental disadvantages of students of color by identifying and labeling them for mild disability services. Conversely, if γ does not lose considerable size relative to β and maintains significance, it is seen as evidence that race/ethnicity affects categorization above and beyond class, which is interpreted as an indication that mild disability categorization is racially/ethnically biased. Findings based on this approach have been persistently mixed. Some studies report race effects smaller than class effects (e.g., Hosp & Reschly, 2004; Yeargin-Allssopp, Drews, Decouflé, & Murphy, 1995), while others show the opposite (e.g., Skiba, Poloni-Staudinger, Gallini, Simmons, & Feggins-Azziz, 2006; Sullivan & Artiles, 2011). Findings are more uncertain when disproportionality in specific categories are considered, as the effects of race/ethnicity and class on the risk of ID, LD, and ED vary considerably (e.g., Shifrer, Muller, & Callahan, 2010; Oswald, Coutinho, Best, & Nguyen, 2001). Mixed findings are partly associated with the use of different datasets, but a more basic problem is the functional form of conventional regression itself.

In casting race/ethnicity and social class as empirically competing predictors, conventional regression models can fail to effectively account for the conflation of these two factors. Race/ethnicity and social class are conflated in the United States because, as a racialized society, its economic, political, and social hierarchies are structured in part by assigning actors to racial categories (Bonilla-Silva, 1997). The evolving racial structure of society functions as a system for allocating social privilege, socioeconomic advantage, and political power (Marable, 2015). Given this conflation, it is possible for a student of color to grow up in low-income conditions and thus be subject to higher risk of developmental problems, and, at the same time, *also* attend a school where the mild disability identification and labeling process are racially biased. In other words, a larger social class effect than the race/ethnicity effect on the risk of mild disability does *not* necessarily indicate the schools are unbiased. In fact, class disadvantage combined with educational discrimination is a highly plausible condition for students of color, as these groups can face adversity in multiple institutional spheres.

One way to account for conflation is to introduce interaction terms between race/ethnicity and social class measures. For instance, being Black may have a different effect at high and low levels of SES. However, specifying interaction terms presumes a priori assumptions about how many interactions to introduce and the particular form of the interactions (e.g., two-, three-, or four-way interactions). The question of non-linear interactions is also contingent on a priori assumptions (e.g., the interactive effect of SES and race may be different at different levels of SES). Optimal model specification can be elusive, given the range of assumptions involved and potentially limited theoretical bases to justify each interaction. Omission biases further complicate problems in accounting for conflation. These issues are important reasons why existing research on racial/ethnic disproportionality in mild disability categories offers mixed evidence.

The Propensity Score Method

The PS method is widely used for estimating the average treatment effect under conditions of non-random assignment to a treatment condition. Non-random assignment violates experimental principles in evaluating outcomes. Such violations are ideally resolved by means of randomized controlled trials, which can be costly and impracticable. For instance, it is often implausible to randomly assign students, educators, or schools to a treatment condition. The PS method approximates an experimental design using observational data. It involves multiple steps. First, assignment to a treatment is predicted as a function of observable covariates (e.g., personal and institutional traits). Predicted values (PSs) from this selection function are then typically used to match individuals in the treatment condition to those in the control condition with similar propensity to be in the treatment condition; unmatched cases are omitted. This is the propensity score matching (PSM) procedure (for details, see Luellen, Shadish, & Clark, 2005; Caliendo & Kopeinig, 2008; Lane, To, Henson, & Shelley, 2012; Guo & Fraser, 2014). When predictors in the selection function in step 1 (where PSs are estimated) are thoroughly specified, PSM creates treatment and control groups with similar means on predictors in the selection function, groups that can be compared for the treatment effect. An alternative to PSM is to use PSs as the basis to weight *all* observations in a way that homogenizes the weighted means of treatment and control groups on predictors in the selection function. This is referred to as propensity score reweighting (PSR) (DiNardo, 2002). In step 2, the outcome of interest is regressed on group membership. In the PSM context, only the matched observations are used. In the PSR alternative, all observations are used, but estimates are based on weights that homogenize group means for predictors in the selection function. PSR can be useful for overcoming small sample size and cell size problems since, unlike in PSM, no observations are omitted.

The PS method is superior to conventional regression in examining disproportionality because it effectively deconflates the effect of class in examining the role of race/ethnicity in mild disability categorization. This is accomplished by substituting (empirically) race/ethnicity (e.g., student of color status) as a *treatment* condition (the dependent measure) in step 1, where a rich array of class measures and other related covariates are used as predictors. Such a model produces PSs to be a student of color, which can be used to specify treatment (student of color) and control (White) groups with equal means for social class measures and related covariates (PSM); or, to specify weights that homogenize these means across the two groups (PSR). This is more effective than conventional regression models because it reduces the need for specifying class and race/ethnicity as empirically competing factors in the *same* model predicting disability categorization, a model that can require complex interaction terms and non-linear predictors which may need to be theoretically justified. Thus, the PS method removes the need for a restricted functional form in controlling for class effects. It is particularly effective when the analysis incorporates a rich array of class measures and related covariates in producing PSs.

Moreover, PS method offers a more robust basis to make inferences about bias. Such inferences ideally require an experimental design where educators are asked to make identification and labeling decisions on White students and students of color who are equal in terms of all traits except for racial/ethnic identity. If such students are subject to different decisions, this would suggest bias. Yet such a design is not only complex but must also overcome the issue of social desirability in decisions when racial/ethnic identity of students are not hidden from educators. The PS method approximates such an ideal design far better than conventional regression models do. Its ability to do so (in the case of analyzing mild disability identification) is importantly related to array of class measures and related covariates used to estimate PSs. If only a few social class measures and related covariates are used in the selection function, this would be a poor approximation of random assignment (which adjusts for all possible traits). But if the selection function involves a rich set of social class measures and related covariates, the PS method can yield results that support better inferences about bias than those made based on conventional regression designs (for more on the importance of all specified selection functions to estimate PSs, see DiNardo, Fortin, & Lemieux, 1996; DiNardo, 2002).

Examining Racial/Ethnic Disproportionality in Mild Disability Categorization

We illustrate the utility of the PS method by analyzing the federal Early Childhood Longitudinal Study—Kindergarten Class of 1998–1999 (ECLS-K). The base year (kindergarten) cohort includes 21,250 students. We focus on White, Black, and Latinx students (total base year $n = 18,713$), since much of the literature on racial/ethnic disproportionality in mild disability identification and labeling addresses bias against Black and Latinx students relative to White students.[1] For illustrative purposes, we address dynamics only in kindergarten and first grade (students were followed through eighth grade). ECLS-K is important for two reasons. First, it is the only student-level, large, longitudinal, national dataset that consists of detailed disability information as well as a wide array of social class measures and related covariates. Second, it recently has been analyzed by Morgan et al. (2015) who used a conventional regression design and found that students of color were underrepresented in mild disability categories. Our analysis of the same data using the PS method offers a critical contrast.

Information on six mild disabilities are available in ECLS-K: (1) speech and language impairment (SLI), (2) autism (AU), (3) ID, (4) ED, (5) LD, and (6) other health impairments (OHI, comprised largely of students diagnosed with attention deficit hyperactivity disorder [ADHD]). We operationalize class based on (1) ECLS-K's SES quintile measure involving household income and parental education level and occupation, (2) low birth weight (less than 5 lbs., which can be common among poor children), (3) family structure (one/two-parent household), (4) parental social capital (whether the parent talks to the child's classmates' parents regularly, and whether the parent attends parent-teacher conferences), (5) a parent-reported ordinal neighborhood safety measure (1 = not at all safe, 3 = very safe), and (6) percentage of college-educated adults in the student's residential census tract (for details, see Tourangeau, Nord, Le, Sorongon, & Najarian, 2009). We also include two class-related covariates, student behavior (externalization and self-regulation) and achievement (standardized mathematics test score) (for more on these, see Morgan et al., 2015). Both factors play a role in labeling. Finally, we control for gender and state fixed effects. The latter is important as identification and labeling practices vary by state (Scull & Winkler, 2011).

In step 1, we estimate odds of being a student of color (R_i) with the following *logistic regression* model (the selection function, using PROC LOGISTIC in SAS 9.4):

$$\log\left[P\left(R_{i(s)}\right)/1-P\left(R_{i(s)}\right)\right]=\alpha+\beta C_{i(s)}+\gamma A_{i(s)}+\delta B_{i(s)}+\varepsilon_{i(s)}, \qquad (19.2)$$

where, for student i with grade-specific sample weight s, C represents social class variables, A represents academic achievement, and B represents behavioral measures. This model produces predicted values or PSs (p_i) for being a student of color. We fit the model separately for kindergarten and first grade. For first grade, we include lagged values of predictors (except for low birth weight) as these may play a role in categorization later (i.e., the developmental effects and related outcomes of low birth weight may take time to manifest themselves more acutely over time).

PSR offers key advantages over PSM in examining mild disabilities, which are observed for a limited number of students (e.g., between 2000 and 2010, students labeled as ID or ED represented no more than 0.8 to 1.3 percent of all students [for details on trends, see Scull & Winkler, 2011]). Since unmatched cases are omitted in PSM, small cell sizes for certain disability labels can result in loss of statistical power. Thus, PSs are used to weight all observations to homogenize group means for A, B, and C in Eq. (19.2). Individuals in the treatment group (African Americans and Hispanics) are assigned $1/p_i$ for analytic weights, and those in the control group (White students) are assigned $1/(1 - p_i)$ (Nichols, 2008). The following scheme for PSR analytic weights (w_i) also accounts for original sampling weights:

$$w_i = s_i \times \left(1/p_i\right) \quad \text{when } R_i = 1 \quad \left(\text{student of color}\right), \qquad (19.3a)$$

$$w_i = s_i \times \left(1/\left(1-p_i\right)\right) \quad \text{when } R_i = 0 \quad \left(\text{White}\right), \qquad (19.3b)$$

where, for student i, s is the grade-specific sample weight and p_i is the PS (from Eq. (19.1)). These weights are used in step 2 to estimate group differences in disability categories by way of the following multinomial regression model (using PROC CATMOD in SAS 9.4):

$$\log\left[P\left(D_{i(w)}\right)/1-P\left(D_{i(w)}\right)\right]=\alpha+\beta W_{i(w)}+\gamma G_{i(w)}+\delta S_{i(w)}+\varepsilon_{i(w)}, \qquad (19.4)$$

where, for student i with analytic weight w, D is a nominal disability indicator with the baseline group specified as "nondisabled" students. W is a dummy indicator for being White, G is an indicator for gender (1 = male), and S is a vector of dummy indicators for state of residence.

Findings

Table 19.1 shows the odds ratios (ORs) from the model in Eq. (19.4) across kindergarten and first grade. The ORs for White students (over students of color) are in the first panel followed by the ORs for males (over females). Due to space limitations, we do not report ORs for state fixed effects. Our discussion of the table addresses ORs for race/ethnicity. With few exceptions, these ratios are well below 1.000,

Table 19.1 PSR-adjusted multinomial estimates for odds of mild disability labels

		Kindergarten		First grade			
				Model 2		Model 3	
		Model 1		Students labeled previously removed		Students labeled previously retained	
		Coefficient	OR	Coefficient	OR	Coefficient	OR
White (v. nonwhite)	OHI	0.262***	1.300	−0.245***	0.783	−0.280***	0.756
		(0.004)		(0.005)		(0.004)	
	LD	−0.241***	0.786	−0.061***	0.941	−0.574***	0.563
		(0.005)		(0.005)		(0.004)	
	ED	−0.433***	0.649	−1.504***	0.222	−0.883***	0.414
		(0.009)		(0.022)		(0.011)	
	ID	0.002	1.002	−0.083***	0.920	−0.111***	0.895
		(0.013)		(0.015)		(0.011)	
	AU	−0.046***	0.955	−0.052	0.949	0.294***	1.342
		(0.002)		(0.072)		(0.017)	
	SLI	−0.361***	0.697	−0.355***	0.701	−0.278***	0.757
		(0.003)		(0.004)		(0.003)	
Male (v. female)	OHI	−0.038***	0.963	0.032***	1.033	0.141***	1.151
		(0.004)		(0.005)		(0.004)	
	LD	0.171***	1.186	0.128***	1.137	0.445***	1.560
		(0.005)		(0.004)		(0.003)	
	ED	0.694***	2.002	0.714	2.042	1.869***	6.482
		(0.011)		(0.548)		(0.027)	
	ID	0.541***	1.718	−0.506***	0.603	0.050***	1.051
		(0.014)		(0.016)		(0.010)	
	AU	0.046**	1.047	0.624	1.867	0.719***	2.052
		(0.018)		(0.801)		(0.020)	
	SLI	0.509***	1.664	0.453***	1.573	0.465***	1.592
		(0.002)		(0.004)		(0.003)	
State		...	...	...	...	...	...
LR		220,330***		266,181***		339,841***	
N		16,201		13,094		13,684	

Note: Odd ratios (ORs) are shown for each coefficient. Standard errors are in parentheses. Estimates of state fixed effects are not shown. Sample sizes (N) and likelihood ratios (LR) are shown below each model
***$p \leq 0.010$, **$p \leq 0.050$

indicating that African Americans and Hispanics are broadly *overrepresented* in mild disability categories. Given the PSR-adjustment, the pattern in ORs suggests that race/ethnicity has a considerable role in mild disability identification and labeling above and beyond social class, behavior, and achievement. Later we focus first on the issue of student of color overrepresentation, followed by the exceptions to that pattern.

As seen in Model 1, in kindergarten, White odds, compared to that of students of color, are about 22 percent lower for LD (OR = 0.786, $p \leq 0.010$), 35 percent lower for ED (OR = 0.649, $p \leq 0.010$), and 30 percent lower for SLI (OR = 0.697, $p \leq 0.010$). These differences indicate significant overrepresentation of African Americans and Hispanics in LD, ED, and SLI in kindergarten. White odds for AU is also lower, but only about 5 percent (OR = 0.955, $p \leq 0.010$). This suggests, in kindergarten, schools are less likely to overidentify students of color for AU. A similar dynamic is observed for ID, for which the group difference in ORs is non-significant (OR = 1.002, $p \geq 0.100$). This could be because of a general reluctance to identify any child with ID in kindergarten to avoid premature and potentially self-fulfilling labeling (Danaher, 2011). Alternatively, schools may be normatively or politically inclined to refrain from using this category for students of color in particular, given the highly stigmatizing nature of the ID label and its historical overuse for students of color (particularly African Americans) (Skiba et al., 2008). As for OHI—a category in which more than two-thirds of the students between 1998 and 2002 were diagnosed with ADHD (Forness & Kavale, 2002)—White odds are 30 percent greater than that of students of color (OR = 1.300, $p \leq 0.010$). ADHD is a socially acceptable label (Reid & Knight, 2006) that provides academic and behavioral services (e.g., tutoring, behavior intervention) and accommodations (e.g., modified and time-extended tests) (Schnoes, Reid, Wagner, & Marder, 2006). Thus, being identified in kindergarten with ADHD (within OHI) is a way to increase the likelihood of elementary-grade success in a minimally stigmatizing way (Ong-Dean, 2009).

For first grade, we fit the multinomial model in Eq. (19.4) twice. First, we removed students labeled in kindergarten (Model 2), focusing on those labeled in first grade, which provides a *discrete* (grade-specific) analysis. Next, we used the full first-grade sample (Model 3), retaining students labeled in kindergarten, which provides a *cumulative* analysis. The difference in sample sizes for the discrete and cumulative runs is 590 students (see Ns at the bottom of the table: 13,684–13,094). The findings for Model 2 and Model 3 are similar to those from the kindergarten analysis (Model 1) with regard to LD, ED, and SLI. Students of color are overrepresented in all three of these categories. Unlike in kindergarten, though, students of color are also overrepresented in OHI, as the White odds for this label is more than 20 percent below that of student of color odds (in Model 2, OR = 0.783, $p \leq 0.010$; in Model 3 OR = 0.756, $p \leq 0.010$). This may be because White parents are more likely to be given efficacy to recognize their child's needs early and advocate for the best label (OHI) and grade level (kindergarten) to begin addressing them (Ong-Dean, Daly & Park, 2011), making first-grade OHI more vulnerable to student of color overrepresentation. It may also be because schools are more receptive to

White parents' efficacy than they are to student of color parents' efficacy regardless of any true efficacy difference between White and student of color parents. Another key finding about kindergarten is the racialization of ID. Compared to students of color, White students are about 8 percent less likely in Model 2 (OR = 0.920, $p \leq 0.010$) and 10 percent less likely in Model 3 (OR = 0.895, $p \leq 0.010$) to be labeled ID. This suggests that as age-related barriers (professional and political) against the use of ID label weaken, this label may be more vulnerable to overrepresentation of students of color. Finally, our first-grade analyses reveal a striking finding about AU. The OR in Model 2 (discrete analysis) is similar to that in Model 1, but it is non-significant, suggesting no racial/ethnic overrepresentation (OR = 0.949, $p \geq 0.100$). But the ratio in Model 3 (cumulative analysis) is significant and indicates that White students are 34 percent more likely than students of color to be labeled AU (OR = 1.342, $p \leq 0.010$). This suggests three possibilities: (1) White first graders labeled AU in kindergarten and White first graders labeled AU in first grade *together* are enough to make White students overrepresented in the AU label in first grade, (2) at least some White kindergartners with disability labels other than AU may switch to AU in first grade, and (3) a combination of both possibilities underlie the observed pattern. Our findings are consistent with research showing that, from 1998 to 2006, AU increasingly became a disproportionately White label (Travers, Tincani, & Krezmien, 2011).

Discussion

In this chapter, we demonstrate the PS method for examining racial/ethnic disproportionality in mild disability categorization. Because disproportionality is present after deconflating class and related achievement and behavior indicators, our findings may be indicative of racial/ethnic bias in the categorization process. Our approach has implications for other domains such as academic tracking, access to extracurricular options, and discipline. In each of these domains, factors cast as competing with the demographic trait in question (e.g., gender, race/ethnicity) can be used to produce PSs for the demographic trait. The scores can then be used for a robust comparison of groups on the relevant categorization. For instance, achievement, ability, and social class can be used as predictors of race/ethnicity (or gender) in step 1 of the PS procedure to estimate academic track as a function of race/ethnicity (or gender) in step 2. Likewise, achievement, ability, social class, school characteristics, and disciplinary infractions can be used as predictors of race/ethnicity in step 1 for examining disciplinary punishment as a function of race/ethnicity in step 2. In the absence of experimental data, the PS method is a novel alternative to conventional regression which may result in biased estimates of group differences. Our findings on mild disability identification and labeling illustrate the advantages of the PS method. While other studies that analyzed ECLS-K using conventional regression models report that students of color are underrepresented in mild disability categories, our findings suggest the opposite. We find not only that most labels are racialized, but also that in some cases, the racialization is pro-White. Ultimately, it appears that racially/ethnically neutral labels are a rarity at best in kindergarten and first grade.

Suggested Readings

Guo, S., & Fraser, M. W. (2014). *Propensity score analysis: Statistical methods and applications*. Thousand Oaks, CA: Sage.

This is a rigorous book on the PS method, particularly PSM, covering foundational and advanced topics. It reviews PSM's origins, history, and statistical foundations, illustrating how it can be used for solving evaluation and causal-inference problems. This book thoroughly addresses the pros and cons and practical applications of various user choices regarding specific matching alternatives and related diagnostics. It is a highly accessible source for scholars and applied researchers.

Busso, M., DiNardo, J., & McCrary, J. (2014). New evidence on the finite sample properties of propensity score reweighting and matching estimators. *Review of Economics and Statistics, 96*, 885–897. https://doi.org/10.1162/REST_a_00431

This study compares PSR and PSM, showing that the two methods perform similarly. Expanding on previous work on the finite sample properties of reweighting and matching estimators of average treatment effects, the authors show that reweighting is competitive with the most effective matching estimators, especially when PS estimation model is not misspecified.

DiNardo, J. (2002). Propensity score reweighting and changes in wage distributions. *Working paper*. University of Michigan. http://www-personal.umich.edu/~jdinardo/bztalk5.pdf

This study applies PSR to estimate changes in wage distributions. The author's propensity examines the effect of changes in covariates on the distribution of wages, and relates this to the literature on estimating "average treatment effects" and Blinder/Oaxaca decompositions. The paper also discusses some key limitations and uses of reweighting.

Nichols, A. (2008). Erratum and discussion of propensity-score reweighting. *The Stata Journal, 8*, 532–539.

This article reviews alternative weighting schemes for PSR. To our knowledge, this is the most accessible source that explains the properties and the rationale for each of the various weighting schemes using PSs. For each scheme, the author illustrates applications in STATA with particular command notation.

Note

1. African American students are the most overrepresented group in virtually all states (Parrish, 2002). They have been and continue to be overrepresented nationally in categories of intellectual disability (ID), emotional disturbance (ED), and learning disability (LD) (Skiba et al., 2008). Hispanic students have been overrepresented historically in LD and speech and language impairment (SLI) in some states (Waitoller et al., 2010), but recent reports indicate they are overrepresented in those categories nationally (e.g., U.S. Department of Education, 2015).

References

Artiles, A. J., Kozleski, E. B., Trent, S. C., Osher, D., & Ortiz, A. (2010). Justifying and explaining disproportionality, 1968–2008: A critique of underlying views of culture. *Exceptional Children, 76*, 279–299. https://doi.org/10.1177/001440291007600303

Bonilla-Silva, E. (1997). Rethinking racism: Toward a structural interpretation. *American Sociological Review, 62*, 465–480. https://doi.org/10.2307/2657316

Busso, M., DiNardo, J., & McCrary, J. (2014). New evidence on the finite sample properties of propensity score reweighting and matching estimators. *Review of Economics and Statistics, 96*, 885–897. https://doi.org/10.1162/REST_a_00431

Caliendo, M., & Kopeinig, S. (2008). Some practical guidance for the implementation of propensity score matching. *Journal of Economic Surveys, 22*, 31–72. https://doi.org/10.1111/j.1467-6419.2007.00527.x

Clotfelter, C. (2002). Interracial contact in high school extracurricular activities. *The Urban Review, 34*, 25–46.

Danaher, J. (2011). Eligibility policies and practices for young children under Part B of IDEA (NECTAC Notes No. 27). Chapel Hill, NC: The University of North Carolina, FPG Child Development Institute, National Early Childhood Technical Assistance Center.

DiNardo, J. (2002). Propensity score reweighting and changes in wage distributions. *Working Paper*, University of Michigan. Retrieved from http://www-personal.umich.edu/~jdinardo/bztalk5.pdf

DiNardo, J., Fortin, N. M., & Lemieux, T. (1996). Labor market institutions and the distribution of wage, 1973–1992. A semiparametric approach. *Econometrica, 64*, 1001–1044.

Forness, S., & Kavale, K. (2002). Impact of ADHD on school systems. In P. Jensen & J. Cooper (Eds.), *Attention deficit hyper activity disorder: State of the science, best practices* (pp. 24-1–24-20). Kingston, NJ: Civic Research Institute.

Guo, S., & Fraser, M. W. (2014). *Propensity score analysis: Statistical methods and applications*. Thousand Oaks, CA: Sage.

Heilburn, A., Cornell, D., & Lovegrove, P. (2015). Principal attitudes regarding zero tolerance and racial disparities in school suspensions. *Psychology in the Schools, 52*, 489–499. https://doi.org/10.1002/pits.21838

Hochschild, J., & Skovronick, N. (2003). *The American dream and the public schools*. New York, NY: Oxford University Press.

Hosp, J. L., & Reschly, D. J. (2004). Disproportionate representation of minority students in special education: Academic, demographic, and economic predictors. *Exceptional Children, 70*, 185–199. https://doi.org/10.1177/001440290407000204

Klingner, J. K., & Harry, B. (2006). The special education referral and the decision-making process for English language learners: Child study team meetings and placement conferences. *Teachers College Record, 108*, 2247–2281.

Lane, F. C., To, Y. M., Henson, R. K., & Shelley, K. (2012). An illustrative example of propensity score matching within education research. *Career and Technical Education Research, 37*, 187–212. https://doi.org/10.5328/cter37.3.187

Loveless, T. (2017). *Racial disparities in school discipline*. Washington, DC: Brookings Institution. Retrieved from https://www.brookings.edu/blog/brown-center-chalkboard/2017/03/24/racial-disparities-in-school-suspensions/

Luellen, J. K., Shadish, W. R., & Clark, M. H. (2005). Propensity scores an introduction and experimental test. *Evaluation Review, 29*, 530–558. https://doi.org/10.1177/0193841X05275596

MacMillan, D. L., & Reschly, D. J. (1998). Overrepresentation of minority students: The case for greater specificity or reconsideration of the variables examined. *The Journal of Special Education, 32*, 15–24. https://doi.org/10.1177/002246699803200103

Marable, M. (2015). *How capitalism underdeveloped Black America: Problems in race, political economy, and society*. Chicago, IL: Haymarket Books.

Morgan, P. L., Farkas, G., Hillemeier, M. M., Mattison, R., Maczuga, S., Li, H., et al. (2015). Minorities are disproportionately underrepresented in special education: Longitudinal evidence across five disability conditions. *Educational Researcher, 44*, 278–292. https://doi.org/10.3102/0013189X15591157

Murray, C. (2009). *Real education: Four simple truths for bringing America's schools back to reality*. New York, NY: Three Rivers Press.

Nichols, A. (2008). Erratum and discussion of propensity-score reweighting. *The Stata Journal, 8*, 532–539.

Oakes, J. (2005). *Keeping track: How schools structure inequality* (2nd ed.). New Haven, CT: Yale University Press.

Ong-Dean, C. (2009). *Distinguishing disability: Parents, privilege, and special education*. Chicago, IL: University of Chicago Press.

Ong-Dean, C., Daly, A. J., & Park, V. (2011). Privileged advocates: Disability and education policy in the USA. *Policy Futures in Education, 9*, 392–405.

Oswald, D. P., Coutinho, M. J., Best, A. B., & Nguyen, N. (2001). The impact of sociodemographic characteristics on the identification rates of minority students as mentally retarded. *Mental Retardation, 39*, 351–367. https://doi.org/10.1352/0047-6765(2001)039%3C0351:IOSCOT%3E2.0.CO;2

Parrish, T. (2002). Racial disparities in the identification, funding, and provision of special education. In D. J. Losen & G. Orfield (Eds.), *Racial inequity in special education* (pp. 15–37). Cambridge, MA: Harvard Education Press.

Quinton, S. (2014). The race gap in high school honors classes. *The Atlantic*. Retrieved from https://www.theatlantic.com/politics/archive/2014/12/the-race-gap-in-high-school-honors-classes/431751/

Reid, D. K., & Knight, M. G. (2006). Disability justifies exclusion of minority students: A critical history grounded in disability studies. *Educational Researcher, 35*(6), 18–23.

Schnoes, C., Reid, R., Wagner, M., & Marder, C. (2006). ADHD among students receiving special education services: A national survey. *Exceptional Children, 72*(4), 483–496.

Scull, J., & Winkler, A. M. (2011). *Shifting trends in special education*. Washington, DC: Thomas B. Fordham Institute.

Shifrer, D., Muller, C., & Callahan, R. (2010). Disproportionality: A sociological perspective of the identification by schools of students with learning disabilities. In S. Barnartt (Ed.), *Disability as a fluid state* (pp. 279–308). Bingley, UK: Emerald Group Publishing.

Skiba, R. J., Michael, R. S., Nardo, A. C., & Peterson, R. L. (2002). The color of discipline: Sources of racial and gender disproportionality in school punishment. *The Urban Review, 34*, 317–342. https://doi.org/10.1023/A:1021320817372

Skiba, R. J., Poloni-Staudinger, L., Gallini, S., Simmons, A. B., & Feggins-Azziz, R. (2006). Disparate access: The disproportionality of African American students with disabilities across educational environments. *Exceptional Children, 72*, 411–424. https://doi.org/10.1177/001440290607200402

Skiba, R. J., Simmons, A. B., Ritter, S., Gibb, A. C., Rausch, M. K., Cuadrado, J., et al. (2008). Achieving equity in special education: History, status, and current challenges. *Exceptional Children, 74*, 264–288. https://doi.org/10.1177/001440290807400301

Strauss, V. (2005, February 1). Decoding why few girls choose science, math. *The Washington Post*, p. A07.

Sullivan, A. L., & Artiles, A. J. (2011). Theorizing racial inequity in special education: Applying structural inequity theory to disproportionality. *Urban Education, 46*, 1526–1552. https://doi.org/10.1177/0042085911416014

Tourangeau, K., Nord, C., Le, T., Sorongon, A. G., & Najarian, M. (2009). *Early Childhood Longitudinal Study, Kindergarten Class of 1998–99 (ECLS-K), Combined user's manual for the ECLS-K eighth-grade and K–8 full sample data files and electronic codebooks.* Washington, DC: National Center for Education Statistics.

Travers, J. C., Tincani, M., & Krezmien, M. P. (2011). A multiyear national profile of racial disparity in autism identification. *The Journal of Special Education, 47*(1), 41–49.

U.S. Department of Education. (2015). *37th Annual report to Congress on the implementation of the individuals with Disabilities Education Act.* Office of Special Education and Rehabilitative Service, Washington, DC.

Wagner, M. (1995). *The contributions of poverty and ethnic background to the participation of secondary school students in special education.* Menlo Park, CA: SRI International.

Waitoller, F. R., Artiles, A. J., & Cheney, D. A. (2010). The miner's canary: A review of overrepresentation research and explanations. *The Journal of Special Education, 44*(1), 29–49.

Wong, A. (2015). The activity gap. *The Atlantic.* Retrieved from https://www.theatlantic.com/education/archive/2015/01/the-activity-gap/384961/

Yeargin-Allssopp, M., Drews, C. D., Decouflé, P., & Murphy, C. C. (1995). Mild mental retardation in Black and White children in metropolitan Atlanta: A case-control study. *American Journal of Public Health, 85*, 324–328. https://doi.org/10.2105/AJPH.85.3.324

Chapter 20
Transformative Mixed Methods: A Missed Opportunity

Carey E. Andrzejewski, Benjamin Arnberg, and Hannah Carson Baggett

Abstract In this chapter, we argue that our current sociopolitical context, rife with partisan ideology and 'post-truth' discourse, is fertile ground for transformative mixed methods in education research. We draw on a specific example of an application for grant funds to study school discipline policy and practice in Alabama; we unpack reviewers' responses to the application to highlight the ways that a transformative mode of inquiry not only reconciles tension in method, and the paradigmatic foundations thereof, but positions researchers to engage in work that is situated in sociopolitical commitments toward justice and equity. Moreover, we underscore the ways in which a rejection of findings supported by both narrative and numeric data must prompt critics to acknowledge that their opposition is rooted in ideology rather than onto-epistemology and methodology.

Methodological Tensions

Once upon a time, methodological conversations centered on the 'paradigm wars' (Guba & Lincoln, 1994); attempts were made to legitimize and instantiate one methodology at the expense of all others (i.e., quantitative vs. qualitative methods). Research and research approaches were debated, contested, and dismissed on onto-epistemological grounds. These debates continue in some circles, and rhetoric swirls among education researchers about qualitative methods as 'loose,' 'just stories,' 'anecdotal,' and 'hocus pocus,' and quantitative methods as 'benign,' 'detached,' 'dehumanizing,' and even 'unethical.' As scholars, we are concerned, however, with

All authors contributed equally to this manuscript

C. E. Andrzejewski (✉) · B. Arnberg · H. C. Baggett
Auburn University, Auburn, AL, USA
e-mail: cea0011@auburn.edu; benjamin.arnberg@auburn.edu; hcb0017@auburn.edu

© The Author(s) 2019
K. K. Strunk, L. A. Locke (eds.), *Research Methods for Social Justice and Equity in Education*, https://doi.org/10.1007/978-3-030-05900-2_20

the ways that research for social justice, and in particular studies of race/racism in education, are seen as partisan on ideological as well as paradigmatic grounds. That is, critics of justice-oriented research in education may use methodological arguments to reject the work, or they may reject the underlying assumption of the work— that institutionalized oppression and discrimination are the sources of systematic disparities. Critics often explain disparate outcomes with deficit perspectives (moral, cultural, and/or intellectual) of students, families, and other stakeholders in education. In this chapter, we build on the work of Mertens (2007, 2010) to explore the ways that transformative mixed methods approaches may be powerful avenues for educational change, particularly regarding research about and with marginalized groups, in that they position researchers to be responsive to both onto-epistemological and methodological critiques.

Historically, critical education researchers have rejected the use of quantitative methods to generate knowledge about social outcomes, as these methodologies are rooted in positivist/postpositivist (i.e., colonizing) traditions; the objective stance of discovering some absolute 'truth' about social causes and effects has been regarded as fallacious by those who position themselves as critical scholars. Reducing individuals and social outcomes to numbers may serve to create seemingly causal relationships between and among demographic backgrounds and outcomes where none are present, thus reinforcing deficit perspectives of certain groups (e.g., how education research has promulgated discourse about the 'achievement gap' between White students and students of Color). Moreover, numeric data and inferential statistical analyses may often conceal dominant discourses and 'encode' information about societal processes, particularly with regard to structural and institutional racism in education (Gillborn, 2010, p. 253) and oppression of historically marginalized groups. Critical race theorists, for example, are skeptical of using numbers to create a narrative (Parker & Lynn, 2002), given the emphasis in critical race theory (CRT) on the experiences of individuals and 'counterstorytelling,' which provide alternative perspectives to dominant discourses (Solórzano & Yosso, 2002). Similarly, critical feminist researchers often rely on narrative data to privilege and lift up the everyday lived experiences of women navigating oppressive contexts (St. Pierre & Pillow, 2000). Since all knowledge is value-laden, value-mediated, and shaped by hegemony (Kincheloe & McLaren, 1994), it follows that interpretivist methods are more commonly used by critical (and feminist, queer, decolonizing, etc.) scholars to highlight discourses that are marginalized in positivist/postpositivist approaches to education research.

Narratives, however, are vulnerable to critique. For example, while CRT emphasizes (counter)stories as valid ways of constructing knowledge about race and racism (Bernal, 2002; Delgado, 1995), "legal criticisms have dismissed the use of narrative and storytelling in CRT, positing that stories about racism are unreliable, unverifiable" (Parker, 1998, p. 49). Further, education policymakers rely predominantly on 'hard numbers' to make decisions that ultimately affect public schools and teachers' and students' experiences in the classroom. In the wake of No Child Left Behind and Race to the Top initiatives, this emphasis on quantitative methods and 'evidence-based strategies' (wherein the evidence is derived from large-scale, quantitative studies) is now well established in educational research (Ravitch, 2016). Caracelli (2006) issued a call to include ethnographic data in program and policy evaluation studies, making them inherently mixed methods. This call, however, has been largely unheeded, rendering narratives from students and teachers as somehow separate and distinct from formal policymaking. (More broadly, researchers have called for the use of critical mixed methods in efforts to offer 'hard numbers' and simultaneously highlight and validate the experiences of individuals; see, for example, DeCuir-Gunby & Walker-Devose, 2013 for an explanation of critical race mixed methods). In this emphasis on numeric data and trends at the expense of narrative methods, researchers may "neglect dynamic conditions in the field of practice" (Carter & Hurtado, 2007, p. 27) that come with the inherent complexities of understanding the social world. Moreover, a focus on numbers and statistics may serve to obfuscate and ultimately dehumanize participants and perspectives represented by those data. Thus, here we focus on exploring the utility of complementary quantitative and qualitative methods, with emphasis on both numeric and narrative data in transformative mixed methods designs.

Overview of Mixed Methods

As with any mode of inquiry, there are differing views on what constitutes mixed methods research (see Johnson, Onwuegbuzie, & Turner, 2007, for an overview of conceptualizations). In this section, we position our understanding of mixed methods inquiry as it relates to Greene's (2006) four domains for social inquiry, which must be addressed regardless of method: (1) philosophical assumptions and stances (i.e., paradigmatic matters); (2) inquiry logics (i.e., what is traditionally thought of as methodology); (3) guidelines for practice (i.e., methods and procedures); and (4) sociopolitical commitments (i.e., arguments for the location and purpose of inquiry in society). Mixed methods research, particularly transformative mixed methods research as defined by Mertens (2007, 2010, 2012), positions researchers to address these domains in ways that are compelling and persuasive to a variety of audiences.

Creamer (2018) synthesized four philosophical foundations and arguments for the use of mixed methods that appear in the extant literature. The first, complementarity, suggests that the different paradigms or philosophical commitments that undergird qualitative and quantitative inquiry complement, rather than contradict, one another. The idea of complementarity has a long history in the social sciences. For example, Maslow (1954) asserted that understanding human behavior required both measuring and observing it (i.e., numeric data) alongside gaining first-person perspectives about the behavior (i.e., narrative data). Similarly, both Cooley (1930) and Weber (1949) argued for the use of both statistical, or rational, and empathic knowledge. This argument for mixed methods speaks directly to Greene's (2006) call for methodologies of social inquiry to address paradigmatic matters and situates mixed methods work as attending to the paradigmatic positions of multiple audiences.

The second argument for mixed methods is compatibility (Creamer, 2018). The distinction between qualitative and quantitative methods is indeed a false dichotomy: both involve constructing and interpreting meanings (Morrow & Brown, 1994). This addresses Greene's (2006) second domain—logics of inquiry. The third and fourth arguments for mixed methods are combination and triangulation to enhance validity (Creamer, 2018), which directly address Greene's (2006) third domain: guidelines for practice. Both of these arguments are about data and interpretation. Combination means collecting both numeric and narrative data, which results in a more robust data corpus. Triangulation/convergence focuses our attention on the ways in which numeric and narrative data can point to the same conclusions, rendering the case for their validity stronger. Of course, Mertens (2010) reminds us that one of the powers of transformative mixed methods is the discovery of divergence, which may be particularly meaningful in research contexts focused on oppressed or marginalized individuals and groups. Mixed methods, be they focused on convergence or divergence, position researchers to address multiples audiences' preferences for how research should be done.

These four arguments for mixed methods, as presented by Creamer (2018), do not, however, directly address Greene's (2006) fourth domain—sociopolitical commitments (i.e., ideology), which has become a site for contestation in research. We suggest that mixed methods research has the potential to be more persuasive, even in the face of ideological opposition, because mixed methods positions researchers to satisfy multiple audiences with regard to the other three domains. That is, as our example below demonstrates, critics may reject work on what they claim to be methodological or paradigmatic grounds, but that argument may really be a mask for an ideological qualm. Inasmuch as engaging explicitly in transformative mixed methods positions researchers to address methodological and paradigmatic critiques, detractors are then pushed to acknowledge that their rejection is ideological or political (e.g., rooted in White supremacist cisheteropatriarchy). Furthermore, the use of transformative mixed methods positions researchers to respond to Giddens' (1979) calls to: (1) provide alternative perspectives to dominant narratives and opportunities for participant empowerment, and (2) attempt to make findings accessible and credible to those who do not share a critical worldview, or who may see the findings as a threat to their protected or privileged status.

Our Example

To restate, transformative mixed methods reconciles tension in method, and the paradigmatic foundations thereof, and positions researchers to engage in work that is situated in sociopolitical commitments toward justice and equity (Mertens 2007, 2010, 2012). Mertens (2010) posits that "the transformative ontological assumption recognizes that there are many versions of what is considered to be real...it holds that there is one reality about which there are multiple opinions" (p. 470). This ontological grounding has implications for the questions that transformative researchers ask, including: (1) "Whose reality is privileged in this context?"; (2) "What is the mechanism for challenging perceived realities that sustain an oppressive system?"; (3) "What are the consequences in terms of who is hurt if we accept multiple versions of reality or if we accept the 'wrong/privileged' version?" (pp. 470–471). In our study of school discipline policy and practice in Alabama public schools, we sought to highlight how current discipline policies and practices affect students of Color in dehumanizing ways, and how school-based practitioners have the power to disrupt those practices. Our project positioned us to develop a counternarrative to the accepted ostensibly colorblind/colormute 'reality' in education spheres that some students are inherently bad and behave in ways that deserve punishment and exclusion from their peers; sometimes that behavior is so bad that a student warrants contact with a law enforcement official who may be stationed in their school (i.e., a school resource officer). In accepting that privileged 'reality' or dominant narrative in public school discourse, however, we neglect to account for the ways that school officials in Alabama routinely and unjustly suspend and exclude students of Color via in- and out-of-school suspension, referrals to alternative schools, and referrals to law enforcement officials. School officials also often mete out corporal punishment to students of Color, a practice which is still legal in Alabama as in many other states.

A few semesters ago, we submitted an internal grant proposal for funding of a multiphase, mixed methods analysis of discipline policy and practice in Alabama. We had much of the data we planned to work with in the study: numeric data about school discipline practices in public schools retrieved from the Alabama State Department of Education, interview and observational data collected from alternative school students about their experiences with school discipline, and interview data from school administrators and school resource officers about their discipline philosophies and practices. As we crafted our proposal, we anticipated that the evaluators would be from colleges and departments on our campus where quantitative methods and positivistic perspectives were privileged. That is the norm on our campus, as it is at many institutions. Thus, we focused on including pilot study findings and extant literature that were grounded in numeric data and analyses; we did so at the expense of the inclusion of the narrative data and findings we had generated from our work with school-based practitioners and students. Ultimately, the proposal was rejected, and the feedback we received contested the methods by which we proposed to collect additional data and conduct further analyses. This rejection of method was also accompanied by a stronger, more explicit rejection of the ways in which we conceptualized school discipline: that is, we took a critical lens to data generation and analyses, centered on the foundational assumption that school discipline policy and practice are inherently racialized and function as part, and products, of institutionalized racism and the school-prison nexus (Meiners, 2007).

In retrospect, we realize in crafting the grant proposal to privilege numeric data, we first missed an opportunity to illustrate the power of mixed methods research by including both numeric and narrative data that pointed to similar conclusions (i.e., triangulation). We also missed an opportunity to humanize the students adversely affected by school discipline practices, thus undermining our goals for research to advance equity and justice. Mixed methods appeal to audiences because the mix illuminates numbers with stories, and each strand (numeric and narrative) is stronger in concert than solo (i.e., complementarity). This epistemic synergy is especially true in education research, where teacher and student voices are often lost in conventional statistical modeling. As evidenced by the feedback on our proposal, which we explore later, the sociopolitical context in which we live and research now may increasingly be a space wherein it is easier for both laypeople and scholars to dismiss approaches to and findings of research, depending on whether they align not only with one's paradigmatic commitments but also with one's partisan ideology. Thus, our current sociopolitical context, rife with partisan ideology and 'post-truth' discourse, is fertile ground for transformative mixed methods in education research. That is, it is more difficult to reject findings supported by both narrative and numeric data, regardless of paradigmatic or partisan commitments. To do so requires critics to disclose that their opposition is to the lived experiences of the research participants, experiences which are represented in the aggregate from numeric data and humanized via narrative data.

When we developed our proposal, we thought we were navigating territory still shaped by the paradigm war. Assuming (post)positivists would review our internal grant proposal, our strategy was to front-load and emphasize numeric data. What we did not anticipate was that our interpretation of those data would be rejected, not only on paradigmatic or methodological grounds but seemingly on ideological grounds. First, our reviewers did not see justice-oriented scholarship as research. Second, they took issue with our assumption that discipline disparities are the result of systemic inequity and institutionalized racism. Had we situated our work in a transformative mixed methods approach, with more balance between numeric data and individual stories that emphasized triangulation across data sources to warrant our interpretations, it may have been more difficult, or at least uncomfortable, for the reviewers to dismiss our work on these grounds.

We reflected on reviewer comments extensively to determine where the feedback might be useful for future grant proposals and manuscripts. We learned from one review that observation/description might not be viewed as research, despite the fact that much research rooted in the humanities and social sciences is descriptive. The reviewer began, "They know already what they plan to gain further evidence for in order, hopefully, to evoke change. Again, worthy goals. But not research goals." These statements positioned an issue of social justice (exemplified through examining and disrupting the effects school discipline has on students of Color) as a "worthy goal" but not a "research goal." The crux of the reviewer's criticism rests on the absence of an identifiable 'hypothesis' or 'thesis to be tested.' The work we articulated was 'descriptive,' even as description was seen as incompatible with research. There is much to unpack within these epistemic assertions. We wondered: can social sciences, specifically social justice research, begin with hypotheses? Perhaps, but hypotheses imply eventual experimentation to render the hypothesis true or null; what does it mean to position research as capable of 'nullifying' the narratives of participants? In other words, a rejection of description and a refocusing on experimentation do not serve the interests of justice- and equity-oriented work if it renders (in our case, students') lived experiences (with often violent school discipline policy and practice) as possibly 'null.'

Field work, which forms the basis of the qualitative component(s) in mixed methods studies, does not start with a hypothesis. Researchers in the field start by observing and talking to people. From observations and conversations (which include method conventions like interviewing, thick description, reflection and audit journaling, member checking, and data assemblage), researchers in the field begin to piece together a vision of the context of their research. As this vision develops, a researcher may hypothesize about correlations (patterns) within the context. Inferential statistics, then, become useful to determine *the extent to which* those speculated correlations may be present or even causal. Here we can see the fundamental flaw in the strategy we enlisted in our proposal: by foregrounding an inferential analytical plan, we put the cart before the horse. Hypotheses follow holistic, immersive field work and using that work to construct holistic, immersive narratives. We should have first given voice to the population before presenting a proposal meant to illuminate correlations between those voices and the institutional violence that often stifles and disciplines them. The reviewer targeted a core component of our proposal for comment. They quoted us:

> In some of the poorest school systems in the western part of Alabama, no students were referred to law enforcement. Further, there were few referrals (25 of 671 total referrals; ~4%) in the counties that comprise what is known as the 'Black Belt,' where African American students often attend highly segregated, drastically underfunded schools. These preliminary findings suggest that African American students who attend schools with more White students may suffer harsher consequences for disciplinary infractions than their White peers across Alabama, than their African American peers who attend predominantly African American schools.

We must point out that we articulate a hypothesis in this statement, which the reviewer did not recognize. The term 'suggest' is the identifier; we observed that there were more referrals to law enforcement as a disciplinary consequence in schools with high White populations, and we knew, based on the analyses of other researchers in other locations as well as media coverage, that students of Color are considerably more likely to be arrested at school than their White peers. We then hypothesized that these outcomes were due to the ways in which students of Color are likely to be perceived as misbehaving (e.g., Gilliam, Maupin, Reyes, Accavitti, & Shic, 2016) rather than an inherent inclination to misbehave; indeed, there are decades of research on the racialized nature of school discipline to support this hypothesis. The reviewer's reaction to this quote was: "I would think that it shows that 'they do suffer harsher penalties,' but it tells us nothing about why that is."

Had we been given an opportunity to respond, we would have argued: we already know why that is: White supremacy and institutionalized racism are the culprits. The purposes of our proposed study were to explore just how egregious these problems are (there has been little to-date exploration of school discipline in Alabama) and to work toward disrupting those patterns by confronting school-based practitioners with both numeric and narrative data. We also realized that our absence of vivid, emotionally laden narrative in the proposal obfuscated some of the 'why.'

The Missed Opportunity

When one examines the history of corporal punishment in the United States, for example, it is easy to see how the absence of contextual narrative alters the interpretation of the numeric data. In the landmark Supreme Court case on corporal punishment, *Ingraham v. Wright* (1977), the plaintiff alleged that '20 licks' with a paddle violated the 'conscience-shocking' standard by which state agents are liable for cruel and unusual punishment. Without contextual and personal detail, 20 licks may not necessarily sound traumatizing. In *Archey v. Hyche* (1991), a student received 'five licks' for a disciplinary infraction, far fewer than the 20 received in the Ingraham case. It would be easy to conclude, based on numeric data, that Gary Shane Archey, Jr.'s case was less severe than James Ingraham's. What would their narratives have revealed? Archey received 'five licks' for humming in the bathroom. The 'licks' caused a hematoma on the buttocks. Ingraham was accused of tardiness and, because he refused to turn his back to the principal to be paddled, he was held down and paddled 20 times. He too suffered a hematoma and was treated at a hospital. In *Peterson v. Baker* (2007), a teacher administered 'one lick' to Jonathan Peterson, who has a hearing impairment. This 'lick' involved choking him as a consequence for not responding to the teacher's instructions. None of these events was found by the courts to 'shock the conscience.' These examples demonstrate why narratives are essential when communicating the complex psychosocial ramifications of school discipline policies on children. When numbers are stripped from context, they may seem less frightening than reading a more holistic account that includes imagery such as hematomas or deaf students being choked or, in *Neal v. Fulton County Board of Education* (2000), an eye dislodging from its socket when a White coach struck an African American student on the head with a metal lock. Without the narrative to accompany the number, Durante Neal's experience is summed: 'one lick.'

At this point, one might read our methodological reflection as an earnest (and maybe even bitter) attempt to improve our mixed methods modeling and reporting. However, the reviewer's final comment left us bewildered and pessimistic about the possibility of our social-justice-oriented work ever being seen as legitimate by this and other similarly minded colleagues, reviewers, or readers. The reviewer wrote:

> You would expect at least that we would see some attempt to correlate those geographical areas where punishment in high schools seem disproportionately imposed on blacks and areas where judicial punishment seems disproportionately imposed on blacks. *But even this won't be enough, not nearly enough*, to justify the causal claim in the first paragraph. (Emphasis ours)

In short, even if we demonstrated a correlation between school discipline and subsequent incarceration, that would not be enough to convince that a school-to-prison pipeline exists, or at the very least, that exclusionary discipline contributes to the school-to-prison pipeline and that exclusionary discipline is racially biased. The reviewer closes, "Nothing in the proposed study will begin to show this." What evidence could be produced to identify the school-prison nexus? This reviewer suggests that no form of evidence will be enough to conclusively identify a correlation, much less causation. If they are reluctant to trust numeric data, which already point to a correlation, would fuller mixed methods approaches suffice? And, if not, what methodological options remain? When the methodological options are exhausted, and readers still refuse to view research claims as legitimate, it can be assumed the rejection stems from ideological rather than onto-epistemological and methodological qualms.

Conclusion

In this chapter, we have highlighted the ways that transformative mixed methods are useful in research for justice and equity, especially in addressing and situating research as reflective of sociopolitical commitments. As Greene (2006) argued:

> One vitally important role for mixed methods social inquiry is to trouble taken-for-granted understandings of assumed common meanings of constructs by incorporating a diversity of perspectives, voices, values and stances. In this role, mixed methods inquiry honors complexity alongside diversity and difference, and thereby resists simplification of inherently contextual and complex human phenomena. (p. 97)

In our research about school discipline policy and practice in Alabama, we sought to trouble the common assumption that students of Color who are more frequently and severely punished in K-12 schools somehow deserve those punishments, including exclusion and corporal punishment. We aimed to capture and describe students' experiences with racialized school discipline practices in a way that humanized the numeric trends and added depth and nuance to understandings about (perceptions about) student (mis)behavior. By unpacking the ways that reviewers responded to a grant proposal, we reflected on our 'missed opportunity' in putting forth numeric data about school discipline trends at the expense of narrative data that captured the lived experiences with school discipline practices of students of Color in Alabama public schools. We suggest that, in the unification of both numeric and narrative data, it becomes more difficult for critics to reject research on the basis of onto-epistemology and methodology; instead, mixed methods may push critics to reckon with the ideological and partisan worldviews that they bring to their evaluation of research. When data are humanized, as when numeric and narrative data are combined in transformative mixed methods research, rejecting the claims made with them is a dehumanizing act that reflects more on the critic than the research.

Suggested Readings

We suggest the following readings for researchers interested in developing mixed methods research for justice and equity. First, Donna Mertens has written a comprehensive body of scholarship on transformative mixed methods where she positions this mode of inquiry, in particular ontological, epistemological, and axiological beliefs:

Mertens, D. M. (2007). Transformative paradigm: Mixed methods and social jus-
tice. *Journal of Mixed Methods Research, 1*(3), 212–225.
Mertens, D. M. (2010). Transformative mixed methods research. *Qualitative
Inquiry, 16*(6), 469–474.

Next, we join Mertens in suggesting these three exemplar articles that feature transformative mixed methods:

Hodgkin, S. (2008). Telling it all: A story of women's social capital using a mixed
methods approach. *Journal of Mixed Methods Research, 2*, 296–316.
Huato, J., & Zeno, K. W. (2009). Class, race, and the spousal income gap: The
effects of family income, educational attainment, and race-ethnicity on the
husband-wife income ratio in the United States, 1980, 1990, 2000. *American
Behavioral Scientist, 53*, 261–275.
Silka, L. (2009). Partnership ethics. In D. M. Mertens & P. E. Ginsberg (Eds.),
Handbook of social research ethics (pp. 337–352). Thousand Oaks, CA: SAGE.

Finally, for further readings about mixed methods, more broadly, we suggest:

The Journal of Mixed Methods Research, SAGE.
Tashakkori, A., & Teddlie, C. (Eds.). (2010). *SAGE handbook of mixed methods in
social and behavioral research* (2nd ed.). Thousand Oaks, CA: SAGE.

References

Archey v. Hyche, 935 F.2d 269 (1991).
Bernal, D. D. (2002). Critical Race Theory, Latino Critical Theory, and Critical Raced-Gendered
epistemologies: Recognizing students of color as holders and creators of knowledge. *Qualitative
Inquiry, 8*(1), 105–126. https://doi.org/10.1177/107780040200800107
Caracelli, V. J. (2006). Enhancing the policy process through the use of ethnography and other
study frameworks: A mixed-methods strategy. *Research in the Schools, 13*(1), 84–92.
Carter, D. F., & Hurtado, S. (2007). Bridging key research dilemmas: Quantitative research using
a critical eye. *New Directions for Institutional Research, 133*, 25–35.
Cooley, H. E. (1930). *Sociological theory and social research.* New York, NY: Scribner's.
Creamer, E. G. (2018). *An introduction to fully integrated mixed methods research.* Los Angeles:
Sage.
Decuir-Gunby, J. T., & Walker-Devose, D. C. (2013). Expanding the counterstory: The potential
for critical race mixed methods studies in education. In *Handbook of critical race theory in
education* (pp. 268–279). New York, NY: Routledge.
Delgado, R. (1995). *Critical Race Theory: The cutting edge.* Philadelphia, PA: Temple University
Press.
Giddens, A. (1979). *Central problems in social theory: Action, structure, and contradiction in
social analysis* (Vol. 241). Berkeley, CA: University of California Press.
Gillborn, D. (2010). The colour of numbers: Surveys, statistics and deficit-thinking
about race and class. *Journal of Education Policy, 25*(2), 253–276. https://doi.org/
10.1080/02680930903460740
Gilliam, W. S., Maupin, A. N., Reyes, C. R., Accavitti, M., & Shic, F. (2016, September). *Do early
educators' implicit biases regarding sex and race relate to behavior expectations and recommendations of preschool expulsions and suspensions?* Yale Child Study Center. Retrieved from

http://www.addressingracialmicroaggressions.com/wp-content/uploads/2016/10/Preschool-Implicit-Bias-Policy-Brief_final_9_26_276766_5379.pdf

Greene, J. C. (2006). Toward a methodology of mixed methods social inquiry. *Research in the Schools, 13*(1), 93–98.

Guba, E. G., & Lincoln, Y. S. (1994). Competing paradigms in qualitative research. *Handbook of Qualitative Research, 2*(163–194), 105.

Ingraham v. Wright, 430 U.S. 651 (1977).

Johnson, R. B., Onwuegbuzie, A. J., & Turner, L. A. (2007). Toward a definition of mixed methods research. *Journal of Mixed Methods Research, 1*(2), 112–133. https://doi.org/10.1177/1558689806298224

Kincheloe, J. L., & McLaren, P. L. (1994). Rethinking critical theory and qualitative research. In N. K. Denzin & Y. S. Lincoln (Eds.), *Handbook of qualitative research* (pp. 138–157). Thousand Oaks, CA: Sage.

Maslow, A. (1954). *Motivation and personality*. New York, NY: Harper.

Meiners, E. R. (2007). *Right to be hostile: Schools, prisons, and the making of public enemies*. New York, NY: Routledge.

Mertens, D. M. (2007). Transformative paradigm: Mixed methods and social justice. *Journal of Mixed Methods Research, 1*(3), 212–225. https://doi.org/10.1177/1558689807302811

Mertens, D. M. (2010). Transformative mixed methods research. *Qualitative Inquiry, 16*(6), 469–474. https://doi.org/10.1177/1077800410364612

Mertens, D. M. (2012). Transformative mixed methods: Addressing inequities. *American Behavioral Scientist, 56*(6), 802–813. https://doi.org/10.1177/0002764211433797

Morrow, R. A., & Brown, D. D. (1994). *Critical theory and methodology*. Thousand Oaks, CA: Sage.

Neal ex rel. Neal v. Fulton County Board of Education, 229 F. 3d 1069 (2000).

Parker, L. (1998). 'Race is race ain't': An exploration of the utility of critical race theory in qualitative research in education. *International Journal of Qualitative Studies in Education, 11*(1), 43–55. https://doi.org/10.1080/095183998236881

Parker, L., & Lynn, M. (2002). What's race got to do with it? Critical Race Theory's conflicts with and connections to qualitative research methodology and epistemology. *Qualitative Inquiry, 8*(1), 7–22. https://doi.org/10.1177/107780040200800102

Peterson v. Baker, 504 F. 3d 1331 (2007).

Ravitch, D. (2016). *The death and life of the great American school system: How testing and choice are undermining education*. New York, NY: Basic Books.

Solórzano, D. G., & Yosso, T. J. (2002). Critical race methodology: Counter-story-telling as an analytical framework for educational research. *Qualitative Inquiry, 8*(1), 23–44. https://doi.org/10.1177/107780040200800103

St. Pierre, E. A., & Pillow, W. S. (Eds.). (2000). *Working the ruins: Feminist poststructural theory and methods in education*. New York, NY: Routledge.

Weber, M. (1949). *The methodology of the social sciences*. Glencoe, IL: The Free Press.

Part III
Developing a Research Agenda

Chapter 21
Writing, Race, and Creative Democracy

Timothy J. Lensmire

Abstract My chapter traces how my critical teaching and scholarship has sought to contribute to what John Dewey called creative democracy—first, in my explorations of how the teaching of writing might serve radical democratic ends and, second, in my examination of the complexities and conflicts of Whiteness and White racial identities. Along with sustained intellectual engagements with the writings of Mikhail Bakhtin and W.E.B. Du Bois (among many others), my hatred of school and my love of basketball are noted as significant influences on my living and learning.

One way to narrate my journey as a critical education scholar would be to emphasize *disjunction* rather than cohesion. If you split my career as a researcher roughly in half, then in the first part I established myself as a critical literacy scholar. I investigated and theorized the teaching and learning of writing in public school classrooms, paying particular attention to how gender and social class constitute children's writing and their interactions with each other. Then, telling the story this way, in the second part I left the study of literacy to focus on race and education—specifically, how White people learn to be White in our White supremacist society and what this means for antiracist efforts in schools and teacher education.

However, I do not think of the story of my work this way. For me, my scholarship, throughout my career, has been grounded in, and has attempted to articulate commitments to, radical and creative democracy. By democracy, I do not mean a political system or form of government. The image or sound of democracy I have been pursuing is both humbler and harder. I have been guided by John Dewey's (1951) sense of creative democracy as a "way of life"—a way of life that Dewey thought was "controlled by a working faith in the possibilities of human nature" (p. 391).

T. J. Lensmire (✉)
University of Minnesota, Minneapolis, MN, USA
e-mail: lensmire@umn.edu

K. K. Strunk, L. A. Locke (eds.), *Research Methods for Social Justice and Equity in Education*, https://doi.org/10.1007/978-3-030-05900-2_21

In other words, my current work on race and education expresses the same long-term commitments as my earlier work—to better understand what helps and hinders democratic education and living.

***

I was born and raised in a small, rural, working-class community in Wisconsin, and I am sure that many different aspects of what I lived and learned there contributed to what became my radical commitments. For now, I will highlight two. First, I grew up among people who talked things over, together, as they responded to problems and challenges confronting them. Though I could not have described it this way at the time, I listened to and eventually joined my parents, aunts, and uncles in meaningful versions of what Dewey called *deliberation*. For Dewey, deliberation was a playing out, a rehearsal, of what would happen if we pursued this or that path. However, this deliberation was not some mechanical projection of profit or pleasure or pain. Instead, as Dewey (1922) wrote:

> To every shade of imagined circumstance there is a vibrating response; and to every complex situation a sensitiveness as to its integrity, a feeling of whether it does justice to all facts, or overrides some to the advantage of others. Decision is reasonable when deliberation is so conducted. (p. 194)

A second (and perhaps even more powerful) influence on me, growing up, was school—or more precisely, *my trouble with school*. For me, from the beginning, school meant adults attempting to control my body, making me sit still, face forward; school meant adults demanding that I talk quietly and not laugh, loudly (like my father did). I put it this way in an autoethnographic piece I wrote about Whiteness and social class:

> I was already engaged in the struggle that has defined my life in school, all the way from elementary through graduate school, and on into my life as a professor. I was struggling with the offer, made by school, to join the middle class. I was struggling with its demand that I remake (or at least hide) my working-class insides. (Lensmire, 2008, p. 310)

It is not so surprising, then, that in my early teaching (with 7th graders) I gravitated toward approaches that rejected the tight control of student bodies and voices, which rebelled against machine and factory qualities of schooling. My first guides in experimenting with alternative pedagogies were advocates of writing workshop or process approaches to the teaching of writing—approaches that emphasized experience and non-conformism, and with strong affinities to Ralph Waldo Emerson, Henry David Thoreau, and American Romanticism. Later, as I began teaching in college classrooms, my progressive teaching practices would be built upon and radicalized in engagements with critical pedagogy and feminist teaching and theory.

If my teaching was grounded, in part, in a rejection of traditional schooling, my eventual research was as well—and not just in terms of the *what* I was studying. I started my doctoral program at Michigan State University in 1986. And even though there was a well-established, year-long sequence in educational ethnography that I took in the college of education my first year, quantitative approaches to the study of education—especially what were called "process-product" studies—certainly felt dominant. They also felt like traditional schooling to me, felt hostile to life.

Thus, it is surely *not* the case that I *chose* ethnography after a careful weighing of the merits of various methodologies or that I *chose* ethnography because it was an appropriate methodology for the questions I wished to answer. Instead, I chose it quickly, instinctively, and for the same reasons, I think, that I had tried to teach in progressive ways.

I did a critical ethnography for my dissertation, which became my first book, *When children write: Critical re-visions of the writing workshop* (Lensmire, 1994). I wrote myself into enough problems in that first book that I needed to write a second book, *Powerful writing/Responsible teaching* (Lensmire, 2000), in order to work myself out of at least some of those problems. In this second book, I explored and criticized the learning environments created within writing workshops by imagining them as *carnivals*, as theorized by Russian philosopher and literary theorist Mikhail Bakhtin (1984b). This analysis enabled me to both affirm and question the guiding vision of these approaches to teaching and learning literacy—children writing themselves and their worlds on the page, within a classroom setting that liberated student intention and association.

I also examined teaching and the teacher's role in such spaces. Bakhtin's work was again important—this time, his celebratory reading of Fyodor Dostoevsky's fiction. For Bakhtin (1984a), Dostoevsky's novels featured strong characters who, in dialogue with each other and the author, articulated a plurality (a *polyphony*) of worldviews and truths—and this in sharp contrast to the *monologic* novels of most other writers, novels with a single worldview (that of the novelist) mouthed by servile characters. I looked to Bakhtin's appraisal of Dostoevsky in order to criticize how progressive and critical approaches to literacy have envisioned teaching and the teacher. I imagined the teacher as a novelist—a Dostoevskian novelist—who created a polyphonic classroom-novel and took up dialogic relations with student-characters. With this metaphor, I began to revise the roles and responsibilities of workshop teachers.

***

Over time, I realized that in this work on writing and its instruction, I had been willing to take up issues of social class and gender, but had shied away from race and racism. After finishing my second book, and at about the time that I was leaving Washington University in St. Louis to come to the University of Minnesota, I dedicated myself to learning about race in the United States and its relations to schooling and teacher education.

I did not want to take up race in a cheap or facile way, so it took me a number of years to read myself into and begin to position myself in relation to various and extensive literatures (and, of course, this labor continues). Eventually, I centered my learning about race in critical Whiteness and cultural studies—especially work coming out of labor history that was inspired by W.E.B. Du Bois's (1935/1992) idea, in *Black Reconstruction in America, 1860–1880*, that White workers were paid "a sort of public and psychological wage" (p. 700) by White elites that did little to alter their material condition, but that enabled White workers to think of themselves as different from and superior to Black people. In addition, the writing of Ralph Ellison (1953/1995, 1986) on the scapegoating rituals that fortify White Americans' sense of self, as well as Thandeka's (2001) psychoanalytic and historical rendering of White racial identity, became crucial to my theorizing.

This short account of how I came to race and racism in my scholarship is reasonable enough, but it omits a crucial underpinning to my study and learning. A better way to narrate this would be to add that, during my time as an assistant and then associate professor at Wash U (that's what we called it), I lived in Black neighborhoods and, during the summer, played basketball three or four nights a week on outdoor courts where I was usually the only White player among Black teammates and opponents. I was lucky enough to have Black colleagues at Wash U who wrote brilliantly about race, such as Garrett Duncan and Gerald Early, and I learned much from them. So it is certainly fair to say that my *intellectual* engagement with race and racism had already begun in St. Louis. But the most significant engagements were probably more *bodily* ones. Unconsciously (sometimes more consciously)—as I ate and laughed and hollered with my neighbors in our backyards, and as I coordinated the movements of my White body in relation to Black bodies on the basketball courts in Heman Park—I was learning not only about who my neighbors and friends were, but also about who I was as a White man. As always, my body was ahead of my conscious thought, my experiences ahead of my ability to understand and theorize what was happening and what it meant. As Dewey (1916/1966) put it:

> Activity begins in an impulsive form [and] does not know what it is about; that is to say, what are its interactions with other activities. An activity which brings education or instruction with it makes one aware of some of the connections which had been imperceptible. (p. 77)

As my reading and study caught up with my living, I realized that I would need to go backward to go forward. I knew that I wanted to do an interview study with White people, in order to write about White supremacy and White racial identity. And I knew that I wanted to find a way to write in which I did not, as author, separate myself from or suggest that I was superior to the people I was writing about (something you see, over and over again, in books written about White people by White antiracists). I realized that I should go home.

So I did.

I interviewed 22 White people, aged 18 to 83. Across two or three open-ended interviews totaling three to six hours, we talked about how they thought the German and Polish origins of the town of Boonendam (a pseudonym I created from an Ojibwe word meaning to forget or to give up thinking about something) influenced their lives there. I asked them to try to remember the first time that they realized they were White and to narrate experiences in which race somehow mattered or was important. We talked about how they and their community had responded to people of Color in various situations and across different historical events, including the controversy surrounding Ojibwe efforts in the 1970s to claim fishing rights on nearby lakes and rivers, and their interactions with recent arrivals to the area, especially Hmong and Mexican Americans hired to work on local farms.

Drawn from this larger interview study, as well as autoethnographic writing, my recent book—*White folks: Race and identity in rural America* (Lensmire, 2017)—

focuses on the experiences and stories of eight White people (including me) from Boonendam, Wisconsin, and explores the complex social production of White racial identities. The book is about becoming a White person in a White community, but demonstrates just how dependent White racial identities are on racial others, even in segregated White spaces.

Unfortunately, my book is timely. As racial actors in the United States, White people do not understand themselves or their country very well. We may try to take up colorblindness as a sensible, moral stance and hope that we had achieved a post-racial society with the election of our first Black president. But then how do we make sense of all the violence being waged against people of Color, make sense of all the news (that is not new) in our country?

Furthermore, the current dominant critical framework for understanding racism and Whiteness—a White privilege framework, popularized by writers such as Peggy McIntosh and Tim Wise—provides precious little help to those who want to understand and intervene in how White people learn to be White, how we come to think and feel and act as we do. Within a White privilege framework, White people are conceptualized as little more than the smooth embodiment of privilege.

Something more is needed—a way of conceptualizing White people that is unafraid to confront, head on, the violence at the core of White racial selves, but that also illuminates conflicts and complexities there. What's needed is a way of understanding White people that recognizes the profound ambivalence that characterizes White thinking and feeling in relation to people of Color—not just fear and rejection, but also envy and attraction. If, as Antonio Gramsci (1971) thought, the "starting point of critical elaboration is ... 'knowing thyself' as a product of the historical process to date which has deposited in you an infinity of traces, without leaving an inventory" (p. 324), then in *White folks* I attempt to create inventories and understand traces, as regards the historical process of becoming White in a rural community in the United States. My hope is that the storytelling and theorizing I do in this book will support the development of more effective antiracist pedagogies, and that it will help us imagine and live out better ways of working with and mobilizing White people to take up antiracist and social justice action.

***

Inevitably, unavoidably, narratives reveal some things and hide others. My account of how and why my journey as a critical researcher and educator played out as it did does not escape this fact.

One goal I had in telling my story was not to write as if ideas and books were the only important characters. I love reading. Serious, sustained study has been crucial. Without the writings of Du Bois and Bakhtin and many others, I would not have written what I have written, done what I have done, and become what I have become.

That said, my hatred of school and my love of basketball have been just as important in propelling my life (and story) forward.

And, of course, once I say this, once I assert this, it becomes apparent immediately that there is more going on in this hatred and love than is immediately apparent—that this love and hatred must be interpreted, theorized, become educative so I can see how they interact and connect with other things and activities.

Lurking in my hatred of schooling is a working-class kid's nascent critique of capitalism. And my love of basketball surely expresses, among other things, an attraction to Black ways of moving in the world and the fact that playing basketball has taught me about what it means to be free—where freedom is not the absence of constraint but the power to do something, create something, in community with others.

My story is one of movement, then, of the thinking body leaping forward, half aware of what it is doing and why, and of movement among story and interpretation, practice and theory, living and learning.

Suggested Readings

Ellison, R. (1995). *Shadow and act.* New York, NY: Vintage International. (Original work published 1953).

I have found Ralph Ellison's collection of essays to be incredibly helpful in understanding race and Whiteness in the United States. Two aspects of these essays that are especially important are how complex and conflicted racial identities are assumed to be by Ellison and the fact that, at every moment, he is concerned with what all of this means for democracy.

Thandeka. (2001). *Learning to be White: Money, race, and God in America.* New York, NY: Continuum.

I would be hard-pressed to name another book that is as effective at theorizing White racial identity—not only in terms of societal structure and history, but also at the level of intimate, everyday relations and interactions.

References

Bakhtin, M. M. (1984a). *Problems of Dostoevsky's poetics.* (C. Emerson, Ed. & Trans.). Minneapolis, MN: University of Minnesota Press.
Bakhtin, M. M. (1984b). *Rabelais and his world.* (H. Iswolsky, Trans.). Bloomington, IN: Indiana University Press.
Dewey, J. (1922). *Human nature and conduct.* New York, NY: Henry Holt.
Dewey, J. (1951). Creative democracy—The task before us. In M. Fisch (Ed.), *Classic American philosophers* (pp. 389–394). New York, NY: Appleton-Century-Crofts.
Dewey, J. (1966). *Democracy and education.* New York, NY: Free Press. (Original work published 1916).
Du Bois, W. E. B. (1992). *Black reconstruction in America, 1860–1880.* New York, NY: The Free Press. (Original work published 1935).
Ellison, R. (1986). *Going to the territory.* New York, NY: Vintage International.

Ellison, R. (1995). *Shadow and act*. New York, NY: Vintage International. (Original work published 1953).

Gramsci, A. (1971). *Selections from the prison notebooks*. New York, NY: International Publishers.

Lensmire, T. (1994). *When children write: Critical re-visions of the writing workshop*. New York, NY: Teachers College.

Lensmire, T. (2000). *Powerful writing/Responsible teaching*. New York, NY: Teachers College.

Lensmire, T. (2008). How I became White while punching de tar baby. *Curriculum Inquiry, 38*(3), 299–322. https://doi.org/10.1111/j.1467-873X.2008.00410.x

Lensmire, T. (2017). *White folks: Race and identity in rural America*. New York, NY: Routledge.

Thandeka. (2001). *Learning to be White: Money, race, and God in America*. New York, NY: Continuum.

Chapter 22
Beyond White: The Emotional Complexion of Critical Research on Race

Cheryl E. Matias

Abstract Exposing life in the academy while doing racially just work is difficult. For one, those who relay their experiences in the academy as a way to improve the professoriate are incorrectly labeled whistleblowers and are often met with resistance, passive aggressive bullying tactics, or find themselves and their scholarship constantly under scrutiny. Second, instead of listening and learning from the stories shared about academy life, administrators who do have the power to make changes belittle and minimize the stories as if they are just mere whines of a baby. To combat this, I share three essays that paint a picture of academy life while doing racially just work. I do so to share the trials, tribulations, and simple successes of this path so that professors and administrators can create more racially just educational systems that are inclusive to faculty of Color and scholars of race.

Introduction

This chapter shares emotional essays from my personal journey of engaging in a racially just research agenda, methodologies, and activism inside the academy. Embedded in this chapter are several deliberate emotional juxtapositions to capture forever the complex struggles of engaging in such work, especially when your complexion is beyond white.

Special Note: To mi nina grande, La Dona. May you experience the full range of beautiful and healthy emotions in an unhealthy emotional world.

C. E. Matias (✉)
University of Colorado Denver, Denver, CO, USA
e-mail: Cheryl.Matias@ucdenver.edu

© The Author(s) 2019
K. K. Strunk, L. A. Locke (eds.), *Research Methods for Social Justice and Equity in Education*, https://doi.org/10.1007/978-3-030-05900-2_22

The Frustratingly Discomforting Realization of Race Justice

During my much-needed year-long sabbatical, I attended a Research Apprentice Course (RAC) that was *sadly comforting* to my heart. The course was offered by my former professor at my doctoral granting institution, and despite having graduated eight years prior and living in another state for those eight years, I oddly felt home in a space I have not been in for years. The physical space has not changed much. In fact, the same droning beige walls still came alive with the bright overhead projector displaying terminologies from critical race theory (CRT) and critical whiteness studies (CWS). The chiming of the local bell tower at the top of the hour and the constant whirring of helicopters above provided the same white noise that immediately faded into the background as intellectual dialogues of race ensued. And, the warmth of a summer day in Los Angeles in a room without air-conditioning embraced us all, as if it were one of those welcoming hugs that warmed the entire body. In all, I sat there in the space staring, listening, laughing, tearing, speaking, and living. It was then that I realized the space was sadly, gut-wrenchingly comforting. That is, though we, as former graduate students and now professors, have left the nest, so to speak, and end up in all parts of the nation, being back in this physical, spiritual, and emotional space was uplifting and healing, yet, at the same it, it was oddly saddening. Let me explain.

A plethora of literature explicates the hostile climate toward racially just educators in the ivory towers, particularly for women of Color who engage in race research. Berry and Mizelle (2006), for example, suggest how academia has created habits, practices, and curricula that are often microaggressive to women of Color. In describing her lived reality as a woman of Color in the academy, Berry exasperatedly writes, "It's always something (what the fuck?). As a woman of Color, some facet of my multidimensional being is always a problem, a dilemma for someone" (p. xiii). Gutierrez Muh, Niemann, Gonzalez, and Harris (2012) echo this sentiment by highlighting the maltreatment women faculty of Color experience in higher education. From being presumed incompetent to as Lugo Lugo (2012) blatantly describes, "a prostitute, a servant, and a customer service representative" the academy has not often been respectful to women of Color whose research critically focuses on race and gender (p. 40). In fact, Baszile, Edwards, and Guillory (2016) call such treatment spirit murder knowing all too well that academia engages in whiteness so much so that it murders the very soul of women of Color. Suffice it to say then that spaces like the one described at the beginning of this chapter are not often available in academic spaces, even if such spaces proclaim to be socially just in their mission statements and visions.

Therefore, one can better understand my deliberate use of an emotional juxtaposition to describe my experience in that course. On the one hand, the space was comforting because during the five-hour RAC session, we, critical scholars of race, openly discussed methodological applications and theoretical ruminations of racial micro-affirmations[1]; its application, sociohistorical roots, and as a way to counter racial microaggressions people of Color face in a white supremacist world. There were no white tears, protests of "not all white people," emotional projections of one's guilt, or pontifications of one benevolence in "helping" students of Color; for this was not simply a physical space for critical race researchers to gather. No. This was a spiritual, emotional, and intellectual space that allowed us just to be free from all that mess. So I felt home. I felt heard. I felt respected. On the other hand, it was this very realization of feeling home, comforted, and relaxed that I became sad. One, I rarely feel this way when engaging in the work of dismantling white supremacy in the academy, a purpose many scholars would agree with but in which they would rarely invest. Two, despite the academy claiming to want to engage in racially just research and practices, they still refuse to acknowledge the humanity of the very researchers who do this work. And three, as I listened to study after study of micro-affirmations and how they affirm communities of Color as a way to counteract the daily racially microaggressions we experience, I realized how sad it is to need a space just to assert our humanity. Meaning, though the work was comforting, affirming even, to hear it or bear witness to the work that is being done, embedded within its very need to be uttered is an ontological sadness. 'Tis as if we need to find secret pockets within our lives to identify the affirmations because we are too often unaffirmed, unrecognized, disrespected, and dehumanized. Hence, I reassert that sadly comforting emotional state of heart because in recognizing this sentiment I must also realize that it is only true because we are *frustratingly discomforted* in engaging in critical research on race in the "socially just" academy.

Regarding White Behaviors: Shocked and Surprised Versus Frustratingly Predictable

I want to be shocked, floored, awed, and inspired in new ways, especially when it comes to the predictable behaviors of white emotions and emotionalities. Meaning, I want to be shocked and surprised by *not* seeing the predictable behaviors of white emotions. By white emotions I mean those very surface emotions that are expressed as some sort of unhealthy defense or coping mechanism strategically employed to avoid discussions or realizations of race and whiteness. It is captured in verbal expressions like "I never own slaves," "why are you blaming me," or, "not all white people." Or, such white emotions can be captured in behaviors like strategically running to a dean or department chair to presumably "tattle" on a professor who is teaching and learning about race, as if their discomforted emotions have more validity than the doctoral degree of the professor teaching on the topic. Alas, those who employ this strategy know all too well that such white emotions do in fact have power. We need not look further than the employment of this reverse victimization of white women to see how it impacts the lives, and sadly, also the deaths of people of Color, like how it did for Emmett Till. It is as if we, women professors of Color who teach racial justice, are only present to *mammy* the emotional needs of white students. Or, more specific to my case as a brown-skinned Pinay, *nurse*[2] the needs of unfettered white emotions.

Unlike these surface emotions that are eerily and routinely performed each time a racially just educator attempts to teach about race and racism (let alone even scratch white supremacy in any form), more deeply masked are the white emotionalities that dig deep into the abyss of what Thandeka (1999) coins, white ethnic shame. That is, beyond the toddler-like tantrum of these white emotions is a deeper white emotionality that gave it rise—one that has been so repressed that it manifests in almost hysterical or irrational ways (Gonsalves, 2008).

To better understand this, allow me to illuminate. In delivering a keynote about the need to say and talk about race in teacher education, there was one self-identified white woman teacher candidate in the audience. She even began her comment with "I am just like one of those white female preservice teachers in your study." The keynote speaker was listening attentively to this white female as she said, "This thing about culture…" At this, the keynote speaker was frustrated at the predictable maneuver of whiteness to once again deliberately refuse to engage the word "race" after delivering a 1.5-hour talk about race. As such, the speaker refused to allow rhetoric of whiteness to ensue and interjected, "Please, you have to say the word race. We are all here to talk about race." The teacher candidate nodded her head, took a deep breath, cleared her throat, and began with her response again. "OK. This thing about culture…" The keynote speaker was shocked—not in a good way—to hear this candidate's refusal to say the word race so the speaker interjected again saying, "Please. I just got done showing why we must have the courage to say the word race let alone really understand how race operates in teaching and education. It is why I am here at this university. To begin this work, please use the word race." Upon this redirect, the white woman teacher candidate got visibly flustered. Her face turned red, and it appeared her breath became shallow and panicked. She was standing up in a ballroom of close to 150 audience members of faculty, staff, and students from all over the university and surrounding community and began to display a white emotion which, for some, was shocking or surprising, yet, for me, it was frustratingly predictable. She started crying. Through her sobs, she exasperatedly cried out, "I just can't say that word! I just can't say that word!" Her confession of not being able to say the word race was nothing more than a revealing tale of her deep refusal to say the word, for it is ludicrous to presume that a person has a particular speech impediment that physically does not allow one to say the single word, "race." Obviously, the white emotions she displayed are that of extreme distress, sadness, and white tears.

Beyond those white emotions, however, are deeper emotionalities such as the shame of bearing witness to race but suppressing this truth in order to be accepted into whiteness (see Thandeka, 1999), guilt for partaking in whiteness (Matias, 2016), and fear of what happens if they reject the norms of whiteness by asserting and identifying its existence (Matias & Allen, 2013). You see, beyond the frustratingly predictable white tears that are strategically employed to stop mere dialogues of race and racism is a plethora of mechanisms of whiteness. For one, they operationalize white tears because they know that white women's emotions, stereotypes of innocence and purity (via anti-miscegenation laws), and employment of reverse victimization have historically been used to maintain whiteness and relinquish any culpability that white women have had in such maintenance (see Godfrey, 2010). And, beyond this, this strategy has been good enough to incite white men into a frenzy under the guise of "protecting" white women, as if white women are indeed in need of protecting. Therefore, these tears are real, but are not valid because they have for so long been operationally used to reinforce a racial power structure that benefits whiteness, particularly gendered whiteness, at the expense of people of Color.

Second, when white women deliberating employ white tears as a way to feign innocence and victimization, it inadvertently makes anyone who made the white women cry the enemy. White women are held to a false ideal of moral compass and within this white supremacist understanding of humanity, anything that causes emotional "harm" to this all-benevolent being is thus castigated as evil. In this case, the keynote speaker was the evildoer for simply bringing up a topic that the white woman teacher candidate was too unfettered to deal with because of her own issues regarding race. Of course, the candidate's issues regarding race cannot be addressed if she pretends to be the crying victim while projecting her racial angst onto the keynote speaker.

Third, once labeled as the evildoer who caused the white women "harm," whiteness flares up to once again reassert its power and privilege by policing, surveilling, and disciplining the action, speech, tone, and research of the race scholar or scholar of Color. In this case, the tears made its predictable appearance, but what was more frustratingly predictable was the immediate rush to cater to her emotional needs, as if the world needed to pause. One white woman audience member stood up and went on a diatribe about nothingness or gibberish, which is common to whiteness in its irrational logic. Another white woman who sat in the very last row of the ballroom even tried to end the entire lecture by closing with, "Thank you all for coming." Another spoke at lengths at how antiracist she was by showcasing all the organizations she was a part of and all the good deeds she has done instead of taking the time to digest the feelings of whiteness and sit with discomfort. As if, the quick turn to "I'm a good person" is some say deflection of the culpability we should all own. In all, during these pontifications made primarily by white women in the audience, never once was there a real question asked to keynote speaker during this Q & A. Instead, it became a silencing act to dismiss the credibility, respect, and message of the keynote speaker. In fact, it shifted the focus and gaze that was on the keynote speaker and the research delivered to the performance of whiteness. The soliloquies of, "how good I am." The monologues of incoherent logic. The controller of the spotlight. Bravo, whiteness.

The most frustratingly predictable aspect of all this is that this exact scenario plays out too often in various fields across the US. And, in this annoyingly repetitive movie of whiteness, we, the spectators, are so engulfed in the performance that we may overlook two major things. One, how catering to white tears is in and of itself a maintenance of white supremacy because to be too emotionally unfettered to learn about race and racism is NOT the same as to be emotionally traumatized by racism: police brutality, job discrimination, housing discrimination, academic lynching, denial of tenure, and death. Plainly, one's choice to be emotionally unfettered to merely learn about racism is NOT on par with the pain people of Color experience under white supremacy. Catering to these white tears then becomes a giant leap backwards in dismantling white supremacy. In doing so, it suffocates those racially just researchers who try to engage in racially just research, teaching, and service.

Two, when people act as if they are shocked or surprised with some predictable performance of white emotions like "I didn't know about racism" or "My goodness, can you believe she called the cops on those guys who were just barbecuing at a park" it is frustrating. It is as if that person who is acting all surprised or confounded by a particular behavior of whiteness is yet again feigning innocence by employing an ahistorical understanding of our world. Frankly speaking, one cannot be surprised about behavior that is routinely performed. Yes, she will call the cops because white women have done it before. Do not act as if one did not know about racism when they refused to bring their Black boyfriend home or chose to drive around a particular part of town because it was "rough around the edges" (code for too Black). The engagement of whiteness, anti-blackness, and white supremacy are so masterfully executed because in their execution they deny its existence. 'Tis nothing more than an abusive cycle whereby the abuser abuses and then uses his power to deny the abuse ever took place. Therefore, this bewilderment toward acts of white supremacy via white emotions and behaviors are frustrating because although they are so routinely performed we, as a society, are forced to act as if it were the first time ever.

And it is this pre-context that makes researching, teaching, and servicing racial justice in the academy so frustrating. In fact, as social scientists, we are to investigate patterns, understand why they exist, and theorize its maintenance and relation to society. For example, when it comes to exceedingly high, high school dropout rates of Black and Latinx students in US education, one does not hesitate to study this pattern, what existing structures impact its prevalence, or to theorize as to ways it can better support Black and Latinx students. When it comes to bilingual education, we give no second thought of the pattern of white women educators who become the experts of this field, many of whom do not speak another language. Yet, when it comes to whiteness in teacher education, white supremacy in US education, or emotionalities of whiteness that impact teaching and learning of our predominantly diverse student population, naysayers strategically overlook this pattern. To ponder why education is predominated by white women is to engage in an emotional act of whiteness because in that very quandary is a refusal to bear witness to how post-*Brown v. Board of Education* inadvertently socially implied that Black teachers were incompetent and thus many were pushed out of the field of teaching (Tillman, 2004). To ask why women of Color are not supporting white women's marches is a direct slap in the face because it denies the historical realities of white women who have rarely championed the interests of women of Color (see hooks, 1994). To question the competence, teaching practices, research agendas, and servicing projects of women professors of Color who are researching race and racism is a blatant denial of one's own insecurities of accepting that a woman of Color *is* an expert. Thus, they forever attempt to undermine her competence. Meaning, to readily accept that white professors can be experts on bilingual education without knowing another language, educational pipelines of African Americans without ever living in Black communities, or on culturally responsive teaching regardless of a refusal to acknowledge their white cultural selves is narcissistic, especially when those same folks find it difficult to respect the decisions of deans, principals, bosses, faculty, staff, or students of Color who are experts in race, white supremacy, and whiteness. So, to enforce white supremacy these folks who continually choose to undermine racially just researchers will

- sabotage tenure cases,
- engage in workplace bullying or harassment if a researcher continues to do research on race,
- anonymously call the Institutional Review Board (IRB) as a way to start an inquisition and dissuade researchers from their race-related research agendas,
- attempt to ostracize race researchers by putting them in isolated programs,
- discredit their accomplishments perhaps by never citing the glowing letters from external reviewers during a tenure case,
- reduce their counterstories, as proffered by CRT, to mere autobiographies,
- continually try to control the narrative of a racially just researcher by stating they are uncollaborative,
- deny funding opportunities to race-related projects or conferences,
- ignore racially just service projects or teaching so that annual merit pays are overlooked, or
- deny courses specific to race, racism, or whiteness despite having an urban education program with a mission statement that is committed to equity and social justice.

These strategies are NOT shocking or surprising for they are no different than the tactics historically used to ostracize, marginalize, and delegitimize groups of people in the past. As such, they are frustratingly predictable in the resoluteness of whiteness. Yet, I forever hope that I can be shocked or surprised by someone who diverges from this patterned behavior—that shows true humanity. Because in that emotional space we can begin down an excitingly unpredictable path toward racial healing.

Hope Versus [Side-Eye]: The Annoyingly Methodological Side-Step

The field of education is quick to draw upon the now famous work of John Dewey to understand the state, purpose, and experience of US education. Books, articles, journal even, are written and established in the memory of his scholarship. Common parlance within educational circles are talks of pragmatism, educational experience, and democratic education. In fact, these concepts are held as truths from which empirical studies then arise. Studies focusing on how democratic education can better be facilitated, how does pragmatism impact student success, or what educational experiences are contributing to the educational attainment of students are common research inquiries that draw from Dewey's foundational scholarship. Clearly, Dewey's educational contributions are long lasting and give education hope in its innovative theories.

In the same vein, when educators and educational researchers engage in the en vogue discussions of social justice, they are astute in citing Paulo Freire. His notions of conscientization, banking education, and pedagogy of oppressed are just a few of his theoretical rumination that are now used as the basis to drive educational policy, teacher preparation programs, and university mission statements and visions. Freire's work has become so commonplace that high school kids at Tucson Unified School District read *Pedagogy of Oppressed*. His face even glitters on the T-shirts of many socially just educators. Freire is not only the man who is given the credence of social justice education, but he has now become the iconic ideal which is now repurposed as a living process of a pedagogically hopeful education, so captured when researchers engage the word, "Freirean." Meaning, to engage in Freirean approaches to education is beyond Paulo Freire the man. In doing so, the hope for socially just education lives on.

These are but two examples of scholars who have greatly influenced educational practices, thoughts, and research agendas. Indeed there are many more like Karl Marx, Max Weber, or even modern scholars like Michel Foucault, Henry Giroux, or, my own mentor, Zeus Leonardo. Suffice it to say that understanding the complexities of education builds upon the research of yesteryear; research that is popularly accepted as truths and applicable to education. As a subset of the entire discipline of education, teacher education is no different. Echoed in mission statements and visions is the need for democratic, socially just, and equitable education. Research agendas within teacher education continually explore new teaching practices, curricular approaches, and pedagogical applications in order to meet the meets of a growing linguistic, cultural, racial, sexual, and gender diversity found in US K-12 schooling. Needless to say, teacher education and all its belief system, practices, operation, and evaluation are built upon truths first defined in theoretical postulations of past scholarship. Meaning, within teacher education, it is common practice and widely accepted to build research agendas off the need for social justice or to enforce democratic education. With this in mind, one would have no disagreements in saying these past theorizations, ideas, and assertions from scholars like Dewey or Freire are relevant to the state of US teacher education today. Yet, when one attempts to push the theorizations of yesteryear to the twenty-first century in teacher education, there is *empiricist* pushback, especially with regard to those educational scholars who research race, racism, and white supremacy. By empiricist I specifically identify a group of educational gatekeepers or an educational epistemology that actively limits what constitutes educational research. They do this by defining educational research as empirical studies only. Let me explain.

CRT and CWS operate as critical social theory has done before yet are not often given the same credence. Like Marx and other critical theorists from the Frankfurt School—many of whom were white men—the theoretical contributions were widely accepted in various academic disciplines; teacher education is no different. In the scholarship of critical theory, they critique society knowing that observing society itself is in and of itself a wonderfully rich canvas for which to generate theories. These theories are then applied to teacher education as a way to engage in socially just teaching. In fact, Freire himself often cites Erich Fromm, who was originally a part of the Frankfurt School. Therefore, the idea of accepting theoretical research is not foreign to teacher education for its very foundations, pursuits, and missions are guided by them.

In the same likeliness, CRT is a formidable analytic tool first used in the discipline of law and then applied to education to investigate society and its maintenance of white supremacy and racism. As a great complement to CRT, CWS deconstructs hegemonic whiteness and how its operations ultimately uphold white supremacy. Both theories or theoretical fields of study are like critical theory, in that they begin with a point of contention. More precisely, just as conflict theory so describes for critical theory, society is not benign, produced or interacted within a vacuum, or absent of conflict over power. Similarly, society is not colorblind, post-racial, or free of the competing powers found in a racial hierarchy. As such, CRT and CWS do not preoccupy themselves in empirically demonstrating whether or not racism exists. It is a fact embedded in its application just as the observation of a conflicting society is embedded in critical theory. So you would think that teacher education that builds its very foundation on theorization would welcome further theorizations as applicable to nowadays. Unfortunately, that has not been my experience.

First, when engaging in the theorization of the emotionalities of whiteness, there were several pushbacks. First, the idea of studying whiteness in a field that has been determined to have an overwhelming presence of whiteness (Sleeter, 2001) was difficult. White teachers, white professors of teacher education, and white administrators could not fathom a different narrative to their existence and presence as white educators other than the Hollywood depictions of the white savior. Merely, positing the idea that perhaps they are not helping was too unfettering. Second, the study of emotionality was difficult because although male scholars have had the liberty to study "affect," the same study on emotions was considered biased when researched by a woman, let alone a woman of Color. But the worst pushback was what I call the methodological side-step. This process was often nonlinear and convoluted but eerily very predictable.

I first noticed one application of the methodological side-step when I submitted manuscripts that employed theory as a method or engaged in theoretical investigations to understand society's patterns of racialized emotions. On one of my manuscripts, the infamous reviewer two predictably reacted to the topic of whiteness *and* emotionality placing comments throughout the manuscript that were just objections to every idea. They refused to engage in the topic, argument, and literature and flat out wrote emotional responses to each claim. Knowing that one cannot deny a manuscript based upon one's emotional response to it, the reviewer then wrote a lengthy paragraph that discredited the entire manuscript based on methods alone. In speaking with other critical race scholars or critical whiteness scholars, I noticed this was becoming a more commonplace practice. Clearly, it became a new strategic maneuver to discredit and silence the work on race, particularly whiteness. Yet, in the same journal, I saw published articles of how white teachers became antiracist upon simple learnings of race and racism. It was as if research can never critique whiteness unless it was given a heroic ending just like the Hollywood films depict.

It was annoying because my research is not about proving that racism, whiteness, and white supremacy exist just as feminists do not have to prove that gender bias exists. Instead, my research agenda was focused on how does the emotionality of whiteness look in teacher education and how might it impact a teacher's teaching such that it also affects her students of Color. The inquiry and research was not to demonize any one being, but to tackle the problem of racial bias in teacher education—a field which is predominated by white women—in new ways so that education actually becomes racially just. If by chance my research ever held up a mirror to a reflection that one detests, then that is not my problem. The problem becomes why someone would refuse to see their own reflection.

However, the methodological side-step grew even worse in its institutional presence. During my tenure process, a rubric was designed after the start of my professoriate. It was developed to ascertain the excellence of our research as faculty. Included was a simple word that defined what constitutes as research. The word inserted was "empirical" which was later footnoted to be defined as "not just theoretical." Interesting. Here are educational researchers who are okay with accepting theorizations made by white men but disavowing, discrediting, and even discouraging the expansion of epistemological, ontological, philosophical thought, especially during a time when newer faculty are more diverse in gender, race, ability, and sexuality than ever before. It is as if education refuses to allow diverse people to generate philosophy of their own while readily citing Dewey, a philosopher by training.

Even the largest professional educational research organization, American Educational Research Association (AERA), released a 2009 memorandum affirming the use of what they coined "humanities-based research" which officially recognized the importance of theoretical research in education. To honor this, AERA even updated their online submission interface, allowing a drop-down tab to indicate whether the proposal is methodologically theoretical. So it is quite telling when the leadership of a school of education makes the decisions to limit the definition of research to empiricism when it readily applies theoretical research to undergird their missions and visions. I mean, honestly, who did Freire or Dewey interview? And, beyond this line of questioning, why is it that some folks in teacher education, or education writ large, is averse to accepting newer theorizations like the emotionality of whiteness from scholars of Color? Crooms (2003) answers this by positing how women of Color, particularly Black women, are not given the credence of engaging in theory building, as if the job is only open to white men, or men in general.

In addition to this is the fact that CRT and CWS are not preoccupied with providing empirical evidence that racism or white supremacy exists. It is a fact embedded in its very employment. Thereby, to limit the scope of what constitutes research for a scholar's tenure process to only empirical research is also to limit the ability for scholars to engage in CRT or CWS. In the end, this limitation is but another attempt to once again silence racially just research. Furthermore, CRT's method of counter-storytelling, parables, or testimonies are also not given credence because if administrators continue to redefine what constitutes research during the tenure process, they will revert back to the good old, "but that's only your story," or "this is just autobiography," as a way to minimize the relevance of counterstories.

Therefore, when this methodological side-step is applied to you, the reader, in any of your racially just scholarship, recognize that this is not about your research and it should not deter your hope in a racially just system; instead, it is about one's own insecurity to accept you as a scholar with formidable ideas, theories, and contribution to education. In fact, it is about one's insecurity to see its own complexion. Because, alas, education is already run by queen bees refusing to share the hive while enforcing, perhaps more precisely reinforcing, the whitened complexion of education.

Suggested Readings

Fanon, F. (1967). *Black skin, white mask*. New York: Grove Press.

This book provides great insight in the psychoanalytic behind race and how it impacts folks of color. Though written in 1967 it is still relevant today.

Matias, C. E. (2016). *Feeling Whites*. Netherlands: Sense Publishers.

This book provides great insight into how race and, more specifically, whiteness, impacts emotionality and how this all plays out in education.

Thandeka, T. (1999). *Learning to be white*. New York, NY: Continuum International.

This book provides great insight into how white children become white and how that impacts their identity.

Notes

1. Per Danny Solorzano and Lindsay Huber (2018).
2. In reference to the US Exchange Visitor Programs that funneled mass droves of Filipina nurses into the US since 1940s. Hence, the prevalence of Filipina nurses in US hospitals, hospices, and domestic health care services.

References

American Educational Research Association. (2009). Standards for reporting on humanities-oriented research in AERA publications. *Educational Researcher, 38*(6), 481–486. https://doi.org/10.3102/0013189X09341833

Baszile, D., Edwards, K., & Guillory, N. (Eds.). (2016). *Race, gender, and curriculum theorizing: Working in womanish ways*. New York, NY: Lexington Books.

Berry, T. R., & Mizelle, N. D. (Eds.). (2006). *From oppression to grace: Women of color and their dilemmas in the academy*. Stylus Publishing, LLC.

Crooms, L. A. (2003). "To establish my legitimate name inside the consciousness of strangers": Critical race praxis, progressive women-of-Color theorizing, and human rights. *Howard Law Journal, 46*, 229–581.

Godfrey, P. (2010). "Sweet little (white) girls"? Sex and fantasy across the color line and the contestation of patriarchal white supremacy. *Equity & Excellence in Education, 3*(3), 204–218. https://doi.org/10.1080/10665680490491506

Gonsalves, R. (2008). Hysterical blindness and the ideology of denial: Preservice teachers' resistance to multicultural education. *Counterpoints, 319*, 3–27.

Gutierrez Muh, G., Niemann, Y., Gonzalez, C., & Harris, A. (2012). *Presumed incompetent: The intersections of race and class in women in academia*. Boulder, CO: University of Colorado Press.

hooks, b. (1994). *Teaching to transgress: Education as a practice of freedom*. New York, NY: Routledge.

Lugo Lugo, C. (2012). A prostitute, a servant, and a customer representative: A Latina in the academy. In G. Gutierrez Muh, Y. Niemann, C. Gonzalez, & A. Harris (Eds.), *Presumed incompetent: The intersections of race and class in women in academia* (pp. 40–49). Boulder, CO: University of Colorado Press.

Matias, C. E. (2016). *Feeling White: Whiteness, emotionality, and education*. Netherlands: Sense Publishers.

Matias, C. E., & Allen, R. L. (2013). Loving whiteness to death: Sadomasochism, emotionality, and the possibility of humanizing love. *Berkeley Review of Education, 4*(2). https://doi.org/10.5070/B84110066

Sleeter, C. (2001). Preparing teachers for culturally diverse schools: Research and the overwhelming presence of whiteness. *Journal of Teacher Education, 52*(2), 94–106. https://doi.org/10.1177/0022487101052002002

Thandeka. (1999). *Learning to be white: Money, race, and God in America*. New York, NY: Continuum International.

Tillman, L. C. (2004). (Un)intended consequences? The impact of Brown v. Board of Education decision on the employment status of Black educators. *Education and Urban Society, 36*(3), 280–303. https://doi.org/10.1177/0013124504264360

Chapter 23
I Pulled Up a Seat at the Table: My Journey Engaging in Critical Quantitative Inquiry

Lolita A. Tabron

Abstract Historically, statistical research has been used as a tool of oppression attempting to "prove" the intellectual and cultural inferiority of communities of color (i.e., bell curve, Tuskegee Syphilis Study, eugenics, IQ testing) and obscure the reality of racism. Such scientific racism is the foundation of the US education system and contextualizes many of the contemporary issues of racial and social stratification today. Consequently, there is a widely held belief that "quantitative methods are antithetical to social justice," which situates the problem with statistical methods rather than the users of the methods (Cokley & Awad, *Journal for Social Action in Counseling and Psychology*, *5*, 26–41, 2013, p. 27). In this chapter, I discuss the need for critical quantitative inquiry, where researchers disrupt and push for the re-imagining of ways to engage in more culturally inclusive and sustaining approaches to quantitative inquiry. I argue that statistics is a powerful tool that can be used to resist oppression through community-driven, justice-oriented work.

There is a great African proverb that states, "Until lions have their historians, the tales of the hunt will always glorify the hunter." This proverb has in many ways reflected traditional academic research, where the research narratives continue to legitimate hegemonic ways of thinking and doing, especially in quantitative inquiry. Historically, statistical research has been used as a tool of oppression attempting to "prove" the intellectual and cultural inferiority of communities of color (i.e., "the bell curve," Tuskegee Syphilis Study, eugenics, IQ testing) and obscure the reality of racism (Cokley & Awad, 2013; Gillborn, 2010). Such scientific racism is the foundation of the US education system and contextualizes many of the contemporary issues of racial and social stratification today. Too often communities of color are over-researched, exploited for capital gains, and dehumanized as a statistic

L. A. Tabron (✉)
University of Denver, Denver, CO, USA
e-mail: lolita.tabron@du.edu

© The Author(s) 2019
K. K. Strunk, L. A. Locke (eds.), *Research Methods for Social Justice and Equity in Education*, https://doi.org/10.1007/978-3-030-05900-2_23

(Leong, 2013). Further, findings from statistical studies often remain unchecked due to the perception that numbers represent objectivity, truth, and real evidence (Gillborn, 2010). Consequently, there is a widely held belief that "quantitative methods are antithetical to social justice," which situates the problem with statistical methods rather than the users of the methods (Cokley & Awad, 2013, p. 27).

In this chapter, I share how this history and ongoing tension has shaped my journey as an African American woman and scholar toward critical quantitative inquiry. I begin by sharing two short narratives that were pivotal educational experiences and examples of how the mobilization of bias and shaping of consciousness prevalent in K-12 settings is perpetuated in higher education classrooms. I then share how the dynamics of racism experienced as a student led to my path as a faculty member teaching statistics through a critical lens and conducting critical quantitative inquiry as a researcher. I continue the conversation by discussing what I view as the strengths and challenges to critical quantitative inquiry. I end the chapter with recommendations for those currently engaged in or desire to be engaged in critical quantitative inquiry.

Pivotal Educational Experiences

I know firsthand the magnitude of educational inequities and its consequences. My lived experiences as a student in both a poverty-stricken school that faced state closure and a wealthy, state award-winning school were influential in my research agenda. In my research, I study the ways that systemic racism and other forms of oppression are perpetuated, reproduced, and sustained through policy, politics, and statistical data. I became interested in this work not only because of my lived experiences but also my heightened critical consciousness of the racist narratives and tools used to not only frame the achievement gap but create it (Kendi, 2017). Such deficit narratives and approaches to inquiry are implicit forms of power that breed *epistemic injustice*, the mobilization of bias, and the shaping of consciousness. I share how these forms of power manifested in two pivotal educational experiences that led me to critical quantitative inquiry.

The N-word

The first pivotal experience occurred when I was in elementary school. I was born on the southside of Chicago, in the Englewood neighborhood, and was prepared to attend schools in the Chicago public school system. Understanding the challenges with the Chicago public school system, my parents decided to move to Indiana and enrolled me in the neighborhood elementary school. My parents believed that outside of the city, I would receive a better education, especially since I entered the school one year ahead in math and reading. This meant that I stayed with my age group for all social activities such as lunch and recess, but I joined the grade ahead for math and reading instruction. There is no question that I arrived at the school confident in myself and my academic abilities. Unfortunately, it did not take long before my spirit was broken by the consistent racism even at the elementary level. As the only Black child in the school, I was the victim of racist slurs and bullying almost daily. One day, I got into an argument with a classmate who called me the N-word, and I retaliated verbally. We were both disciplined. However, my classmate received a verbal warning and phone call home to her parents, and I was removed from advanced level math and reading courses. I never shared that incident with my parents until adulthood due to my fear of my part in the altercation and retaliation by the teachers and administrators. As an elementary student, this behavior incident shook my confidence academically. While I still performed well academically, maintaining high honor roll throughout my elementary and secondary experiences, I remember feeling like I had to work really hard in my courses to get back what was stripped from me and to prove that I was good enough.

"Blacks and Latino Students Are Not Good at Math"

Fast forward to one particular graduate school experience as a doctoral student. I remember the excitement and pride I held as a first year PhD student. Like many students, I had no clue what my dissertation would be about, but I knew it would be a study focused on equity for marginalized communities. As my colleagues and I exchanged ideas for topics, I quickly realized a methodological divide by race. Most of my Black and Latinx colleagues had already predetermined that they would use qualitative methods without even knowing their research question, and many, though not all, of my White colleagues were intrigued by quantitative inquiry. Despite this early commitment to methodological approaches by my peers, I remained open and tried to take as many quantitative classes as I could. Aside from introduction to statistics, a required course, I was often the only or one of few students of color in advanced statistical classes. One day, I attended office hours to seek clarification about a lecture in one of my advanced statistical courses. To this day, I am not sure how the conversation shifted and made room for this comment, but it is a comment that I will never forget and the culminating factor that confirmed my pursuit of critical quantitative inquiry. During that office hour appointment, that professor stated,

> I don't see why we are pushing for Black and Latinos in STEM. Black and Latino students are not good at math. They are better at the arts and are good with people...[the professor goes on to say] please don't think I'm racist, that's just what the statistics show.

These external racial microaggressive experiences fueled an imposter syndrome that is not my own psychological tensions but a dominant exercise of power working to shape consciousness and mobilize bias to affect the behavior of another. A poignant illumination of the intent and effects of this implicit form of power is reflected in an excerpt from Lukes ([1974] 2005) which states, "Is not the supreme exercise of power to get another or others to have the desires you want them to have—that is, to secure their compliance by controlling their thoughts and desires?" (as cited in Fowler, 2000, p. 35). The racial and gender segregation in advanced level statistics along with the identities of those who were teaching these courses and how they presented the content definitely displayed this dimension of power. In other words, deficit messages and fallible statistics socialize Black and Latinx students to not perceive themselves as mathematicians or future statisticians.

Occasionally these challenges resurface in my current work. Ford (2015) said it well when she stated, "too often the mind (e.g., intellectual abilities and expertise) of Black female faculty and administrators is minimized, obscured, or ignored, while the body is literally and symbolically exploited to achieve diversity-related institutional objectives"(p. 191). However, I am reminded of what Former First Lady Michelle Obama shared at the Pennsylvania Conference for women. She said, "If you are scared to use your voice, then you've got to get up and give it to someone who isn't afraid to use the spot." It is this charge and conviction that compelled me to move from being a character in someone else's narrative to being an author who changes the narrative through critical quantitative inquiry.

Critical Quantitative Inquiry

Critical quantitative inquiry requires that we, as producers and consumers of research, disrupt and push for the re-imagining of ways to engage in more culturally inclusive approaches to quantitative inquiry that will drive us all to critically interrogate and self-appraise our beliefs, probe our research designs, humanize the data, and approach understanding the story behind the data with curiosity and humility. Distinct from traditional quantitative inquiry, researchers engaged in critical quantitative work are called to

> Use data to represent educational processes and outcomes on a large scale to reveal inequities and to identify social or institutional perpetuation of systemic inequities in such processes and outcomes.....[and to] question the models, measures, and analytic practices of quantitative research in order to offer competing models, measures, and analytic practices that better describe experiences of those who have not been adequately represented. (Stage, 2007, p. 10)

Critical quantitative inquiry is about the "judicious and socially conscious use of quantitative methods in our research" (Cokley & Awad, 2013, p. 37). Researchers engaged in critical quantitative work are concerned about research questions asked and decolonizing research designs and interpretations that reproduce oppression and maintain the status quo (Stage, 2007; Stage & Wells, 2013).

Challenges to Critical Quantitative Inquiry

While there is great opportunity for equity with critical quantitative inquiry, there are also challenges. One challenge is that method courses in educational programs are often the breeding grounds for epistemic injustice. Those underrepresented in the academy, particularly scholars of color, might have experiences similar to my own where the educational process and content objectified me and my cultural community. The narratives shared about my cultural community were often ill-understandings of our marginalized experiences. Worse is the weighted responsibility and urge to correct these narratives only to have these counter-narratives denied as legitimate knowledge sources, while the false interpretations and misleading arguments propagated through statistical research is seen as factual and remain unchecked (Gillborn, 2010). Santoro and Kumar (2014) refer to this as testimonial injustice, where

> prejudice causes the hearer to give a deflated level of credibility to a speaker's word…This is not only a denial of the claim of a resource as a valid knowledge, but it also undermines the community's claim to knowledge. It is an injustice done to an individual by virtue of them being part of that community. This likely leads to a feeling of inferiority in the student, as well as a lack of confidence in one's own ability to learn. (pp. 4–5)

This injustice is perpetuated when diverse experiences, histories, and contexts of diverse groups are not represented in the curricula. Their participation in pedagogical activities are controlled by a hegemonic narrative, and they are denied equal participation in the knowledge process. Another manifestation of this is when methodological instructors serve as epistemic gatekeepers by discouraging or criticizing students from studying certain populations or using methodological approaches in a way that is incongruent with hegemonic ways of knowing and doing (Yee, Carey, & Gamble, 2015). Gillborn (2010) spoke to this when he wrote, "Statistical work will be automatically privileged above qualitative research unless it dares to name racism, in which case it will be subject to the same dismissive attacks as any other anti-racist scholarship" (p. 260). He goes on to argue that anti-racist quantitative research is often criticized and scrutinized unless there is an abundance of control variables to explain inequity in a way that points to the individual and their families instead of racism and systemic inequity.

Another challenge in critical quantitative inquiry is the missing and erased narratives of marginalized groups, such as Indigenous communities, because of small sample sizes. Students may be encouraged to become complacent with this explanation of why the narratives of Indigenous communities are often missing in quantitative analysis. However, this should not be the message communicated in methods classes. We, as researchers, must commit ourselves to findings solutions to challenge the systemic exclusion of Indigenous communities in research instead of being complicit in the erasure of Indigenous groups from the narrative.

We must be committed to making our data and interpretations accessible to broad audiences, especially understanding the prevalence of the shaping of consciousness and mobilization of bias that keeps marginalized communities and other "nonstatisticians intimidated by the numbers. They don't have the confidence or expertise to challenge the conclusions or the methods that generated them" (Gillborn, 2010, p. 267). This means we have to act to ensure our work is inclusive, accessible, and relevant.

Concluding Thoughts

Finally, there is a need for more members of historically underrepresented groups, particularly students of color, to engage in critical quantitative inquiry. Social justice is not only difficult without members of these communities, but it is incomplete without our voice, our perspective, and our work. My advice for members of marginalized communities engaged in this work is to remember that we are not tokens, and our excellence is not aberrant behavior of our cultural groups and lineage. Let your excellence be a form of protest. For those reading this in a methods course and questioning yourself—we are not imposters. I know that being in these spaces is not always easy, but being authentically you is necessary and important in social justice work. We are our ancestors' wildest dreams. We have a duty not only to take the opportunity to sit at the tables where our ancestors were previously denied, but we must do so with the conviction of course correcting the injustices that still remain. It is impossible to break down a structure when you do not understand what gives that structure its fortitude. Quantitative analysis is one of the most powerful engines of the system. Statistics is a powerful tool that can be used to resist oppression through community-driven, justice-oriented work. Pull up a seat. Let's prepare to reverse engineer. We need to have a seat at the table.

Suggested Readings

Bonilla-Silva, E. (2015). More than prejudice: Restatement, reflections, and new directions in critical race theory. *Sociology of Race and Ethnicity, 1*(1), 73–87. https://doi.org/10.1177/2332649214557042.

In this article, Bonilla-Silva critiqued framing racism as a matter of individual private prejudice. He pushed readers to understand that race still matters because racism is systemic, evolving, and firmly rooted in power differentials based on socially constructed categories of race.

Cokley, K., & Awad, G. H. (2013). In defense of quantitative methods: Using the "master's tools" to promote social justice. *Journal for Social Action in Counseling and Psychology, 5*(2), 26–41.

In this article, Cokley and Awad challenged the notion that quantitative methods are antithetical to social justice. They argued that the reproduction of oppression through quantitative analyses should be situated with quantitative users and their misuse rather than the methods themselves.

Fendler, L. (2014). Bell curve. In D. C. Phillips (Ed.), *Encyclopedia of educational theory and philosophy* (Vol. 1, pp. 83–86). New York, NY: SAGE Publications.

In this encyclopedia entry, Fendler discussed the history of the bell curve and its intended use to display binomial probability density in the hard sciences, specifically astronomy. Fendler poignantly illustrated the misinterpretations and the erroneous application of the bell curve since its crossover in the social sciences.

Gillborn, D. (2010). The colour of numbers: Surveys, statistics and deficit-thinking about race and class. *Journal of Education Policy, 25*(2), 253–276. https://doi.org/10.1080.02680930903460740

In this article, Gillborn illustrated through narrative how traditional approaches to quantitative inquiry can obscure the reality of racism, which sustains and reproduces hegemonic assumptions.

Stage, F.K. (2007). Answering critical questions using quantitative data. *New Directions for Institutional Research, 133*, 5–16. https://doi.org/10.1002/ir.200

In this special issue, Stage described the evolution of critical quantitative inquiry, addresses early critics, and discusses the need for more quantitative criticalists.

Stage, F. K., & Wells, R. S. (2013). Critical quantitative inquiry in context. *New Directions for Institutional Research, 158*, 1–7. https://doi.org/10.1002/ir.20041

In this special issue, Stage and Wells provided an overview of the development and evolution of critical quantitative inquiry, with an introduction to researchers currently engaged in this work.

Zuberi, T. (2001). *Thicker than blood: How racial statistics lie.* Minneapolis, MN: University of Minnesota Press.

In this book, Zuberi discussed how statistics has been used to promote racists narratives and ideologies. This dangerous use of racial statistics must be understood and challenged to ensure social and racial justice for all.

Zuberi, T., & Bonilla-Silva, E. (Eds.). (2008). *White logic, white methods: Racism and methodology.* New York, NY: Rowman & Littlefield Publishers.

In this edited book, Zuberi and Bonilla-Silva challenge the perceived objectivity, color-blindness, and infallibility of statistics. They further argue that the color-blind treatment and understanding of race as static and a social constant rather than a social construct that sustains power differentials in statistics is undergirded by logic and methods grounded in white supremacy used to justify racial stratification, which further perpetuates racism.

References

Cokley, K., & Awad, G. H. (2013). In defense of quantitative methods: Using the "master's tools" to promote social justice. *Journal for Social Action in Counseling and Psychology, 5*(2), 26–41.

Ford, K. A. (2015). Exploiting the body and denouncing the mind: Navigating a Black female professional identity within the academy. In K. J. Fasching-Warner, K. A. Albert, R. W. Mitchell, & C. M. Allen (Eds.), *Racial battle fatigue in higher education: Exposing the myth of post-racial America* (pp. 189–196). Lanham, MD: Rowman & Littlefield.

Fowler, F. C. (2000). *Policy studies for educational leaders: An introduction.* Upper Saddle River, NJ: Merrill.

Gillborn, D. (2010). The colour of numbers: Surveys, statistics and deficit-thinking about race and class. *Journal of Education Policy, 25*(2), 253–276. https://doi.org/10.1080/02680930903460740

Kendi, I. X. (2017, January 21). Racial progress is real. But so is racist progress. *The New York Times.* Retrieved from https://nyti.ms/2jKFsNC

Leong, N. (2013). Racial capitalism. *Harvard Law Review, 126*(8), 2151–2479. https://doi.org/132.174.254.116

Lukes, S. ([1974] 2005). *Power: A radical view* (Vol. 1). London: Macmillan.

Santoro, D., & Kumar, M. (2014). Being bound to fail. How epistemic injustice fails educational opportunities. Retrieved from https://imera.univ-amu.fr/sites/imera.univ-amu.fr/files/being_bound_to_fail.how_epistemic_injustice_fails_educational_opportunities_draft_0.pdf

Stage, F. K. (2007). Answering critical questions using quantitative data. *New Directions for Institutional Research, 133*, 5–16. https://doi.org/10.1002/ir.200

Stage, F. K., & Wells, R. S. (2013). Critical quantitative inquiry in context. *New Directions for Institutional Research, 158*, 1–7. https://doi.org/10.1002/ir.20041

Yee, L. S., Carey, R. L., & Gamble, W. S. (2015). Navigating the academy, creating counterspaces: Critically examining the experiences of three PhD students of color. In K. J. Fasching-Warner, K. A. Albert, R. W. Mitchell, & C. M. Allen (Eds.), *Racial battle fatigue in higher education: Exposing the myth of post-racial America* (pp. 7–16). Lanham, MD: Rowman & Littlefield.

Chapter 24
Working with Intention and in Tension: Evolving as a Scholar-Activist

Kristen A. Renn

Abstract In this chapter, I recount the pathways I followed in developing a line of LGBTQ research and my identity as a queer researcher. I study higher education, specifically college students, and do so in ways that connect to my professional background as a university administrator. Here I trace the parallel pathways of becoming an LGBTQ activist and focusing my research on LGBTQ topics, in the process coming to terms with the ways that I was socialized to follow rules, not draw attention to myself, and not cause trouble. I describe how I came to understand myself as a scholar who works intentionally to create a more socially just version of higher education while also being in tension with the idea that higher education is itself inherently unjust.

I work in a fairly small field within education research: I study higher education, and in particular I study college student learning, development, and success, broadly defined. My research centers on students who are minoritized by their social identities, with a long-standing commitment to conducting studies of LGBTQ student experiences and identities. My commitment to this topic arises from my own experience as a White, lesbian, cisgender woman and my belief that colleges and universities can be places of transformation for students. After my own transformative experience as an undergraduate at a women's liberal arts college, I knew that I wanted to work in higher education and started down a path into student affairs administration. While pursuing a PhD in higher education, with the goal of becoming a vice president of student affairs, my head was turned in the direction of research on higher education and the possibility of a faculty career as an education researcher.

K. A. Renn (✉)
Michigan State University, East Lansing, MI, USA
e-mail: renn@msu.edu

© The Author(s) 2019
K. K. Strunk, L. A. Locke (eds.), *Research Methods for Social Justice and Equity in Education*, https://doi.org/10.1007/978-3-030-05900-2_24

My career in the academy has existed in the tension that forms where my urge to conform meets my urge to refute, resist, and reject injustice. This professional space is a continuation of the same tensions I experienced as a young person trying to work out how to be a respectable Connecticut girl while enacting a youthful feminist agenda. From kindergarten onward, I never cared to fit gender norms very well, and with my sporty demeanor I took charge of the classroom and playground, always with an eye to step in and speak out when someone—first me, then increasingly I saw others—was being treated differently, unfairly, unjustly. Yet, I still wanted to conform to social norms of the well-behaved suburban girlhood that dictated one should not draw attention to oneself or make trouble for others. I carried these dispositions forward into my work as a student affairs professional, my doctoral program, and now into my scholarship, teaching, and mentoring as a faculty member. I live within the tension or misalignment of enacting a social justice agenda from within an unjust system of higher education that is not equally accessible to all and that perpetuates racism and social stratification, even as it serves as engine of social mobility for some. I wonder and worry about how my scholarship and subject positions as a White, lesbian, cisgender woman who is a tenured professor at a public research university act to reinforce the inequities and injustices I seek to illuminate and eliminate. Can I simultaneously be a participant in and critic of the neoliberal academy? Is my scholarship *enough*?

I conduct a lot of research in the areas of queer theory and the experiences of LGBTQ people in higher education. In these projects, I am an insider and bear negative and positive consequences of insider positionality, such as familiarity with cultural norms (positive) and risk of taking for granted what I know about the topic (negative; see Chavez, 2008). I am keenly aware of how my ability to be an out-lesbian academic and conduct queer research was enabled by a generation of scholars before me (e.g., Bill Tierney, Toni McNaron, Tony D'Augelli) and is now elaborated, challenged, and supported by scholars of my generation and those after us (e.g., Cris Mayo, Juan Battle, Catherine Lugg, Dafina-Lazarus Stewart, s. j. Miller, Erich Pitcher, Ed Brockenbrough, Carrie Kortegast, and too many more to name).

Because LGBTQ people remain the object of substantially inequitable treatment, discrimination, and violence, my scholarship itself reinforces my desire to resist norms and work for justice. Early in my professional career as a student affairs professional at Brown University (from 1989 to 1999, critical years in queer civil rights and AIDS activism, as well as campus climate improvements), in graduate school (Boston College [BC], 1994–1998), and even early in my faculty career (beginning in 1999), queer research and work in what was at the time called "gay and lesbian issues" pushed boundaries. It entailed professional and personal risks and interacted in uncomfortable ways with my enculturated disposition to work within the system, my inclination to seek a seat at the table as a well-behaved White cis lesbian who was sure she would "lift as she climbed" and make space for other (well-behaved) queer folks. Yet daring as it seemed, it was still well within the boundaries of acceptability, as demonstrated by those institutions' willingness to co-opt the work as evidence of *their* progressive commitments.

Because I was working half-time (at Brown) while going to my doctoral program (at BC), I had the opportunity to explore when and where in academe I might behave differently as a scholar-activist. Brown students were far more adventuresome in their activism than I was as an undergraduate. My Brown job, which was in the administration and therefore not protected by tenure, entailed inaugurating what is now a full-fledged LGBT campus resource center, and so I often found myself well on the "well-behaved" side, negotiating between activist students and an administration that was fairly liberal but wary of rapid change. At the same time, as a student at BC—a university that featured paradoxically liberal Jesuit values and conservative Catholic administrative viewpoints—I embraced whatever degree of academic freedom graduate students enjoy to push the university to be more inclusive of LGBTQ students. The unusual opportunity to contrast these two academic personae, often on the same day, opened up space for thinking about how I could perhaps take more risks in my research with LGBTQ topics and queer theory.

I also hit a turning point when being well behaved seemed to have hit a limit. After an article appeared in the Providence newspaper about my LGBTQ work at Brown, resulting in my being let go from a summer job at a Girl Scout camp, I testified four years in a row at the Rhode Island legislature to help convince them to pass non-discrimination bills. This experience was enough to get me over the misconception that being well behaved was going to be a satisfying way to have a career. Whether in the hearing room or rallying in the capitol rotunda with hundreds of queers and queer supporters, I was disrupting the status quo—perhaps not in the same way as street activists in the AIDS Coalition to Unleash Power (ACT UP)— but the shiny suburban gloss of respectability politics was wearing off. I faced a decision point, whether to continue my career in university administration—fulfilling work in which one can make a real difference in policy and programs that benefit LGBTQ students, but which does require a lot of "good behavior"—or turn to a faculty career. The decision to take up the latter was based in part on the opportunity to focus less on being a well-behaved bureaucrat and more on undertaking scholarship that could also make a real difference in supporting policy, programs, and curriculum to benefit LGBTQ students. That I could be considered at least somewhat edgy among education scholars in my choice of topic was an added appeal for a reforming follower of convention.

Twenty years later, LGBTQ research in higher education has reached a point at which it is no longer edgy or particularly risky to undertake, at least for someone like me who is a tenured professor in a good-sized and generally good-natured department. Out-lesbians and gay men—though not necessarily scholars of other minoritized sexual orientations and certainly not transgender scholars—are fairly commonplace in my field (higher education), and each generation brings forward more talented queer scholars. Observing their scholarship, it seems to me that the edginess, the riskiness, has shifted from simply conducting research on LGBTQ topics to pushing epistemological and methodological frames through more explicit use of queer theory and by posing challenges to established, "acceptable" LGBTQ research. When Darris Means (2017) "quares" his analysis of spirituality among Black gay and bisexual college students he not only risks seeming like a less-than-well-behaved Black man, but he also risks being seen as an early career scholar who takes on established queer scholarship, holding it to account for its epistemological racism. Z Nicolazzo (2017) pushes back on the cisnormativity and cisheterosexism of social science research—even ostensibly queer scholarship—by arguing for a trans* epistemological stance in higher education research. And while they are unlikely to lose their jobs for doing queer research, it is indeed a risky decision to point out epistemological shortcomings of (or, depending on one's perspective, simply differences with) the very scholars who are likely to have opportunities to promote (or derail) one's career.

So if I have contributed in any way to the possibilities for these newer scholars to challenge and re-shape the field, where is the tension I feel now? It lies at the point where I have become if not well-behaved at least "established" as a scholar and in ways that make me wonder if I have perhaps fallen behind in my duty to use the privileges granted institutionally through tenure and systematically by my race, social class, ability, cisgender identity, and nationality. I feel the tension when I design my own studies and consider where to publish the results and think, "Is *that* journal a little…too…'out there'?" and "What will establishment scholars—even those on the ideological left—think of my work if I do it in an unproven way?" These questions, of course, really mean, "What will they think of me? Am I too 'out there'?" My press to do cutting-edge work that matters in improving the lives and life chances of LGBTQ people runs up against the press to stay in the lines, or mostly so.

Where those lines are depends a lot on one's field and method, and I am not alone in trying to understand what it means to cross them. Jay Garvey (see Garvey et al., 2017; Garvey, Mobley, Summerville, & Moore, 2018), for example, is mapping the terrain of queer-inclusive critical quantitative research in higher education. In this vein, I am co-leader of the National Study of LGBTQ Student Success, a mixed-methods study that includes critical quantitative methods (see Nguyen, Brazelton, Renn, & Woodford, 2018; Nicolazzo, Pitcher, Renn, & Woodford, 2017; Pitcher, Camacho, Renn, & Woodford, 2018; Woodford, Chonody, Kulick, Brennan, & Renn, 2015).

This project has also become a place in which I can deal with and work out the tension between being a "well-behaved" researcher (Look at those *p* values! Check out our qualitative trustworthiness!) and challenging neoliberal academic norms that are now as much an object of my resistance as homo-, bi-, and transphobia have been. For example, adopting the example of National Study co-lead investigator Michael Woodford, we developed an open stance to participation in the research team (e.g., to design protocols and collect data) and use of data by colleagues and students across a number of US states, Canadian provinces, academic programs, and institutional types. By queering the traditional practice of holding data close in a competitive market for publishing, we serve LGBTQ students better by letting more people use the data and press back against norms that would pit us all in competition. It is a way to use the privileges of my position (which comes with resources to conduct large-scale LGBTQ research) to benefit others. I am aware that this method of creating seats for others at the academic table is just that—creating seats, not changing out for something other than a table—but it feels at least somewhat better than throwing elbows to keep others from coming to the table at all. Getting them to the table while we and others continue to chip away at the table itself is something, though not enough.

I end where I began: in the tension of trying to work for justice from within a fundamentally unjust structure. I was socialized to be comfortable working within the system, and, to a great extent, my academic career reflects this approach. I was also socialized to see injustice and to try to act upon and against it, and my ongoing research projects—both the topics and the ways that I undertake them—reflect to an increasing degree my will to do so. If an end goal of the field of education research is to create better lives and life chances, then I think it is best served by a steady supply of "well-behaved" scholars, scholar-activists, activist educators, students, and communities who demand more and better knowledge, and by people like me who walk in and across those lines.

Suggested Readings

Ladson-Billings, G., & Donnor, J. (2005). The moral activist role of critical race theory scholarship. In N. K. Denzin & Y. S. Lincoln (Eds.), *The Sage handbook of qualitative research* (3rd ed., pp. 279–301). Thousand Oaks, CA: Sage.

This chapter provides several examples of moral and ethical dilemmas imposed on minoritized scholars and calls the reader to re-consider the role of the academic and intellectual. The authors argue that a critical race theory perspective requires engagement in activist scholarship and offer a view of a "reconstructed university" (p. 295) that would reflect this approach.

Quaye, S. J., Shaw, M. D., & Hill, D. C. (2017). Blending scholar and activist identities: Establishing the need for scholar activism. *Journal of Diversity in Higher Education, 10*(4), 381. https://doi.org/10.1037/dhe0000060

In this article the authors provide and analyze an example of scholar activism, specifically the case of Black faculty taking up a call to address racism and injustice on their campus and beyond. The authors participated in an activist group on their campus and offer insight into the challenges and rewards scholar-activist work entails.

Rasmussen, M. L., Gowlett, C., & Connell, R. (2014). Interview with Raewyn Connell: The cultural politics of queer theory in education research. *Discourse: Studies in the Cultural Politics of Education, 35*(3), 335–346. https://doi.org/10.1080/01596306.2014.888839

In this article, a dialogic interview of Connell by Rasmussen and Gowlett, Australian sociologist Connell traces how she has theorized gender from the 1970s women's movement through present conceptions of queer theory. The interview provides an historical overview of the emergence of queer theory and demonstrates the complexity of defining it as a static term.

References

Chavez, C. (2008). Conceptualizing from the inside: Advantages, complications, and demands on insider positionality. *The Qualitative Report, 13*(3), 474–494.

Garvey, J. C., Hart, J., Hoffman, G. D., Iverson, S. V., Metcalfe, A. S., Mitchell, T. D., et al. (2017). Performing critical work: The challenges of emancipatory scholarship in the academic marketplace. *Critical Questions in Education, 8*(2), 138–162.

Garvey, J. C., Mobley Jr., S. D., Summerville, K. S., & Moore, G. T. (2018). Queer and trans* students of color: Navigating identity disclosure and college contexts. *The Journal of Higher Education*. Advance online publication. https://doi.org/10.1080/00221546.2018.1449081

Means, D. R. (2017). "Quaring" spirituality: The spiritual counterstories and spaces of Black gay and bisexual male college students. *Journal of College Student Development, 58*(2), 229–246. https://doi.org/10.1353/csd.2017.0017

Nguyen, D. J., Brazelton, G. B., Renn, K. A., & Woodford, M. R. (2018). Exploring the availability and influence of LGBTQ+ student services resources on student success at community colleges: A mixed methods analysis. *Community College Journal of Research and Practice, 42*(11), 783–796. https://doi.org/10.1080/10668926.2018.1444522

Nicolazzo, Z. (2017). Imagining a trans* epistemology: What liberation thinks like in postsecondary education. *Urban Education*. Advance online publication. https://doi.org/0042085917697203

Nicolazzo, Z., Pitcher, E. N., Renn, K. A., & Woodford, M. (2017). An exploration of trans* kinship as a strategy for student success. *International Journal of Qualitative Studies in Education, 30*(3), 305–319. https://doi.org/10.1080/09518398.2016.1254300

Pitcher, E. N., Camacho, T. P., Renn, K. A., & Woodford, M. R. (2018). Affirming policies, programs, and supportive services: Using an organizational perspective to understand LGBTQ+ college student success. *Journal of Diversity in Higher Education, 11*(2), 117–132. https://doi.org/10.1037/dhe0000048

Woodford, M. R., Chonody, J. M., Kulick, A., Brennan, D. J., & Renn, K. (2015). The LGBQ microaggressions on campus scale: A scale development and validation study. *Journal of Homosexuality, 62*(12), 1660–1687. https://doi.org/10.1080/00918369.2015.1078205

Chapter 25
Collaboration, Community, and Collectives: Research for and by the People

Erica R. Dávila

Abstract This chapter is a reflective piece on my research trajectory rooted in collaboration, community, and collectives. I provide a discussion of my development as a scholar-activist and my work with justice-centered research projects. This chapter aims to: (1) highlight work with and for our people; (2) highlight lived experiences grounded in struggle and hope; and (3) complicate the power that schools/universities have to liberate and oppress. I have consistently worked on these three goals, and yet they continue to guide my work and I understand there is no finish line; this work is not static, it is the work of humanity that is always evolving.

My path in educational research began at a very young age, probably around the fourth grade, when I started noticing that school policies and practices were simply unfair and discriminatory, albeit without a conscious or deliberate awareness of the reasons why. Some of the injustices I recall include my (and my peers) transition to a monolithic English curriculum, unjust disciple policies for very young children, and teachers and principals that devalued my home culture. Collection of data for my dissertation brought me back to my public high school to recruit potential interviewees and conduct some formal observations. This was not only a physical return but also an emotional and cognitive one. As I walked the hallways, I began some much-needed *introspection*. Recalling the days, I navigated my neighborhood high school with all the beauty and pain that came with those few but vital years in my life. For my dissertation studies (Dávila, 2005), I conducted a qualitative research study that provided an in-depth analysis of the experiences of Puerto Rican students in the Chicago Public Schools (CPS), and the narratives of my participants have shaped most of my research agenda for the past three years. Some of my findings included the priority of a Eurocentric curriculum resulting in the erasure of Puerto Rican history at best and demonization of those racialized or othered bodies at worst

E. R. Dávila (✉)
Lewis University, Romeoville, IL, USA

© The Author(s) 2019
K. K. Strunk, L. A. Locke (eds.), *Research Methods for Social Justice and Equity in Education*, https://doi.org/10.1007/978-3-030-05900-2_25

(Spring, 2016), and the desire for more teachers and counselors who understood their lived realities and valued their cultural capital. Another key finding uncovered the value one's Puerto Rican home identity provided as they navigated their schooling experiences as youth of color and for many, learners of the English language. Hearing these stories and reflecting on my experiences with schooling, my role as a scholar become clear—I was to investigate the curricular issues, inclusive of the nuances that come with these realities, while highlighting and learning from the stories of resistance, hope, and love. From this early research through today, my positions as researcher and scholar-activist have become critical to my work in three specific ways: (1) working with and for *our* people; (2) highlighting lived experiences grounded in struggle and hope; and (3) complicating the power that schools/ universities have to liberate and/or oppress.

First, I want to define what I mean by "working with and for *our* people," the *our* is contextual and varies depending on my role in various educational environments. For example, my first cousin (Ann M. Aviles, PhD) and I have worked together to lift the experiences of our own *familia* and as an extension we have worked to expose the inequities embedded in our hometown of Chicago and even more specifically investigated the CPS where we both matriculated from K-12. One piece that has been significant in our scholarly trajectory is an article titled, "Examining Education for Latinas/os in Chicago: A CRT/LatCrit Approach" (Dávila & Aviles, 2010). In this article, we explore the sociopolitical context of education policy, particularly as it relates to Latinx education, highlighting the status of Latinx students and teachers within CPS using a Latina/o critical race theory framework. This publication is part of a larger project that began in the early 2000s, where, as graduate students, we worked with community leaders and educators across Chicago to assemble two reports (Aviles, Capeheart, Davila, & Miller, 2006) on the status of Latinos in the CPS; this was my entry into the world of research. I was intentional in working with this group of researchers because I experienced the problematic ways research is conceptualized and disseminated in academia. This research experience was empowering, as I was able to see firsthand how research can impact policies and practices, it restored my hope in research and led to my grounding as a scholar-activist. In this work, I had the honor of being mentored by an amazing scholar-activist who has passed on by the name of Angela Perez Miller, her ancestral wisdom from countless years in CPS as a parent, teacher, and principal was invaluable then and now; her presence in the landscape of Latinx educational research is far and wide, and we miss her every day. In addition to Perez Miller's mentorship, this committee also worked with other elders in the community who had been fighting for equity in CPS for decades prior to this project.

Some of the specific practices of this collective that I have carried in my work include translating the reports in Spanish, collective reading and writing, and grass-roots dissemination. Currently, I ask every publisher I work with if we can provide a Spanish version (for scholarship specifically about Latinx people); although these publishers do not often or always take on this charge, simply making this request creates awareness, and it is my intention that it leads to a change in broadening readership that is more inclusive. In community spaces, when creating flyers, reports, and conference programs, the idea to translate is not only welcome. I have seen some researchers who themselves pursue this translation, taking their own time; most recently, I witnessed Ramona Meza, a Latina doctoral candidate at the University of Illinois Chicago also studying CPS take on an arduous translation task for the good of our people. Although the collective has changed over the last 13 years, what I have witnessed is the power of *our* people fighting for CPS, who are alums, parents, teachers, and counselors, on the ground. More recently, we have assembled a larger collective of Latinx academics who have lived experiences in Chicago and who have built their scholarship in an effort to challenge inequities and lift the beauty of resistance in our city. Together we assembled an edited volume titled, *Latinx education in Chicago: Historical trajectories, contemporary realities and transformative possibilities*, which is in submission with University of Illinois Press, and three fierce Latina scholars who are editing this volume are leading this collective. I have made it a point to lift other women of color in the academy because we are underrepresented and undervalued (Gutiérrez, 2012).

This lived reality has pushed my "prima scholar" and me to move our work into the sphere of investigating our firsthand experiences as Puerto Rican women in academia; we are undergoing a critical autoethnography. In a recent publication, we reflect on our identity and positionalities in higher education as Puerto Rican women. We have generated two scholarly publications as part of this intellectual journey. In the summer of 2018, a book chapter entitled "Afro-Puerto Rican Primas: Identity, Pedagogy, and Solidarity," where we weave together our personal and professional narratives to highlight the struggle of our work as academics as well as the hope and love embedded in our work, was released. The second piece that has come out of this project is an article submission scheduled to be published in spring of 2019 for *Taboo* titled "Un réquiem para la lucha Afro-Boricua: Honoring moments of decolonization and resistance to white supremacy in academia," which has a similar framing, but we focus more on our lived experiences in higher education; we close this article stating:

> Continuing to build upon the mentorship and work we have been inducted into, we seek to continue to create opportunities that build solidarity amongst Black and Brown faculty as an act of resistance and self-determination within institutions of higher education. Often these collaborations lead to networks and professional organizations that provide literal and figurative space(s) to collaborate and grow through shared community. Other times these networks provide support when we are resisting the oppressive symptoms of white supremacy and its subsequent microaggressions. One of those instances occurred several years ago as one of the authors struggled to keep teaching courses that unpacked concepts of institutional racism and white privilege primarily to middle-class suburban students at a PWI.

One practice that Aviles and I undertake is being strategic about our order of authorship. Since we think and write together, we struggle with the traditional notion in higher education of ranking the weight of our work, in other words the common practice is that the person with a better rank and power takes the top spot in order of authorship, or in more equitable circumstances, the person who does more work and provides guidance for co-authors may be appointed as first author. However, we challenge these norms because we recognize the way academia values the order of authorship, which demonstrates a practice that pits scholars against one another, which we resist. As we state:

> As an act of solidarity, resistance and healing/love to the mistreatment of women of color in the academy, we discuss and consider each other's positionality when making decisions regarding authorship order. Our approach to shared authorship is grounded in a pedagogy of collectivity and familial relationships. We do not view the project as something to be "completed"; instead we view it as an opportunity to learn, grow, and nurture each other's scholarship and humanity. We consider factors such as: where is our co-author(s) in their tenure process?: what is their teaching/workload?, etc. Further, as part of the writing process, we consciously and deliberately take time to check in with one another about personal situations (partnerships/marriage, divorce, children, familial responsibilities, etc.), centering and honoring our humanity—people over product; process over outcome. What we do in community with colleagues informs the ways in which we understand and interact with our larger social world, including personal relationships and struggles. While these actions may appear minor, it is these "small," but important acts of humanity that help us to nurture and heal. Our discourse guides our actions, and we are continually working to implement restorative and healing practices in spaces that too often dehumanize and objectify us and our work. (Aviles & Davila, 2018)

In the fall of 2016, I received an invitation to co-write a chapter for a book titled *The Long Term* which was published in the summer of 2018. This invitation came to a collective of activists in Chicago known as People's Education Movement, a chapter of a larger national collective. This work is mostly connected to my recent work investigating the school-to-prison pipeline because it connects to my own research interests, but also in my experience, working with doctoral candidates who are professionals in the police force, we aim to bridge the conversation with school officials and the Department of Corrections. This chapter, which was crafted in partnership with Free Write Arts & Literacy (www.freewritechicago.org), is titled "Redefining the Long Term: Schooling and the Prison Industrial Complex." And in this chapter, we state:

> We listen to the youth writers who are affiliated with *Free Write Arts and Literacy*, a project based in Chicago that engages incarcerated and court-involved youth in the performing, visual and literary arts. By designing creative space for their students, *Free Write* incarcerated and court-involved youth to "become the narrators of their own stories and the authors of their futures" and in turn, supports young people in "developing educational and career opportunities that reduce recidivism. (Davila et al., 2018)"

Writing this chapter was an empowering experience as I was able to work closely with activists from all across the Chicago area. In this chapter we complicate power dynamics, collectively trying to understand and analyze the school-to-prison pipeline and the positionality of researchers/community folks working together to resist hierarchies of power embedded within institutions of higher education and other institutions such as prisons. Especially exciting was being able to publish with one of my mentors, David O. Stovall, PhD, Professor at the University of Illinois Chicago, who served on my dissertation committee 13 years ago, and while we have worked together on multiple projects, this is the first publication in which I was able to work with him at this level. This project was a collaborative research study where seven of us ranging from professors to youth writers, to community workers worked together to highlight the experiences of youth who are resisting the oppressive nature of the prison system through writing and the creative arts.

Another research project that I am currently working on aims to bridge our scholar-activist work in academia to our predecessors conducting activist work in Chicago, specifically connected to the Communiversity and the Chicago Young Lords. This partnership came after what Aviles and I wrote about in the forthcoming *Taboo* issue (discussed above) that mentions our familial connection to the Chicago Young Lords, and Richard D. Benson, II, PhD, an educational historian, invited us to collaborate with him on this project. Our first publication from this work was an invited chapter that is currently in press with Lexington Books titled ""Our political line was to *serve the people*": Community education and the transformational praxis of the Chicago Young Lords Organization." This archival research project has been in the works for years as the three of us have participated in writing retreats where we have supported one another as we navigate academia. Our identities are grounded in our lived experiences as kids of color growing up in Chicago during the 1980s and 1990s; not only is this an opportunity to understand the work of our people in Chicago communities better, but it also serves to inform our collective aim to make our city better for the kids of color who are navigating/negotiating many of the same issues such as police brutality, Eurocentric curriculum, disinvestment, gentrification, and racial/ethnic and gender discrimination.

Overall, reflecting on my development as a scholar-activist, I am both humbled by the powerful humans I have been able to work with and eager to keep pushing my justice-centered research projects. As highlighted at the onset of this chapter, my work aims to: (1) work with and for *our* people; (2) highlight lived experiences grounded in struggle and hope; and (3) complicate the power that schools/universities have to liberate and/or oppress. Finally, as expressed in this chapter, I have consistently worked on these three goals, and yet they continue to guide my work. I understand there is no finish line; this work is not static, it is the work of humanity that is always evolving.

References

Aviles, A., Capeheart, L., Davila, E., & Miller, A. P. (2006). *Dando Un Paso ¿Pa' Lante o PaTras?: Latinos in the Chicago Public Schools* (2nd ed.). Chicago: Second Legislative District's Education Committee. Retrieved from https://www.chicagoreporter.com/wpcontent/uploads/2017/06/Dando-un-Paso-2006.pdf

Aviles, A. & Davila, E. (in press). Un réquiem para la lucha Afro-Boricua: Honoring moments of decolonization and resistance to white supremacy in academia. *Taboo*

Davila, E. R. (2005). *Educational policies and practices in lived context: Puerto Ricans schooled in Chicago*. PhD thesis, University of Illinois at Urbana-Champaign.

Davila, E. R., & Aviles, A. M. (2018). Afro-Puerto Rican primas: Identity, pedagogy and solidarity. In J. Ewing Flynn, S. Shelton, & T. Grassland (Eds.), *Feminism and intersectionality in academia: Women's narratives and experiences in higher education* (pp. 117–130). New York, NY: Palgrave Macmillan.

Davila, E. R., & Aviles, A. M. (in press). Brown spaces: Latinx education in Chicago. In I. Pulido, A. Rivera, & A. M. Aviles (Eds.), *Latinx education in Chicago: Historical trajectories, contemporary realities and transformative possibilities*. Urbana, IL: University of Illinois Press.

Davila, E. R., Aviles, A. M., & Benson, R. (in press). "Our political line was to *serve the people*": Community education and the transformational praxis of the Chicago Young Lords Organization. In T. R. Berry, C. A. Kalinec-Craig, & M. A. Rodriguez (Eds.), *Latinx curriculum theorizing*. Race & Ed. Series. Lanham, MD: Lexington Books.

Davila, E. R., & Aviles de Bradley, A. (2010). Examining education for Latinas/os in Chicago: A CRT/LatCrit approach. *Journal of Educational Foundations, 24*(1–2), 39–58.

Davila, E. R., De Dios, M., Gamboa-Turner, V., Pantoja, A., Pulido, I., Shony, A., et al. (2018). Redefining the long term: Schooling and the prison industrial complex. In A. Kim, E. Meiners, J. Petty, A. Petty, B. Richie, & S. Ross (Eds.), *The long term* (pp. 228–237). Chicago, IL: Haymarket Books.

Gutiérrez, M. G. (2012). *Presumed incompetent: The intersections of race and class for women in academia*. Boulder, CO: University Press of Colorado.

Spring, J. (2016). *Deculturalization and the struggle for equality* (8th ed.). New York, NY: Taylor and Francis.

Terminology[1,2]

Acceptance Goes beyond "tolerance" by suggesting that, in addition to tolerating those different from oneself, one would accept those different from oneself as completely valid and worthy.

Agender An individual who does not identify with any gender identity category.

Antiessentialism Refers to the rejection of essentialized social identities, recognizing the unique experiences and diversity across communities carrying the same identities.

Asexual An individual who does not experience sexual attraction to any gender. May or may not experience romantic attraction.

Banking concept of education Stemming from the work of Paulo Freire, is a way of describing and implicitly critiquing traditional education. In the banking concept of education, an expert teacher "deposits" knowledge via lectures, readings, and other means into passive learners. In this concept of education, the learner is a passive recipient of knowledge, much as a bank is a passive recipient of money.

Bias The cognitive or emotional state of preferring certain identities, or of avoiding and/or denigrating other identities. This is an internal state of preference, judgment, emotional reaction, or biased beliefs about certain identities. For example, bias in hiring might involve feeling uneasy about a Black candidate, or assuming a White candidate will be more intelligent. Bias can lead to discrimination. However, bias is the cognitive or emotional state, while discrimination is behavior.

Binaries The conceptualization of categories as dichotomous rather than fluid or multifaceted. For example, binary conceptions of gender dichotomize human gender into man/woman or male/female.

Bisexual In the narrowest sense, an individual who is sexually and/or romantically attracted to both men and women. However, in practice, is often used interchangeably with pansexual.

Census A collection of data where the sample includes the entire population.

© The Author(s) 2019
K. K. Strunk, L. A. Locke (eds.), *Research Methods for Social Justice and Equity in Education*, https://doi.org/10.1007/978-3-030-05900-2

Cisgender A person whose sex as assigned at birth is congruent with their gender identity.

Civic engagement Participating in a society as an active member working to improve the quality of life in a community, and developing the necessary skills and knowledges to do so.

Civil Rights Movement The movement occurring primarily in the 1950s and 1960s in the US in which Black citizens, as well as citizens from other marginalized groups and non-marginalized groups, worked together for legal protections, voting rights, nondiscrimination laws, and to end Jim Crow laws and de jure segregation.

Civil rights Typically refers to basic legal rights, such as voting rights, public accommodations, housing, and employment. For example, civil rights laws are intended to protect marginalized groups from discrimination in these categories.

Colonialism The practice or philosophy of domination or subjugation of one group of people by another. Perhaps most visible in the subjugation of non-European and non-Western peoples and ideas to European and Western (and therefore, White) peoples and ideas. Involves the false assumption that non-European, non-Western, and/or non-White peoples and ideas are somehow less civilized, casting domination and erasure of those peoples and ideas as legitimate aims. This dynamic is linked to expansion of European control and its various entanglements (death, violence, and displacement) that unfolded as a result of colonization. In a research setting, these same colonizing assumptions can come to frame research questions and data analysis, furthering the erasure of marginalized communities and knowledges.

Complementarity As applied to mixed methods research, refers to the idea that the different paradigms and philosophical commitments of qualitative and quantitative inquiry complement one another. This is in contrast to the view (as articulated in the paradigm wars) that qualitative and quantitative approaches are inherently contradictory.

Conscientization The process whereby individuals develop a critical consciousness, wherein they become aware of social realities around power dynamics. Involves reflection on the ways in which social knowledge is driven by power and oppression, and action toward liberation.

Counterculture A way of being in a society that is opposed to or different from the dominant social norms. In research, this might involve diverging from traditional methods, strategies, paradigms, research models, grammars, and theories in educational research.

Counternarrative Broadly speaking, a narrative that counters another. In this text, narratives which counter the dominant and oppressive cultural narrative.

Critical pedagogy An educational paradigm and educational philosophy in which education is conceived as a place for critical examinations of power and oppression, and the goal of which is conscientization.

Critical race theory A theoretical framework that critically analyzes the effects of race and racism in modern society. Originating in legal studies and drawing from critical theory, Critical Race Theory scholarship is characterized by empha-

sis on several central tenets that fundamentally critique liberal meritocratic ideologies regarding race, and highlight the pervasive embedded nature of racism.
In addition, Critical Race Theory is a praxis-based framework that focuses on
both studying and challenging white supremacy and its intersected systems of
oppression.

Cultural capital Assets other than financial assets that can be mobilized for liberation and social change. May include cultural features such as resiliency, education, appearance, and other non-financial assets.

Culturally relevant education Approaches to pedagogy, curricula, and research
that center the experiences, histories, and knowledges of traditionally marginalized students and communities. The aim is to identify and cultivate individuals'
unique cultural strengths within educational practices.

De facto segregation Segregation by race that, although not enforced by laws,
exists in fact due to economic, cultural, and social conditions. For example, due
to issues such as income inequality and White flight, large portions of the US,
though not legally enforced, remain deeply segregated.

De jure segregation Segregation by race as enforced by the laws of a municipality,
state, or nation. See also Jim Crow laws.

Decolonizing methodologies Research methods that challenge dominant, traditional research paradigms by privileging participant voices, co-constructing
with participants, and emphasizing an emancipatory lens. Includes an intentional
attempt to both make transparent and resist colonially situated perceptions of
value and worth.

Deficit approach Sometimes referred to as deficit thinking or deficit mind-set, this
approach to understanding difference assumes differences from the dominant
cultural norms, practices, and values are the result of deficiencies in the individual and/or cultural group.

Desegregation A process in which schools, which had been previously segregated by student race, are no longer legally designated as single-race facilities.
Desegregated schools are not necessarily integrated, however, as desegregation
is only a change in the legal status of a school.

Discrimination The act of providing additional rights or privileges or denying certain rights or privileges based on identity. For example, discrimination in hiring
might involve choosing to hire a White person over a person of Color on the
basis of race. This goes beyond bias, which is a cognitive or emotional state.
Discrimination involves behavior (or lack thereof).

Disparity Differences in outcomes, like health, educational, financial, or employment outcomes, that are driven by systemic oppression. Disparities involve both
the element of differential outcomes and the connection to systems of power and
domination.

Economic capital Financial assets, such as money, property, and credit, which can
be mobilized for liberation or social change.

Emic An interpretive research lens wherein researchers seek to understand from
within the community or culture being studied, or to take an insider point of

view. Provides descriptions and analysis from the perspective or with the voices of participants or members of the community being studied.

Epistemic violence Violence inflicted on ways of knowing or generating knowledge, usually by dominant ways of knowing (e.g. post-positivism and empiricism) on marginalized communities' knowledges and ways of knowing. In the extreme, can be referred to as epistemicide, which involves the complete erasure of alternative knowledges and ways of knowing.

Epistemology An individual's theory of knowledge, comprising what they believe to be knowable, how knowledge can be generated and validated, and the limits of knowledge and knowledge production.

Equality Rooted in concepts of equal access or equal opportunity. For example, equality in higher education might mean that students of varying backgrounds are subject to admissions on equal grounds, and able to enroll in courses equalty. Equivalent access to resources no matter the ascriptive characteristics of the person. Equality requires equalizing inputs.

Equity Goes beyond equality, to include fairness and equal inclusion. Equity can include measures beyond equal access or equal treatment as a way to remedy injustice and historical underrepresentation. Where equality might require equal access, equity involves inclusion and correcting disparities. Equity requires equalizing outcomes, which might necessitate unequal inputs.

Essentialism The belief that characteristics of an identity are set or natural, and that particular group of characteristics defines what it is to be a member of that identity category. For example, essentialized notions of gender ascribe static and discrete characteristics to masculinity and femininity, presuming intrinsic differences in characteristics between masculine and feminine identities. Assumes extreme in-group homogeneity.

Ethic of care Nel Noddings coined this phrase, and it speaks to the relationship between a student and their teacher. Educators need to display a consistent level of love and caring for their students as their work to address their needs.

Ethnicity A designation based primarily on social or cultural affiliation. Though related to race, ethnicity often includes finer distinctions, and is not based solely on physical characteristics, but social sense of belonging. In the US, the federal government defines ethnicity solely as "Hispanic" and "non-Hispanic," though that definition is not well aligned with scholarship.

Etic A normative research lens wherein researchers seek to study phenomena from outside of the community or culture being studied, to take an outsider positioning, or to impose outside theoretical frames on the data.

Gay Usually refers to a man whose sexual and/or romantic attraction is primarily or exclusively to men. However, this term is also sometimes applied more broadly to any individuals who experience same-gender attraction.

Gender identity The sense of self that one has as a man, woman, nonbinary, genderqueer, trans, or another gender category.

Gender The culturally and socially determined attributes (such as behavior, emotions, beliefs) that are associated with masculinity/femininity. It is a social construct often conflated with sex.

Genderqueer Variously used to refer to individuals who do not define themselves on the gender binary (man/woman), or for whom gender identity is more fluid, and thus not easily categorized.

Heat map Shows the density of participant responses. Deeper color patterns represent more frequent responses.

Hegemony The dominance of societal norms, values, and practices by one group. Hegemony typically involves the reproduction of those norms, values, and practices in new generations. For example, US norms, values, and practices are dominated by White, cisgender, straight, and masculine practices. Education serves to reproduce those norms, values, and practices by treating them as "normal" or even "desirable," by favoring the stories and writings of White, cisgender, and straight men, and by teaching cultural systems established by White, cisgender, and straight men. Importantly, hegemony involves the structuring of social relations such that the oppressed group may participate in their own continued oppression.

Heteronormativity A term used to describe the way in which societal norms, expectations, and practices normalize straight/heterosexual identities while othering queer identities.

Heteropatriarchy A societal system which systematically privileges straight cisgender men while systematically oppressing LGBTQ people, trans people, and women.

Heterosexism Systematic bias and/or discrimination against people of sexual orientations other than straight/heterosexual. Although straight people might experience bias and/or discrimination on the basis of sexual orientation, they are systematically privileged, while queer people are systematically oppressed.

Human Capital Those assets centered in human people that can be mobilized for liberation and social change. May include the experiences, knowledge sets, and skills of a group of people.

Imposter syndrome A socioemotional pattern in which one feels as though their success, accomplishments, or position of authority are unearned and unwarranted. It is often experienced as an internalized fear that one will be discovered to be a fraud—as if one is an imposter in their position or accomplishments.

Integration A process, usually occurring alongside or following desegregation, in which students of various racial backgrounds are enrolled in the same schools. While desegregation involves removing single-race designations for schools, integration involves the actual enrollment of multiple races at a school.

Intersectionality At its core, the idea that bias and discrimination can occur across intersecting marginalized identities (e.g. a company that promotes White women and Black men into management might still discriminate in promotion against a Black woman based on her intersecting social identities). In research, it is a tool of analysis centered on the interconnected relationships across multiple marginalized social identities and overlapping forms of oppression.

Intersubjectivity Refers to shared or mutual understandings. Intersubjectivity denotes that, while meanings and knowledges might be subjective, individuals can share a common understanding. This mutual understanding is usually reached via dialogue.

Lesbian A woman who is primarily or exclusively sexually and/or romantically attracted to women.

Life history methodology A research paradigm consisting of a collective of life stories that comprise the main data source. Life history methodology consists of a theoretical analysis of the method-life stories and the sociocultural, socioeconomic, and political aspects and assumptions related to these methods.

Liquid modernity A time after post-modernity; one that is marked by disposability, rampant consumerism, a constant fluidity which results in a lack of solid bonds, and a complete blurring of the lines between public and private lives. Additionally, liquid modernity is marked by a constant surveillance, one that is often self-imposed.

Logistic regression A regression procedure where the outcome measure is a binomial (0/1) indicator (e.g. rain versus no rain). It estimates the odds of an event (1) over non-event (0) as a function of specified predictors.

Metanarrative A general story (a grand narrative about smaller stories) that is meant to give meaning, structure beliefs, or give context to experiences for people. Metanarratives serve to legitimize existing social structures and systems by contextualizing them as part of a larger progressive shift.

Microaggression Small, regular, and common acts or experiences that serve to reinforce bias, stereotypes, and discrimination, as well as oppression. Often, microaggressions are so slight or common that individuals question whether they really happened at all. However, when added up, the variety of these brief and commonplace insults or biased acts result in a cumulative oppressive and harmful effect.

Misogyny The systematic oppression and denigration of women and/or femininity within a societal context that privileges men.

Mixed methods Research that includes a combination of both qualitative and quantitative strands in a single study. Differs from multi-method research, in that there is a "mixing" of qualitative and quantitative strands in design, data collection, and/or interpretation.

Mobilization of bias The structuring of systems and policies that restricts or limits participation of certain groups or the raising of certain issues. By structuring processes to enact this exclusion or limitation, the operation of those systems to produce bias is rendered invisible.

Modernity As a time period, modernity refers to changes and trends in Western society during the late nineteenth century and stretching into the early twentieth century. As a philosophical or analytic concept, it refers to shifts in social developments associated with the modern era such as focus on individualism, the embrace of capitalism, professionalization, and belief in granting social, scientific, and moral progress as inevitable.

Multinomial regression A regression procedure where the outcome measure is a multinomial indicator (e.g. 1, 2, and 3, respectively, representing rain, snow, and neither). One of the categories in the outcome (e.g. neither rain nor snow) is specified as the baseline category. The odds of each remaining category over the baseline category are estimated as a function of specified predictors.

Neoliberalism At the simplest definition, it involves the move from public control of systems to private control of systems, perhaps most notably schools, but also other systems that were traditionally publicly controlled. Neoliberalism also involves the commodification of ideas such as student learning, teacher quality, and other concepts not traditionally considered commodities. This results in the definition of learning as the ability to produce profit, and schools as places for individuals to develop their profit potential. In other words—neoliberal philosophies of education result in schools conceptualized as businesses, and students conceptualized as commodities. In higher education, the concept is used to describe the ways that competition for resources (e.g. students, faculty, revenue) creates a "market" that emphasizes efficiency and production, individualism and brand promotion.

Nonbinary An individual whose gender identity and/or gender expression is outside or beyond the traditional male/female or man/woman binary.

Opportunity gap Disparity in educational opportunity, often divided by race. Which schools students have access to, for example, presents students with very different sets of opportunities. Because of de facto school segregation, educational opportunities such as advanced courses, highly qualified instructors, college preparation, and other opportunities are split by race, creating a gap in opportunity. This opportunity gap, in turn, drives achievement gaps. In other words, gaps in achievement might be better explained by gaps in educational opportunity.

Oppression The state in which dominant groups, acting as oppressors, subjugate and restrict other groups. Those dominant groups use power structures to ensure they remain dominant by controlling non-dominant groups, restricting opportunities, enacting bias, and attenuating their capital.

Panopticon A metaphor used by Michel Foucault to describe diffuse mechanisms of surveillance as a means of social control. The panopticon, a reference to earlier European prison designs, involves the constant threat of surveillance and an inability to determine when one is being surveilled or by whom. The threat of surveillance, then, becomes a tool for policing individual behavior and attitudes.

Pansexual An individual whose romantic and/or sexual attraction is not based on gender, who may thus be attracted to individuals of any gender identity.

Paradigm wars A period in which researchers debated the value of various paradigms. This period was marked by conflict between qualitative and quantitative methodologists with deep animosity developing between paradigmatic approaches. Similar conflicts arose between humanities scholars and social scientists as well.

Paradigm A philosophical approach to research that includes ontology, epistemology, methodology, and axiology.

Participatory action research A community-based research method that emphasizes action and broad participation and seeks to co-create new knowledge between researchers and participants by attempting to produce change in the community.

Patriarchy A societal system which privileges men and masculinity, while oppressing women and femininity.

Photo-elicitation Involves either inviting research participants to take photographs of a space (e.g. a school) under a broad prompt (e.g. places where you like to have fun), or researchers selecting photographs and asking participants to respond. Researchers then ask questions to fully elucidate participants' experiences.

Photovoice The use of community-produced images to critically explore community needs.

Position taking The process of trying to understand another person's experience or social position.

Positionality Involves critical examination of a researcher's social position, especially as positioned within power structures, as it relates to research participants and research questions.

Postmodern A time period beginning in the mid-twentieth century, and a set of beliefs or philosophies that involve critique of modernity and its investment in rationality and professionalization. Involves the fragmentation of authority and counter-empirical movements. There is disagreement regarding when it began and when or if it ended.

Praxis Involves critical reflection and thinking directed toward transforming educational practice.

Propensity score matching A procedure that helps estimate the effect of a treatment, policy, or other intervention by accounting for factors that predict receiving the treatment. It is a common approach to using observational (non-experimental) data to estimate treatment effects when assignment to the treatment condition is non-random. Cases in treatment and control groups are matched based on similarity of propensity scores, and unmatched cases are omitted.

Propensity score reweighting A contemporary alternative to propensity score weighting, particularly useful in overcoming small sample and/or small cell size problems. In propensity score reweighting, propensity scores are used to control the influence of each participant by weighting his/her responses based on his/her propensity to receive the treatment. Since no cases are omitted, considerable statistical power can be retained when working with limited datasets.

Quare As a noun, refers to a lesbian, gay, or bisexual person of color. As a verb, "to quare" something is to acknowledge the intersection of race, class, gender, and sexual orientation in one's identity and social location, as well as account for racism in the White LGB community.

Queer theory A theoretical approach that aims to deconstruct and critique binary notions of identity, perhaps most notably around gender and sexual identity. Its approach is oppositional and antiessentialist, refusing binaries as intrinsically attached to hegemonic power relations.

Queer Traditionally a slur against LGBTQ individuals, but it has more recently been adopted as an affirmative identity category. Can refer to sexual orientation or gender identity, but typically includes identities other than cisgender straight individuals.

Race A designation based primarily on physical characteristics, including skin color. Can be thought of as the physical or biological differentiation, though genetic differences do not appear to exist. For example, a person might be categorized as "Black" based on skin color.

Racial battle fatigue The psychological, physiological, and behavioral responses to the socioemotional conditions that arise from struggling against racism, such as slights, microaggressions, inequitable treatment, threats, and so on.

Racism Denotes systemic bias and/or discrimination on the basis of race or ethnicity. Racism does not require the presence of racists (individuals biased based on ethnicity), and can instead be the result of systems, policies, practices, and laws that privilege the dominant racial or ethnic group. Because racism is systemic, dominant or majority group members cannot experience racism. While those in the dominant or majority group might experience bias or discrimination based on race, without the systemic element, such bias or discrimination would not be considered racism.

Reflexivity An analysis of researchers' positionalities within a study. They interrogate their social positioning and social location, especially in relation to the purpose of the study and their participants. Reflexivity can and should be used throughout the research process, and helps to establish the validity of research.

Resegregation The gradual process by which many US schools, though desegregated and at least partially integrated at one point in time, have become de facto segregated. This has the net effect of creating some schools that are mostly or entirely Black, while others are mostly or entirely White.

School-to-Prison Pipeline Refers to the overwhelmingly disproportionate numbers of young people of Color who find themselves incarcerated due to zero-tolerance policies and harsh discipline procedures in schools.

Sex Typically refers to biological status, or sex as assigned at birth between male, female, and intersex. This designation is usually based on the external appearance of genitalia at birth.

Sexism Systemic bias and/or discrimination on the basis of sex or gender. In societies where men are the dominant group, sexism refers to bias and/or discrimination against women and trans people. Cisgender men may experience bias and/or discrimination on the basis of their gender, but because such bias and/or discrimination is not systemic in nature, it would not be considered sexism.

Sexual orientation A broad term usually used to describe the gender to which one is romantically and/or sexually attracted.

Shaping of consciousness Inculcation of beliefs and values through messages, explicit and implicit, to shape one's consciousness and the way one sees the world.

Social capital Often refers to relationships and social networks in which one operates. These assets could be used for liberation and conscientization.

Straight In the context of sexual orientation, a woman who is sexually and/or romantically attracted to men, or a man who is sexually and/or romantically attracted to women.

Student voice The ways in which all students have opportunities to participate in and influence the decisions that will shape their lives and the lives of their peers.

Subaltern Often used in postcolonial studies, these groups are marginalized and stripped of agency within hegemonic and imperialist power structures. These marginalized populations are those whose epistemologies and cultures are colonized and subjected to epistemic violence.

Tokenization Symbolic effort to include members of underrepresented groups to create the impression of social inclusiveness and diversity, without ongoing or meaningful inclusion.

Tolerance A popular way to describe and conceptualize the existence of multiple perspectives, identities, and backgrounds. Tolerance implies that, while one might not affirm or embrace those different from oneself, one is tolerant of such differences.

Trans A person whose sex as assigned at birth is not congruent with their gender identity.

Transmisogyny The systematic oppression and denigration of trans people within a societal context that privileges cisgender individuals.

Unusual disempowerment A shaping of consciousness that disempowers individuals or groups with messages that communicate low status and unsuitability for leadership.

Unusual empowerment A shaping consciousness that empowers individuals or groups with messages that communicate high status and suitability for leadership.

Validity claims As used in qualitative research, the degree to which knowledge or truth claims made as part of a communicative act can be understood as valid, based on the conditions necessary to achieve consensus. Conditions for achieving validity differ for objective, subjective, and normative-evaluative claims.

White supremacy The belief, or actions consistent with the belief, that White lives and experiences are superior to those of people of Color. White supremacy can be an individual's belief that White lives and experiences are superior, but the term is used to describe systems, laws, and policies as well. In the US, White supremacy is visible in policies, practices, and laws that provided affirmative action, preferential treatment in housing and jobs, and other benefits to White individuals at the expense of people of Color.

Whiteness Describes the ideologies, epistemologies, emotions, behaviors, rhetoric, and semiotics that promote notions of White superiority, normalcy, and dominance. It can be individually or hegemonically enacted, and upholds White supremacy, which in turn denies the rights, equity, and humanity of people of Color.

Notes

1. Portions of this section have been adapted from Strunk, K. K., Locke, L. A., & Martin, G. L. (2017). *Oppression and resistance in Southern higher and adult education: Mississippi and the dynamics of equity and social justice*. New York, NY: Palgrave.

2. We provide a list of terms used in this book which might not have widely understood meanings. Our purpose is not to provide a definitive meaning for each term, but rather to explain how those terms are used in this text.

Index[1]

A

Academic achievement, 100, 132, 228, 229, 233
Accountability, 4, 7, 94, 128, 145, 168
Activism, 6, 130, 132, 222, 263, 284, 285
Agency, 19, 20, 36, 61, 86, 88, 99, 110, 111, 126, 132, 169, 191
Antiracism, 255, 258, 259, 267, 271, 279
Assumptions, 11, 12, 21, 26, 34, 48, 52, 63–65, 71, 93, 140, 141, 143, 144, 168, 170, 171, 178, 186, 192–194, 196, 205, 206, 211, 228, 230, 242–246, 249
Autoethnography, 97, 99, 256, 258, 291
Axiology, 93, 118

B

Bias, 16, 17, 19, 20, 24, 26, 121, 143, 144, 155, 192, 203, 204, 229, 231, 232, 236, 276, 278, 279
Black, 18, 20, 46, 47, 49, 50, 52, 62, 94, 177–180, 183, 185, 195, 219, 228, 230, 232, 257–260, 268, 272, 277–278

C

Categorization, 213n1, 227–236
Cisgender, 21, 30, 74, 283, 284, 286
Civic engagement, 126, 129, 130, 132
Colonialism, 51, 164, 165, 173
Colorblindness, 17, 21, 245, 259, 271

Conscientization, 270
Counterculture, 178, 183, 187
Covariate(s), 228–232
Critical consciousness, 76, 96, 126, 130, 132, 276
Critical pedagogy, 50, 72, 76, 256
Critical race theory (CRT), 45–52, 71, 198, 242, 264, 269–271, 290
Critical theory, 78, 270, 271
Critical whiteness, 51, 78, 271
Cultural insurgency, 178
Culture, 4, 6, 19, 20, 25, 26, 28, 35, 48–50, 61, 82, 95, 97, 100, 101, 127, 128, 130, 131, 138, 139, 142, 145, 154, 177, 178, 181, 183–185, 193–194, 242, 257, 266, 269, 270, 275, 279, 280, 284, 289

D

Decolonizing, 19, 92, 96, 97, 126, 127, 165, 278
Deliberation, 256
Democracy, 255–260
Democratize, 4, 9, 12
Dialogic, 5, 9, 11, 257
Disability, 48, 227–237
Discourse, 5–7, 23, 26, 39, 48, 73, 74, 87, 92–95, 98, 101, 127, 137, 153, 173, 178, 183, 185, 187, 192, 195, 242, 245, 246, 292
Discrimination, 15, 37, 141, 198, 228, 230, 242, 267, 284, 293

---

[1] Note: Page numbers followed by 'n' refer to notes.

© The Author(s) 2019
K. K. Strunk, L. A. Locke (eds.), *Research Methods for Social Justice and Equity in Education*, https://doi.org/10.1007/978-3-030-05900-2

Disjunction, 255
Disproportionality, 227–237
Domination, 73, 74

E

Early Childhood Longitudinal
        Study—Kindergarten Class of
        1998–1999 (ECLS-K), 232, 236
Emancipatory, 4, 16, 92–101, 104, 127, 132,
        141, 145, 146
Emic, 181, 182
Emotionalities, 265, 266, 268, 271, 272
Emotion(s), 65, 265, 266, 268, 271
Empiricism, 60, 61, 66, 183, 193, 269, 272
Epistemicide, 184, 185
        epistemic violence, 184
Epistemologies, 4, 5, 26, 93–95, 97–99, 104,
        118, 125, 127, 132, 154, 166, 177,
        179, 181, 184, 193, 196, 241, 242,
        270, 272, 285, 286
Equality, 62, 152, 204, 205, 209–212
Equity, 5, 16, 33, 34, 41, 50, 60–65, 74,
        81–88, 92, 95–97, 117, 118, 129,
        137, 140, 152–153, 155, 157, 159,
        167, 186, 192–198, 204, 205, 209,
        212, 220, 227, 244–246, 249
Ethics, 5, 15–30, 35, 40, 85, 139, 155, 156
Ethnocentric, 182
Ethnography, 23, 33, 35, 40, 92, 100–101,
        126, 156, 164, 243, 256, 257
Etic, 181, 182
Exclusion, 95, 153, 165, 168, 211, 217, 245,
        248, 249, 279
Experimental, 97, 99, 120, 191, 194, 198,
        228–231, 236

F

Feminism, 23, 28, 50, 51, 62, 91–96, 98–100,
        103, 104, 141, 242, 256, 272, 284

G

Gender, 4, 17, 18, 20, 23, 25, 26, 29, 59–64,
        72, 73, 78, 93, 96–98, 100, 101,
        137–139, 146, 167, 170, 185, 193,
        194, 196, 198–200, 208, 223, 224,
        228, 232, 233, 236, 255, 257, 264,
        267, 270, 272, 278, 284, 293
Globalization, 19
Grassroots, 126, 129, 290
Grounded theory, 66, 143, 156

H

Heat map, 219
Hegemony, 19, 51, 75–76, 92, 94, 96, 138,
        177–178, 192–194, 242, 271, 279
Heterosexism, 64
        cisheterosexism, 75, 286

I

Ideological domination, 46, 74, 75
Ideology, 16, 17, 34, 48, 65, 74–78, 185, 193,
        244, 246
Implicit bias(es), 198, 228
Inclusive, 48, 50, 95, 97, 137, 152, 153, 157,
        165, 182, 204, 220, 223, 224, 245,
        278, 280, 285, 286, 290
Indigenous, 52, 102, 103, 126, 127, 165, 184,
        208, 279
Intentionality, 9, 35, 65
Interaction(s), 7, 21, 38, 65, 77, 86–88, 166,
        169, 171, 220, 222, 224, 230, 231,
        255, 258
Interpretivism, 122, 155, 194, 242
Intersubjective, 3, 5, 9, 11, 12
Interview(s), 4, 6–8, 10, 11, 16, 27, 28,
        35–39, 41, 95, 99, 101, 104, 113,
        128, 130, 131, 152, 154–159, 167,
        169, 180, 218, 220–224, 245,
        258, 272

K

Knowledge(s), 4, 5, 16, 17, 20, 26–29, 40, 46,
        47, 51, 73, 75, 77, 92, 93, 98, 118,
        120, 122, 126–128, 130, 132,
        152–155, 164–166, 173, 182, 183,
        186, 187, 193, 197, 242, 243,
        279, 287

L

Latinx
        Hispanic, 102, 167
        Latina/o, 102, 129, 277, 290, 291
LGBTQ
        LGBT, 285
        LGBTQ+, 60–62, 219
Liberation, 34, 40, 63, 74, 76, 78, 181
Life history, 177–188
        methodology, 177–188
Liquid modernity, 81–88
Literacy, 52, 127, 255, 257, 292
Longitudinal, 232

M

Marginalization, 15–18, 30
Mass incarceration, 180, 193
Meaning-making, 12, 84, 102, 166
Member checking, 9, 12, 29, 95–97, 99, 102, 104, 120, 122, 247
Microaggression, 51, 198, 264, 265, 277, 291
Minoritization, 15, 17, 46, 49, 51, 102, 144, 145, 177, 178, 185, 218, 219, 283, 285
Misogyny
Model specification, 230
Multinomial, 233, 235

N

Narrative, 29, 38, 39, 47, 51, 52, 62, 99, 100, 103, 144, 145, 167, 179–181, 224, 242–249, 259, 269, 271, 275, 276, 278, 279, 289, 291
Neoliberalism, 48, 73, 82, 83, 94, 100
Normative, 7, 11, 101, 181, 182, 218

O

Objectivity, 26, 98, 117–119, 122, 186, 191, 192, 276
Observational, 165, 229, 230, 245
Odds ratios, 234–236
Ontology, 93, 97, 103, 118, 244, 265, 272
Oppression, 20–22, 33, 35, 40, 46, 48, 49, 52, 63–65, 71–78, 88, 125–127, 141, 242, 244, 270, 275, 276, 278, 280

P

Panopticon, 82, 83
Participatory research
    participatory action research (PAR), 28, 119, 125, 153
    participatory methodology, 127
Patriarchy, 185
Pedagogy, 72, 73, 126, 166, 181, 256, 270, 279, 292
People of Color
    Communities of Color, 165, 265, 275
    Students of Color, 228–232, 234–237, 245, 249, 265, 269, 272, 277, 280
Photo-elicitation, 151–160, 166

Photovoice, 8, 29, 92, 97, 128, 153, 155–157, 163–173
Positionality, 3–12, 15–30, 77, 86, 97, 117, 118, 120–121, 144, 187, 195, 197, 284, 291, 292
Position-taking, 5, 9, 10, 12
Positivism, 92, 193–194
Postmodernism, 50, 88, 98
Post-positivism, 155, 194, 196, 242
Poststructuralism, 34, 64, 65, 138, 141, 145
Power
    power dynamics, 7, 11, 16, 28, 93, 96, 121, 138, 155, 164, 167, 169, 170, 292
Praxis, 49, 52, 126, 180, 183, 184, 293
Predictor(s), 194, 229–231, 233, 236
Prejudice, 152, 279
Prison-industrial complex, 128
Privilege, 15–23, 26–28, 30, 33–35, 51, 63, 65, 72, 140, 153, 166, 170, 173, 217, 227, 230, 242, 245, 259, 267, 286, 291
Propensity score analysis
    propensity score matching (PSM), 198, 231
    propensity score method, 227–237
    propensity score reweighting (PSR), 231
    propensity scores (PS), 229, 231–233, 236

Q

Quantitative, 52, 99, 118, 119, 122, 163, 164, 179, 181, 183, 191–198, 203, 204, 209, 228, 229, 241–245, 256, 275–280, 286
Quares, 285
Queer, 59–66, 78, 129, 242, 284–286

R

Race, 46, 50–52, 72, 242, 257, 258, 266, 267
    ethnicity, 17, 60, 62, 63, 185, 228–231, 234–236
Randomized controlled trials, 193, 230
Reconstructive horizon analysis (RHA), 3–12
Reflectivity, 9, 26, 183, 249
Reflexivity, 3–12, 17, 24, 26, 27, 29, 35, 65, 77, 96–99, 122, 127, 143, 144, 153, 155, 195, 197
Regression, 228–233, 236, 237
Rural, 167, 256, 259

S
Sample, 119, 143, 144, 179, 181, 196,
        206–208, 231, 233, 235, 279
Social class
    poverty, 153, 229
    socio-cultural, 178, 180, 183
    socioeconomic, 178, 180, 183,
        185, 230
    socioeconomic status (SES), 18, 141, 229,
        230, 232
Social justice, 5, 15, 22, 29, 30, 33–41, 45,
        46, 48, 49, 52, 59–66, 81–88,
        91, 94–96, 98, 99, 104, 117,
        118, 126, 127, 137–147, 152,
        153, 155, 157, 159, 164, 177–188,
        191–198, 203–212, 213n1, 220,
        242, 246, 259, 269, 270, 276,
        280, 284
Socio-cultural, 178, 180, 183
Sociolinguistic, 39
Subaltern, 40, 184, 185
Subjectivities, 77, 102, 138, 141, 142, 182,
        191, 197
Subjugation, 72, 127

T
Theory of Communicative Action, 6
Tokenizing, 159
Transgender, 146, 207, 285, 286

U
Urban education, 76, 179, 269

V
Validity, 3–12, 24, 29, 96–98, 101, 120–122,
        185, 186, 204, 222, 244, 265
Validity horizon, 7, 8, 10, 11

W
White, 17, 18, 20, 22, 24, 29, 30, 33, 46, 47,
        50, 52, 72–76, 78, 99, 102, 183,
        187, 192, 193, 195, 204, 210, 218,
        228, 231–236, 242, 244, 247, 248,
        255, 257–259, 263–273, 277, 283,
        284, 291
Whiteness, 47, 51, 71, 75, 78, 193, 197, 198,
        256, 257, 259, 264–269, 271, 272
White supremacy, 72–76, 99, 192, 193, 218,
        244, 255, 264, 267

Y
Youth Participatory Action Research (YPAR),
        125–133, 153, 166

Z
Zero-tolerance, 228